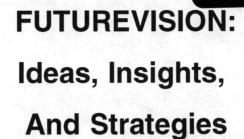

FUTUREVISION:

Ideas, Insights,

And Strategies

Edited by
Howard F. Didsbury, Jr.

Preface by
Jerome Karle

World Future Society
Bethesda, Maryland
U.S.A.

Editor: Howard F. Didsbury, Jr.

Editorial Review Committee: Deirdre Banks, James J. Crider, Howard F. Didsbury, Jr. (Chairman), Theodore J. Maziarski, Andrew A. Spekke and Claudia Spekke.

Staff Editor: Frances Segraves

Editorial Consultant: Edward Cornish

Project Director: Susan Echard

Project Assistants: Gladys Archer, Robert Schley, Lisa Mathias

Cover Art: Mark Stutzman

Published by: World Future Society
7910 Woodmont Avenue
Suite 450
Bethesda, Maryland 20814
USA

CB
161
.F88
1996

International Standard Book Number: 0-930242-53-X

Printed in the United States of America

Contents

iv

Dedicated to the fond memory

of

Masuda Yoneji (March 4, 1909-August 28, 1995)

One of the early pioneers of Japanese computerization and forecaster of the significance of the advent of the information society

H.F.D.,Jr.

NOTE

FUTUREVISION: Ideas, Insights, and Strategies was produced in conjunction with the World Future Society's Eighth General Assembly held in Washington, D.C., July 13-18, 1996. The Eighth General Assembly marks the 30th anniversary of the founding of the Society. The assembly chairman was David Pearce Snyder. Susan Echard was staff director. The assembly program coordinator was Robert M. Schley.

The papers presented here were selected from a very large number submitted to the Editorial Review Committee prior to the General Assembly. They are not necessarily papers presented by their authors at the assembly.

A number of distinguished papers whose subject matter did not lie within the limits of the volume could not be included.

As is our practice in general, footnotes and other academic paraphernalia have been minimized to avoid interruption in the flow of the author's ideas and insights.

PREFACE

THE HUMAN AND PLANETARY CONDITION

by

Jerome Karle

The past few hundred years of human history have witnessed remarkable developments in science and technology. Humanity's scientific understanding and technological facility have expanded very rapidly. At the present time, it continues to accelerate, affecting greatly almost all aspects of people's activities in all but the least developed areas. Medical diagnostics and treatments, pharmaceuticals, appliances, transportation and communications facilities are examples of the ongoing scientific and technological revolution that greatly affect individual lives on a daily basis. The advances in health, comfort, convenience, and personal well-being are most evident.

Despite these inspiring accomplishments, the future is more and more threatened with a deterioration of the quality of life and the proliferation of social inequities. It is therefore imperative that societies make planning for the future a high priority consideration. Appreciation of this need is increasing, having become much more widespread in recent years as people find the various manifestations of the pressing problems part of their own life experience. In looking toward the future, it is incumbent on us to consider our past and present circumstances in order to establish key issues, priorities and necessary action. In this way, the impact of the threats may be minimized and cultural, ethical and humane values may not prevail but even be enhanced. Many individuals and organizations have already devoted much effort to these questions. Much still needs to be done to bring societies and governments into effective action. It is my intention here to present some impressions obtained from a number of the studies that have already been made while emphasizing the degree to which many of the current and potential problems are interconnected.

The objective is to identify major factors that contribute to or generate the conditions that threaten our planet. Such factors must be controlled so that their harmful effects may be minimized or

---

Jerome Karle *is a Nobel Laureate in Chemistry.*

reversed. Failure to do so could lead to great harm to the earth and life upon it. When we think of problem areas, we think of the environment, of human violence and warfare, of the many failings of human character, of the failings of leadership, of the interactions of economics, population and human psychology, of health and food supply, and we wonder about the extent to which many of these problems are interconnected and whether the interconnections can be sorted out so that there may be some hope of dealing with the problems effectively.

ENVIRONMENT

Much discussion has appeared in the literature of organizations dedicated to preserving a healthful and humane environment concerning the many human activities that have severely degraded it. These activities threaten the habitability of major portions of the earth and perhaps all of it. How far do we have to look to find examples? Polluted air, waterways and oceans, ravaged lands, erosion, desertification, deforestation, and radioactive and chemical wastes are by now either common experience or common knowledge. Even the more esoteric threats which may not be as broadly appreciated or sensed such as the depletion of the ozone layer and the accumulation of hothouse gases have been brought to our attention. At what point does the damage become irreversible? How great an insult can the earth take and still bounce back? Have we passed the point of no return already with some of these issues? Possibly, possibly not. It would be prudent, nevertheless, to take immediate steps to minimize the effects of the various threats. This requires no less than world cooperation among societies as well as their governments. Can this be achieved?

There is another aspect of a proper environment that is important to consider, namely, quality of life. This means various things to various people, but it may be broadly described as an aspect of life that goes beyond the minimal requirements of subsistence, shelter, and basic health needs. For many of us, quality of life involves artistic, esthetic and intellectual components, human decency, high standards of behavior, peace, trust, kindly interactions among peoples with a respect for human dignity, and sufficient space in which to dwell. The amount of space for comfort may vary considerably among us, but I believe that most of us need room for privacy, thought and contemplation. This is not to be found readily in congested cities and congested living conditions brought on by high density population.

High density population impacts profoundly on the environment and all aspects of the quality of life. It is difficult to imagine an environmental problem that would not be improved by a decrease in population and made worse by an increase in population. Since the current trend is manifested by an explosion of population in many parts of the world, it is clear that this factor in environmental problems demands immediate attention.

NATURE'S STOREHOUSE

There are many reasons for not destroying huge ecological areas such as the rain forests. A main one is that such areas are vast biological storehouses of substances having important potential to benefit humans. This derives from the fact that living organisms, including both flora and fauna, develop chemical mechanisms that protect them from hostile environments, predators, infectious agents and disease. Such problems have been solved in nature in a great variety of ways, most of which are yet to be discovered. The compounds involved can possibly serve humanity in many ways, as antibiotics, insecticides, herbicides, fungicides, preservatives, drugs such as anticancer agents and antimalarials, heart drugs and many other types of physiologically active substances. Destruction of ecological systems destroys the opportunity to learn their secrets forever.

ECONOMICS AND WAR

The earth is finite and the number of people whom the earth can support is finite, under the best of circumstances. As a consequence, people have developed the concepts of a sustainable economy and a sustainable earth. Rarely is the expression "sustainable economy" heard. The term "economic growth" predominates. Certainly activities that replace other ones can grow and, to an extent, new activities can grow. Growth can also be associated with a raising of the average quality of life in the world. There are limits, however, and the limits arise from limits on natural resources, limits on need and demand, limits generated by environmental considerations, and constraints on total population. The latter statement provides a clear indication that future economic policy must be in harmony with the finiteness of resources and population, and the requirements for a wholesome environment.

Economic competition is often enhanced by limited resources and markets. In the extreme case, it leads to warfare. A major component of many wars has been economic competition. There have been, of course, additional issues, but it seems fair to say that economic motivation has predominated. Economic competition should not be expected to cease when warfare ceases. The experience of the post World War II period, for example, is testimony to the fact that its underlying aspects of economic competition never disappeared, but simply have taken on another form. If and when the major players in industrialized states decide to confront economic reality by supporting and developing their human, humane and industrial capacities consistent with the broad concepts of sustainability and a large measure of self-sufficiency, they may be able to save their countries and future generations from severe economic hardship, if not destruction.

There is not much to say about warfare *per se*. It is enormously destructive, it dehumanizes and brutalizes survivors, damages the environment, wastes resources and many leave legacies of great potential harm to future generations. nevertheless, warfare has been all too common a phenomenon in this century. Societies must find other ways that are nonviolent to deal with their economic stresses and other perceived inequities. Certainly, pouring arms into those societies that are most likely to use them offensively does not help matters. the large and apparently irresistible profit motive in the selling of arms makes control very difficult. the economic gain may be short range but the harm can be major and long-lasting. there is not likely to be a net gain for any society in the long run.

There are other circumstances in which perceived short-term economic gains motivate inappropriate behavior and result in net economic loss and harm to society. Industrial pollution is an example. From my contacts with the various news media in Europe, I have the impression that it is rather popular to blame chemists for pollution because often some sort of "chemicals" are involved. Although, there may be on occasion a chemist sufficiently high in industry to do so, chemists as a class have not been in a position to make decisions that determine how environmentally safe a manufacturing plant will be. In fact, in very many cases, chemists know what to do to protect the environment but have no way to implement it. Pollution often occurs because industry makes short-range economic decisions, or because appropriate legal regulations are not in place or are not enforced. I have made a point of this not simply to exonerate chemists, but, more importantly, to emphasize that economic and environmental problems require clear thought on the part of all concerned. The problems that threaten the world involve everyone. Solutions to the problems may require expert help but the implementation of the solutions involves us all, societies and governments must be strongly involved and come together.

GAINFUL EMPLOYMENT IN THE AGE OF AUTOMATION

I recall reading an article several years ago that characterized a present economic dilemma, namely, that a new revolution is taking place in manufacturing, without being accompanied by a subsequent reduction in the work week. A main generator of this revolution is automation with its accompanying efficiencies. The author asserted that this is the first time a major manufacturing advance in efficiency was not followed by a reduction in the work week. The consequence of this circumstance is that advanced societies are becoming remarkably incapable of providing meaningful employment for a large fraction of its citizenry. Expanding populations can certainly add to the problem. In the present economic climate in many developed countries, the industrial response to monetary problems is to dismiss large numbers of employees and overwork others.

It would be most appropriate for societies to analyze the social and economic implications of the rapidly developing technologies, changing markets in the world economy, and other powerful forces that affect the quality of life in their communities. The problems are not insolvable. It would seem that successful societies would need to have a sustainable plan in which all the population would have the opportunity to make a contribution and thereby earn enough compensation to enjoy what most people would recognize as a decent standard of living. Can this be achieved in the atmosphere of competition that has characterized the industrial revolution up to this time? Is it possible to achieve sustainable economies and decent living standards without inhibiting the various aspects of individual initiative and creativity? There are a myriad of questions that societies may consider. The world, however, can not possibly benefit from continued procrastination in facing these issues or wait for the results of endless debate and deliberation. Too much debate and little testing is as bad for societies as it is for science.

What would need to be done, were governments willing, would be to take a careful look at resources, human and otherwise, set goals on the basis of high and presumably workable ideals and implement them. There would be the need for flexibility so that, in learning from experience, corrections could be made in a stepwise process. This would require governments to be composed of people, or advised by people, of the highest intelligence and personal standards and whose greatest satisfactions would derive from the good results that they could achieve. This is not as difficult to secure as may seem. There are many such people. The important step is for governments to be open to accepting well-motivated, well-thought-out plans and make the difficult, selfless decisions, for the good of society unencumbered by parochial considerations.

A view of the history of the 21st century suggests that the world is more than ready but ill-prepared for such high-minded developments. That certainly seems to be broadly true. Nevertheless, there are a few countries that have renounced war and appear to have pursued, for long periods, steps toward a humane society. It is very important for those who would have high-minded thoughts concerning the future of world societies to realize that there is little chance of accomplishing very much without the help of high governmental leaders who would have the decision-making power to proceed with new approaches.

There is an aspect to these efforts that I do not understand. This concerns the concept that developed nations would provide help, conceptual, financial and technical, to developing nations to enhance their progress. Developed countries have a long way to go to reach environmentally sound, sustainable economies in their own countries. They must stem the trend toward larger discrepancies between the richer and poorer members of their societies and must find useful and productive roles for an increasing number of their citizens in the age of automation. It is legitimate to wonder, under present circumstances, just what it is that developed nations would be exporting to developing ones.

MULTICOMPONENT PARTICIPATION

Many of the problems associated with a deteriorating environment can be readily corrected by applications of science and technology. Examples are replacement of current energy sources by renewable ones that do not add to the carbon dioxide burden in the atmosphere, and technologies and processes that minimize pollution. Science and technology also continue to make major contributions to the health and well-being of people as well as enhancing many other aspects of the quality of life. With all the wonders of science and technology that have developed over the past few centuries and are currently appearing at an accelerating pace, the fact remains that science and technology are not enough to solve all the world's problems. There are matters of ethics, governmental leadership, economics and social philosophy that must play an active role in addition to science and technology, a truly multicomponent participation.

The question arises concerning whether high levels of technology should be the goal of all societies on this earth. That is a rather difficult question, if for no other reason than the fact that high levels of technology are currently very remote from the lifestyles of many areas. In such areas, perhaps present goals should be to assure sustainable, humane and healthful communities consistent with current levels of development.

There is a feature of science and technology in its effects on society that is a cause for special concern. As societies depend more and more on complex technology, it takes only one individual to commit an error or one component to break down to jeopardize the functioning of a major portion of a community. An extreme case is a deliberate act of terrorism or sabotage in which individuals take advantage of products of technology to cause harm and destruction. Thus, modern technology can enable very few people to cause highly disabling events to occur, intentionally or otherwise.

ETHICS AND EDUCATION

It is important that young people be trained from an early age to question contemporary concepts and ideas that swirl around them. They should be taught how to think and draw rational conclusions. Together with this, the development of high ethical standards needs to be emphasized in the educational process. Although such standards should come from the home as well as the school, if they do not come from the home, they must come from the school. The learning of purely factual material is, of course, indispensable, but education obtained in the absence of fine-tuned reasoning and an ethical sensitivity is probably a major contributor to current societal ills.

Valuable leadership qualities are the ability to apply sound intellectuality to problems and to use the results in an ethical fashion. It is, to be expected that an educational system that emphasizes such qualities in general would raise the standards and the quality of life for society as a whole. In addition to learning how to think, a very worthwhile feature of an educational system is for it to be broadly based. Everyone who attended my liberal arts college was required to study mathematics through calculus, attend a "science survey" course, take a particular science course of one's choice, attend courses on subjects such as government and history, public speaking, English literature, music appreciation, hygiene and develop language skills. There were undoubtedly other requirements that I do not recall. Other courses taken by the students were at the students' choice. High standards and broad requirements were also maintained in elementary and high school. Ethics, *per se*, was not taught, but there was a no-nonsense, respectful atmosphere in which the business of the schools was conducted. In elementary school there were two report cards, one for the scholastic accomplishments and one for personal behavior. Although I attended college (all male and free of charge) during the height of the depression years of the 1930s, students attended classes as respectable gentlemen, generally dressed in suits.

An educational system such as the one I was fortunate to attend, the New York City system, provided students with a broad education, literacy in many intellectual areas, and the preparation to go into the world with heightened insights and understanding. The graduates were rather clear about their choices for further specialized studies, confident about their own capabilities and by and large good citizens, many have had outstanding careers. The school system also served people well who did not go to college or preferred to learn a trade while in high school. I attended school in New York City during the 1920s and 1930s. Perhaps there are historical records extant that could serve as a worthwhile model. There may be many individuals in the field of education who would surpass such a model. This is perhaps so and should also be considered. I look, however, at the challenges and the discipline that I faced as a student compared to those broadly followed in many locations at present and I must conclude that the older system was, in general, the more successful. My experience as a participant and observer is largely confined to the US. Readers in other countries may perhaps see some similarities to their own views and experiences.

The thought that there should be special graduate institutions to train the leaders of the future on the main subjects of critical importance[1] is a very fine concept. It may even be said that such institutions ought to be regarded as indispensable. Subjects of critical importance have been discussed in many publications during previous decades. Their urgency has become increasingly recognized and publicized, so that many of the issues have become part of public knowledge. Perhaps we may hope that, in the future, training in the proposed graduate institutions will be a prerequisite to appointment to high political office and that the entering students will be among the finest graduates of an educational system that promotes broad scholarship combined with ethical principles. The world can always benefit from great leaders with impeccable standards having broad intellectuality and a good sense for what may be achieved in practice.

CHARACTER

It is evident that if a society were comprised of people who have ethical standards, avoid anti-social behavior, have a deep regard for human dignity and have self-respect that is based on high personal standards, such a society would have the potential to exceed by far current experiences. The actual level of character and morality in present day societies are a matter of concern. Anti-social behavior at all levels can defeat attempts to raise the average standard of living, solve economic and environmental problems and achieve humane and cultured civilizations throughout the world. There are many areas of our world in varying degrees of strife and otherwise sorry state.

The serious implication is that it is not possible to assume that governments and societies are necessarily readily willing to correct the problems of the world or to try to do so within a thoughtful, rational and humane framework.

We are told by behavioral scholars that it is important to start to instill character into children at a very young age, otherwise, in general, it is not particularly successful. This appears to be a subject that merits careful consideration, since it seems to be vital for the achievement of more humane and ethical societies in the future. In addition to building character, it is important to teach young people to have inquiring minds and well-ordered priorities. They must learn to think, gather information and draw rational conclusions based on the information. A common impediment in reaching people is their tendency to draw conclusions based on emotion or other motivations, rather than information and analysis. They will often proceed by trying to justify the conclusions and insist on their validity in the absence of careful thought. Societies' preoccupation with trivia and self-endangering behavior reflects questionable value systems. Such value systems are, however, a mark of the 21st century. Considering the threats to future existence, it is self-defeating to persist in maintaining many current societal priorities and values. There needs to be, of course, flexibility and respect for a variety of opinions, but when ethical standards, for example, are quite low, it should be possible to decide on which standards should be raised and in what way. We make laws to try to correct or prevent unacceptable behavior. It is much better when people's ethics, humane principles and self-respect make laws unnecessary.

SUMMARY REMARKS

Interconnections

There are a number of issues concerning the interactions of humans with the earth and with each other that have been briefly noted. Some of the more important ones are listed in alphabetical order below:

> Economic matters
> Education
> Environment
> Ethical, humane and wholesome behavior
> Finiteness of resources
> Health care
> Population
> Priorities and values
> Quality of life
> Sustainability

These issues are far from independent of each other. They are, rather, grossly interdependent. This interdependence leads to the concept of "indispensables," namely, those issues that are particularly indispensable to the achievement of widespread improvements in the human condition. In fact, without proper handling of the indispensables, the attempt to achieve improvements in a broad sense by appropriate treatment of the other issues has little chance of success.

INDISPENSABLES

Population control is an indispensable. I am in agreement with many others who have indicated that unless population is brought under control, it will not be possible to enhance the hum,an condition on a broad scale. Any progress will be eliminated by the huge numbers of people who must be supported if the unbridled increase in overall population persists. Population control must be achieved. A second indispensable is sustainability. The concept of sustainability must be brought into the handling of environmental problems. activities that degrade the environment can no longer be tolerated. Renewable energy sources, for example, must replace the burning of fossil fuels. Economic decisions impact greatly on the sustainability of an economy. It was pointed out in a talk that I hear recently that the inhabitants of Easter Island, located off the west coast of South America, use up all the resources of the island to the extent that they did not have enough food to subsist and did not have enough wood to build boats on which to escape from the island.

Proper human behavior is an indispensable. The amount of animosity of various groups toward their neighbors in many areas of the world is a serous impediment to progress. The ease with which seemingly cultured societies can be transformed to behave in a barbaric fashion is another sad lesson of the 20th century. Such threats of unbridled hostility and violence must be curtailed if a proper environment for peace and stability is to be achieved.

BARRIERS

There are various barriers that can interfered with the bread attainment of a quality existence. The problems that need to be overcome are formidable. They are manifold and extensive. Great leadership in the world is required to overcome societal indolence, selfish motives, lack of character, perverse priorities and values, widespread unwholesome life styles, lack of cooperativity, extreme poverty, educational limitations, violence, and the lack of suitable mechanisms to settle disputes peacefully, exploitation of the earth and of people and a population explosion that is out of control.

Societies whose survival is marginal can not readily give much attention to the issues that are raised in this article. It is very difficult for societies or individuals on the edge of survival to change the patterns of their lives. Many marginal societies are overpopulated, are under severe economic pressures, and have low levels of health care.

As recent history shows, large portions of the world can be brought into war by extremely antisocial governments. Considering the number of such governments, it seems to be all too easy for them to form. In order to achieve any semblance of world order, it is necessary to prevent or at least largely minimize such occurrence. Could some form of world government with a world constitution be capable of achieving this with perhaps a number of other benefits? Further study is merited.

CONCLUDING QUESTION

We live in a world in which there re major inequities within societies and among societies. It is also a world whose future is greatly threatened. Do we want nature to take its course, a path that is often extremely harsh, or will the world's population and leadership be willing and able to take the major courageous steps required to mitigate nature's harshness, preserve the earth and generate a more equitable and humane future?

NOTE
1. Kaoru Yamaguchi. *Creating a Higher Institution for Future Oriented Studies.*

INTRODUCTION

by

Howard F. Didsbury, Jr.

The 25 papers in this volume have been divided into eight categories: The Future of Work; Education; Management; Sustainability; Reflections on the Future; Decline or Revitalization; Medical Ethics and the Future; and The Global Scene. Without doubt, there is an arbitrary character in this eightfold scheme and we regret that fact. However, this seemed to represent the best arrangement which limited the number of categories. It is hoped that the reader will find this arrangement generally helpful.

THE FUTURE OF WORK

A valuable function of futurist speculation is that of attempting to foresee likely harmful or undesirable results of scientific advances and technological ingenuity. In this role, futurist speculation serves as "early warning signals" that are designed to elicit prudent reflection and timely action. This is a major theme of many of the papers in this volume. To take one example, whose importance will no doubt increase in concern as we enter the 21st century, is the threat of persistent technological unemployment in high-tech societies: Simon Head's "The New, Ruthless Economy: *The New York Review*, February 29, 1996; Ethan B. Kapstein's "Workers and the World Economy," *Foreign Affairs*, May/June 1996; and Louis Uchitelle's article "We're Leaner, Meaner and Going Nowhere Faster" in the May 12, 1996 *The New York Times* are symptomatic of the concern. Dr. Mercedes M. Fisher's "The Last of the Baby Boomers and Their Prospects for Climbing the Corporate Ladder of Success" is one of the four papers in this section. Though concerned with the future of work, her concern in this paper is of a narrower focus than those discussed in the sources cited above. She is especially concerned with "how organizations will meet the challenge of appeasing younger workers who are faced with job plateaus brought on by the immense number of baby boomers who preceded them in the job market; and how these same businesses will cope with the shrinking labor pool as their older employees approach retirement." She highlights a variety of "alternatives available to businesses in both the private and public sectors" to meet the challenge. Professor Frederick C. Thayer's paper, "The Growth Profession of the 21st Century: Unemployment," succinctly states the national and global challenge.

"The growth of unemployment as a lifetime profession is sneaking up on us, and for reasons that are so contradictory that we badly need to straighten out our thinking before dangerous social collisions overwhelm us as, indeed, they have been threatening to do for some time. For example: Our democratic political traditions, dating back at least to the time of Aristotle, long assumed that the management of public affairs should be entrusted to white males who are so rich that they need not "labor," but should run government as a hobby or avocation, perhaps even a "duty" that they owe society for their good fortune.

"Over a long period of time, technological progress has been acting to reduce the number of available jobs relative to increases in the size of the labor force. While it is often said that 'technology creates more jobs than it replaces,' our policy actions have said otherwise. We have shortened the work week, prohibited child labor, made secondary education compulsory, and provided social security payments to the elderly if they promise not to work between ages 65-70."

"In recent decades, we have developed a bipartisan economic policy to maintain high unemployment (a jobless rate of 6.0 to 7.0 percent) in order to control inflation by effectively preventing wage increases, even if productivity improves. While many commentators pretend that this policy does not exist, the interest rate increases made by the Federal Reserve Board are designed to slow economic growth and prevent job creation."

"Looked at more broadly, the immediate future promises to quickly become one in which there is exponential growth in the number of people that are *surplus* to the needs of society. There will be no 'work' for many, it is likely that many will be asked or compelled to avoid reproducing themselves, and the world may be unable to feed them all. But first things first. What can we do to accept unemployment as a dignified career that will transition us to a world in which work and income may have to be separated."

The purpose of Bertrand H. Chatel's, "Unemployment and Underconsumption in the Twenty-first Century," is "to analyze some of the causes of world unemployment and to propose a few solutions." For example, the concept of "Workers in reserve (WIR) is offered as "a step in the cycle of work, where professional associations and job describers would play an important role." He also discusses the national and international financing of WIR and the creation of an "Underconsumption Fund." Needless to say, a radically different approach than that of Professor Thayer or David Macarov.

"Poverty Has a Rich Future!" according to Professor David Macarov. "More than a billion persons in the world today--about one fifth of the human race--live below an income level that does not furnish them with adequate food, safe water, secure shelter, and access to education and health care...As the amount of human labor needed for production of goods and services diminishes there is every indication that poverty will continue to spread and deepen, with resultant threats to the stability of civilization. Only a basic change in the economic and social paradigms that underlie income distribution offers any possibility of averting the ominous future."

EDUCATION

Professor W. Warren Wagar shares thoughts as a teacher of futures courses which have attracted large enrollments since 1974! In "Teaching the Future: A Memoir," he shares details as to how the courses are organized, taught, and the ground covered. He concludes that "it should be possible for teachers in many disciplines to help futurize the curriculum, if high academic standards are preserved and a liberal dash of imagination is injected into the process."

"Most approaches to foresight, futures study, have concentrated on one or other aspect of the field." Dr. Richard A. Slaughter "argues that in order to create a futures-responsive culture, foresight will need to be implemented in a series of stages." These stages "correspond to five layers of understanding and capacity. The *layered quality* of applied futures work has been widely overlooked. However, an understanding of these layers and how they work provides the key to more effective implementation of foresight at the social level."

According to Dr. Slaughter, "In this approach, foresight emerges from the raw capacities and perceptions of the human brain/mind system and its higher-order consciousness. These capacities and perceptions are taken to a new level, or stage, by the careful use of futures concepts and ideas. These enable a futures discourse, which itself is the key to further developments. Next, futures tools and methodologies add an analytic capability and a wide variety of procedures to enhance futures understanding. When the resulting processes, projects and structures are embodied in specific applications and purpose-designed contexts (such as a twenty-first century study) foresight can be routinely applied within many organizations."

The subtitle to John L. Anderson's, "Strategies for Using Human Intuition," is "A Beginning Exploration" and raises some fascinating questions. "Nearing the millennium we have a complex mix of problems, change forces and futures that often appear to require greater mental abilities than we possess," observes Anderson. However, he goes on to point out that "Progenitors of future solutions, technological revolutions, great movements and even some 'obvious' answers to today's dilemmas do already exist. But they are embryonic at best, frequently masked and may be increasingly unrecognizable by our normal and historical means of evaluation. In our past we have become highly skilled at rational process and analytical inference, but little has been accomplished in developing strategies of intuitive inference." The question then is raised: "...Suppose we could develop strategies for using our intuitive faculties--these would provide a doorway to entirely new levels of human thought and achievement." The author then "describes the

Horizon Mission Methodology and its results as a structured means of using intuitive thinking."

"Specialist or Generalist?   A False Dichotomy; An Important Distinction" by P.J. Hartwick and Caela Farren, is designed "to provide a useful perspective of the underlying process of specialization and its implications for ongoing learning, the value of specialists in organizations, as well as the proper role and contribution of the so-called 'generalist.'" The authors stress the special importance in "the emerging relevance of the findings and implications of neurobiological research having to do with brain development that accompanies learning, and the broader implications for individual and organizational learning."

Dr. David Passig in his "Virtual Literacy: In Virtual Learning Environments" sets out to clarify "the areas of cognitive and motor skills which will be required for studying virtual environments." He first surveys "a number of applications in learning" and analyzes "the character of expression in virtual environments." He then defines "the character of virtual literacy" and ends with "the character of the areas of literacy in virtual reality."

"Cyberspace Versus the Endangered University: The Prospects for the 21st Century Education" is a stimulating and provocative paper by Professor Joseph N. Pelton. The educational challenge we face is to change the traditional role of the university for the future in order to reach and educate another two billion inhabitants on the planet. Professor Pelton offers ten reforms which question conventional educational thinking. Some of these reforms are already in use at conventional institutions of higher education.

MANAGEMENT

In their essay "Strategic Management Response to the Challenge of Global Change" by Professor James L. Morrison and Ian Wilson, the authors note "turbulent times require a planning model that allows us to anticipate a rapidly changing future and to use this information in conjunction with an analysis of our organization--its culture, mission, strengths, and weaknesses--to define strategic issues, to chart our direction by developing strategic vision and plans, to define how we will implement these plans, and to evaluate how well we are implementing these plans." The authors describe "the strategic management model, particularly the environmental tools in this model, as this model is designed to assist us in anticipating and shaping the future of our organization."

"New techniques developed by practitioners of Strategic Management" are discussed by Dr. George Korey in his paper, "Technique for Strategic Management." According to Dr. Korey, "the ideal organization system should be operations-oriented." After all, an organization's structure is "only a vehicle for accomplishing results."

The author discusses "the concept of LRC--Linear Responsibility Charting" and describes the symbols employed and lists numerous practical applications in "Functional Organization Analysis."

A practical suggestion for service business or industry managers is offered by Professor Charles H. Little in "Investing in Attitude Capital to Improve Service Quality." All too frequently when confronted with the growing ranks of "service" providers one cannot help but ask: "Where is the service in the service industry?" Professor Little's paper offers some advice on how to improve "services."

"The service sector is an integral part of today's economy, and service quality needs to be improved. Service quality depends largely on the attitudes prevailing at the time a service is rendered, that is, on how the provider approaches the problem and how the recipient perceives the service provided. The attitudes of service workers must be improved in order to improve service quality. Workers need the people skills necessary to deal with messy situations and unhappy people, and this training is just as important in today's business world as the technical training currently offered in the education system. Improving the educational offerings to better train service workers amounts to an additional investment in human capital, and this investment in attitude capital will improve service quality." "This paper attempts to view the situation from an economics perspective. An attempt to improve service offerings amounts to an investment in the business that will offer returns commensurate with the level of investment."

In "The Future of Mobile Computing" Ralph Menzano writes about mobile computing and how it will change the way we work and live. He "provides a summary of a mobile computing project gone astray and detail[s] how similar projects can attain success and avoid common project problems in the near future." The project in question was entitled "Branch-in-a-Briefcase" and "involved mobile loan officers who dealt with borrowers at a point of sale similar to other industry's point of sale activities."

SUSTAINABILITY

"Sustainable agriculture programs provide measurable environmental improvements. By making sure that their farming programs are ecologically sound, sustainable farmers contribute to the solution of problems caused by overuse of chemical pesticides and synthetic fertilizers." This is the subject of Clifton E. Anderson's "Politics, Science, and Sustainability: The Prospects for Agriculture." The author makes a most important observation: "Political support for sustainable farming must come from non-farmers who value the environment. For their part scientists can expand the knowledge base and managerial skills of sustainable farmers.

"Generating concepts for new products that represent minimal impact to land, water, and air requires new and different thinking than that which created conventional products[in the past]. Thinking that is more in tune with nature can help. Such is the major thesis of Jacquelyn A. Ottman's "Growing Greener Products: What We Can Learn from Pea Pods and Apple Peels in Sustaining Creativity in Environmental-related Innovation." Ottman describes a new innovation process called *Getting to Zero*^{sm} that relies on nature as a stimulus for creating concepts for products and packages that approach zero environmental impact. "This paper discusses the implications for nature-based thinking to the packaging industry."

REFLECTIONS ON THE FUTURE

Frederik Pohl's "Thinking About the Future" is a fine practical insight into the area of futures predicting and forecasting. Pohl does not take himself too seriously when discussing possible future scenarios. He avoids falling into the trap of championing one methodology over another while discussing futures predicting in general non-technical terms.

In trying to predict and possibly "invent" the future, according to Pohl, it is not only important to know more than just some methodologies but to take into account social, emotional, economic forces that come into play when trying to affect change on a regional, national or global level. Pohl's paper ends on a positive note: "The only good reason for trying to predict the future in the first place is so that now, in the present, we can try to shape it to our heart's desire."

"Why the Future Belongs to Smaller Sized Humans" is certainly a title that will catch the eye of any adventuresome reader. In this paper, Thomas T. Samaras presents "a provocative and unique exploration of the advantages and disadvantages of increasing human size over the last 200 years." "The impact of a world of larger size people is quantified in terms of food and water needs, resources, energy, economics, pollution, health, and performance." Samaras "shows that smaller human size is one of several approaches needed to preserve the environment and to improve our chances of surviving the inevitable shortages that mankind will face. A practical method currently within the power of modern science is given for reducing the size of future generations."

Professor Allen Tough takes a novel approach to the future by trying to imagine what future generations might say to us today if we were able to cross the span of time that separates us. As he notes, "Individually and collectively, we struggle with the need to set priorities for our society. Amidst the clamor of competing needs and solutions, we have to choose the most important priorities of all and focus our efforts particularly on them. When choosing societal priorities, one useful perspective is provided by listening to the friendly advice that future generations would send to us if they could. This message from future generations urges us to focus our efforts on six priorities:

- A long-term perspective
- Future-relevant research and teaching
- Weapons and warfare
- Planet and population
- Significant knowledge
- Learning, caring, and meaningfulness.

DECLINE OR REVITALIZATION

"One constant in the decline of nations is the inability to effectively reform the institutions and systems that are causing the decline," notes former three-term governor of Colorado, now director of the Center for Public Policy and Contemporary Issues at the University of Denver, Richard D. Lamm. In his essay on the need for "Futurizing America's Institutions," he examines some of the areas where imaginative reform is imperative: the United States has "half of the world's lawyers, the highest drug and alcohol abuse in the workplace, the largest number of functional illiterates, the highest health care costs, an increasingly dysfunctional educational system, and retirement systems that promise to bankrupt our children." The message is clear: "Futurize" America's institutions or prepare for a truly grim future.

MEDICAL ETHICS AND THE FUTURE

In "Some Reflections on the Future of Medical Ethics" Dr. Robert B. Mellert draws our attention to the fact that advances "in the field of medicine have begun to affect previously defined roles for both the health professional and the patient. New technology provides more options and increased costs. In addition, legal forces have brought about a growth in malpractice litigation and the legalization of living wills. As a result, a new tension is emerging between the primacy of curing versus that of caring.

Medical ethics can help clarify the scope of this tension, provide moral justification for each of the contending positions, and suggest the core issues that must be confronted if we are to move towards resolution [of the issues involved].

THE GLOBAL SCENE

According to Gary S. Schofield in his essay entitled "Avoiding the Future of War," in the next 50 years social and political forces will collide. The end of the bipolar world will create a world outside of our personal experience. There is an immediate need for complete understanding and prediction of countries' behavior and yet current models [of the behavior of nations] are limited and contradictory.

In Schofield's view "science uses hypothesis and the future to test its models but we, as futurists, are all trapped in *one frame of the historical movie.* We are dependent on an accurate accounting of the past to predict the future. Unfortunately history is fatally flawed. "Avoiding the Future of War" not only presents a fresh view of the past but also presents practical steps for the future. The paper questions widely held beliefs about war, atrocity and human nature. Extraordinary claims require extraordinary evidence and so clear examples are cited through human history. Schofield's model introduces "a model incorporating science, economics, psychology and military strength. His approach dismisses "self-serving myths" that he believes contributed to the perpetuation of human conflict on an epic scale through the ages.

"A central characteristic of the modern world consists of the growing dominance of artificial over natural problems. Human accumulation of power means that we are now capable of creating and destroying many things, including ourselves. Unfortunately our destructive capacity is out-pacing our creative ability; so the threats to humanity become more awesome than the promises. As a result problems multiply faster than we are able to solve them and the lead-time for making decisions shrinks into nothingness.

In response to this critical situation, Professor Paris Arnopoulos offers a "Prolegomena to Problemology [or a way of] Defining Global Problematics." "This study initiates a rigorous definition of complex problems as the first step in an emerging science of problematics." The present paper "is a prerequisite to any scientific treatment of problems, because it lays down the foundation for further systematic and systemic work by outlining the concept, structure, and process of problems and by doing so answer the questions related to the nature, meaning, type, location, time, and solution of the world's most critical issues."

Dr. John M. Francis is deeply concerned with the need to revitalize the idea of civil society as exemplified in "Reformation and Enlightenment--The Reconstruction of Civil Society for the 21st Century." Historically, he notes, "The idea of civil society sprang from the writers and thinkers of the Scottish Enlightenment who advanced the view that the autonomous and moral individual provided the very foundation of the social order. In the present era our capacity to live with difference in terms of traditions, cultures, religions, and values is the key to the viability of civil society. It is the means by which the power of the state is balanced by the self-organization of strong and autonomous groups, while the individual is free to express and to sustain core values at a personal level.

"We need to give more attention to methods and procedures for resolving conflict, building consensus and strengthening democracy on a wide range of social issues which pose problems for the future. At present large numbers of people are obliged to cope with major policy shifts affecting the provision of services but remain largely confused about the reasoning behind these changes. The pace of technological change is unrelenting and all too frequently the capacity of individuals, groups and whole communities to adjust to the continuing patten of change is taken for granted. Representations by voluntary groups and associations as custodians of the public interest are therefore essential if the vestiges of a civil society are to be retained."

"Africa and the New Globalization: Challenges and Options for the Future" by Professor Julius O. Ihonvbere "examines the paradoxical location and role of Africa in the emerging complex and competitive international divisions of labor and power. It examines the historical origins of the African predicament; the implications of the region's experiences for power, politics, production, and exchange relations; and locates the region in a discussion of the features of the new globalization."

THE FUTURE OF WORK

THE LAST OF THE BABY BOOMERS AND THEIR PROSPECTS FOR CLIMBING THE CORPORATE LADDER OF SUCCESS

by

Mercedes M. Fisher

BACKGROUND

A demographic occurrence has been developing which will affect nearly every business institution and worker across the US--the nation's work force is getting older. This trend is not new, but part of a gradual progression over the last half of this century.

Since 1900, our life expectancy has increased by twenty-eight years, from forty-seven to seventy-five.[1] In the year 2000, some 54 million persons will be older than the age of 55.[2] If current birth rates are kept constant, by the year 2035, nearly a quarter of the US population will be *elderly* people.[3] This segment of the population will grow the most during the first two decades of the next century when the post World-War II *baby boom* generation, those individuals born between 1946 and 1964, reach older ages. The transformation in population becomes obvious when one considers that nearly a third of America's total population was born during this period. However, what precipitated the situation was the subsequent baby bust that followed the mid-1960s. People began to have fewer children. During the 1970s the population under 18 decreased by eight million and decreased by another three million in the 1980s.[4] Subsequently, the median age of the United States population was 30 in 1980; by the year 2000 over half the population will be over 35.[5] This rapid decline in the birth rate has had an equally significant effect on our country's overall age composition.

The impact on the nation's labor force is even more drastic. During the 1970s, the pool of human resources grew at a rapid rate of 2.9% annually, but it is only expanding by one-third of that pace today.[6] In the work force, the average age increased from 36 to 39 over the same time period.[7] This slower growth rate has resulted in a natural tightening of the labor market.

Not surprisingly, politicians have been taking credit for the recent drop in unemployment during the past decade, but the main cause of the labor shortage is the baby bust. As the last of the baby boomers migrate past their entry-level jobs, holes will be left in the labor market. Businesses which have depended on inexpensive entry-level employees are just now beginning to experience labor

---

Mercedes M. Fisher *is assistant professor of educational technology, School of Education, Marquette University, Milwaukee, Wisconsin.*

shortages. Census figures indicate that there are 5 million fewer 18-24 year-olds today than there were in 1989. During this same period, according to the US Department of Labor, the economy has generated 16 million new jobs. Based on these and similar statistics, there is a major skills shortage anticipated for this country before the end of the century.

While the ramifications of these events have not yet become fully evident, are they unavoidable? The decline of young people in the labor market can have both positive and negative implications. For instance, the older work force will be more experienced, stable, and reliable. More importantly, surveys show that one-third of all retirees aged 65 and older would prefer to be working. Today, that represents a potential pool of some 35 million experienced, willing workers--more than double the amount of new jobs expected to be generated. All that is certain is that much is dependent on the way business organizations structure their policies, programs, and services in order to meet the challenges of an older work force.

ANALYSIS

Younger Workers

Before one can analyze the implications of the nation's maturing labor force on younger workers, a concrete definition of *younger* needs to be specified. Though there is no concrete age which delineates *younger* from *older*, for the purposes of this paper, younger workers should be interpreted as those employees who were born after the baby boom period from 1946 to 1964. They are sometimes referred to as *baby busters*. Accordingly, *older workers* are defined as those individuals who were born before or during the baby boom generation.

Because older workers will continue to comprise an increasing majority of America's labor force, there will be less room at the higher levels of management within organizations for the number of available candidates. There is less room at the top levels of management for this generation simply because of the huge numbers of baby boomers who preceded them in the labor force. According to the Bureau of Labor Statistics, during the 1980s the number of workers between 35 and 44 years of age has doubled in comparison to available management jobs.[8] Anthony Carnevale, chief economist of the American Society for Training and Development says, "the leading edge of the baby boom has just turned 40 and won't be retiring for another thirty years. Over that period of time, employees will face a curious demographic twist in their internal labor markets."[9]

This demographic twist caused by the large number of baby boomers and the relative shortage of younger workers entering the work force results in *job plateaus*."[] In other words, younger workers

4

will be caught in dead-end jobs or waiting longer for promotions. As Arch Patton, a former McKinsey and Company management consultant puts it, "they will spend more time on each plateau up the promotion climb."[10] Thus, in general, younger workers will have to change their expectations in terms of professional advancement and redefine their timeframe for success.

Younger workers will definitely need patience to handle the developing problem of longer waiting times for advancement. Though this younger group may be able to demand higher salaries for the plethora of entry-level assignments which will be available, each new job assignment will be extended before the next opportunity to move up on the organizational chart. Therefore, increased frustration and disenchantment among employees may occur within companies. One study suggests that plateaued workers tend to either withdraw from their jobs entirely or spend more time thinking about home or leisure.[11] These types of findings can only increase the concern over America's growing competitiveness problems. In addition, Ed Masse, dean of the Temple University School of Business Administration says, "American business, in general, is staying lean and mean. Two or three managers are being asked to do jobs that took at least five in the past. Foreign competition and the fast-changing economic climate have kept corporations from staffing up.[12] This can only frustrate new entrants into the labor markets as they attempt to climb the corporate ladder of success.

In order to cope with this discouraging scenario, younger workers will have to redefine their timetable for success and try to be more patient in waiting for advancement. This country's social values have historically emphasized progressively upward mobility and increasing compensation. Success, which has traditionally been defined in monetary terms, will have to change to reflect new expectations. For workers, this means modifying values to appreciate the continuum of work life, encompassing upward and horizontal mobility without increased pay, and even downward mobility with reduced responsibility and reward.[12] With the higher education levels of most managers, emphasis should be shifted to personal challenges and growth opportunities--not exclusively money. This may sound extremely idealistic, but it is possible through innovative ideas and methods implemented by today's top management.

OLDER WORKERS

A natural development which partially resolves the younger worker's disenchantment with the *system* and their impatience for quicker entry into the upper levels of management is the retirement of older cohorts. In this respect, younger workers tend to favor earlier retirement for older employees as a way to move them out of the labor force to create and maintain room for their own advancement. However, with the shrinking number of young workers entering the job market, businesses will be hard-pressed to find replacements for their departing older employees. In addition, the social and psychological importance for older workers to maintain their identity and retain a sense of usefulness in terms of work can not be overlooked.

For some employees, retirement is an advantage, permitting them to escape hated jobs, to spend more time on activities they have always enjoyed, or to fashion new roles consonant with their energies, interests, and financial resources.[14] In addition, there are many other reasons for retiring as early as possible. First, individuals retire because they are tired of what they are doing and see no other worthwhile alternatives. Older workers who have grown up expecting to have one career in their lifetime, don't think they can start a new career late in life. Also, work schedules today are structured so that they generally require full-time work if one is to work at all. Many older people would like to continue working, but not at the pace they kept when they were younger. Finally, the more physically demanding the work, the more likely it is that the worker will retire as soon as possible. A lawyer or judge is seven times as likely to keep working as the laborer, and the college professor is four times as likely as the cafeteria employee to continue working.[15]

On the other hand, retirement can also be marked by lowered self-esteem and a lack of stimulation that can lead to apathy or depression, jeopardizing vigor and effective functioning.[16] Today, workers are finding themselves spending one-quarter of their adult lifetime in retirement as compared to only 7% in 1940.[17] Furthermore, there is ample evidence that when middle-aged workers lose their jobs or seek to change them, they find it more difficult than younger workers to find new employment; and despite legislative attempts to prevent age discrimination, various practices by employers can make it difficult for older workers to keep their current jobs.[18] Fortunately for older workers, several social forces are now converging that will allow many people to continue working past the traditional retirement age. First of all, more older people want to work. A national poll conducted by the research firm Public Agenda shows that a majority of Americans want to work one way or another after the age of 65 even if they had enough money to be comfortable for the rest of their lives.[19] Second, older people today are healthier and work is becoming less physically demanding. Health continues to improve through findings concerning diet, lifestyle, and exercise while the post-industrial economy is becoming more based on knowledge and experience.[20] Also, it should be recognized that elderly individuals will comprise the majority of the country's consumer base, thus, the value of the older worker's judgment is magnified.[21] Third, older people will need to work. Due to the shifts in worker-to-retiree ratios, there will be changes in Social Security, including a rise in the age of eligibility, the taxing of benefits, a reduction in protection from inflation, and the elimination of some benefits to the financially secure. With less of a financial base for later life, the elderly must remain in the work force to survive.[22] Fourth, mid-life changes, as well as regular exits from and re-entries to the workplace, are becoming more common due to increased career education.[23] Last, older workers will become more desirable and necessary. Most importantly, the strength and eagerness of younger workers must be balanced by the sound judgment, personal skills, accumulated experience, and availability of older cohorts.[24]

Because of these societal trends, retirement as we now know it will soon disappear.[25] The past tendency toward early retirement will slow and finally reverse itself, at first in a few industries, and eventually across the whole work force.[26] The companies that initially recognize these patterns will have a head-start in sustaining the size of their current human resource pool.

BUSINESS ENVIRONMENT

The decreasing availability of higher level positions within companies is already appearing in the private-sector of business. Service companies such as Marriott and McDonalds have made significant changes in their commitment to rounding out their work force in response to the changing composition of the labor force.[27] In the years to come, there will be an increasing number of older people working in a variety of other service positions, such as security guards, hotel clerks, receptionists, limousine drivers, small-company consultants, airline reservation agents, and insurance claims adjusters. However, when profit margins are tight, lower and middle management cuts become attractive for quick cost savings. This only makes things more difficult between companies and their employees. For instance, low-growth businesses like the computer and automobile industries are staying lean as a way to free capital resources. Peter Van Hull, an automobile industry expert predicts that overall employment will fall 5% a year through the 1990s and most of the cuts will be mid-level or clerical staffs. He states, "There is a view that middle-management and clerical groups are involved in work that doesn't add value to the product."[28] Regardless, the changing labor market will require considerable adaptation on the part of these employers. Because of the relative scarcity of young workers to older employees, businesses will have greater incentive to encourage older workers to remain in the labor force longer. Therefore, it is expected that private industry will increasingly provide better information about job openings to employees, increased amounts of training and retraining, and more flexible working arrangements, especially for older workers.[29]

However, private-sector efforts will not be enough in themselves. With the strong role the public-sector plays in funding and administering many employment and training programs, in shaping incentives and disincentives for labor force participation, and in determining the quality of preparation for employment that our public educational system provides, changes in public policy must also be necessary.[30]

Public-sector employment clearly illustrates the severity of the plateau problem. After growing from 7 million in 1955 to a peak of 17 million in 1980, federal, state, and local employment had fallen back to 15 million by the end of the decade.[31] As public management expert James Wolf writes, "it is impossible to avoid the conclusion that baby boom demographics and the public employment bust will severely constrict career opportunities in the public sector. The obvious, and perhaps most damaging, consequence will be the number of plateaued public employees whose potential for movement into positions in the organizational hierarchy will be severely limited. Opportunities for career success, as currently defined by title, status, and a bigger paycheck will diminish.[32]

In view of this outlook, public and private sectors must implement policy changes before the front-end of the baby boomers begin to reach retirement age.

ALTERNATIVES

Historically, our economy has derived much of its strength from the flexibility of its work force, that is the willingness of the current labor pool to make job changes and the large resource of new entrants who can more easily be directed into appropriate jobs and areas. Now, because of the changes previously mentioned, the work force is less likely to adapt as quickly.

Currently, no guidelines are available to direct us on what path to follow or who should take the lead. Historically, removal of older people from the labor force has not solved any of business's problems. Therefore, policies must incorporate values which are consistent with the changing attitudes among older workers. These include:[33] (1) A basic belief that all persons, regardless of age, can continue to be productive members of the labor force, should they be physically or psychologically able and willing to participate; (2) A belief in the heterogeneous nature of the older population and a commitment to making options available, without penalty, to participate in paid or unpaid activities in the labor force that reflect this heterogeneity; (3) A recognition that older people can and do function differently, regardless of age; and, (4) A recognition that in order to understand the differential participatory nature of older people in the labor force, there needs to be an ongoing program of basic research to guide policy makers. Such research will need to be designed to allow for a high degree of specificity regarding description, explanation, and prediction concerning the group of persons under consideration.[34]

As many older individuals wish to seek new or second careers, education-work programs will be needed. D.O. Cowgill, author of

The Aging of Populations and Societies, suggests that the increased motivation for extended education throughout one's career combined with the general concerns about older workers as unused resources, are signs that today's workplace is rapidly moving toward maturity.[35] While retraining of workers has become more popular among public and private sectors, it is still confined to mostly the upper and lower ranks on the organizational chart. Efforts must be made to encourage training and retraining with the emphasis placed on improving the flexibility of workers in service industries, including government. This segment of business will represent the greatest portion of national employment and output in the next century. As this continues, it will create significant impacts toward changing and developing attitudes about older workers and their work roles.

Much is dependent on whether the young labor market will be ready and willing to accept the re-entry of older workers with the potential sacrifice of their own advancement. What is needed is a national policy which encourages business to identify new and innovative ways to involve older people in the productive activities of work. One pressure that has resulted in retirement not being re-defined is the desire of companies to maintain employment for younger workers. If financial and social policy disincentives to employment could be reduced, there is no reason to believe that the economy would be unable to expand gradually to accommodate more "retired" persons, especially in part-time, self-employment, and service capacities.[36] This does not imply that unlimited expansion is possible, but to point out that intergenerational job competition is not direct, and job-for-job substitution of younger for older employees is not common.[37]

With this in mind, the following alternatives should be considered.[38]

- Re-educating and training programs for older workers in order to prolong careers and enable job flexibility. This should especially be used in industries where recruitment of trained personnel is difficult and costly.
- Phased-retirement designed to permit job retention by older employees. This arrangement provides reduced work schedules with partial retirement.
- Part-time work which enables re-entry into the workplace for employees. This approach usually entitles workers to basic wage rates and minor fringe benefits.
- Annuitant pools involves the employment of a company's own retirees for temporary, full, or part-time assignments.
- Contract work using older persons as independent contractors on a fee-for-service basis. This is often used in the field of sales, technical consulting, and temporary personnel services.
- Multiple flexible work arrangements are practical when experienced, older employees have long-standing clients who value the "wisdom" of the elderly worker.

These options are viable because older people have the time, the hours are right for them, and they are willing to be active participants. At the same time, they do not directly conflict with younger worker's job plateau concerns. Therefore, it seems predictable that pressures from old people and from the public at large will modify the existing work and retirement roles.[39]

Before any judgment can be made on the effectiveness of these policies, more data is needed regarding the employees involved in these programs. Systematic organization of this information would facilitate interpretation of results and suggest appropriate education programs to meet the different needs of workers--both young and old.

CONCLUSION

This paper is not intended to be a pessimistic view of the future for America's workers. Instead, it has attempted to point out the ramifications of our country's aging labor force so that actions can be taken to smooth this transition. If ignored, these developments may result in personal and social tension among the baby bust generation and their elderly counterparts and, consequently, American industry's productivity will suffer. Today's managers, by addressing this issue now, can create the opportunity for American business to reach its full potential throughout the next century.

NOTES

1. Bronte, L. and A. Pifer. *Our Aging Society, Paradox and Promise,* New York: W.W. Norton & Company, 1986, p.4.
2. Brotman, H. *US Chartbook on Aging in America,* Washington D.C.: Bureau of the Census, 1981, p. 2.
3. Bronte, L. and A. Pifer. *Our Aging Society, Paradox and Promise,* New York: W.W. Norton & Company, 1986, p.4.
4. Brotman, H. *US Chartbook on Aging in America,* Washington D.C: Bureau of the Census, 1981, p.4.
5. Ibid., p.4.
6. Johnston, W.B. "Workforce 2000: Work and Workers for the 21st Century", US Department of Labor, Indianapolis: Hudson Institute, 1987, p. 75.
7. Ibid., p.75.
8. Light, P. *Baby Boomers,* New York: W.W. Norton & Company, 1988, p. 258.
9. Ibid., p. 258
10. Ibid., p. 257.
11. Near, J. "The Career Plateau: Causes and Effects" *Business Horizons,* No. 10, 1980, p. 53-57.
12. Light, P. *Baby Boomers,* New York: W.W. Norton & Company, 1988, p. 260.

13. Bronte, L. and A. Pifer. *Our Aging Society, Paradox and Promise*, New York: W.W. Norton & Company, 1986, p. 359.

14. Ibid., p. 61.

15. Dychtwald, K. and J. Flower. *Age Wave, The Challenges and Opportunities of an Aging America¨*, Los Angeles: Jeremy P. Tarcher, Inc., 1986, p. 174.

16. Bronte, L. and A. Pifer. *Our Aging Society, Paradox and Promise*, New York: W.W. Norton & Company, 1986, p. 61.

17. Ibid., p. 388.

18. Ibid., p. 60.

19. Mowsesian, R. *Golden Goals, Rusted Realities*, New Jersey: New Horizon Press, 1986, p. 175.

20. Ibid., p. 176.

21. Farrell, C. "The Age Wave--And How to Ride It", *Business Week*, 1989, p. 112-116.

22. Mowsesian, R. *Golden Goals, Rusted Realities*, New Jersey: New Horizon Press, 1986, p. 177.

23. Mowsesian, R. *Golden Goals, Rusted Realities*, New Jersey: New Horizon Press, 1986, p. 179.

24. Ibid., p. 180.

25. Ibid., p. 183.

26. Ibid., p. 183.

27. Dychtwald, K. and J. Flower. *Age Wave, The Challenges and Opportunities of an Aging America*, Los Angeles: Jeremy P. Tarcher, Inc., 1989, p. 182.

28. Light, P. *Baby Boomers*, New York: W.W. Norton & Company, 1988, p. 261.

29. Dychtwald, K. and J. Flower. *Age Wave, The Challenges and Opportunities of an Aging America*, Los Angeles: Jeremy P. Tarcher, Inc., 1989, p. 183.

30. Bronte, L. and A. Pifer. *Our Aging Society, Paradox and Promise*, New York: W.W. Norton & Company, 1986, p. 374.

31. Light, P. *Baby Boomers*, New York: W.W. Norton & Company, 1988, p. 260.

32. Ibid., p. 260.

33. Mowsesian, R. *Golden Goals, Rusted Realities*, New Jersey: New Horizons Press; Includes four points listed, 1986, p. 239-240.

34. Ibid., p. 240.

35. Ibid., p. 126.

36. Bronte, L. and A. Pifer. *Our Aging Society, Paradox and Promise*, New York: W.W. Norton & Company, 1986, p. 357.

37. Ibid., p. 357.

38. Ibid., p. 358.

39. Ibid., p. 64.

REFERENCES

Abbott, J. "Those Aging Boomers", *Business Week*, (May, 1991), p. 106-111.

Bronte, L. and A. Pifer. (1986), *Our Aging Society, Paradox and Promise*, New York: W.W. Norton & Company.

Brotman, H. *US Chartbook on Aging in America*, Washington D.C.: Bureau of the Census, 1981.

Dychtwald, K. and J. Flower. *Age Wave, The Challenges and Opportunities of an Aging America*, Los Angeles: Jeremy P. Tarcher, Inc., 1989.

Farrell, C. "The Age Wave--And How to Ride It", *Business Week*, (October, 1989), p. 112-116.

Johnston, W.B. "Workforce 2000: Work and Workers for the 21st Century", US Department of Labor, Indianapolis: Hudson Institute, (June, 1987).

Light, P. *Baby Boomers*, New York: W. W. Norton & Company, 1988.

Mowsesian, R. *Golden Goals, Rusted Realities*, New Jersey: New Horizon Press, 1986.

Pampel, F. *Social Changes and the Aged*, Lexington Books, 1981.

Parker, J.F. (Oct. 1991), "Workers Have a Goal for 2000: A 40-hour Week", *Chicago Tribune*, Sec. 8, (October, 1991), p. 1.

Rice, F. "Tougher Customers", *Fortune*, (June, 1990), p. 39-48.

Walker, A. "Aging and Intergenerational Conflict", *Aging and Society*, Cambridge University Press, (December, 1990).

Wise, D. *The Economics of Aging: A National Bureau of Economic Research Project Report*, The University of Chicago Press, 1987.

UNEMPLOYMENT AS THE 21ST CENTURY GROWTH PROFESSION: PRELUDE: "WELFARE REFORM" AS A COMIC OPERA

by

Frederick C. Thayer

"Welfare reform," one of the grander comic operas ever staged in Washington, features an unusual array of principal players who appear at first hearing to be singing in harmony. "Liberal" and "conservative" politicians who are, or were, likely 1996 presidential candidates, Christian Evangelical Protestants, quasiscientists who echo the l9th century British Fabian socialists, and a few cheerleaders for American "virtue" and "morality" do the singing. Stage manager and Federal Reserve Chairman Alan Greenspan has the gigantic task of keeping a very large wagon at the back of the stage filled with a silent chorus of eight million unemployed Americans, many of them the welfare recipients that the principal players repeatedly accuse of such sins as laziness and promiscuity.

The best-known aria in this opera is Senator Phil Gramm's "I will ask able-bodied men and women riding in the wagon on welfare to get out of the wagon and help the rest of us pull." When some of them pay attention to Gramm and find jobs, Greenspan is stirred to action. He immediately raises interest rates to slow down the economy and increase unemployment. As Greenspan finds the people who have just lost their jobs, he sweeps them into the wagon as replacements for those who paid attention to Gramm's request and his assurance that "we love you." President Bill Clinton, singing the most harmonious line ("the welfare system is broken"), nudges his economic coach, Laura D'Andrea Tyson, who reminds Greenspan that he must keep the unemployment rate above 6.0 percent, and he does indeed announce on February 22, 1995, that he thinks he may have to cause more workers to lose their jobs so he can keep the wagon completely full.

The huge chorus of the unemployed is silent because, as sinners, they are expected to keep quiet, but also because they are thoroughly confused. They know from experience that if some of them "get off the wagon," as Gramm asks, Greenspan will push them back onto the wagon or find others to replace them. Meanwhile, they must listen to the biblical melody of the Evangelicals ("no work, no eat"), the solemn chant of the quasiscientists ("you have inherited stupidity, and you should not have children"), the plaintive weeping of secular and religious moralists ("no sex before marriage, no matter what

Frederick C. Thayer *is professor emeritus, Graduate School of Public and International Affairs, University of Pittsburgh, Pittsburgh, Pennsylvania, and senior fellow for Education Policy, Phelphs Stokes Fund, New York.*

age"), and the vocal exercise of the economists that has so much immediate influence on public policy ("we must maintain high unemployment").

A major growth profession of the 21st century is likely to be unemployment, in this country and elsewhere. Except for the very rich and very poor, unemployment is usually not so considered. From Aristotle to Washington and Jefferson to some of the Rockefellers to George Bush, "democracy" has embraced the idea that the rich should manage public affairs as an avocation or hobby, even a duty that repays society for their good fortune. Presumably, they have no need for a salary; John Kennedy did not accept his presidential salary. Also presumably, they are incorruptible and, sometimes, even can finance their own campaigns, as Steve Forbes and Ross Perot demonstrate.

Those of the poor considered incapable of working are, even so, mildly resented as a drag on the economy. Many of them are thought to have character traits, inherited from parents and other ancestors, that make them lazy enough to not even bother looking for jobs. If we find them holding out cups as we walk by them on the streets, many of us may mumble, "Get a life!" or "Get a job!" The traditional view is that work, or labor, is available for all, and the jobless are *choosing* to be jobless. Worse yet, they are "unproductive" in that they are not making goods to sell in the marketplace. Many have been labeled "tramps." "hoboes," "vagabonds," "vagrants" and, let us remember, "pioneers." In virtually all cases, they should not be "spoiled" with welfare benefits. English clergy once argued in sermons that if each parish were to send one of these people to the "colonies" each month, the parish would be left with only its productive citizens.

As we move into the next millennium, we now confront the phenomenon we have been trying to wish away for a long time. Work, or labor, will not be available for many citizens, especially if we insist that labor is legitimate only when producing goods to sell. In theory and bookkeeping systems, working for government is considered only a form of welfare, no matter how necessary the jobs. There are obvious and overlapping reasons.

As David Macarov has brilliantly been outlining for some years, the ability of technology to increase productivity has been accelerating so fast for so long that it more and more outstrips the need for jobs by those entering the labor force. This can be labeled "overpopulation" if you choose, and we have hidden it by using many devices to officially remove people from the labor force. The 40-hour week is one such example, so are child labor laws, so is compulsory high school, and so is social security. These actions have often been described as altruistic in that they provide for more comfortable old age, and better-educated and more highly skilled workers. Even the G.I. Bill that introduced mass higher education following WW II reflected, at least in part, a fear that jobs would not quickly be found for the millions suddenly being demobilized.

The current furor about "welfare reform" is perhaps the best possible example along these lines. In the Great Depression, when unemployment rates stayed in double digits until 1942, it was widely understood that it made no sense to ask women raising children on their own to look for jobs. Common sense required that they be paid to stay home and raise the children, a form of public service and, indeed, an assigned duty. Politicians, of course, cannot be given all the blame for such silly rewriting of history. My fellow intellectuals deserve much of the credit, for they provide the underpinning for political hypocrisy.

The most important corollary theory that intellectuals have produced is that society, acting through its government, cannot afford to pay citizens for not working, nor even take action to keep them healthy enough to perform whatever duties society might one day have to ask them to perform. In a nutshell, there is no evidence at all to support the widespread agreement that deficit spending by government damages the economy, and that the national debt is a threat to our future. Indeed, deficit spending has *never* damaged the economy, but *cuts* in deficit spending *always* harm the economy. The national debt, at its peak in 1946, was 127.5% of Gross Domestic Product; in 1995, it was 70.3% of Gross Domestic Product. As for annual deficits, they ranged from 20 to 31% of GDP in the early to mid-1940s. The highest deficit since 1946 was 6.3% of GDP in 1983. How could such a trivial deficit do any damage, when deficits many times larger in the 1940s won a war and ended the Great Depression?

INTRODUCTION THE CAST

The background themes that play on and on as the principals sing their individual arias are those that drive "welfare reform." These themes are old ones, and they were written centuries ago, first by Christian Protestants, later by secular intellectuals, in such fields as public law, government and economics, who put slightly different words to the same music. The Protestant approach is dedicated to the notion that *all* human decisions are "voluntary," even for the individual who is threatened with eternal damnation or starvation for not working, in that the individual "chooses" to respond to the Savior or to Satan. The secular intelligentsia of this country preaches "independence," "individual freedom" and "free will" decision-making, ascribing inner motivation to genes. Taken together, these themes proclaim that all unemployment *must* be "voluntary," even if the government *announces* that its policy is to maintain an unemployment rate of 6.0%. The economists, having told presidents to keep people out of work but also providing the background theme that involuntary unemployment is impossible, are the most agile of all. There is every reason to conclude that this secular theme of voluntarism was deliberately written to avoid challenging the Protestant version.

The attack on the jobless poor is a by-product of the dedicated effort by Protestants, especially Evangelicals, and the modern secular intelligentsia to preserve the religious, political and economic myths that the very presence of millions of unemployed workers demonstrates to be false myths. The jobless cannot be blamed for being out of work unless these defenders of the myths pretend that public policies to *compel* workers to remain out of work cannot possibly exist and, in fact, do not exist. When true believers must ignore evidence that contradicts the myths, they become especially angry at the bearers of the evidence, in this case the unemployed. Disingenuousness and even outright lying become common when the defenders of the myths feel threatened, and this is true, unfortunately, for both secular and religious defenders. The pretense that all unemployment is voluntary is one such example, and I cite one other at this point.

Understandably, there is considerable worry about the increase in out of wedlock births, allegedly an example of uniquely American, and perhaps British, immorality in recent decades. True, nonmarital births in this country jumped from 11% of all births in 1970 to 30% in 1991, and from 8 to 30% in Britain, but also from 10 to 29% in Canada, from 11 to 47% in Denmark, from 6 to 15% in Germany, from 18 to 48% in Sweden, and from 7 to 30% (1990) in France. "Illegitimacy," the favorite word among those who see themselves as the standard-bearers of morality and do not hesitate to stigmatize the children along with their parents, is not unique to any one or two societies. The data may show only that nonmarital births are now carefully recorded instead of being carefully hidden as they used to be; the literature considers the old data anything but trustworthy. Now that politicians and other celebrities, including heads of state, publicly acknowledge fathering children out of wedlock, nobody should be surprised that the poor do the same thing, especially since procreation has long been a *duty* assigned women because of the presumed need to increase population.

Given the myths that drive public policy and undergird the theme music of this comic opera, the word "duty" seldom makes the headlines. The "welfare reformers," however, are indeed outlining what they claim to be the *duty* of all members of the labor force to *work*, a duty to themselves, to their families, to society at large and, perhaps most of all, to God. House Speaker Newt Gingrich, a principal player, has explicitly inserted the religious theme by designating a particular book, and not a widely known one, as the best source for understanding the "welfare problem" and what to do about it. Written from a Christian Evangelical perspective, the book demonstrates how far true believers will go in attempting to avoid the question of *involuntary* unemployment because the Bible presumably asserts that all unemployment is voluntary. The book's author, as I shall indicate in more detail later, is unable by virtue of his world view to see Chairman Greenspan pushing people onto the wagon of involuntary joblessness. Along with "education reform," "welfare reform" is an issue that cannot be fully addressed unless the religious questions are opened to scrutiny. As I see it, the unwillingness to do this is a major reason for the "voluntary unemployment" theme of this comic opera.

I find it impossible to avoid the conclusion that because the holy books of the great religions, including the Bible, are collections of principles, rules and regulations for the management of societies, those directives were applicable to the societies then existing, but can no longer be considered automatically applicable. The duty to work, the belief that productive work is always available, and associated questions such as sex education, sexual abstinence and reproduction are matters taken up in the Bible. Many "reformers" believe that Biblical instructions must be obeyed to the letter, even when those instructions are wholly compatible with the widespread slavery of biblical times. Speaker Gingrich has endorsed an author who looks back approvingly on whipping, solitary confinement and bread and water diets as "tough love" motivational techniques for dealing with workers, including slaves, who do not give maximum effort. This perspective, shared by many "reformers," sees the entire problem as one of rehabilitating sinners, and "fallen women" are particular targets.

POOR WOMEN, TRADITIONAL DUTY, AND EUGENIC DISCRIMINATION

Some "reformers" argue that poor women have children out of wedlock in order to collect larger welfare checks, and may even be predators who seduce males for that purpose. Teen-agers are the primary targets, other reasons for the rise in such births are discounted, and one important reason isn't mentioned at all. Sex education, free condoms and encouraging abortion might help, but "reformers" generally accept sexual abstinence as the only acceptable solution. Ironically, many of these "reformers" seem unaware of the tradition that childbearing is a painful, heroic, life-threatening *duty* of women that parallels the *duty* of men to fight and die in wars so that society may survive. Women are beginning to share the *duty* to fight and die, but men cannot perform the *duty* of childbirth. The "right to life" for women and men has much lower priority, no matter the Declaration of Independence. The "reformers" ignore the likelihood that many poor women have children because they have been taught that God and society want them to.

In abortion decisions, the Supreme Court has more than once observed that the country's interest in life is rooted in society's *need* for a larger population. The *duty* of women, not a "right," is to bear children, as many and as quickly as possible. Traditionally, a child becomes an adult upon entering puberty, and marriage and child-bearing immediately follow. Traditionalists should be asking that young people marry and produce children while in junior high school, but neither the tradition nor the abstinence now make sense. Justice Brennan once dissented from the majority's restatement of the tradition, arguing that the state of Connecticut, a party to the case, had not argued that it needed more people. In another case, Justice O'Connor asked if procreation was a Constitutional "right," suggesting that the need to regulate population growth might make it necessary to restrict such a "right."

Traditional family *duty* has long been supported by public policy. The current tax exemption for the parents of dependent children, $2,450 per year for those with taxable incomes up to $83,850, graduated thereafter, is a taxpayer subsidy for producing babies, a cash bonus. Democrats and Republicans now want to provide more rewards for non-poor parents, a form of "welfare benefit" for those who perform the *duty*. Some middle-class families doubtless count on such bonuses when planning families; the baby born in December is an exemption for that entire year. The welfare checks given to poor women also have subsidized the social *duty* they learned when their only toy, perhaps, was a doll. Some "reformers" now want the upper classes to increase their child production, but want the poor to stop, a rather obvious form of discrimination that can only be based upon the presumed "inferiority" of the poor.

Encouraging poor women to avoid pregnancy will amount to an official renunciation of the traditional population principle, and of a core "family value" as well. Poor males and females will be told that society does not *need* their children, even though different "reformers" are providing different reasons for delivering the message. Simultaneously, however, the same "reformers" are trying to keep alive the corollary tradition that the only legitimate purpose of sexual activity is the production of babies.

SEX AS DUTY OR RECREATION?

Prostitution, homosexuality, masturbation and contraception have long been condemned or reluctantly accepted because they do not produce children. Recreational sex, traditionally improper, is immoral and inefficient because it wastes precious resources; husbands are expected to husband their sperm for legitimate use. Holy books prescribe execution for homosexuals, dictionaries link masturbation with "self-abuse," and youngsters still are instructed that masturbation can cause everything from poor eyesight to epilepsy and bed-wetting. Traditionalists deplore the distribution of condoms in schools, condemning the belated decision of American pediatricians to support it. Former Surgeon General Joycelyn Elders was a favorite target of traditionalists because she would not pretend that absti nence was a sufficient policy for dealing with unwanted pregnancies and the spread of disease.

Traditionally, pleasure has been an irrelevant by-product for males performing sexual *duty*, but unpredictable and irrelevant for women. Poor young American women and men, unable to climb out of poverty for reasons soon to be mentioned, will now be instructed to commit themselves to a lifetime of sexual abstinence, even though they learned in church that child production is a traditional *duty*. Worse yet, political leaders across the board now praise the concept of having six or seven employers in a working lifetime, because "flexibility" and "mobility" are more prized than ever. With job security giving way to insecurity, stagnating wages that do not keep up with inflation, and sub-poverty minimum wages, how can families *know* they will be able to support children? The "reformers" want to put strict time limits on benefits, then blame the jobless for having children and not working. If life expectancy had been longer in biblical times, post-menopausal sex also might have been condemned.

The Christian Evangelicals who were a dominant force in the 1994 elections, and who list "welfare reform" as their top priority, are awash in such contradictions. They do not want poor women to produce children because society does not need them but, once pregnant, poor women must give birth because society *does* need the children. The "right to life" of the fetus is to be defended, even if it was earlier declared unneeded by society. While implicitly supporting a form of "planned parenthood" for the upper classes, they will permit only planned *unparenthood* (abstinence) or *unplanned* parenthood (no abortion) for the poor. The contradictions are intensified by the important players who do not want the poor to perform the *duty* of having children, but also do not want them to perform the *duty* of working.

"WELFARE DEPENDENCY" AND THE POLICY OF COMPULSORY UNEMPLOYMENT

The endlessly repeated "dependency" argument is shared by such certified policy intellectuals as former Rhodes Scholar and law professor Bill Clinton, former university president and now Secretary of Health and Human Services Donna Shalala, Senator Phil Gramm and House Speaker Newt Gingrich, both with Ph.D. degrees, Gramm's in economics. The "welfare system," so it is said, has created a "culture of dependency" that has encouraged the jobless to believe they are "not responsible" for "self-help," that they are the "victims," and that they might as well become lazy, shiftless, uninterested in training, addicted to drugs and sex, antisocial and involved in crime; the way to end this cycle is to shut down the system in a demonstration of "tough love." In announcing his presidential candidacy in February, 1995 Gramm declared that the system should end because "we love them and want them to have the opportunity to participate in the American dream."

While this is not the only explanation for why people are on welfare (innate stupidity, a propensity to be sinful, and general moral decay also are mentioned), this most popular version of "dependence" reinforces the myths of "self-reliance" and "independence," but the argument is silly. The youngster who "grows up" and leaves home may appear to assert "independence," but a new *dependence* is immediately needed. Anyone who works for a living is *dependent* upon the income supplied by an employer if a living standard is to be maintained. Traditionally, a wife is *dependent* upon the husband who is also her employer. Those on welfare are indeed *dependent* upon society as a whole, and government is the agent of society. Those now unemployed are government employees because they are performing the *duty* of not working as a matter of public policy.

Presidents, their economic advisers, Congress and the Federal Reserve have agreed for years that an unemployment rate of not less than 6.0% is necessary to prevent inflationary wage increases. As an economic concept widely known in the profession, this agreement has its own title--Non-Accelerating Inflation Rate of Unemployment, or NAIRU--and no public official of any consequence opposes the agreement. The most recent public expression of the policy is an essay in the *New York Times* of April 15, 1994, by Laura D'Andrea Tyson, President Clinton's chief economist, arguing that inflation does indeed become a threat when the jobless rate falls into a range of 5.9 to 6.3%. The standard view of 6.0% translates to eight million job-seekers, but does not include those "temporarily" laid off, working part-time because full-time work is unavailable, or so "discouraged" that they have stopped looking for work.

The policy has been highly effective. The Federal Reserve has raised interest rates on many occasions in efforts to "slow down" an "overheating" economy. There is little interest in prohibiting employers from hiring replacement workers and firing strikers who seek higher wages. There is only symbolic effort to raise the minimum wage above poverty levels. Policy-makers do not loudly proclaim their success; when Secretary of Labor Robert Reich announced in 1994 that full-time workers earning "low pay" had increased from 12 to 18% of the labor force since 1979, he labeled this a "problem," not the intended result of a policy he has not publicly questioned. Now that 6.0% unemployment is repeatedly labeled "full employment," even sophisticated analysts do not notice what has happened; in a recent book, Gertrude Himmelfarb refers to 1949, 1958 and 1961 as "high-unemployment years" because the jobless rates were "6 or 7%," unaware that such rates are now considered normal, and even an explicit policy objective.

Some of the principal effects of this successful policy of compulsory unemployment are regularly reported as "good news." When the unemployment rate increased from 5.4% in December, 1994, to 5.7%

in January, this showed that the Federal Reserve was "succeeding" in slowing the economy, and might not immediately raise interest rates again. The stock market rallied because the prospect of low inflation would cause banks to reduce interest rates on savings accounts, prompting depositors to move into the stock market. The *New York Times* of Feb. 25, 1995, had a front-page article headlined "Why Wall St. Cheers as Economy Slips." President Clinton repeatedly promises "job growth," failing to mention that new jobs take care of increases in the labor force, but without reducing the unemployment rate. He has bragged of an "economic boom" during his Administration, but a real "boom" would not include the "welfare problem" that worries him.

Understandably, those performing the *duty* of unemployment are disproportionately young. Among white males, 20% of those in the labor force, ages 16 to 19, are jobless, 10% of those 20 to 24. Among white females, 16 to 19, 17% are out of work. Among African-American males, 16 to 19, 40% can find no work; for ages 20 to 24, the rate is 23%. By way of comparison, the worst unemployment rate of the Great Depression was 25% in 1933, but 38% for non-farm workers. More than half of those working for today's sub-poverty minimum wages are adults, many of them the "unmarriageable males" that William Julius Wilson has studied. The sustained unemployment of recent decades has been exceeded only twice in the past century, during the Great Depressions of the 1890s and 1930s, and those periods were much shorter.

It is absurd and tragic that "welfare reform" became the immediate issue for President and Congress at the precise time unemployment was *less* than President,Congress and Federal Reserve want it to be. When the unemployment rate is *less* than desired, those out of work are involuntarily unemployed, they are indeed the victims of a policy of compulsory unemployment, it makes no difference why any one individual believes she is out of work, jobs are not available, and policy-makers want the unemployed to continue to do what they are doing. If three million of today's jobless were suddenly to find jobs, others would have to lose jobs in order to preserve the NAIRU. And, of course, a steady unemployment rate constantly increases the number of people kept out of work.

Policy-makers stumbled into this multi-decade debacle of forced joblessness after taking a number of other policy decisions, one by one over many years, without thinking ahead to the ultimate blind alley. Not until the 1930s, for example, did our high schools enroll 50% of the youngsters in age group 14 to 17. Compulsory high school kept them out of the labor force during the Great Depression, as did the prohibition of child labor. This improved national intelligence and discouraged teen-age marriage, but also implicitly promised that jobs would be available for graduates. The expansion of higher education following World War II also delayed entry into the labor force, and may have kept unemployment down, encouraged still later marriage, and implied that parents would be able to support their offspring through college. Combined with the almost forgotten Employment Act of 1946 and the Humphrey-Hawkins Act of the late 1970s, the tacit guarantee was decent jobs for parents, high school graduates and college graduates.

Policy-makers have long since decided that high unemployment is necessary, regardless of education, skill levels and parental support responsibilities. The *actions* of the policy-makers show unmistakably that parents, high school graduates and college graduates are in many cases *not needed* to perform the *duty* of working but, because the same policy-makers cannot bring themselves to admit they are at the end of that alley, they attack the jobless for performing the assigned *duty* of not working. Making things worse day by day, these policy-makers, whether Democrat, Republican, "liberal," "conservative," deny the *obligation* to create jobs that can sustain families, promise to compel the "able-bodied" to move from compulsory unemployment to forced labor, and identify them as the "voluntarily" unemployed who would not work until forced to wear the "scarlet letter."

The notion that high unemployment acts as a "cap" on production costs, and "disciplines" workers, is anything but new. A British Poor Law Commission concluded in 1909 that a pool of unemployed labor was necessary to the "Management of Men." Employers admitted that "the foreman...who has to get work done is much helped if he is always conferring a favor upon the man he employs, and a very marked favor upon those whom he employs frequently..." Supervisors were "afraid to give the men security of tenure, for fear lest it weaken their power over them." Today's NAIRU policy, buttressed by sub-poverty wages and potential replacement workers, is only a slightly more sophisticated version of the management principle that the fear of losing a job makes the worker afraid to ask questions.

The policy of compulsory unemployment is not a secret and, inasmuch as all public officials of consequence accept it, the agreement is not a "conspiracy." Sadly, the policy is overlooked even by those who oppose the "reforms" on grounds of "cruelty," because the myth that chronic unemployment is voluntary remains very powerful. It is embedded in economic theories that hold "business cycles" to be unavoidable and beyond human control but very temporary, in religious doctrines that consider unemployment evidence of individual sinfulness, and in broader social and educational concepts that individuals must be "blamed" for their failures if others are to be "praised" for success. The failure of the intelligentsia to acknowledge the policy of forced joblessness leaves the "welfare reformers" free to become hyper-moralistic. Some of them now pose as enemies of the "welfare system", an *environmental* explanation that absolves the poor, if only in part. Others pose as scientists who can explain the innate genetic deficiencies of the poor, the hereditary explanations.

"War on Poverty," "Counter-Culture," "Bell Curve"

Lyndon Johnson's woefully underfunded 1964 election-year gimmick, the War on Poverty, is now scorned for its part in creating "dependency." This puny "war," of course, could not have been launched in the absence of already abundant poverty, unemployment and malnutrition. It is, therefore, wholly dishonest, if politically convenient, to label the *cause* of that "war" (poverty) as the *effect*. Actually, a pointed early critic was Senator Robert F. Kennedy who, running as an anti-war presidential candidate in 1968, proclaimed "We Can Do Better!" in references to poverty. Aside from its puniness, the "war" also suffered from the misleading identification with "welfare rights" that do not exist. The appropriate question is whether society *needs* those who are currently poor and jobless, and what to do if they are unneeded. To reiterate, the current anti-jobs policy assumes that the unemployed are indeed *needed* to perform the *duty* of threatening the jobs of those at work, but the policy does not answer the question of how to reward the jobless for performing that *duty*.

The "counter-culture" argument blames "the 1960s" for an alleged decline in moral standards, an increase in recreational sex and out of wedlock births, and other sins traceable to feminism, civil rights, affirmative action, rock and roll, pot smoking and pornography. Today's "reformers" choose to forget the dominant event of the 1960s--the Vietnam War. Those drafted into military service to fight and perhaps die were given a week of "rest and recreation" half-way through their single year of combat duty, and delivered to the various flesh-pots of Asia at public expense. This military tradition, long associated with wars considered "morally just," was yet another public acceptance of recreational sex that today's hyper-moralists said nothing about at the time. Some of those not called to arms, whether by luck or deliberate evasion, are now among the loudest "welfare reformers" who blame the jobless for sinful idleness. The rise of a "counter-culture" in the 1960s should not have surprised anyone, especially given a seemingly endless war.

Blaming Lyndon Johnson and the "counter-culture" might make sense if widespread poverty and large-scale unemployment never had existed before the 1960s, and if such problems were unique to this country. Yet, except in big wars, the problems have been chronic since industrial concentration made them impossible to hide except through endless repetition of religious and intellectual mythology. Giving money to the poor and permitting them to even hear about recreational sex ("make love, not war") presumably "teaches" them bad habits, an *environmental* motivation. The opposite explanations point to the "innate sinfulness of the heart of man" and a quasiscientific *hereditary* view that blames parents and more distant ancestors for the perpetuation of low intelligence.

To the authors of *The Bell Curve*, Charles Murray and the late Richard Herrnstein, "welfare dependency" refers to those who, by virtue of inherited subnormal intelligence, are likely to be unemployable, bear out of wedlock children and, therefore, be "dependent" on charity or public assistance. The conclusion is not racially based, but the authors point out that the average intelligence scores of African-Americans are lower than those of whites and other groups such as Asians and Jews. While Murray, of necessity the book's defender, claims that the data should not lead to immediate panic, his long-term crusade against welfare belies his claim that he has no interest in policy. In a C-Span discussion of the book, he observed that "if you have people with low IQs having more babies than people with high IQs, you end up with downward pressure on human capital." While this "does not mean that you must start advocating eugenic schemes," he added, "it's time to get serious."

As Charlotte Allen notes, Murray's current argument is the opposite of his 1984 attack on welfare, one that blamed the "system". He now blames innate stupidity and unemployability, and only then the welfare that "subsidizes births among poor women who are disproportionately [stupid]." America, he says, does indeed have "fertility policies" that "social-engineer who has babies, and [they] are encouraging the wrong women." To give Murray and Herrnstein their due, they oppose subsidies for any births, but they do not attack tax exemptions, their focus being the poor and procreation. If poor stupid women, clever enough to produce babies for money, are to be stopped from reproducing, Murray clearly implies a "eugenic" policy is needed. His new stance meshes with racial stereotypes about sub-human intelligence and lust, including the view of Biblical literalists that slavery was a "natural" relationship of "superior" and "inferior" peoples, but the literalists also are committed to maximum population growth.

Murray's shiftiness, however, is less important than the long fascination of intellectuals with the "heritability" argument; a recent case is almost a perfect example. Campus uproar immediately followed when the president of Rutgers University blamed "genetic hereditary background" for low admissions test scores among minorities. His statement was wholly compatible with "democratic" myths about "independent" citizens motivated by "inner selves" and genetic endowment to make "free will" decisions. The myths conveniently overlook the commands that parents or their surrogates issue to children, that teachers issue to students, that traditional husbands issue to wives, and that employers issue to employees. These are the basic forms of *environmental* motivation. "Free will" is a leisure time concept, and only then for adult males with enough resources to enjoy that leisure, often by paying others to obey them.

Men, and increasingly women, make their greatest contributions at work; sadly, the environment can be oppressive, and employees are subject to dismissal and exile. There is no distinction between the employee punished for "insubordination" in a "democratic" society, and one punished for "dissidence" in an "authoritarian" regime. Humans are taught from birth to obey legitimate authority, and even Murray, noting that intelligence scores stabilize by age six, implies that tests do not assess pre-birth intelligence, but only what has been taught since birth. The reaction of the Rutgers president and his supporters (an "inadvertent remark") demonstrates that they do not understand the difference between "environmental disadvantage" and "stupid parents" as causes of low test scores. Ironically, intellectuals who have the *duty* of sustaining social myth give excessive weight to genetic factors in order to reinforce "individual freedom," but the same argument reinforces the idea that the rich are "superior." Worse yet, doctrines of "genetic deficiency" justify undemocratic policies to maintain "caste" systems and a "permanent underclass."

Essentially, Murray argues that innate stupidity prevents some citizens from performing the *duty* of work, but also makes it socially undesirable that they perform the *duty* of procreation. In this context, they are non-citizens. If ending cash payments does not halt procreation, what about compulsory abortion, compulsory sterilization and similar solutions? The Evangelicals and Murray are unlikely to remain complete partners, because the former are still believers in the population principle and will not want to discourage or prevent the birth of potential recruits for the churches. Further, there is no reason to assume that all poor women are unintelligent and will produce unintelligent children. The hereditary argument is a weak one and, given the policies of compulsory unemployment and sub-poverty wages, arguments about the War on Poverty and the "counter-culture" are just as weak, as history demonstrates. The country had little trouble finding useful things for millions of the unemployed to do in World War II, either in factories or in the military, technology has not changed all that much in recent years, and intelligence levels are higher. The record of history, however, almost always gives way to the power of myth, religious or secular.

Science and Religion: The New Fabian Socialists, the Evangelicals and "Voluntary" Unemployment

The implied agenda of *The Bell Curve* resembles the 19th century efforts of the Fabian Socialists to breed a superior British race that would expand the Empire. The most famous of the originals were Sidney and Beatrice Webb, George Bernard Shaw and H. G. Wells, who supported the new "science" of eugenics that appeared in the 1880s. The Fabians wanted an "intelligent purposeful selection" that would "insure the rearing of an Imperial race," in Sidney Webb's words. Thoroughly documented by Gertrude Himmelfarb, who admires the moralism of the Fabians if not their socialism, the Fabians were quite forthright. The Webbs condemned the "feeble-minded mother of illegitimate children, the feeble-minded vagrant wandering along the road, and the feeble-minded parasite of urban soup-kitchens and free shelters." Wells attacked the "mean-spirited, under-sized, diseased little man, quite incapable of earning a decent living...married to some under-fed, ignorant, ill-shaped, plain, and diseased little woman, and guilty of the lives of ten or twelve of ugly, ailing children." Such people, the Webbs added, should be "permanently segregate[d], under reasonably comfortable conditions and firm but kindly control" in government facilities because, if they had more children, they would "hasten our undoing as a nation." Sidney Webb feared that if "race deterioration or suicide" continued, Britain would be "falling to the Irish and the Jews," and Wells included the "black, or yellow, or mean-white squatter," quite a different collection of the "feeble-minded" than Murray and Herrnstein have now given us.

In a book that Beatrice Webb lavishly praised, Wells proposed that the undesirables live "on sufferance." If they produced babies, they should be killed for "an ideal that will make killing worth the while," but humanely, "with an opiate." He hoped that "half the population of the world, in every generation, [would be] restrained from or tempted to evade reproduction." Shaw, advocating a "eugenics religion," asserted that "we must eliminate the Yahoo or his vote will wreck the commonwealth." The Webbs, believing that some of the destitute might be salvaged, asked that a new public authority set up "Training Establishments" that could transform some of the poor into willing workers. For those with "morbid states of mind," "Detention Centers" would supplement existing lunatic asylums. All services should be provided "in kind," cash being given only to those too old to work. "Without an obligation to good conduct, or to seek and keep employment," Beatrice Webb argued, cash would "encourage malingering and a disinclination to work," a 19th century version of the "welfare dependency" argument.

In taking up "the most important of all questions, the breeding of the right sort of man," as Beatrice Webb described it, husband Sidney asked for an "endowment of motherhood," a system of government-provided family allowances. These cash subsidies might reverse a declining birth rate among the "abler classes" by encouraging "the procreation of what is fine and efficient and beautiful to humanity -- beautiful and strong bodies, clear and powerful minds, and a growing body of knowledge," the Wells ideal. In fathering two children out of wedlock, he doubtless believed they were the "beautiful" ones society needed. The New Fabians of the 1990s follow the same path: they want to discourage or prevent the poor from having children, and provide new bonuses for affluent parents.

If old and new Fabians have blamed "feeble-mindedness," religious "reformers" always have blamed the human propensity to commit sin by failing to work when jobs always are plentiful. Their biblical doctrine of "no work, no eat" is identical to "workfare," but they do not approve anti-procreation initiatives. Speaker Gingrich's favorite expert is Marvin Olasky, author of the Evangelical-oriented *The Tragedy of American Compassion*, an all-out attack on secular public welfare systems, and an attempt to show that earlier religious charities always were able to handle welfare problems. In his Preface to Olasky's 1992 book, Charles Murray still was blaming public welfare, not genes, for creating an "underclass," defined by Olasky as "pauperism," a condition of "unnecessary dependence".

Murray was arguing that without the "welfare system," the jobless poor would have looked for jobs and easily found them. Olasky is arguing that the jobless poor are sinners who cannot be helped by impersonal and bureaucratic public welfare, but only by religion-driven charities who will rehabilitate them with "tough love" approaches, because "until Christianity pervades and renovates the habits of social and civic life, there is no reliable foundation for prosperity." If "every able-bodied man" does not "support himself and family comfortably, [it is] owing to idleness, improvidence, or intemperance." As to what treatment regimes might include, Olasky cites 18th century workhouses whose masters could "punish...the idle, stubborn and disobedient by immediate confinement [with only] bread and water" and with "whipping," acts that were "not seen as oppressive" because the poor were "members of the community," not "animals." This is a formula for dealing with reluctant slaves, as the Bible itself makes clear.

Slaves who became Christians were free to consider themselves no longer slaves to their masters (1 Corinthians 7: 22-23), but this identity was so compelling that it did not require literal freedom. Slaves were expected to look upon their owners as their "benefactors" and, if the owners were Christians, work as hard as possible (1 Timothy 6:2). Christianity, therefore, incorporated its recruitment techniques with enhancements of slave productivity, especially useful to rulers of the Roman Empire. The immediate point is that dedicated believers such as Olasky simply cannot imagine that any unemployment is involuntary, no matter the data in government reports.

A favorite Olasky source is Jacob Riis' 1890 book, *How the Other Half Lives*, because it praised the work of charities that had "accomplished what no machinery of government availed to do" in helping the poor in New York tenements. Riis acknowledged that "New York is today [1890] a hundredfold better, purer...than ten years ago" but, as Olasky does not mention, this was only with regard to charitable operations seeking to improve the lot of children who lived in the tenements. Olasky, filling his book with minute data on charity-by-charity accomplishments in the 19th century (a Pittsburgh church had a visiting nurse who made 8,000 visits to 800 patients in three years, 43 of the patients having typhoid fever) uses Riis to demonstrate that the poverty problem should be turned over to such charities, but this was not Riis' conclusion at all. He praised the charities, but concluded that the only ways to deal with New York's tenement problem were by law, remodeling the houses and building model tenements. Contrary to Olasky, who uses Riis' account of a landlord who complained that tenants did not take care of renovated buildings, Riis concluded that the use of "competent agents on the premises," normal in modern apartments, already had solved the problem, and tenement dwellers were indeed competent to use reasonably priced and upgraded housing that only government regulation might make possible. Riis provided hard data that Olasky chooses not to mention; the 14,872 tenements with 468,492 people in 1869 had grown by 1890 to 37,316 tenements with more than 1,250,000, and the rate of growth was increasing. Riis did not at all suggest that the Evangelical preference for unfettered free markets and private charities could deal with the tenements that included 75% of the city's population.

Olasky uses a single reference to a survey of "charity experts" in 1892 to conclude that throughout the 19th century, only in "rare" or "very exceptional circumstances" were "honest and sober men" forced to spend "more than a short time out of work." There are mountains of evidence in the huge literature on poverty and unemployment to show that this cannot be true and that, contrary to Olasky and Murray, the private charities that tried long ago to cope with such problems could not do so and, indeed, were ill-equipped by their religious-based doctrines to do so. While data collection was primitive then, the economic collapse in 1837 left more than 50,000 jobless and 200,000 without adequate support, in a New York City population of 300,000. There were long depressions in the 1870s and 1880s and, at the time of the 1892 survey mentioned above, the violent steel strike in Pittsburgh announced the arrival of the depression of the 1890s. The official unemployment rate for nonfarm workers remained between 20 and 30% for the 1890s, and above 10% for most of the years from 1900 to 1915. In the early part of this century, more than 60% of the males employed in industry were paid less than $626 per year, at a time when $825 seemed the minimum necessary to support families. A New York commission, including members of Olasky's favorite 19th-century charities, concluded after a state-supported investigation that 69.9% of New York's tenements in 1884 had no water closets. In other works, Jacob Riis reported that serious crime was epidemic, especially among the young, in the tenements that housed 75% of New York's population.

Understandably, Olasky does not take into account some of the factors relevant to understanding poverty and unemployment in the 19th century. In church-dominated villages and parishes that are now suburbs of New York City, those designated as "paupers" were auctioned off to citizens who, for the lowest bid, would promise to house and feed them for specific periods of time, in exchange for work. Ironically, there was some suspicion that the "winning" bidders entered the contests only to get a little extra money, and there were no methods for examining the treatment given the paupers. Because workers earned very low sub-poverty wages, and were not protected at all against death, injury or illness incurred at work, the charities were indeed under pressure to keep the unemployed at even lower living standards so they would take any jobs they could find. On many occasions, especially when severe depressions suddenly threw many out of work, the charities were in no position to help everyone, and this reinforced their religion-inspired tendency to brand many of the unemployed as "undeserving."

While acknowledging that "some involuntary unemployment" occasionally existed, Olasky's insistence that it was very temporary ignores other evidence. In the 1890's, the papers of the *American Economic Association* were including articles showing that most unemployment was involuntary and not due to the character defects of the jobless. Nor does Olasky indicate any familiarity with the evidence as to why the private charities of the 19th century gave way more and more to the professional social workers of this century. Fairly accurate government data began to demonstrate the involuntary nature of unemployment, data that over the years has come to focus only on involuntary unemployment (those not seeking work are not counted). The huge immigration of the final decades of the 19th century, especially given the rampant poverty in the tenements, was beyond the ability of the charities to handle. Worse yet, these foreigners were often from Eastern Europe, and were emphatically not candidates for recruitment by the Protestant Evangelical missionaries who were looking for souls to save. A charity official whom Olasky repeatedly praises, Charles L. Brace, declared as early as 1869 that most new immigrants were of poor quality, "being either paupers, or criminals, or diseased, ... or whose labor, as destitute women, has not supported themselves." The over-supply of such people made their value to society less than their cost as non-producers, he added.

The religious thrust that is prominent among today's "welfare reformers" is a throwback to the pre-Civil War days and the belief that unemployment is a conscious sin. It would not be worth much space here except for the increasing prominence of Christian Conservatives in the Republican Party, and Speaker Gingrich's endorsement of the Olasky book. Olasky, even while admitting to involuntary unemployment in the Great Depression, attacks a 1930's social worker who dared question the prevailing concept that "people are in need through some fault of their own, a belief rooted in our culture, fostered by religious injunctions, nourished by education." Committed to supporting that old concept, Olasky even speculates that some of the social programs instituted during the Great Depression "may have prolonged economic misery," a view that accurately reflects the Christian Conservative belief system. The concept of voluntary unemployment, clearly developed in pre-industrial and slave conditions, is absolutely necessary to the support of that belief system.

Olasky, probably a perfect example of Protestant Evangelical thinking, might be surprised to learn that his prescriptions for dealing with the jobless poor are, except for procreation issues he does not mention, also like those of the old and new Fabian Socialists. Murray, agile as always, essentially agrees with both the Evangelicals and Fabians. With conservative capitalist Gertrude Himmelfarb stirred into the mix, welfare clearly is not an ideological issue. Nor should any of us forget that during the Great Depression, Franklin Roosevelt constantly worried that "relief" and the "dole" would become a "narcotic" unless benefits were connected with work. The religion-based myth of voluntary unemployment is so strong that even those who admire the old Fabians for their moralism--Himmelfarb is a good example--have not noticed that Sidney and Beatrice Webb concluded, in a massively documented three-volume *English Poor Law History* published in the late 1920s, that their earlier arguments had been incorrect.

After careful study, they decided that "involuntary Unemployment on a large scale [is] the characteristic disease of the modern industrial system in all countries," that it exists even in the best of times, and that when workers are "denied even the opportunity to work, and are reduced to destitution through no fault of their own, they become bitter and angry, as well as a danger to the existing social order." They also reported incontrovertible evidence that "the assumed category of the Unemployable was meaningless." Most of those classed as "morally and physically" incapable of work were, in fact, "usefully and even profitably employed" over a significant period of time that included World War I. The British Government itself described the "unprecedented mobilization, in the ranks of labour, of the decrepit and the unfit, the septuagenarian and the child," including "all those between 14 and 70 who were not absolutely incapacitated." The Webbs decided that what had been known as "work-shyness" ["welfare dependency"] was "amenable to nothing more recondite than a keener demand for labour and a higher rate of remuneration." Almost to their own astonishment, the Webbs discovered that the unemployed went to work when jobs were available, even if they were officially designated "unemployable" and could have retained that label.

Before they thoroughly researched the question, the Webbs had fought Winston Churchill, then a young government official who, in 1909, recognized that it was futile to insist that benefits given the poor be contingent upon their adherence to moral standards, the unbending Fabian position of that time. There was no way to know, said Churchill, if a man had lost his job "through his own habits of intemperance or through his employer's habits of intemperance." There was no need, then, to establish moral standards that Fabian eugenicists might devise, and to look for administrators who could distinguish between the "deserving" and "undeserving" poor. Twenty years later, the Webbs caught on, but their new evidence did not overcome accepted myth.

The Fabians were at least willing to admit that their moral stance had been a mistake, but it is sadly typical that today's "reformers" ignore the array of evidence that long-term unemployment is indeed involuntary, and quickly can be overcome. The American experience in World War II is just as convincing as the data the Fabians collected in the 1920s, but just as widely ignored. It is as though the social scientists remain afraid to contradict the dogma, and end up accepting it without serious question. As for the increasingly powerful Evangelicals in this country, a concept that does not exist in the Bible cannot possibly be discovered. In the world of slavery that gave rise to religious dogma, there could be no "involuntary" unemployment, only insubordination punishable by whipping or even starvation that would remove the offenders. We now face a form of "moralism" that, shared by secular and religious believers, is itself unbelievable.

Former Secretary of Education William Bennett and historians Himmelfarb and Olasky insist that the jobless poor be compelled to return to the "virtues" that fell victim to the 1960s or to "the deviousness of the human heart." Himmelfarb even argues that we must build into the social system the necessary "moral, social and, if possible, religious sanctions," but without saying how and by whom "religious" sanctions should be imposed. James Q. Wilson, co-author with Herrnstein of an earlier book linking genetic deficiencies, including intelligence, with criminality, has toyed with ideas of "preventive detention" for those "scientifically" shown to have such deficiencies. More recently, he has suggested removing children from "unfit" parents at the earliest possible age, presumably at birth, in the hope that their deficiencies in intelligence and "moral sense" might be corrected by high-intensity indoctrination in group homes or orphanages, bringing to mind Speaker Gingrich's endorsement of *Boys Town*, the motion picture about an orphanage that was filmed in the 1930s. Sociobiologist Edward O. Wilson argued in 1978 that "innate motivators exist in the brain" and "from these roots, morality evolved as instinct" or, as James Q. Wilson puts it, "moral sense." Such concepts, the ultimate products of the "free will" thesis, have the effect of dismissing without comment the function of social structures and legitimate authority to impose behavioral "norms" and "standards." Unless "innate" moral standards are identical in all humans, how are decisions made about "immoral" instincts?

The agreement among all the moralist "welfare reformers," including the eugenicists, may be enough to pass ugly legislation, but the agreement is superficial, with many issues left as yet untouched, especially the precise punishments to be administered to the immoral unemployed. "Thrift" is a favorite "virtue" of the moralists because its practice could make citizens responsible for their own survival when unemployed, their own pensions, and the proverbial "rainy day." Yet the most secularly religious social scientists, the economists, hold that high unemployment and stagnating wages are indispensable to economic stability. Unfortunately, these conditions prevent thrift, and also discourage the home ownership and 30-year mortgages important to the social stability that cannot be achieved without decent and steady incomes. From their perspective, economists are both moral and altruistic in prescribing how to help consumers by keeping prices as low as possible. In this standard view, "consumers" and "workers" are viewed as different people, yet another holdover from the age of slavery, and workers must be paid as little as possible if consumers are to get maximum benefits. Meanwhile, the contemporary Fabian eugenicists pose a question that Biblical literalists cannot accept, at least not yet. If it can be discovered at a very early age, or before birth, which citizens *are not needed*, what should be done to prevent their birth?

WHERE TO BEGIN?

In a careful survey released in March 1994, the Massachusetts Department of Public Welfare discovered that 70% of current recipients of Aid to Families with Dependent Children had been on welfare for longer than two years, 57% for more than three years, and 28% for at least five years. David T. Ellwood, Assistant Secretary of the US Department of Health and Human Services, a major architect of the Clinton Administration's "reform" proposals, had concluded while a professor at Harvard that more than 65% of such families would be on welfare for eight years or more. Yet in August 1994, his boss, Secretary Donna Shalala, insisted in Congressional testimony that it was absolutely essential to "cap" welfare benefits at two years so that recipients and caseworkers would know exactly when working would have to replace welfare. In an interview a few months earlier, Shalala repeated her long-standing insistence that "we should [not] subsidize poor mothers to stay out of the work force...we ought to do everything we can to move everyone into the workplace...we shouldn't have a different standard for one group of women." The "welfare establishment" of public agencies, social workers, and professors of social work had been insisting for years that the vast majority of those on welfare "went off welfare" in less than two years, even though any such assumption is obviously nonsensical in light of the *permanent policy of compulsory unemployment*. Shalala, trying to "help" those on welfare, was sticking to the widely accepted two-year "norm" because she believed it accurate and, therefore, believed that all the jobless could find work within that period. Does Shalala know that her positions make little sense in light of the anti-jobs policy?

Worse yet, the academic "experts" on welfare and poverty, perhaps as empathetic a group of intellectuals as can be found, have long been the unwitting allies of the economists who smilingly describe the need for high unemployment, and the political scientists who perpetuate the myths of "freedom" that produce such spin-off concepts as "welfare dependency." Among the intellectuals, the economists have the toughest time; they must acknowledge the theoretical need for public policy action to maintain high unemployment, but they also must pretend that all unemployment is voluntary. Saying things that appear to make sense while trying to remain true to both silly positions is very stressful, but relatively easy for those in academe who do not have to publicly comment on economic trends. The economists who work in Wall Street financial firms are more direct; they routinely announce, whenever the Federal Reserve raises interest rates to slow down job creation, that "what is good for Wall Street is not good for workers." The fully qualified economists at the center of public policy-making, however, know they lie about "putting people to work", and they are not alone. When President Clinton's chief economist publishes her estimate that a 6.3% unemployment rate is necessary, that is a policy statement, and the President must be assumed to know about it. Senator Gramm, a former economics professor, must be familiar with the NAIRU principle and the NAIRU policy. These people, and doubtless many others, are duping the public about "welfare reform."

The policy of compulsory unemployment assumes that those prevented from working are "able-bodied," "able-minded," and "ready and willing" to work, for that is the only way they can be used as instruments of public policy to threaten the jobs of those already at work. They are "riding in the wagon" awaiting a call to jump out and take the jobs of others. They are, to repeat it yet again, performing the *duty* they have been commanded to perform, and this is the key to understanding how to replace the comic opera of "welfare reform" that also features the Christian Conservatives dedicated to saving souls. "Our main purpose is winning people to Christ," says the founder of a Dallas organization that sponsors housing, recreation, education and summer job training for 9- to 13-year olds who, traditionally, are on the verge of adulthood. These organizations are the most dedicated to working in the inner cities that now resemble the tenements of the 1890s, and they are attracting both foundation grants and even some government grants.

What *duties* do we expect the poor to perform? Is it to be a *duty* to remain sexually abstinent for life if they cannot become self-supporting? Is it to be their *duty* to remain unemployed or, if we now compel them to perform the stigmatized *duty* of forced labor, will they be counted as "employed" or "unemployed?" If we put them all to work, what are policy-makers expected to do about the NAIRU policy of compulsory unemployment? If we keep them out of work and also demand that they not have children, what other *duties* do we have in mind for them? Except in cases of all-out war, do society and its government have an *obligation* to achieve full employment by creating jobs in such underfunded areas as health, environmental quality, infrastructure, transportation, education and a host of other areas usually labeled "public sector," even if this requires more public spending? None of these questions can be addressed until all of those now preaching the gospel of "reform" acknowledge that "welfare dependency" has been created by the *long-term public policy of compulsory unemployment.* This is not an easy task to achieve; traditional religious dogma will have to be swept away in the process of acknowledgement, and the same is true for the corollary sexual issues.

In the 1930s, movie stars Loretta Young and Clark Gable saved their careers by pretending, in traditional fashion, that they did not have a daughter who was born nine months after they had been together on location while making a film. Young went into hiding for months before giving birth, with press releases announcing her "illness." The baby was separated from her mother for several months, christened at a church ceremony in which priests knowingly used false names for the parents, and then raised as her own mother's "adopted" child. She had no contact with her father, and lived in stressful pretense that ultimately led to permanent estrangement of mother from daughter, and long-term psychological confusion for the daughter. It is not at all clear that dreadful harm is done to society at large if such individuals as former Canadian Prime Minister Pierre Trudeau, President François Mitterrand of France, miscellaneous members of Congress and other celebrities admit to having out-of-wedlock children, homosexuality or "living in sin," a violation that greatly disturbed President Jimmy Carter when he learned that some public officials were sharing homes without benefit of marriage.

The written rules and regulations that appear in holy books of the great religions may have made some sense in the early years of the civilized era. Job training for the 9-year olds who would be married and producing children by age 13 or 14 was logical enough, but job training for the same 9-year olds makes less sense today, other than as indoctrination in the *duty* of paying taxes ("gifts") to churches. Similarly, efforts to prohibit recreational sex until males and females marry at, say, age 30 and above, and to pretend that sex is only a *duty* that should not be treated as pleasure are simply absurd. And, as the global society seemingly moves toward acknowledging that overpopulation may be a problem, there may develop very logical arguments for encouraging recreational sex and "alternative life-styles".

Much of the present difficulty, I reluctantly conclude, is traceable to an understandable and deep-seated fear of being identified as "anti-religious." For Christian Conservatives, there are no issues to debate or discuss because their beliefs are beyond question. They often respond to challenges by accusing the challengers of intolerance. The fear of being so branded seems to have caused secular intellectuals to avoid examining their own beliefs because to do so would force them to closely examine religious beliefs as well. Rather than admitting to a steady increase in *involuntary unemployment*, for example, the intellectuals pretend they remain committed to the "voluntary" myth that is the same as the religious myth. Yet the only justification for modern intellectualism is that its practitioners will not lie to themselves.

The issues have little to do with supposedly competing ideologies. Producers who compete in the marketplace, the global marketplace included, must treat workers as harshly as necessary, by turning to slavery, forced labor or the maintenance of high unemployment, and individual producers and producing countries are not to blame. The Webbs, having finally decided that involuntary *Unemployment* was the problem, concluded their multi-volume, multi-year study with words that accurately portray the situation that the American anti-jobs policy has created:

> Is there any condition more sordidly tragic than the lot of the youthful Unemployed, to-day counted by the hundred-thous-and--under-nourished, physically undeveloped, empty-minded, lounging in disconsolate groups at street corners ... a prey to all evil influences? Is it seriously contended that by this public neglect the nation is adequately preparing these youths to fulfill their obligations as parents, citizens or producers? ...the fuller development of individual faculty, the finer tone of family life, or the widening grasp of public spirit...must remain the dominant consideration...

THE ULTIMATE CHALLENGE: THE REDEFINITION OF EMPLOYMENT

Our traditional views of work are colored by the long connection of work with slavery, and unbroken history from pre-Biblical times until, our case, the post-Civil War era. In the context of slavery, work is a form of imprisonment, one in which the workers are considered *sub-human* or otherwise fundamentally different than their bosses. Work is punishment, and anything less than what the boss considers top performance is grounds for any punishment desired, including killing. This relationship remains largely unchanged; anything less than top performance is grounds for firing, a form of exile that is similar to deportation, especially if the fired individual can no longer afford rent or the mortgage payment. In the face of these threats, implied or direct, the idea that an individual can come to *love* her work is nonsense. While we know that hostages can indeed *bond* with their captors, this cannot be the type of workplace enjoyment we seek.

Essentially, the very poor and the very rich inadvertently introduce a concept that we must take seriously one day. For them, work is separated from income. In the case of those on welfare, of course, the jobless are paid to act as standby workers who threaten the jobs of those who ask for higher pay. Yet, they are not fully aware of that duty, and the duty is not widely advertised. At the same time, we know that there is no acceptable yardstick for measuring the dollar value of any jobs in society. As it becomes obvious that jobs must be shared, that many needed jobs cannot be related to dollar values, that citizens may have to work in one year on-one year off shifts, it should gradually become clear that the concept of *citizenship* will have to include the separation of work from income. This may have to be done piecemeal, inasmuch as health care will have to be separated from employment, an accident of history that must be corrected. Traditional individualism, which effectively exiles many citizens while pretending not to do so, cannot be sustained. Traditionalists fight hard to maintain those traditions, even the most nonsensical ones, but they will not prevail over time.

Also inevitably, the population question will have to be addressed in light not only of the availability of socially useful labor, but also with respect to such hot issues as abortion and population control. If the planet cannot sustain infinite population growth, how shall we transform religious doctrines that say otherwise? How can we manage a planet that requires many of its inhabitants to ensure that they *not* reproduce themselves? It is sufficient merely to ask the question.

There is one very traditional assumption that may become beneficial in designing new definitions of unemployment, and the assumption already is being modified in ways--that may make sense. Traditionally, an individual is prohibited from attempting suicide because he/she cannot unilaterally withdraw his or her services from society because those services are *needed*. Once again, this is a *duty*, not a "right to life," but are we coming to recognize that there can come a point in time when society and the individual, acting in concert, can agree that the duty has in fact been completed, and that the individual can *voluntarily* "retire" from that duty. Out of such questions have come the concept of "assisted society" and the ethical debates about how much extraordinary health care should logically be provided to individuals who, according to the best judgment available, will die in the very near future. Everyone who is alive, therefore, is in this sense *employed*, and should be so recognized, regardless of the sources of their financial support.

Without elaborating in great detail arguments being developed elsewhere, permit me to briefly recap two eras of American economic history, the first a period from 1817 until War II:

- 1817-21: in five years, the national debt was reduced by 29%, to $90 million. A depression began in 1819.
- 1823-36: in 14 years, the debt was reduced by 99.7%, to $38,000. A depression began in 1837.

- 1852-57: in six years, the debt was reduced by 59%, to $28.7 million. A depression began in 1857.
- 1867-73: in seven years, the debt was reduced by 27%, to $2.2 billion. A depression began in 1873.
- 1881-93: in 13 years, the debt was reduced by 50%, to $1 billion. A depression began in 1893.
- 1920-30: in 11 years, the debt was reduced by 36%, to $16.2 billion. A depression began in 1929.

The listed depressions are the only such major occurrences in American economic history, and the sustained periods of national debt reduction are the only such periods. Even when the debt was virtually wiped out in 1836, a truly major depression immediately followed. Andrew Jackson is still listed as an outstanding president for paying off the debt but Martin Van Buren, who took office in 1837, had no chance at all of winning re-election in 1840 when the depression was only half-way to its conclusion in 1843. It appears that the elections of 1876, 1896, and, of course, 1932, were directly the political outcomes of those depressions.

There have been chronic deficits since the 1930s, and no new major depression; perhaps this is a coincidence, perhaps not. There have been a number of recessions, the beginning and end of each being determined and reported by the National Bureau of Economic Research, the non-governmental arbiter of such matters. In the following table, note that the "peak" is the highest point of economic growth before the economy starts downhill. The "trough" is, technically speaking, the lowest point from which "recovery" begins, but a slow recovery acts to extend the period of economic misery for some time:

PEAK	TROUGH
February 1945	October 1945
November 1948	October 1949
July 1953	May 1954
August 1957	April 1958
December 1969	November 1970
January 1980	July 1980
July 1981	November 1982
July 1990	March 1991

Perhaps coincidentally, perhaps not, each recession was immediately followed by a period in which annual deficits were reduced, relative to Gross Domestic Product. Presidents who sincerely believed that it was good for them, their parties, and the country to reduce the deficits may never have realized that they were setting the stage for a recession damaging to everyone, including themselves:

- The recessions that began in 1957 and 1960 did not help Richard Nixon in a close 1960 election.
- The 1973-75 recession hurt Gerald Ford in 1976.
- The 1980 recession hurt Jimmy Carter.
- The 1990-91 recession hurt George Bush, widely thought to be unbeatable until the slump took over.

Since 1992, the deficit has been reduced from 4.9% of GDP to 2.3% in 1995, with a further cut in progress this year. This reduction, more than 50% relative to GDP, suggests that a recession cannot be far off.

There is every reason to suggest that had the national debt not been so systematically attacked in the early period, and if in recent decades the deficits had grown right along with the economy, the depressions and recessions could have been avoided. I believe the connections can be explained, but I do not take up that issue here. I merely restate the issues we face in blunter terms:

- If we cannot afford to support the old, the young, the sick, students, single mothers, and other citizens for whom "normal" jobs are not available or should not be available, we should simply kill them. If we need them as citizens, we should pay them for doing what we want them to do, a far better choice than turning them into criminals and then warehousing them in prison.

UNEMPLOYMENT AND UNDERCONSUMPTION IN THE TWENTY-FIRST CENTURY

by

Bertrand H. Chatel

UNEMPLOYMENT

Unemployment is a basic feature of our economic system and may be characterized by a few figures.

Some Figures

- In the United States, the unemployed represent 7% of the active population;
- In Western Europe, unemployment reaches 12% in France, and 8 to 10% in England, Germany, Italy, or Spain, totalling 20 million persons;
- In Eastern Europe, in the former Soviet Union, there was no unemployment during that Marxist era; but it has appeared now, in the free enterprise economy of the Russian Federation and the Commonwealth of Independent States (CIS), at the rate of about 20%;
- In China, it is expected that unemployment will affect 200 million persons in the year 2000;
- In the developing countries, the majority of the population lives in a state of unemployment, which afflicts some 60% of the active people, while many workers receive an income often as low as $20 a year.

We can say, accordingly, that in developed countries, unemployment is about 10 to 20%, and in developing countries, it may reach 40% to 60% of the potentially active population. On the whole, it is estimated that our planet suffers from massive unemployment, which strikes 1/2 to 2/3 of its potentially active population, i.e., 2 to 3 billion persons.

Unemployment, consequently, is not an accident or a consequence of a temporary recession. It appears, on the contrary, as a structural component of our present economic system.

Actions

Governments are aware of this problem; they try to quantify it and they publish statistics. They create agencies for unemployment in

---

Bertrand H. Chatel *is an international consultant and a member of the American Council for the Club of Rome, Southampton, New York.*

to publicize opportunities for jobs, to encourage vocational training, or to exhort entrepreneurs to hire idle youth.

The international organizations are also active; the United Nations convened a World Summit for Social Development (Copenhagen, March 1995) to draw attention notably to unemployment; the International Labor Organization (ILO) and the World Bank have also produced valuable studies, programs, and seminars.

The regional governmental organizations (Europe, North American Free Trade Agreement (NAFTA) as well as the Economic Community of the Pacific) are also active in this field, as well as non-governmental organizations (NGOs).

However, the magnitude, permanence and expected increase of the problem have not yet generated a sound theory of unemployment as a key factor of our economic system, in order to study the causes and laws of the phenomena, to present adequate solutions capable of eradicating unemployment in the 21st century, and to build a new society based on full employment for all.

THE THEORY OF UNEMPLOYMENT

Unemployment is created by the mechanics of our present economic system, where incentives tend to eliminate human labor in favor of automatic machines to perform the tasks of production, informatics, and sales. The efforts deployed to ameliorate productivity have been so successful that human work has now been largely eliminated from whole factories, management, sales, and finances.

In addition, the introduction of women on a large scale in the labor force has doubled the demand for work, while the amount of work offered is continuously shrinking.

Since the unemployed are maintained at subsistence or survival levels by small governmental subsidies, they consume less, and sales consequently diminish, provoking recessions owing to a lack of consumption, as result of unemployment. This is a vicious circle and a self-destructive system.

In the developing countries--where the employed often earn only $20 a year, and the unemployed nothing--consumption decreases even more, leading to disinterest on the part of entrepreneurs or investors.

The Cycle of Consumption

Let us take an example. The employed consumers spend their salaries--say $1,500/month--at retail shops. These retailers order supplies from industries, agriculture, or services (see figure 1):

FIGURE 1

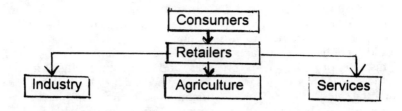

Those suppliers pay salaries which are used as income by the employed to pay for their purchases at the retailers' shops. This is the consumption cycle of the employed (figure 2):

FIGURE 2

Purchase of goods

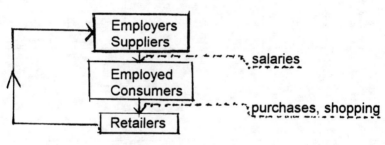

But the unemployed--a majority of the world population--follow another cycle (see figure 3): they receive, sometimes but not all the time, subsidies from their governments, at a survival rate--say $500/month i.e., one-third of the consumption of the employed. The suppliers and retailers pay taxes to the government in order to provide for the unemployment allowances given to the unemployed by the government.

FIGURE 3

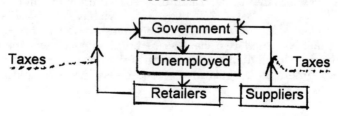

Losses in Sales

This system determines a loss in consumption, in addition to sadness for the unemployed survivors, i.e., the majority of the world population--constrained to misery and poverty, while technology would have had all the capacity to make them happy.

This also provokes a loss in sales, and hence in profits, for the retailers, manufacturers, farmers, and services. This loss is 2/3 of the potential sales, or $1,000/person unemployed in our example. Let us apply this number to our unemployment figures in the table below:

FIGURE 4

Country/Region	Population	Active population	Rate of unemployment	Unemployed population	Lost sales ($1000/unemployed)
USA	200 M	70 M	7%	5 M	5B$.month
Europe	250 M	80 M	10%	8 M	8B$/month
China				200 M	200B$/month
Developing Countries	3 B	1 B	60%	600 M	600B$/month
World	4 B	2 B	40%	800 M	800B$/month

The famous marketing experts who scrutinize the way to increase their sales have never uncovered this tremendous market which lies before them untapped: the market of the unemployed who are confined to consume at survival level or below, when they could become full and happy consumers.

A New Mandarinate

In the traditional Chinese society, the population was divided in a class system by the Mandarins. In India also, as well as in medieval western societies, the social structure was based upon the division of human beings into classes. We believe that we have abolished such archaic systems, but in our present economics of modern times, we have in fact recreated two classes: (a) the employed, who benefit from incomes distributed by the system and who can consume well; and (b) the unemployed--a kind of second-class citizens, the pariahs--

who receive small subsidies from the government and are confined to consumption at survival level:

- The employed class is composed essentially of public civil servants who enjoy the security of their jobs, and of skilled persons from the private sector, corporate employees at various levels with a more limited job security.
- The unemployed--sometimes skilled, often unskilled--are excluded from public and private jobs. Their situation inspires compassion, but is not hopeless if the marketers discover, one day, the loss in sales which they represent, and if they boldly invent a new economic system where, despite their unemployment, they will be authorized to consume above survival/starvation levels.

In this case, the employed will remain the super-consumers, the wealthy, the aristocracy and élite of our future society, but the unemployed will nevertheless have access to a normal consumption, which will provide additional sales of $800 billion/month. Now we are bound by an ethic concept that it is immoral to give money to humans who do not work, because the active workers would resent it. How shall we find a pretext to allot money to the unemployed and thereby transform them into solid consumers?

THE WORKERS IN RESERVE (WIR)

The first step of our endeavor is therefore to discover some pretexts to allocate purchasing power to the unemployed. We have to be careful not to discourage the employed who really work, by preserving their privileges of active workers. But, at the same time, we should find a way to channel money to the second-class citizens, confined at present to mere survival i.e., "the unemployed." First, should we keep that name, which implies a negative connotation? Instead, we shall call them "the Workers in Reserve" (WIR).

We have already used this kind of semantic differentiation when we transformed the "undeveloped" countries into "developing" countries, thus asserting a positive attitude of hope.

In the military sector, a similar classification already exists: an officer is active when young and will enter into reserve status later. If a war occurs, he will come back from the reserve into active duty. Let us examine how this concept could be applied in the cycle of work.

The Cycle Of Work

In the civilian world, this scheme may indeed also be applied. When we consider the cycle of activity of a professional worker, we observe that he starts in school, then enters his active period, which is often followed by unemployment and always by aging (see figure 5):

FIGURE 5

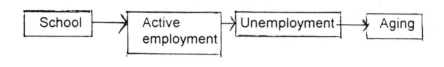

We want to transform this linear process of decay into a loop of recycling and feedback (figure 6):

FIGURE 6

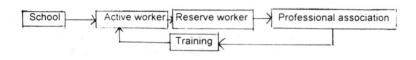

In this type of cycle, the worker, after school and active employment, becomes a "Worker in Reserve." Then, he will be administered by his association or union of his professional category. Hence, he will be oriented towards new training--in his field or in a new one--which will enable him to find a new position. During this process, the reserve worker will be assessed by his professional association and guided towards new technical/professional schooling or to a university as a student or an assistant teacher.

For example, engineers, mechanics, professors, or bankers--after years of professional activity often become obsolete, because their first schooling has been forgotten or discarded by the continuous flow of new techniques, innovations, or computers. Their period of "reserve" happens therefore to become an opportunity for them, for retraining in these new techniques, particularly in informatics and computers. They will be able to afford it because they will be paid as "workers in reserve" in the meantime, as were the veterans after World War I.

The concept of "worker in reserve" injects some balm into the present chaotic careers of the workers passing abruptly from active to nothing status. On the other hand, it keeps their consumption power alive, maintaining sales at the top level in the meantime, whatever misfortunes happen to befall on the workers-consumers.

Role Of Professional Associations

The active workers, when they become unemployed, instead of falling into an abyss, would be recuperated by their professional association which would examine their professional ability, their experience, health and family situation. This assessment will make it possible to formulate a new orientation plan: retraining in the same field or a more thorough change of horizons. The unemployed becomes a worker in reserve and is administered by his professional association or another one if the worker wants to change his profession more radically.

The association, in addition to assisting in professional orientation, will provide a salary to the worker in reserve. For this purpose, the association will receive subsidies from the companies' members of the association and also from the financial system described in figure 7:

FIGURE 7

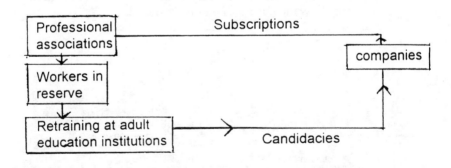

As shown in figure 7, the workers in reserve, administered and paid by their professional associations, are retrained and submit applications to the companies. These companies provide subscriptions through their memberships to their associations.

The companies pay salaries to their active workers and also to their reserve workers through their subscription to their association. The workers of a profession are successively active, on reserve, retrained and rehired by the companies of the profession, which thus maintain their stock of professionals through those successive steps.

Financing The Workers In Reserve

The objective of financing the workers in reserve includes the obvious social purpose of alleviating the misery of the unemployed and their family. But it also contains the famous result of multiplying by three the purchasing power of the needy, thereby multiplying the sales of the retailers and suppliers from industry, agriculture, services, and banks. From this point of view, this is a most powerful leverage in which all the economic actors hold a fundamental interest.

The economic actors will therefore contribute to the financing of the present Underconsumers (UC), in order to transform them into full and loyal consumers, financially backed by a stable income, whether they comply or not with the moral imperative of work. We will review the respective roles of these actors as money-distributors, namely, the retailers, the suppliers, the governments, and the international organizations:

a) Retailers

The retailers are the most interested group of money distributors, since they will be the first beneficiaries of this supplementary consumption coming from the reserve workers and other underconsumers. In our example, they will distribute a consumer allowance of $500/month (see figure 8):

FIGURE 8

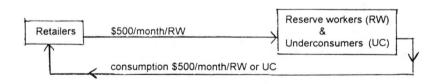

We have to preserve the advantages and privileges of the employed $1,500/month, so we are limiting our injection of consumer money to $500/month. Since the government unemployment subsidy is

$500/month; the worker in reserve will receive a total income of $1,000/month, which will multiply his/her purchasing power by two, hence multiplying the sales also by two.

b) Suppliers (industry, agriculture, services, and banks)

Where will the retailers receive these advances from? From the bankers, industry, agriculture, services, and other suppliers, who will make a loan to the retailers. When the extraconsumption comes in, the retailers will be able to reimburse their advances to the suppliers. This cycle is represented in the following scheme (see figure 9).

FIGURE 9

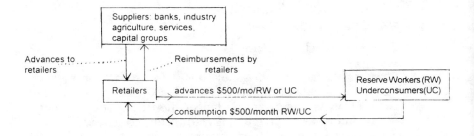

---

c) Government

The government continues to pay its unemployment allowances of $500/month to the unemployed who, in turn, consume this money at the retailer's shops (see figure 10).

FIGURE 10

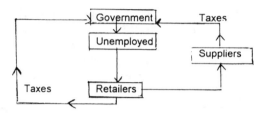

d) International Financing

In order to facilitate these injections of consumption money, international flow of capital will be utilized. This is due to the fact that governments are no longer the richest source where social claims could apply. Governments are overridden by debts; they are "broke;" they are overwhelmed by their deficits and cannot raise their debt limit any more. They can only provide for the small subsidies which they already give to the unemployed. These unemployed allowances are financed by taxes and the taxpayers are already overburdened and weary.

So we have to go to other sources of money which exist and are well endowed--the private international capital flows--thus following the traditional adage: "You cannot comb a devil who has no hair."

• The Tobin Tax

While governments have become poor, private international capital has grown rich. Each day, international flows of currencies are exchanged from or to New York, London, Frankfurt, Tokyo, Hong Kong, or Singapore. Billions of dollars are thus circulating.

Professor Tobin of Yale University has proposed a tax of 0.05% on these flows of capital, which could provide $150 billion/year or $12 billion/month. The United Nations, at its recent World Summit for Social Development (Copenhagen, March 1995), proposed to establish such a mechanism to finance the social needs of the planet, hence increasing consumption and consequently generating growth in sales and the blossoming of the economy.

- **Disarmament**

    The end of the cold war and the progress of peace have induced governments to adopt disarmament programs. The decline in military spending is now observed at a rate of 3% per year. This would yield a global cumulative peace dividend of 3% a year, which may be estimated at $30 billion a year.

- **Special Drawing Rights (SDR)**

    The international Monetary Fund (IMF) could issue, each year, a particular allotment of SDR which would be earmarked for consumer loans to the unemployed and other underconsumers in developing countries.

A NEW ECONOMIC SYSTEM

Our present economic system contains the paradox of its own contradiction, which can be characterized as follows: to punish the unemployed by depriving them of consumption and thereby condemning the producers to reduce sales and profits. Pursuing the goal of increased productivity and sales, our system relegates 2/3 of the population to a status of survival/starvation, instead of consuming all the goods that modern technology can produce. This is a self-destructive scheme; when consumption is reduced, sales diminish by 2/3, leading to recessions and economic stagnation, as well as underutilization of our capacity to produce.

The solution consists of financing the consumption of the unemployed; and the first step is to find "Work Pretexts" to employ the workers in reserve. For this purpose, we will employ a new type of professionals: The "Job Describers."

The Job Describers

In order to call the workers in reserve into active duty, we will find "Work Pretexts" such as public works, community services and other jobs needed but as yet unfulfilled. These are tasks which it would be nice to have done but for which we could not up to now find anybody willing to pay. To define these jobs, we will have a staff of "Job Describers" in each city or county, whose task will be to prepare job descriptions.

The professional associations will also establish a department of "Job Describers" assigned to identify the jobs which could ensure better service by the corporate members of the association. This staff will find gaps in the service rendered by the profession and single out a number of neglected job opportunities.

Financing

a) The Circuit Flow

Retailers will be the main actors for the distribution of the consumption allowances to the workers in reserve and other underconsumers, since they are the direct recipients of any additional consumption. They will become one of the most important groups of money distributors.

For this purpose, the retailers will receive loans from the suppliers' group (see figure 9) including large capital groups from industry, agriculture, services, and banks. These consumption loans will be reimbursed by the retailers to the suppliers when the monthly consumer allowances have been spent by the workers in reserve in the retailers' shops, thus generating additional sales and profits.

In turn, the workers in reserve will reimburse three years later the consumer loans they received after they were recruited and have become active workers anew. Additional capital will be loaned by the World Bank and the International Monetary Fund (IMF) by calling for additional special drawing rights (SDR) devoted to stimulating consumption among underconsumers, the hungry and workers permanently in reserve in the developing countries.

The Tobin tax of 0.05% on international capital flows would also finance capital for loans to the retailers. Other international taxes on disarmament and pollution may also contribute to the financing of additional consumption.

b) The Underconsumption Fund

All these monies will have to be channeled through a new institution: "The Underconsumption Fund" (UCF), similar to the World Bank, but specialized in financing the underconsumption business--a new market to explore--with a view to eradicating underconsumption in the 21st century.

The UCF will have regional branches in the European Community, the North Atlantic Free Trade Agreement (NAFTA) area, the Pacific region, the former Soviet Union (CIS), and China, as well as other countries in Asia, the Middle East and Africa. There will also be national branches which will target underconsumption at the country level and which may be called the "National Funds for Underconsumption" (NFUC).

The purpose of these funds is to combat underconsumption, regardless of the causes, such as unemployment, low salary, inability to work for health reasons or lack of skills.

This new attitude will contribute to disconnecting the traditional link between work and consumption, which we have to loosen since the work offered is shrinking while the consumers' needs are expanding rapidly owing to population growth and technological progress.

The financial institutions and particularly the Underconsumption Fund will have to define the specific roles of the money distributors-- retailers and other groups--as shown in the consumption circuits of figure 11 below. This is due to the fact that governments are no longer the sole money distributors to the unemployed, since governments are now too impoverished. This money therefore has to come from the private sector, where wealth has moved.

c) The Limits of Consumption Allowances

In order to avoid resentment from the employed who really work, we have to keep the monies allotted to the reserve workers and other underconsumers below the salaries received by the employed, but above the present survival/starvation levels of the allowances now received by the unemployed. This concept defines the upper and lower limits of the underconsumption allowances.

Taking our previous example, the WIR/UC will receive a total monthly allowance of $1,000/month: Unemployment allowance ($500) + consumption allowance ($500), well above the present survival/starvation levels, but much below the salaries of $1,500/ month received by the real workers.

Thus the workers in reserve and other underconsumers will become strong and useful consumers, able to support the sales of the retailers, suppliers, and bankers. But, at the same time, the position of the employed--real active workers, the wealthy and much envied élite of the nation--will remain well above that of the unemployed.

We discover that two new rights emerge from this discussion: first, the right of the employed to enjoy their privileges as real workers; and second, the right of the unemployed and other underconsumers to consume at a level compatible with the output which modern technology can provide, as well as with their basic needs. The harmony of the new modern world which is emerging now resides in respect for these two rights. The main reason for the present devastating unemployment is lack of consideration of the second right which has disrupted the sales, production, employment and consumption systems. We have to avoid this mistake in the 21st century.

The Consumption Circuity

FIGURE 11

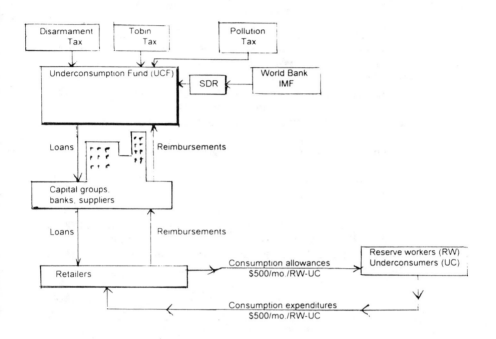

The Underconsumption Fund (UCF) provides capital drawn from the international taxes listed above to the banks and suppliers' groups (industry, agriculture, and services) which, in turn, advance loans to the retailers. These retailers provide a consumption allowance ($500/month) to the reserve workers and other underconsumers so that they can spend it at the retailers' shops, in addition to the unemployment allowance they already receive from the government.

The reserve workers will reimburse the retailers three years after they have obtained a new employment. The retailers will reimburse the capital groups when they receive additional sales and profits.

The capital groups will reimburse the national underconsumption funds which, in turn, will reimburse the world underconsumption fund.

The Inflation Caveat

Injections of money for consumption purposes have always had an inflationary effect. This is due to the fact that a sudden increase in the demand for goods generates an increase in prices, until the offer of goods can meet the accrued demand. This is done by expanding production and creating factories which will increase the supply of goods on the market and finally counteract the increases in prices.

We will therefore have to control and limit the injections of consumers' money so that inflationist pressure on prices does not occur. For this purpose, we will have to increase production before the money injections, instead of after. Since we know when the injections will occur, we will be able to anticipate them and suggest that production increases be placed on the market in advance of the introduction of the consumption allowances. This shows that the manipulation of consumer credit will have to be synchronized with the level of consumer goods production in order to avoid inflation.

The control of inflation in periods of accrued demand and the manipulation of production levels in anticipation of consumer money injections will be the subject of a further study.

OBJECTIVES OF THE UNDERCONSUMPTION FUND (UCF)

The problems of unemployment have been traditionally dealt with by governments, which provide welfare allowances. This system has become obsolete because governments are now deficit-ridden; they are "broke." On the other hand, taxpayers are weary of diverting additional funds from their scarce family budgets.

Entrepreneurs and banks have always considered that providing allowances to the unemployed is somewhat immoral since the recipients remain idle. Such allowances are also irrelevant to the terms of reference of entrepreneurs and banks which are to make profits and to get back the money they have advanced.

Thus, they have neglected the aspect of underconsumption which is linked to unemployment. The magnitude of the unemployed population has a deteriorating effect on sales and is at the root of recessions which, in turn, generate other decreases of sales. We are witnessing the following sequence (see figure 12).

FIGURE 12

| Productivity increases | → | Unemployment | → | Underconsumption | → | Recessions | → | Decreases in Sales |

Since governments are unable financially to provide additional unemployment allowances to maintain active consumption and sales, we have to turn to the vast amounts of capital which have evaded the national circuits of taxation and have become concentrated in the hands of private investors, corporations, and financial institutions which manipulate, each day, billions of dollars from New York, London, Frankfurt, Hong Kong, Tokyo, or Singapore and vice versa. These monies are in search of profits. If we create an incentive to attract these capital amounts into the underconsumption business, we will reinvigorate sales and generate additional profits accordingly.

This is the purpose of the Underconsumption Fund (UCF), whose objective is to pump the money available in the international capital flows into the vast and untapped domains of the underconsumption markets. We will illustrate this point by an example.

The Lake

When algae grow too high above the surface of a lake, they are cut and the rivers below evacuate the cut algae. In this process, some algae flow through the mainstream, but others are stuck on the banks. We have to push them back into the mainstream of consumption. This is the purpose of the Tobin tax: to bring back the billions of dollars stuck in international speculation in order to attract them into the mainstream of consumption and underconsumption.

Money: Purpose and Diversion

The basic purpose of money is to enable a consumer to buy the goods and services he/she needs. This money is created when these goods and services are produced and has to be used to buy them.

But when the money thus created is diverted by huge amounts to the financial circuits--national or international--it is no longer available for the consumers's purchases. Therefore the products are not consumed, since the money to buy them has been diverted from consumption purposes.

This is called a diversion of the money flow and is acceptable on a small scale. But we are witnessing it at present on a large scale; most potential consumers have been deprived of their purchasing power because that money has disappeared from consumption to the national and international circuitry. We have found good reasons to justify this diversion, such as unemployment, but the diversion remains.

NOTES

1. A similar analysis has already been made by the famous economists Keynes and Schumpeter. In order to resolve the economic crisis of the 1930s, they encouraged governments to stimulate consumption, even at the price of budgetary deficits. Here, in this project, we do not burden governments whose wealth is passé. Rather, we rely on the private sector, the banks, and the international capital flows, where wealth has definitely been driven.

2. Kelso, another eminent economist, observed that the present evolution of the economy towards unemployment is due to the further progress achieved by machines and automation in the production process, while the human share is decreasing. For instance, in the past, the value added by manufacturing was, say, 80% due to human labor and 20% to machines. Now, this has reversed. The contribution of human work has been reduced to 20% while the share of machines, computers, and capital provide 80% of the added value. Kelso's proposal is to extend the ownership of stocks to a larger part of the population.

3. Such proposals may complement the programs described in the present project and contribute to solving the problems of unemployment and underconsumption in the 21st century.

POVERTY HAS A RICH FUTURE!

by

David Macarov

THE MEANING OF POVERTY

Being poor in America today means not being able to afford a meal costing more than $1.18, with all other necessities of life extrapolated on the same level.[1] It should be no surprise, therefore, that poor people are generally hungry, as well as suffering deprivation in most other areas, including housing, medical care, and decent clothing. Although some other countries define poverty in relation to other people; or as a percentage of average income, or of wages or wealth, the American definition is based upon an absolute figure: the costs of a food budget originally designed for an emergency, short-term period, not to exceed four days.[2] That budget allowed for 2,300 calories per day, although it has been estimated that a male laborer would require at least 3,500 calories.[3] Thus, poverty in the United States is not simply a comparison with other people; or being unable to acquire what one fancies; or a faceless statistical abstract such as the lower 10% of the income distribution, but individuals beset with belly-gripping, face-grinding poverty[4] -- "a condition of life so limited by malnutrition, illiteracy, disease, squalid surroundings, high infant mortality, and low life expectancy as to be below any reasonable definition of human decency."[5]

THE EXTENT OF POVERTY

Such poverty is experienced by approximately 15% of the American population, including about 22% of its children and over 12% of the elderly.[6] Even if food, via Food Stamps, and housing and medical benefits, are included as income, the percentage of the poor still remains over 11%, and the number at about 28 million.[7] Although in Europe between 55 and 60 million people live in poverty, with about a third of them in the United Kingdom,[8] a study of seven industrial countries found the United States to have more poverty than any of the other countries studied.[9]   And, in addition

---

David Macarov, *emeritus professor at the School of Social Work at the Hebrew University in Jerusalem, is program chairman of the International Council on Social Welfare's conference to be held in Jerusalem in 1998.*

56

to the approximately 35 million vey poor people in the United States, over 60 million others are considered "near poor," with incomes slightly above the poverty line.[10] It is clear that although the former are in abject poverty, the latter are also deprived of many of the aspects of healthy, happy living.[11] Worldwide, poverty ranges from 10% in Germany to almost 70% in Bangladesh.[12] In the former Soviet Union 13% of the people are poor, but the definition of poverty is 5-10% higher than that in the West. Were definitions comparable, the percentage would be higher.[13]

Definitions differ in other countries, too, but using their own definitions, 1,100 million people in the world live in poverty, and more than 600 million of them are extremely poor.[14] In the developing countries alone, excluding China, between 350 and 510 million people are seriously undernourished.[15] Stated differently, one-fifth of the human race lives in acute poverty, and up to 40% of the world population does not have a standard of living that includes adequate food, safe and sufficient supplies of water, secure shelter, and access to education and health care.[16]

LIVING WITH POVERTY

How do people manage as they sink deeper and deeper into such poverty? One study found the following progression: People look for better-paid work or full-time work; spend their savings; claim social welfare benefits; sell their non-essential possessions; use more credit; delay paying bills; take casual badly-paid jobs; cash their insurance policies; pawn their valuables; sell their essential possessions; ask for charity; beg; and finally engage in petty crime.[17]

Another study found a slightly different progression, but the same end result. People acquire income from: Additional payments; income from other household members; casual earnings; saving, credit and loans; sale of goods; help from family and friends; and stolen goods[18].

A more graphic description is Dear's: "Some welfare mothers ransack supermarket garbage bins (called 'garbaging')...to get enough food for their children. Others sell their blood plasma twice a week for about $10 a pint to gain some desperately needed additional income. Still others pilfer Good Will dropoff bins to get clothing for themselves and their children...Some mothers, in absolute desperation, resort to prostitution to get money."[19]

In short, poor people live a hand-to-mouth, scrabbling, trying to make-do, existence. Although the existence of a universal "culture of poverty" has been generally disproved, most poor people spend the major part of their time dealing with the fact and results of their poverty. Far from being the happy, lazy, exploiters of society as portrayed by some popular myths, most poor people are desperately trying to move out of poverty, or, at least, to manage to live with it.

THE CONSEQUENCES OF POVERTY

The consequences of continuing poverty exhibit themselves on both the personal and the societal levels.

Societal consequences: Poverty results in homelessness, begging, substance abuse, crime and vandalism, which are threats to society. In addition, fighting incipient or present poverty, which is the goal of many social security programs, takes up the major part of many nations' total budgets.[20] Further, environmental degradation, which often is a cause of poverty as natural resources dwindle or are exploited for other goals, is also sometimes caused by poverty, through efforts to use whatever resources can be found, such as trees and water, without regard for environmental considerations.[21]

The personal level: On a personal level, it is estimated that 31 million Americans do not have basic health care and 30% of American children have never seen a dentist.[22] Estimates of the homeless in the United States range from 238,000 to 600,000 a night, of which 100,000 are children.[23] Five and a half million children a year experience hunger.[24] Poor people go to hospitals more often and stay longer -- 80% more in one study. The average number of days a person is bedridden increases as income comes down and work-related injuries are more common among the worst paid.[25] Further, mild retardation is fifteen times more likely to occur in impoverished areas[26] and poor people suffer from four to twenty-eight times more health conditions attributable to living conditions than do the non-poor.[27] In addition, 50% of the homeless are in that condition due to economic reasons.[28] Poor children do not do well in educational settings, do not have the stimulation at home that the non-poor do, and do not have successful role models they can emulate. Poverty not only creates an uneducated, unskilled underclass, but "increased poverty results in homelessness, begging, repossession of homes and appliances, electricity disconnections, reappearance of sweatshops and casual labor -- including illegal child labor -- rising number of accidents and deaths at work, deterioration of housing, a sharp increase in thefts and crimes of violence, deterioration in the public's health, and vandalism. Ill-health,

58

disability, and premature death have been linked to material and social deprivation. In short, poverty kills."[29]

EFFORTS TO ALLEVIATE POVERTY

Efforts to eradicate or to alleviate poverty date back at least to Biblical days. The prohibition on gleaning -- that is, picking over -- the orchards and fields, and the requirement that the corners of produce fields be left unharvested were specifically so that the poor could use the leftover products for themselves.[30]   In the days of absolute monarchs, the poor were often the wards of the crown, as well as the concern of the clergy. When constitutional states arose, some provisions were invariably made for the poor, even if these were the deplorable almshouses.   Indeed, one of the earliest governmental attempts to relieve poverty took place in Speenhamland, in England, in 1795, when the government decided to make up the difference between wages and the cost of bread. The experiment failed, however, as employers dropped wage levels, increasing their own profits while requiring larger and larger subsidies of the government.[31]

Despite such incidents, the bulk of social welfare provisions were left to church and voluntary groups until the Great Depression in the United States led to massive governmental intervention in the form of the original Social Security programs. In Great Britain the determination which grew during World War II to create a "home fit for heroes" led to a comprehensive insurance program to "insure everybody against everything." Despite such programs, poverty continued to grow, and in the United States was "rediscovered," so to speak, in the 1960's, primarily due to a book by Harrington called *The Other America*;[32] and an article by MacDonald, entitled "Our Invisible Poor,"[33] that appeared almost simultaneously. The result was a plethora of programs called "The War on Poverty," including Head Start, Upward Bound, Mobilization for Youth, low-cost housing, and others.

However, with political changes, such as the accession of Ronald Reagan in the United States and Margaret Thatcher in Britain, both of whom felt that a general increase in prosperity, to be brought about by supply-side economics, was the best way to aid the poor, cuts began to be made in the funding of such programs. Since 1981 American government spending for social programs, as a percentage of the Gross National Product, has shrunk from 4.2% to 3.7%,[34] and from 1979 to 1990 the number of people in poverty increased by 4 million.[35]   In 1993 there were almost 7 million more people in poverty than there was in 1989. Indeed, in 1993 alone the number of poor people grew by 3.3 million.[36]

Trickling Down: The "trickle-down" effect, despite its logical attractiveness, does not necessarily accompany economic growth. "A rising tide lifts all the boats," is the metaphor used by those who believe that prosperity benefits everyone. However, the fact that a rising tide also creates a powerful undertow that drowns many people is evidenced by the fact that in the 1980s, for every individual in the United States who joined the middle class, two joined the group of the poor.[37] Further, for every $70 increase in income among the richest 20% in the United States between 1979 and 1989, the poorest 20% lost a dollar.[38] In the United Kingdom during the same period, for every 5,000 pounds sterling increase among the upper 10%, the lowest 10% lost 200 pounds. Put differently, while the income of the top fifth of the population in the United States increased by 13% from 1978 to 1987, the income of the bottom fifth declined by 8%.[39] Seen over a longer time span, whereas in 1967 the aggregate household income of the top 5% in the United States was 18% of the total, and that of the lowest 5% of the income group 4%, in 1993 the top 5% had 21% of the income, and the lowest, only 3½%.[40] American household incomes grew about 10% between 1979 and 1994, but 97% of these gains went to the richest 20% of households.[41] Consequently, disparities in family incomes in the United States are now the greatest since they began to be measured nearly 50 years ago.[42]

On a global basis, whereas in 1960 the richest 20% of the world population had incomes 30 times greater than the poorest 20%; by 1990 this had grown to 60 times greater, when measured between countries. When the gap is measured within countries, the income of the richest 20% is 150 times greater than that of the poorest 20%.[43] In the seven country study mentioned above, the gap between the richest and the poorest parts of the population was found to be greatest in Sweden and in the United States.[44] Part of the increase in the gap between the poor and the non-poor in the United States arises from the fact that the poverty line does not keep up with the cost of living: From 1983 to 1992 the Consumer Price Index went up 40%, while the poverty line went up only 35%.

In short, prosperity does not seem to trickle down as much as it bubbles up. The United Nations, the World Bank, and similar organizations have recently come to the same conclusion: "Growth in national income does not necessarily lead to improvement in well being...Poverty is growing."[45]

WHO ARE THE POOR?

Children: Forty percent of the American poor are children; conversely, 20% of American children are poor. The latter figure is rising: in 1970 only 15% of the children were poor.[46] The poverty of children is usually a function of the incomes of their parents, with the obvious exception of those who have no parents. Although there are areas in which child labor is accepted, and others where it is forbidden but winked at, it is generally accepted that children, and especially very young children, should not work. As a consequence, most countries have some sort of children's or families' allowances, many have maternity grants and paid maternity leaves as well, and some also have paternity leaves.

The United States is a notable exception regarding such programs. Instead, there is the Aid to Families with Dependent Children (AFDC) program, which was established basically to help widows stay at home with their children, but which has become more restrictive and more punitive as the target population became unmarried mothers, and -- at least in the public image -- African-American teenagers   In any case, the median AFDC grant is only 41% of the poverty line, and even when combined with food stamps, becomes only 72%.[47] It is thus understandable that families with children make up 34% of the urban homeless.[48]

A contributing reason for the number of poor children in America is the fact that almost 50% of children living with one parent are poor, as compared to 10% of the others, and whereas in 1979 only 15% of children lived with one parent, in 1989 27% did.[49] In Russia, too, 20% of the children live in families below the poverty line, and 30% of families with three or more children are in poverty.[50]

Gender: Gender plays a part in the determination of poverty. In few countries have women achieved wage equality with men. Given the same tasks and conditions, women's wages are almost always lower. Women hold only 3% of the top jobs in Fortune 500 companies.[51] Today, as more women join the labor force and are mostly assigned to low-paid, temporary or part-time jobs, there has been an inevitable growth in the number of the female working poor. When the number of female single parents receiving meager child support or welfare benefits is added to this group, there is a growing "feminization of poverty."[52] Incidentally, when single mothers marry, they are not automatically better off -- 52% of those who marry remain in poverty.[53]

61

Race: The number of African-Americans among the poor in the United States is beyond their proportion in the population as a whole. Of the roughly 35 million poor people in the United States, 23 million are white and 9 million are African-American, although the latter make up only 12% of the population. African-Americans are three times as likely to experience poverty than is the rest of the population. About 34% of African-Americans are poor, compared to 12% of the whites and 28% of the Hispanics. Nearly half of African-American children live in poverty.[54]

Because of the linkage between work records and welfare programs, as explained below, poverty among African-Americans is maintained by social security programs. The average monthly Old Age Survivors and Dependents Insurance (OADSI) payment in 1990 to whites was $592, but $495 for African-Americans. Similarly, disability payments were $616 for whites, but $537 for African-Americans.[55]

The aged: In many countries elderly people have a higher poverty rate than any other group and make up a large part of the poverty class. They constitute 57% of the poor in England, 40% in Australia and 36% in Israel.[56] Studies in the United States indicate that between 22½% and 37% of the elderly are below or close to the poverty line, as compared to 19% of the non-elderly.[57] The median household income of the elderly is less than half that of the nonelderly. In 1983, almost 43% of households headed by older persons in the United States had total incomes below $10,000, compared to only 17% of nonelderly households.[58]

The replacement rate for the elderly via Social Security in the United States is 66% of previous income,[59] and projections are that in the year 2000 Social Security will pay 54% of the preretirement wage to low earners, 42% to average earners, and 28% to maximum earners.[60] Less than one-half of retirees are able to supplement their income with private pension benefits and current retirees have a real replacement rate less than one-half the purchasing power of their previous earnings.[61] Coupled with this is the fact that medical expenses of the aged average six times more than those for young adults, and these are expected to quadruple by the year 2000.[62] That this will be reflected in the number of poor elderly persons is foreshadowed by the fact that presently one in five elderly households has no net assets, and one in seven has no health insurance.[63]

The working poor: One of the fastest growing groups in poverty is

known as the working poor. These are people who are employed --
some of them full-time and year-round -- who do not make enough
to lift themselves and their families above the poverty line. Sixty
percent of able-bodied poor adults work full-time, part-time, or
seasonally, and of the 9 million working poor in the United States,
2 million work full-time.[64] Measured differently, nearly one-fifth
of America's 85 million full-time, year-round workers earn less than
a poverty wage.[65] Of the 18 to 24-year-old workers in the United
States -- that is, the young workers -- 47% hold jobs that pay less
than a poverty income.[66]

While the poverty line, as outlined above, is over $15,000 per year,
60% of all new jobs created in the United States between 1979 and
1984 paid less than $7000 per year.[67] Since 1975, there has been a
52% increase in the number of full-time workers living in poverty.[68]
About 25% of the homeless are working.[69] Even for full-time
workers, the median wage has decreased by 3% since 1979,[70] and
the average wage has fallen more than 20% in the last 22 years.[71]

One reason for the continuing growth in the number and
percentage of the working poor is the current corporate strategy of
keeping companies "lean and mean" -- that is, maintaining a
minimum permanent staff, and hiring contingent and part-time
workers as needed. In the United Kingdom by the early 1990s
almost 40% of jobs did not involve full-time wages or
employment.[72] Such workers not only do not qualify for many of
the social benefits available to full-time workers, but are generally
paid less.

The legal minimum wage, even when enforced, does not help
many poor families. With hourly average wages in the United States
in 1995 at $11.38,[73] the minimum wage remained at $4.25 an hour.
A wage earner working full time at the minimum wage 40 hours a
week for 52 weeks a year would earn $8,840 per year, while the
poverty line for a family of four is over $15,000. A person making
twice the minimum wage and working 30 hours a week could not
earn enough to keep a family of four above the poverty line.[74]
Current efforts to raise the minimum wage to $5.15 an hour would
change the picture very little, as full-time work would still result in
income about $5,000 below the poverty line for a family of four.

The unemployed: Not all of the unemployed are in poverty, but for
those who depend primarily upon income from work, unemployment
and poverty are often overlapping. In the second quarter of 1995
official employment rates were:

United States	5.7%
Canada	9.5%
Austria	8.4%
Japan	3.2%
Italy	12.2%
Sweden	9.4%
United Kingdom	8.8%[75]
France	12.2%[76]

Worldwide unemployment has been estimated as 820 million, which is one-third of the global labor force.[77] However, since every country uses many devices to minimize unemployment figures,[78] it is generally agreed that the official figures should be raised from 50% to 300% to realistically represent members of the labor market who are willing, ready and able to work full-time, who cannot find full-time jobs.[79] For example, more than 5 million Americans involuntarily work part time, when they would rather have full time work.[80] Using official estimates, 28 million people are out of work in the developed countries, 7½ million in eastern Europe and the former Soviet Union, and at least 70 million in developing countries.[81] Among certain groups, unemployment is much higher than the average: In 1988, more than 90% of African-American young men in New York were unemployed.[82] In the United States, nearly three-quarters of all families have had a brush with layoffs since 1980. In one third of households a family member has lost a job, and more than 40% know a relative, friend or neighbor who was laid off.[83] In Europe, more people are without a job than during the Great Depression in 1933.[84]

Unemployment insurance is no guarantee against poverty. Unemployment compensation coverage is dropping in extent as well as in amount. The ratio of insured unemployment to total unemployment has dropped 60% since 1947.[85] In 1975 75% of American unemployed workers were covered by unemployment compensation plans, but this number had dropped to 25% by the end of 1984.[86] From 1984 to 1990, unemployment compensation covered less than 40% of the unemployed --the lowest figure on record since unemployment insurance began.[87] And benefits in the United States are approximately 50% of the recipient's previous earnings. Further, in all but two states benefits end after 26 weeks.[88] Throughout the world unemployment compensation pays between 40% and 75% of average earnings, and compensation periods range from eight to 36 weeks.[89]

WHY POVERTY PERSISTS

As an examination of the groups in poverty noted above will indicate, most poor people either cannot work, cannot find work, cannot find work which will lift them out of poverty, or are prevented from working by circumstances such as small children at home, or by social norms which forbid the elderly to remain at work, or hold that mothers of small children should stay at home with them -- a norm, it should be noted, that is rapidly changing in some places, either by choice or by coercion. In every case, there is a connection between poverty and work, or lack of work. Since the primary source of income in today's society and economy is from work, lack of income arises from lack of work, in one guise or another.

Similarly, insofar as efforts to overcome poverty are concerned, almost every social security program throughout the world is linked to work efforts and records in some manner. Some social security programs specify that they are for workers, employees, or wage earners. Others base coverage, eligibility, and payment amounts on length of employment or previous earnings. Of 139 countries reporting old-age insurance programs in 1991, 88% were linked to work. Sickness and maternity benefits were available only to workers in 89% of the programs. Even family and children's allowances were only for workers' families in 67% of the programs. And, of course, both unemployment compensation and workers' disability were completely linked to work records.[90]

Nor is coverage the only link to the world of work. Covered persons usually must have worked a minimum length of time to be eligible for compensation, and the compensation itself is subject to a "wage stop." That is the provision in almost all social welfare programs that benefits should not exceed, or even approach, that which could be earned by working. So strong is the link to work that the wage stop also limits the payments to those who obviously cannot work, or cannot find work -- the aged, children, the disabled, and others out of the labor market for various reasons, as well as the unemployed.[91]

The double link between work and welfare -- that poverty arises from inability to work or to find work, and that anti-poverty measures are based on work records -- leads to a situation wherein those who have worked full-time for long periods at relatively well-paid jobs suffer some lowering of their standard of living when they are out of work for any reason, but those whose worklife has been sporadic, underpaid, and short quickly join the ranks of the poor.

THE FUTURE OF POVERTY

The aged: The financial future of the aged is precarious. Lengthening life expectancy throughout the world will result in longer and longer post-work periods, with income mainly from pensions and insurance plans. In 1935, when American Social Security came into being, life expectancy was about 55 years and retirement pensions began at age 65, so there was an understanding that pensions would not be paid out for very long. However, in 1990 life expectancy for men was 71.5 years, and for women 78.3 years,[92] while retirement age remained the same. While there are plans to raise the retirement age in the United States to 66 in 2009 and to 67 by 2027, life expectancy will almost certainly outrace these changes. For example, in 1990 life expectancy worldwide was 63.9 years, and by the year 2000 it is expected to be 75.7 years.[93]

No existing insurance program -- governmental, cooperative, or private -- was or is actuarially based on people drawing benefits for fifteen, twenty, or even thirty and more years. Habib[94] pointed out more than ten years ago that the literature on the economics of aging has not yet come to terms with the implications of this phenomenon. As life expectancy continues to increase -- and it is theoretically possible that this will reach 115 to 120 years[95] -- such plans will be financially unable to continue to pay out the benefits that they originally promised. Even so-called "pay as you go" plans, which use current premiums to pay out benefits, will reach a refusal by the policy-holders to pay the enormous premiums that will be required.

The size of this change is indicated by the fact that the current 31 million Americans over the age of 65 will rise to 51 million by the year 2000.[96] As a consequence of such demographic changes, the British, for one, "will be required to restructure their entire funding mechanism for welfare policies for the aged in the next decade."[97] The financial outlook for the elderly is bleak.

The working poor: Although there seems to be a tendency to think of the poor as not working, a very large part of the poverty group, as outlined above, are working, and some of them work full-time and year-round. The growth in the number of the working poor promises to be substantial. Although futurists may disagree as to whether technology creates jobs or wipes jobs out, there is general agreement that the jobs which remain will be unequally divided between a few highly skilled, powerful, important well-paid jobs, and an overwhelming majority of low-skill, undemanding, badly paid positions. Even if good jobs are simply defined as those that pay enough for a reasonably comfortable lifestyle,[98] the outlook is not promising. Of 140,000 new jobs projected by 2005, one-half will not pay enough to cover a minimal budget for an adult with two children.[99]

One reason to expect an increase in the working poor is the fact that the labor force will increasingly be made up of women and minorities -- 85% of those entering the workplace in the year 2000 are expected to be in these categories.[100] Not only are women and minority members paid less, as mentioned previously, but many of them are employed precisely because they will or must work for such pay. In addition, the "lean and mean" corporations who increasingly use temporary help contribute to poverty, as such temporary jobs usually pay less and, of course, do not last long. During the last decade, the number of temporary workers has tripled in the United States, to over 2 million.[101]

There is another reason to forecast a growth in the working poor. As international trade restrictions are loosened through free-trade agreements and other arrangements, those jobs that cannot be easily or cheaply automated must be accomplished with labor costs not much higher than those in developing countries. Particularly, as international conglomerates increasingly provide goods and services, they are subject to no political, emotional, or humanitarian pressures, but unceasingly seek areas of lowest cost.[102] Indeed, it has been found that American trade laws have an inherent basis toward increasing the incidence of poverty.[103] Sandel[104] points out that such international economic entities erode the importance of local and/or national democracy, which makes the latter incapable of protecting the poor or the potentially poor from such manipulation.

The unemployed: To the three traditional types of unemployment -- frictional, cyclical, and structural -- another has now been added: Permanent unemployment. Or, if not permanent, almost so -- a work life of a few isolated periods, within a context of no work. After centuries of fruitless pursuit of a full employment society, it is now generally recognized that the goal is as distant as ever.[105]

In 1930, Lord Beveridge, in England, saw 2% as the irreducible minimum of unemployment; in 1946, the American Congress could not agree on a definition of full employment, but by 1973 the American Council of Economic Advisors was speaking of 3½% unemployment as the "natural" rate; in 1979 the Humphrey-Hawkins Bill called 4% full employment; in 1983, the same Council of Economic Advisors spoke of 6% to 7% as full employment; a rate slightly below 6% is now seen as the acceptable rate in the United

States.[106] As noted previously, this translates into between 9% and 18% of the labor force who cannot find full-time year-round jobs.[107] In Europe, it is estimated that there is a "silent reserve army" of about 13 million people willing to work, but who are not included in the official unemployment figures.[108]

The constant and irreversible growth in real unemployment rates, despite efforts to disguise this growth through definitional deviousness, statistical subterfuge, and junk jobs -- for example, by defining people out of the labor force through requiring them to undergo training courses where they are called students getting stipends; or by neglecting to count discouraged workers; or by calling two hours a week work "employment" -- has been documented in a number of sources.

Up to the year 2000, between 20 and 25 million fewer jobs will be needed in Europe to create the same level of goods and services.[109] Today, only a minority of adult Europeans have permanent full-time jobs over most of their working life period.[110] The United Nations, for example, notes that the past record has "eroded the assumptions that unemployment would be temporary."[111]

Not only is the number of the unemployed growing, but due to technology, the hours that are worked by those employed are constantly shrinking. Since 1960, weekly working time has been reduced by around one quarter, whereas annual vacation time has increased in about the same measure.[112]

This is not to say that efforts to reduce unemployment are not made. These efforts take three forms. One is to train or retrain the unemployed to undertake different jobs. In some cases, such training courses are elective; in others, such as those forced on welfare recipients, they are coerced. In both cases, they are ineffective, primarily because the jobs for which people train -- of any jobs, for that matter -- are not there. In tacit recognition of this fact, the state of Kansas, for example, anticipated that only 13% of the persons in their vocational training courses would achieve full-time jobs, and only 9% part-time jobs. It was understood that almost 80% of entrants would remain unemployed after training.[113] Even when people get jobs after being unemployed, 65% of them end up with lower pay.[114] Programs like the Comprehensive Employment and Training Act (CETA) made only modest gains, mostly through increasing the number of hours employed, but not by increasing access to better jobs or jobs with higher wages.[115]

The second approach to decreasing unemployment is through better general education. Since it is almost axiomatic that the good jobs in the technological society of the future will require a good education (if not a higher education), then the proposed strategy is to improve early childhood education[116] and the public schools, and increase access to universities. Worthy as these aims are in their own rights, the bulk of the labor force will nevertheless be consigned to low-level, uninteresting, low-paid jobs, with their frustration increased by their unused education; or the unemployed group will have a much higher level of education than formerly -- neither of which will relieve unemployment or poverty.

The third solution proposed for unemployment is continuing and continual increase in part-time jobs. That is, dividing current jobs into smaller segments so more people will be able to work. However, it is clear that part-time work pays part-time salaries, and thereby does not attack poverty. This approach is simply a device to use deliberately-created poverty to obscure the extent of unemployment. Fortunately or unfortunately, there is a natural limit to the extent to which work can be divided and still remain efficient, and this device cannot be used forever..

In an overall perspective, unemployment grows because technology -- in the long run -- destroys more jobs than it creates. Indeed, one of the major reasons for introducing technological change is the desire to reduce or eliminate human labor.[117] As compared to technology, human labor is inefficent, undependable, and costly. There is little evidence or reason to believe that technological change will cease, or that it will even decrease its rate. On the contrary, technology is symbiotic, and each new invention gives birth to even newer inventions and uses. Consequently, the need for human labor will continue to decrease, and with it, the opportunities for gainful employment. Since almost all programs to eliminate or alleviate poverty are based upon or linked to work records, poverty will continue to grow unless and until that link is broken.

In summarizing current efforts to reduce poverty, it is helpful to examine the results of a conference which brought together "the best minds representing the full range of thoughts on the issues."[118] After examining anti-poverty efforts that included improving schooling, empowering people, job training, social intervention, and others, the conclusion was reached: "There do not seem to be any programs that really reduce poverty in a cheap and effective way...no programs seem to be on the horizon that will fundamentally and dramatically reduce the incidence of poverty in the United States."[119] Insofar as the world as a whole is concerned, "The outlook for living standards in Eastern Europe, most Third World countries and the poorest 20% or 30% in the rich EC countries, the United States and Japan is gloomy...poverty is deep-seated in many rich and not only poor countries and seems destined to get worse in both groups of countries."[120]

CONCLUSION

Poverty, as it exists today, gives rise to all the social and personal difficulties outlined above. However, future increases in the extent and depth of poverty, which seem almost inevitable at present, have more ominous implications for all of civilization. As poverty spreads, so does the drug culture, crime, militant and anarchic groups, the search for scapegoats which results in ethnic violence and xenophobia, submission to demagogic rulers who promise quick solutions, fundamentalism of various kinds, and senseless terrorism. All history teaches that when the rich are growing richer and the poor are growing poorer, which is the situation today, the future is fraught with danger.

How can this future be averted? Since almost all poverty arises and continues because income is linked to work, and since the need for human labor is constantly decreasing, continuation of this link will act to create more and deeper poverty. What is urgently required is a new societal paradigm, in which income is distributed through a mechanism which is not based on work.[121] It is true that for generations work has been posited as more than just a source of income, but the basis for self- and other-images, the regulator of time, and the source of satisfaction and friendship, so basing society on some other norm or value -- study, creativity, co-operativeness, or morality, for example -- will require massive resocialization efforts. Similarly, distributing the resources created by a technologized economy on the basis of those values, or through basic minimum income schemes, or through cooperatives or collectives, will demand a complete restructuring of the socio-economic framework.

Decline in the need for human labor will continue, bringing with it one of three scenarios. One is the cataclysmic scenario, in which society is brought kicking and screaming into a new era, with all the attendant dislocations and pain that this contains. The second is the peaceful scenario, in which efforts are made to plan for the inevitable, so as to achieve as painless a transition as possible. The third is the passionate scenario, in which the inevitable is seen as desirable, and every effort is made to achieve the almost-workless world as quickly as possible.

Unfortunately, despite the efforts of several small groups, such as The Basic Income European Network and the Society for the Reduction of Human Labor, there is little evidence of any widespread planning for the future predicted above. Indeed, socialization concerning the supposed importance of human work has acted to create so widespread a psychological denial of the facts and trends that are obvious that what we want to believe about the future supersedes what we know. As long as this denial continues, poverty will have a rich future.

REFERENCES

1.   The poverty line for a family of four was $15,500 in 1995 (see "The 1995 Federal poverty guidelines,"*Social Security Bulletin*, 58(1), 87). Using Orshansky's 1965 formula, this is $42.46 per day; $10.62 per person; $3.53 for food alone; and $1.18 per meal (see Orshansky, Mollie [1965]. "Who's who among the poor." *Social Security Bulletin*, 28[3]). It should be noted that the budget on whch this is based was intended only for an emergency period of a few days -- not the sustained periods now being experienced.
2.   For some difficulties in defining poverty, see Citro, Constance F., and Robert T. Michael (eds.) (1995). *Measuring Poverty: A New Approach.* Washington: National Academy Press.
3.   Doron, Abraham (1990). "Definition and measurement of poverty." *Journal of Welfare and Social Security Studies*, (2), 27-49.
4.   The phrase is from Gans, Herbert H. (1967). "Income grants and 'dirty work'." *The Public Interest*, (6), 110.
5.   *Poverty and the Environment* (1995). New York: United Nations, p. 7.
6.   *Annual Statistical Summary - 1944 - to the Social Security Bulletin* (1994). Washington: Social Security Administration, 152.
7.   Ropers, Richard H. (1991). *Persistent Poverty: The American Dream Turned Nightmare*. New York: Plenum, p. 39.
8.   *Annual Report, 1993-1994.* (1995). London: Child Poverty Action Group.
9.   Achdut, Lea and Orit Cristal (1993). *Poverty in Industrial Nations: A Comparative Perspective*. Jerusalem: National Insurance Institute.
10.   Ropers, op cit., 41.
11.   Moore, Truman (1965). *The Slaves We Rent*. New York: Random House. p. xi.
12.   Townsend, Peter (1993). *The International Analysis of Poverty*. New York: Harvester Wheatsheaf.
13.   Mroz, Thomas A., and Barry M. Popkin (1995). "Poverty and economic transition in the Russian Federation." *Economic Development and Cultural Change*, 44(1), 1-32.
14.   *World Social Situation in the 1990s*. New York: United Nations, p. 76.
15.   *Global Outlook 2000* (1990). New York: United Nations, p. 5.
16.   *Poverty and the Environment*, op cit., p. 7.
17.   Kempson, Elaine, Alec Bryson, and Karen Rowlingson (1994). *Hard Times? How Poor Families Make Ends Meet*. London: Policy Studies Institute.
18.   Ropers, op cit.

19.   Colborn, D. (1992a). "Medicaid: A safety net with some holes."
Washington Post, July 28, p. 19.
20.   Nearly 62 percent of all government spending went for social welfare
purposes in 1992. See Bixby, Ann K. (1995). "Public Social Welfare
Expenditures, Fiscal Year 1992." *Social Security Bulletin,* 58(2), 65-66.
21.   *Poverty and the Environment,* op cit.
22.   Ropers, op cit.
23.   *Poverty and the Environment,* op cit.
24.   *Poverty and the Environment,* op cit.
25.   Colborn, D. (1992a). "Medicaid -- a safety net with some holes."
Washington Post, July 28, p. 19.
26.   Mandelbaum, A. (1977). "Mental health and retardation." In J. B.
Turner (ed.), *Encyclopedia of Social Work.* New York: National Association of
Social Workers.
27.   Colborn, D. (1992b) "Who is poor?" *Washington Post,* July 28, p. 12.
28.   First, R. J., and B. G. Toomey (1989). "Homeless men and the work
ethic." *Social Service Review,* 63(1), 113-126.
29.   Townsend, op cit.
30.   *Leviticus,* xix. 9, 10; *Deuteronomy* xxiv. 20, 21.
31.   Macarov, David (1970). *Incentives to Work.* San Francisco: Jossey-Bass,
pp. 10-12.
32.   Harrington, Michael (1963). *The Other America.* New York: Macmillan.
33.   MacDonald, Dwight (1963). "Our invisible poor." *The New Yorker,*
January 16.
34.   Ropers, op cit. p. 180.
35.   Bixby, op cit.
36.   "Poverty Issues Discussed." (1995). *Monthly Labor Review,* 118(2), p. 2.
37.   Ropers, op cit.
38.   Townsend, op cit., p. 15.
39.   Ropers, op cit., p. 57.
40.   Ryscarage, Paul (1995). "A surge in growing income inequality?"
Monthly Labor Review, 118(8), 51-61.
41.   Sanger, David E., and Steve Lohr (1996). "Searching for ways to avoid
layoffs." *New York Times Fax Edition,* March 9, p. 1.
42.   Lewis, Anthony (1996). "Myths and realities." *New York Times Fax
Edition,* January 12, p. 8.
43.   *Poverty and the Environment,* op cit., pp. 7-10.
44.   Achdut and Cristal, op cit., p. 8.
45.   *Poverty and the Environment,* op cit., pp. 10-11.
46.   Devine, Joel A., and James D. Wright (1993). *The Greatest Evil: Urban
Poverty and the American Dream.* New York: Aldine de Gruyter.
47.   Schneiderman, L. (1992). *The American Welfare State: A Family
Perspective.* Paper delivered at the International Conference on Social
Welfare. Seoul, Korea.
48.   "Security for America's children: A report from the annual conference
of the National Academy of Social Insurance." (1992). *Social Security Bulletin,*
55(1), 57-62.

49.   Kotlikoff, Laurence, and Jagadeesh Gokhale (1994). "Passing the generational buck." *The Public Interest,* 114, Winter, 73-81.

50.   Mroz and Popkin, op cit.

51.   Aronowitz, Stanley and William DiFazio (1996). "High technology and work tomorrow." *Annals of the American Academy of Political and Social Science.* 544(March), 52-67.

52.   Goldberg, S. (1989). "The theory of partriarchy." *International Journal of Sociology and Social Policy,* 9, 15-62.

53.   McKay, Steven and Alan Marsh (1994). *Lone parents and work.* London: HMSO.

54.   Dinitto, D. M., and T. R. Dye (1987). *Social Welfare: Politics and Public Policy.* Englewood Cliffs: Prentice Hall.

55.   *Social Security Bulletin Annual Statistical Supplement.* (1991). Washington: United States Department of Health and Human Services.

56.   Macarov, David (1982). *Worker Productivity: Myths and Reality.* Beverly Hills: Sage.

57.   Fowles, D. (1983). "The changing older population." *Aging,* 339, 6-11; Silverstone, B. and A. Burack-Weiss (1983). *Social Work Practice with the Frail Elderly and Their Families.* Springfield: Charles C. Thomas.

58.   *American Association of Retired Persons Bulletin* (1985), 26(6).

59.   Hokenstad, M. D. (1992). "Cross-national trends and issues in social service provision and social work practice for the elderly." *Journal of Gerontological Social Work,* 12(1/2), 1-15.

60.   Chen, Y-P. (1985). "Economic status of the aging." In R. H. Binstock and E. Shanas (eds.), *The Handbook of Aging and the Social Sciences.* New York: Van Nostrand Reinhold.

61.   "Notes on current labor statistics," *Monthly Labor Review,* 118(8), 2.

62.   Zastrow, C. (1992). *Social Problems: Issues and Solutions.* Chicago: Nelson Hall.

63.   *International Herald Tribune,* June 19-20, 1993, p. 3.

64.   Ropers, op cit., p. 51.

65.   Snyder, David Pearce (1996). "The revolution in the workplace: What's happening to our jobs?" *The Futurist,* 30(2), 8-13.

66.   Snyder, ibid.

67.   Ibid.

68.   Ibid.

69.   Ibid, p. 177.

70.   Sanger and Lohr, op cit.

71.   Snyder, op cit.

72.   *World Social Situation in the 1990s.* Op cit., p. 59.

73.   *Monthly Labor Review* (1995), 118(10), p. 75.

74.   Pear, R. (1993). "Poverty 1993: Bigger, Deeper, Younger, Getting Worse." *New York Times,* October 10, p. IE4.

75.   *Monthly Labor Review,* 118(10), p. 102.

76.   Rosen, Sumner N. (1996). "Jobs: New Challenges, New Responses." *Annals of the American Academy of Political and Social Science,* 544 (March), 27-42.

77. Ibid.
78. Varying definitions of unemployment and the labor force gave figures varying between 2.4% and 10.2% when the official rate was 6.8%. See Bregger, John, E., and Steven E. Haugen (1995). "BLS introduces new range of alternative unemployment measures." *Monthly Labor Review*, 118(11), 19-26.
79. Macarov, D. (1995). *Social Welfare: Structure and Practice*. Thousand Oaks: Sage, pp. 240-241; Rosen, op cit..
80. Ropers, op. cit., p. 177.
81. *World Social Situation in the 1990s*. Op cit.
82. Rosen, op cit.
83. Uchitelle, Louis and N. B. Kleinfield (1996). "Millions of Americans suffer stings of layoffs." *New York Times Fax Edition*, (March 3), p. 1.
84. Marin, Bernd (1995). "For new flexible and shorter working life times." *Eurosocial*, 65/66, pp. 3-9.
85. McMurrer, Daniel P., and Amy B. Chasanov (1995). "Trends in unemployment insurance benefits" *Monthly Labor Review*, 118(9), 30-39.
86. Mishra, R. (1990). *The Welfare State in Capitalist Society: Policies of Retrenchment and Maintenance in Europe, North America and Australia*. New York: Harvester Wheatleaf.
87. Blau, J. (1992). "A paralysis of social policy?" *Social Work*, 37(6), 558-562.
88. McMurrer, op cit.
89. *Social Security Programs Throughout the World 1995*. (1995). Washington: Social Security Administration, Office of Research and Statistics, July, SSA Publication No. 13-11805, Research Report No. 64.
90. Macarov, op cit.
91. See Macarov, David (1980). *Work and Welfare: The Unholy Alliance*. Beverly Hills: Sage.
92. *Demographic Yearbook* (1991)
93. Cetron, M., and Davies, O. (1991). "Trends shaping the world." *The Futurist*, 25(5), 11-21.
94. Habib, Jack (1985). "The economy and the aged." In Binstock, R. H., and Ethel Shanas (eds.), *Handbook of Aging and Social Sciences*. New York: Van Nostrand Reinhold.
95. U. S. Department of Health and Human Services (n.d.)
96. Barton, L. (1995). "Aging and economics: A comparative examination of responses by the United States, Great Britain and Japan." *International Journal of Sociology and Social Policy*. 15(1-3), 120-133.
97. Ibid.
98. Snyder, op cit.
99. Geoghegan, Thomas (1996). "The state of the worker." *New York Times Fax Edition* (January 25), p. 8.
100. Barner, Robert (1996). "Seven changes that will challenge manager -- and workers." *The Futurist*, 30(2), 14-18.
101. Koppel, Ross, and Alice Hoffman (1996). "Dislocation policies in the USA: What should we be doing?" *Annals of the American Academy of Political and Social Science*, 544(March), 126.

102.   Justice Brandeis is said to have remarked, many years ago, "Corporations have no souls."

103.   Deardoff, Alan V., and Jon D. Haveman (1995). "The effect of U. S. trade laws on the incidence of poverty in America." *Journal of Human Resources*, 30(4), 807-815..

104. Sandel, Michael (1996). Democracy's Discontent. (Quoted in Friedman, Thomas L. "Politics in a Nafta Era," *New York Times Fax Edition*, April 7, p. 8).

105. Macarov, David (1996). "The employment of new ends: Planning for permanent unemployment." *Annals of the American Academy of Political and Social Science*, 544(March), 191-202.

106.   Macarov, David (1991). *Certain Change: Social Work Practice in the Future*. Silver Spring: National Association of Social Workers.

107.   Rosen, op cit., p. 34, puts the real rate as 12.5% -- more than twice the official rate.

108.   Marin, op cit., p. 3.

109.   Ibid, p. 5.

110.   Ibid, p. 6.

111.   *World Social Situatin in the 1990s*, op cit., p. 201

112.   Marin, op cit., p. 3.

113.   Silverstein, Gary (1994). "Measuring client success." *Public Welfare*, 52(4), 6-23.

114.   Uchitelle, and Kleinfield, op cit.

115.   Simms, Margaret C. (1996). "Training, work and poverty." In Darby, Michael R.   (ed.), *Reducing Poverty in America: Views and Approaches*. Thousand Oaks: Sage.

116.   Zigler, Edward and Sally J. Styfco (1996). "Reshaping childhood intervention to be a more effective weapon against poverty." In Darby, op cit., 310-336.

117. Macarov, David (1982). *Worker Productivity: Myths and Reality*. Beverly Hills: Sage.

118.   Darby, Michael, R (1996). "Acknowledgements." In Darby, op cit., ix.

119.   Darby, Michael, R. (1996). "Facing and reducing poverty." Ibid., p. 7.

120. Townsend, op cit., pp. 234 and 3.

121.   See, for example, Macarov, David (1980).   *Work and Welfare: The Unholy Alliance*. Beverly Hills, Sage; and Macarov, David (1985). "Planning for a probability: The almost-workless world." *International Labour Review*, 124, 629-642.

EDUCATION

TEACHING THE FUTURE: A MEMOIR

by

W. Warren Wagar

When I started my academic career, I was a proper academician, centered in a major professional discipline and armed with a doctorate from Yale University.   I billed myself as a modern European intellectual historian. I wrote books and articles bristling with footnotes, reviewed the footnote-infested scholarly books of my peers in such eminent journals as *The American Historical Review*, and read papers at the annual conclaves of the American Historical Association. During my first tour of duty as a professor, at Wellesley College from 1958 to 1966, I taught such warhorses as "The History of Western Thought," "The History of England," and "Twentieth-Century Europe."

Yet in the early 1970s, after 16 years of teaching European history, I made the fateful decision to add to my pedagogical repertoire the study of the future. This was a deliberate choice, carefully considered; but it was also like flying into heavy fog. Once I had left the familiar clear skies of the past, I knew I would have no landmarks to measure my progress, no beacons or airfield landing lights to help me home, nothing but the featureless pearly gray of that unknowable time we call the future. In the spring of 1974, I taught the first edition of "History of the Future" at Binghamton University. To my surprise, more than a hundred students enrolled. Somehow, we all survived the semester more or less intact.

Since that time, I have offered "History of the Future" at Binghamton 20 more times, attracting a grand total of nearly 6,000 students. The average enrollment has been 285. Although I keep introducing new topics and eliminating older ones, the basic structure of the course has remained much the same all these years. We begin with a methodological overview, then survey global environmental prospects, then explore the future of society and its institutions (such as the state, the world economy, and the family), and conclude with a prognosis of the cultural future of humankind, from religious life to the fine arts.

The popularity of "History of the Future" also prompted me to develop three other, more specialized futures courses. One is the survey course in European intellectual history, which I transformed into an exploration of utopian and dystopian visions in modern literature, from More to Huxley.   Another, first known as "World

---

W. Warren Wagar, *historian and author, is distinguished teaching professor in the Department of History at the State University of New York, Binghamton.*

War III," and now dubbed "War: Past and Future," explores the prospects for war and peace in the next century. The third is a research seminar, "Alternative Futures," limited to seniors who have taken one of my other courses in futures studies.

I should add that the four courses I teach, although they complement one another, have mercifully never been packaged as a "program" offering a "certificate" or some other pretentious scrap of paper. There is no set of requirements that must be approved by the college council, no subsection in the undergraduate bulletin, no need for letterhead or secretaries, no curriculum committee, no biweekly faculty meetings. I just teach the bloody courses.

Or do I? Is it really that simple? Not quite. First, I had to win departmental approval to offer "History of the Future." A few eyebrows did rise perceptibly when I proposed to teach the future in a history department. As an intellectual historian, my interest had always centered on ideas of human destiny and progress, whether from writers of utopian fiction, theologians, philosophers, or whomever. To my colleagues I put the question: what if that strange impermanent creature, the undergraduate, happened to share some of my enthusiasm for things to come? What if he or she were even more interested in things to come than in things gone by--a dangerous question for a professional historian to ask, but one I could not resist.

The trick up my sleeve, which my colleagues were not slow to spy, is the realization that no one can actually study the future, or know anything at all about it. What futurists do is to study images of the future. They make inventories of possibility, based on the well-informed (or ill-informed) speculations of past and present-day minds, including their own. The future itself remains unseen, wrapped in fog, beyond our grasp.

In the end, my colleagues were supportive, and in particular my chairman, Norman F. Cantor. The college council also approved the course and admitted it to the undergraduate bulletin. Through the years I have heard occasional dark mutterings about resources diverted from "real" History, mutterings that are certainly understandable, but on my journeys to the future I have never been ambushed or cut off at the pass.

Nevertheless, the sheer numbers of students who enroll in the two largest courses, "History of the Future" and "War: Past and Future," have resulted in the evolution of a pedagogical style quite different from anything I employed in my earlier years as a college teacher of European history, when most of my classes were fairly small. Briefly put, the challenge I faced was to teach something that demands imagination and speculative verve to a class of the monstrous size normally associated with the introductory college course in psychology or physics. To make matters even more difficult, the students hail from every class year, every undergraduate major, and every school in our university center. (We have schools of education, management, technology, and nursing, in addition to liberal arts.) This heterogeneity can be a big help in discussions, when students with one kind of expertise can enlighten students with another, and vice versa. Given the phenomenally broad scope of futures inquiry, which draws on virtually every discipline represented in the university catalogue, this is all to the good. But it may also make it difficult to develop a sense of academic community in the classroom.

From the beginning, I decided that students would need a wide variety of experiences. If I just lectured three times a week and assigned a few general works by social scientists or humanists in the relevant fields, students would soon get the idea that studying the future is like studying anything else. They would memorize what they heard or read, and feed it back to me at examination time.

This would not do. To introduce variety and encourage creativity, I settled on a three-part calendar of weekly events. The first component is my lectures, given twice a week--formal lectures well stuffed with data, competing theories, and multiple scenarios. In the third weekly class hour, my graduate teaching assistants lead a discussion of the lecture material and readings, in sections of about 25 students each. I also reserve one evening a week for the screening of science-fiction films set in plausible or satirized future worlds. We see films such as "Soylent Green," "Rollerball," "The Handmaid's Tale," "Dr. Strangelove," "A Clockwork Orange," and "Crimson Tide." Attendance is mandatory. In some years, students submit reviews or comparative review essays explaining how each film did (or did not) stretch their academic imaginations.

Books? At the risk of losing a fair number of students I require six or seven books in both "History of the Future" and "War: Past and Future." Here, too, variety is the watchword. 1 assign two or three non-fiction titles, such as *Global Outlook 2000*, produced by a team of UN futurists, or *Fast Forward* by Richard Carlson and Bruce Goldman. In 1991, I published a textbook of my own, *The Next Three Futures: Paradigms of Things to Come*, which I now use in "History of the Future." But the required reading also includes novels and utopias that explore the future. Among many others, I have adopted Walter Miller's *A Canticle for Leibowitz*, Aldous Huxley's *Brave New World*, Stanislaw Lem's *The Futurological Congress*, Pat Frank's *Alas, Babylon*, Ernest Callenbach's *Ecotopia*, Joe Haldeman's *The Forever War*, and my own *A Short History of the Future*. In addition, students either write a research paper or undertake a creative project, such as a newspaper of the future or a short story about a credible future using ideas gleaned from the course.

In keeping with my policy of strictly respecting the academic freedom of students, the examinations themselves, midterms and finals alike, consist chiefly of open-ended essay questions with no "right" answers. Although I do not make a dark secret of my own preferences, I try to present all points of view fairly and encourage students to use the courses as a way of clarifying their own values and defining the kind of future world in which they might wish to live. But they do have to support their views with relevant evidence and argue their case forcefully. The average grade earned in my courses is a touch below the average for our liberal arts departments.

In the discussion sections, I urge my teaching assistants not to lecture, but to use this time to discuss major issues from the books and films, stage debates, entertain dissenting views on the lecture material, and break students into small problem-solving groups that report back to the class in the second half of the hour. The discussion sections feature student-centered and student-initiated learning. In recent years we have videotaped some of these classes and used the tapes to help improve graduate teaching.

The discussion meetings are in many ways the heart of my futures courses at Binghamton. The department is blessed with a large graduate program that attracts superb students from all over the world, many of whom also develop into fine teachers in their own right. When the undergraduates evaluate the course near the end of the term, not a few tell me they have learned more from the discussions than from any other segment of the class, including the lectures.

Working with my graduate assistants, who teach all the discussion sections and grade all the exams and papers, is one of my biggest jobs in "History of the Future" and "War: Past and Future." In point of fact, it is very much like teaching a graduate seminar. Depending on enrollments, the staff can number anywhere from three to nine people, at various stages in their graduate careers, from neophytes in their first year to seasoned veterans in their fourth. The common denominator linking all but a handful of the more than 150 assistants with whom I have worked since the mid-1970s is a predictable lack of any serious academic interest in futures studies. Our graduate students come to Binghamton to learn "real" history--as is their privilege! I cannot count on anyone having the kind of background preferable for an assignment to my courses.

Yet within a month, the staff has usually buckled down and generated an esprit de corps that ensures good teaching, fair grading, and cordial relations with our undergraduates. Most of this is due to the caliber of graduate students in our program, but I help as much as I can. At least four or five times during the semester, we all meet to discuss classroom procedures, grading practices, films and novels, and other matters of mutual interest. At our first gathering, I distribute a "tip sheet" of things to do and not to do, as well as a day-by-day schedule of classes, assignments, and recommended discussion topics. At examination time, I prepare a detailed set of guidelines to help the assistants cope with the grading of essay answers.

The lecture hall experience that we provide is the exact opposite of the discussion section experience. Although some teachers have the ability to wander through an audience of hundreds, engaging students in animated dialogue with microphone in hand, I prefer to treat the lecture hall as a theater. The lecture itself is a solo performance. Before the class starts, I project an outline of my lecture on the overhead screen. As the students enter the classroom, they hear music, something that illustrates the theme of the day's lecture. For my lecture on the future of the class system, I may play Donna Summer's "She Works Hard for the Money." For my lecture on genetic engineering, it's Zager and Evans's "In the Year 2525." For the future of democracy, Aaron Copland's "Fanfare for the Common Man." A mood is set. Attention is drawn to the day's topic. Students often ask about the music, and several have furnished me with tapes of numbers I can use later in the term.

The music stops two minutes into the hour. After ringing a Swiss cow bell to call the class to order, I start my lecture. Sometimes I offer a brief dramatic reading to introduce the subject matter. But most of each lecture is serious business, rehearsed before class and delivered from an elaborate script that keeps me focused on the matter at hand. The script also supplies cues for words to emphasize, changes of pace, time remaining, and so forth. I may make a few cuts and emendations as I go along, but always within the framework of the script. If possible I end my remarks two minutes before the hour, and as the students make their departure, the day's theme music returns.

Not everyone responds to this lecturing style. People who value spontaneity, lively give-and-take, or flaky charm will find my lectures a dead loss. But I think the majority of undergraduates who enroll in lecture courses want the lectures to be substantive, structured, and cleanly delivered. Lord knows this is what I wanted, and rarely got, when I was a student.

The third course in my futures repertoire, devoted to the utopian/dystopian tradition in modern European thought, is another kettle of fish altogether. Here the enrollment is much smaller, anywhere from 30 to 75 students, mostly juniors and seniors, with a sizable contingent of history majors. The class meets only two days a week, for sessions of one and a half hours each. On a normal day, I lecture for the first half of the class period, taking questions throughout; in the second half, we discuss assigned readings with the help of a sheet of interpretive questions handed out during the previous class. In a recent innovation, students also take turns writing brief opinion papers on selected texts. These papers are due on the day the text is discussed in class. The paper writers constitute a "panel of experts" who have spent extra time on the readings and can help move the discussion along whenever it flags. Since I first began teaching European intellectual history as a study of utopias and dystopias in 1976, I have offered it ten times, with a total enrollment of about 500.

The official business of "Modern European Thought," as the course is entitled in the catalogue, is to trace the flow of thought in

European civilization from the Renaissance to the present. I use utopian and dystopian texts as our primary source materials in part because my students and I find them fascinating and easy to take, but chiefly because no other written materials produced by a culture so comprehensively reveal its underlying assumptions, world views, and values. Utopian/dystopian texts offer systematic critiques of the existing social order and furnish road maps to the future. They epitomize our sense of who we are, and who we would rather be. They are perhaps the richest ores that intellectual historians can mine.

The lectures in this course are intended to provide historical contexts for the assigned texts, not to analyze or interpret the texts themselves. After preliminary inquiries into methods and concepts, I give what I call an overview lecture about once every two or three weeks. The overview lecture introduces students to a particular period, such as the Renaissance or the romantic era, surveying both the general history of the period and its dominant cultural-intellectual paradigms. The rest of the lectures explore the life and times of the thinkers whose work we are reading, with an excursus now and then into other thinkers of the same generation.

We begin, of course, with the *Utopia* of Sir Thomas More, followed sometimes by Campanella's *The City of the Sun* or more often by Bacon's *New Atlantis*. Voltaire's *Zadig* and *Candide* represent the world view of the Enlightenment. The most commonly used 19th-century texts include Morris's *News from Nowhere*, Engels's *Socialism: Utopian and Scientific*, and Wells's *The Time Machine* or *A Modern Utopia*. Occasionally students read bits of Fourier, Cabet, and Comte, although as a rule I prefer to stand clear of abridged or excerpted material. For 20th-century texts, my choices have included Zamyatin's *We*, the obvious classics by Huxley and Orwell, Katharine Burdekin's feminist utopia *The End of This Day's Business*, and postmodern texts such as J.G. Ballard's *The Unlimited Dream Company*. In 1984, the Orwell year, I built the course around *Nineteen Eighty-Four* and other works of Orwell's (notably *Coming Up for Air*). We started with Orwell and finished with Orwell, examining earlier utopian/dystopian works in the broad middle of the course.

To vary the pace and bring students more into the picture, I also like to arrange debates on major interpretive issues, usually six or seven a semester. For example, is More's *Utopia* a protomodern text, or does it hark back to medieval values? One or two students will take one side of the issue, one or two the other. They battle it out for half an hour, and then the class has its chance to interrogate the debaters. We usually bring the debate to a close with a vote to determine which side "won." The balloting is rarely lopsided. Once in a great while, I also play a tape from my minuscule collection of radio dramas, especially a 1956 production of *Brave New World* narrated by Aldous Huxley himself. But so far I have not shown films in this course, in part because nearly all the good films are dystopias, rather than utopias.

Finally, "Modern European Thought" features a term paper in which the choice lies between a conventional research project on utopian/dystopian thought and a scenario, story, or play. Students exercising the second option construct their own models of the good or bad society, using as building material some of the ideas encountered in class through the semester.

The last course regularly offered is "Alternative Futures," a senior research seminar restricted to alumni of my other futures courses. Most of the students in "Alternative Futures" are history majors, fulfilling a departmental seminar requirement. It was created in 1978 in response to student demand for a more advanced course in futures studies. Unfortunately some of those who enroll are not dyed-in-the-wool futures enthusiasts. They simply want to fulfill the requirement that all majors take a senior research seminar.

This drawback aside, we usually have a good time. The seminar enrolls about fifteen students and meets once a week for three hours. The opening weeks are taken up in discussions of futures methodology, with the help of works like Barry Hughes's *World Futures* or *What Futurists Believe*, edited by Joseph F. Coates and Jennifer Jarratt.

In due course, after consultation with their fellow seminarians and with me, students select a manageable topic and spend the rest of the term researching it and preparing a full-sized seminar paper. The topic may be a prominent futurist's life and thought, a body of futurist or utopian fiction, a theme in technological forecasting, an econometric or world-system model with predictive power, next year's US election returns, prospects for the exploration of other solar systems in the galactic neighborhood, or any of a hundred thousand other possibilities. I impose no limits, as long as the topic is not too vast and involves serious research in relevant and available primary sources. For about a month and a half in the middle of the semester, the class does not meet every week, to give everyone the chance to get well launched on their projects. As time goes by, we hear several rounds of progress reports from each student, and then (in the last two or three weeks) final reports on the finished papers.

From almost the beginning, I have actively solicited the opinions of my students, especially in "History of the Future" and "War: Past and Future." I poll them not only for their evaluation of my teaching and that of the graduate assistants, but also for their views of the books and films, and for their own ideas about the future. The results are seldom just what I would like to see. My students do not necessarily prefer the books and films I like best, which, in extreme cases, persuades me to drop a text or a film for which I had entertained high hopes. In their political views they are significantly more conservative than I am, but also rather more optimistic.

The survey on which I have the longest run of comparable data is the poll on "Options for the Future" conducted in "History of the

Future" since 1979. Year in, year out, more students expect a continuation of the present-day capitalist liberal-democratic global order during the next 100 years than any of the other four options I provide. The percentage of first-place votes for global capitalism in 1979 was 40%, rising to an average of 57% through the rest of the 1980s, and rising still higher to an average of 70% in the 1990s. The only serious competition has been offered by what I call the technocratic model of the future, a world order run by businessmen and experts, with democracy only a façade. This future was expected by an average of 25% of students in the 1980s and by an average of 17% in the 1990s.

The other choices, a socialist future, a "countercultural" or "New Age" future, and a future in which civilization is destroyed by warfare or environmental catastrophes or both, have never done well. Over the years a socialist future has been expected by only 4% of my students, a countercultural future by only 5%, and an apocalyptic future by 8%. The apocalyptic future was much more commonly expected in the period from 1979 to 1984, when it attracted an average of 16% of all first-place votes. Since 1987, about the time the Cold War began to loosen its grip, the apocalyptic scenario has been the first-place expectation of barely 4%. The study of the future routinely mirrors present-day hopes and anxieties.

But this is to report only what students expect. What they prefer is a somewhat different story, and I have also systematically surveyed their preferences since 1979. The global capitalist model of the future has never been the first choice of more than 52% of my students. In one year (1982) it dropped to the first choice of only 12%. The average over the years has been 39%, with no discernible trend up or down. Running ahead of global capitalism on the preference side of the survey is the countercultural future, the kind of future that would delight a Fritz Schumacher, a Hazel Henderson, a William Irwin Thompson, or an Ernest Callenbach. Although only 5% of my students have expected such a future, an impressive 46% have preferred it. Again there is no discernible trend at work; the countercultural future is just as popular today as it was in the Reagan era and before. The socialist future has been ranked first by 10% of my students, somewhat more in the early days of the course than in the Reagan years, but the numbers have picked up again since 1987. The technocratic model comes in a poor fourth, and only a few wiseacres (or fundamentalist Christians looking forward to the Rapture?) have given a first-place preference vote to the doomsday scenario.

I have also regularly polled students in my "War: Past and Future" course on their expectations for warfare in the future and their preferred roads to world peace. In the first year I taught the course (in 1983 under the title of "World War III"), 72% of the members of the class expected a Third World War involving the United States and the USSR, although less than half of those foresaw the use of nuclear weapons in such an Armageddon. By 1986, only 61% of the members of the class expected a World War III, and by 1989 only 44%.

So far, no surprises. The détente between the US and the USSR had clearly lowered expectations of global war. Yet in 1990 we returned to our starting point, with an astonishing 71% of all students expecting a Third World War during the next century. In 1992 57% expected it and in 1993 61%. I did not offer the course in 1994, but in 1995 58% of my students still expected a Third World War. I have no ready-made explanation for this increase in pessimism in the 1990s, except to say that obviously the euphoria expressed in many quarters about "peace dividends" and "the end of history" did not carry much weight with the people who took my course. They were not tricked by the apparent end of the Cold War into thinking the Peaceable Kingdom was close at hand.

Nevertheless, it could hardly be argued in the first half of the 1990s that the venerable scenario of a fight to the finish between the United States and its NATO allies, on the one hand, and the former Soviet Union and its former East European satellites, on the other hand, remained a likely prospect. Global war and major regional wars were still eminently conceivable, as the students realized, but with various changes in the imagined cast of characters.

In any event the fundamental structural changes in the world political system in 1989-91 forced me to reconceive the course I had already given seven times under the title of "World War III." In the spring of 1992 I transformed it from an inquiry into the prospects for global nuclear war between the Superpowers to a study of the future of post-Cold War armed conflict, especially in the less developed countries. In short, my emphasis shifted from third world wars to wars of the Third World. The segments of the course devoted to war prevention have also undergone significant change, in the light of recent breakthroughs in nuclear disarmament and the remodeling of US and European policy in the Middle East. Keeping up with the future is hard work at best. In recent years it has become absolutely herculean.

But there is clearly no shrinkage of student interest in war and peace. The 11 editions of my course on the future of warfare (under three different titles) have enrolled almost 2,500 students, and I am already planning the 1997 edition.

So I am convinced that futures studies can be insinuated into the liberal arts curriculum without sacrifice of traditional academic values. If such things can be done in a history department with course enrollments in the hundreds by a teacher of modest abilities and no charisma, they can be done in almost any appropriate department with courses of almost any size by almost any teacher. The Aristotelian golden mean between pedagogical radicalism and pedagogical conservatism can be struck. Students can have fun, but also earn their credit hours in generally acceptable and approved ways. They can run the engines of their imagination at open throttle, but also write term papers and final examination essays that are not just blasts of academic hot air.

Not that we entirely escape the hot air. As often happens in courses that are not required, my giant lecture courses attract people who are looking for ways to be passive and invisible. Since most of our undergraduates ranked in the top 20% of their high school classes, they know how to dodge requirements adroitly and turn in written work that looks pretty good, even if it skimps on substance. Attendance is never 100%, and not everyone buys or reads all the books. We are treated, year in and year out, to our share of windy, repetitive essays at examination time.

Still, I have no doubt that the majority of my students take their work seriously. Most learn a great deal from their journeys into the future, or from their rambles in the lush gardens and spired tenements of utopia. They learn about human aspiration, about fear and anxiety, about the dangers and the golden possibilities that lie before our species as it blunders through space and time. And what, after all, could be more important? The past is over. The present flits by. The only thing we can change is the future.

HOW TO DEVELOP A SOCIAL FORESIGHT CAPACITY

by

Richard A. Slaughter

INTRODUCTION

For most people "the future" is an abstraction. While stereotypical images of futures are widely available in popular culture, few people take them seriously or investigate the much wider range of images and scenarios that can be envisaged. Thus, for the majority, the future might as well be an "empty space" for all the effect it has on their daily lives and decisions, their personal and professional behavior. This is partly why governments around the world continue to pursue short-term issues up to the next election, with little or no thought ·for the longer-term implications of their actions, their policies, the major shifts under way and the nature of the multi-faceted transition collectively facing us early in the 21st century. How, then, can this apparent abstraction, "the future" be made more real, more accessible and influential, more a part of daily life for everyone? How can we develop a social foresight capacity?

This essay outlines a strategy which recognizes *the layered quality* of applied foresight. Here foresight is understood as the capacity to think ahead, to consider alternatives, to model different options and to choose between them. In static or slow-moving periods of history, foresight would only be valuable for personal and informal uses. But in a period of rapid change, uncertainty and profound civilizational challenge--in other words during a period such as our own--social foresight becomes a *structural* necessity. The full costs of social learning by crude experience are becoming unacceptable.

Stage 1: Harnessing Human Capacities and Perceptions

The human brain-mind system is endowed not merely with the capacity for primary consciousness (seeing what is here-and-now) but with *reflexive understanding in time.* This higher-order consciousness is characterized by the ability to remember and to learn, to roam consciously throughout a rich, complex, extended present, to understand responsibilities and consequences, and to speculate on futures yet to come. Edelman writes that:

> The freeing of parts of conscious thought from the con-
> straints of an immediate present and the increased richness

---

Richard A. Slaughter *is director of the Futures Study Centre, Melbourne, Australia.*

of social communication allow for the anticipation of future states and for planned behavior. With that ability come the abilities to model the world, to make explicit comparisons and to weigh outcomes; through such comparisons comes the possibility of reorganizing plans. Obviously, these capabilities have adaptive value.[1]

Human beings, therefore, have an *innate* capacity for speculation, foresight, modelling and choosing between alternatives. They are not stranded, willy-nilly, in a deterministic world. Rather, they are consciously located in a socially-created, but self-actualized, matrix of structures, understandings and forces. Unlike the human body, which is necessarily constrained by biological processes, the human mind, imagination and spirit are free to roam at will among a stunning array of different worlds and world-views, past, present and future.

To put it simply, the "wiring" of the human brain/mind system is sufficiently complex and inclusive to permit at least three kinds of journeys. It permits consideration of past environments that the body and perceptual apparatus were never present to experience directly. It supports knowledge and understanding of events that take place in the historical present but which are displaced in space (for example, the Chernobyl disaster, the Bosnian tragedy, the Oklahoma City bombing, and French nuclear tests in the Pacific). Finally, it enables the forward view--a potentially panoramic outlook on a vast span of alternative futures.

Figure 1 therefore suggests that human capacities and perceptions provide a sound foundation for social foresight. The ability to think ahead is *an emergent capacity* of this beautifully-constructed system. This is why everyone is fundamentally capable of foresight, forward thinking and responsible behavior focused on long-term consider-ations. In contrast to the professional (and professionalized) work of, for example, forecasters and scenario analysts, one does not need a higher degree and an institutional base in order to engage in successful foresight. (However, both are useful for wider social implementation--see below). The key question is: How can these symbolic capacities be developed and enhanced?

FIGURE 1

Stages in Developing a Social Foresight Capacity

Stages		Indicators
	<------ A futures-responsive culture ------>	
Stage 5:	*Social capacity for foresight* as an emergent property	Long-term thinking becomes a social norm
Stage 4:	Futures processes, projects & structures embodied in variety of *applications*	Foresight routinely applied in most organizations
Stage 3:	*Futures tools & methodologies* increase analytic power	Widespread use of standard FS tools & methods
Stage 2:	*Futures concepts* & ideas enable a futures discourse	Futures concepts & ideas become influential via discourse
Stage 1:	Raw *capacities & perceptions* of the human brain-mind system	Unreflective use of forward thinking in daily life of individual
	<------ A past-driven culture ------>	

This Figure illustrates the way that futures study is progressively enabled stage-by-stage from a raw, underutilized, potential to an applied social resource. At level 1, futures thinking is informal at best, and the future seems to be an "empty space." However, concepts, methods and applications augment these capacities. The future then emerges as an active social category brimming with social implications.

Stage 2: Using Futures Concepts to Enable a Futures Discourse

The raw biological capacity of the brain/mind system is insufficient to assure understanding and competence in any field. The rare stories of children raised in sub-human conditions give weight to the view that to become properly human, the young need to be nurtured within a family and inducted into the symbolic social world of language and culture. Beyond that they normally progress to the formal processes of education. So far, so good. Unfortunately, however, those raised and taught in Western, or Westernized cultures, are imbued with the characteristic Western outlook. For example: nature is viewed as a resource; growth is an unquestioned good; scientific and technical systems are seen as primary and the past is authoritative. The future is a largely "empty category" which, if it has any influence at all, seems to loom threateningly. [2]

Critical futures study suggests that these embedded cultural biases and commitments are complicit in the emergence *and maintenance* of the global problematique in all its many dimensions. Therefore, as each generation takes up the standard Western/industrial world-view, seeing it as natural and normal, an unsustainable world order is perpetuated at a very fundamental level. However, as noted, higher-order consciousness is reflexive. It can look clearly on its own presuppositions and, where the evidence is clear, change them. As this occurs, a diagnosis emerges about the global plight of human-kind. The next step is as simple as it is powerful: the acquisition of a futures discourse.

It is tempting to see a futures discourse as simply a matter of acquiring the appropriate language. But this is not the case. As a teenager I read a great deal of science fiction. Without realizing it at the time, I was absorbing a "grammar" of futures imagery which subverted the usual view of the future as a "blank space" and instead filled it with an immense range of images and meanings. Due to the great variety of images and possibilities revealed, my relationship to the future became *active*, rather than passive. Further, I began to wonder why so many futures were populated by cruel aliens, implacably menacing super-computers, rampaging robots and planetary catastrophes. Why, I wondered, could the future not be a desirable place, even in imagination? The answers to that key question led me to the global problematique and the futures field.

When I took up futures studies at university, I discovered a literary and methodological futures discourse. As I began to immerse myself in it, so many aspects of the futures dimension began to clarify and to connect with puzzling features of the present (for instance, the decline of "progress", the fears of young people, the ambiguity of science and technology, defective economic accounting). The insights so gained provided a new purchase on the present. Eventually I saw that society is profoundly affected by a small number of dominant discourses (for example, economic, commercial, academic) which, in

no small way, condition the framing of current issues and concerns--
and hence the priorities and directions adopted at any time.[3]

Set against these established discourses are a number of newer ones
which are engaged in a symbolic struggle to gain influence. They
include a peace discourse, an environmental discourse, and discourse
arising from the women's movement. The futures discourse also
seeks acceptance and legitimation. It highlights the need for a shift
from short-, to long-term thinking, and foregrounds notions such as
sustainability.[4] Beyond this it is not strongly prescriptive. Perhaps
the core concept of "alternatives" mitigates against this. I regard the
lack of a futures discourse in society as one of the structural impediments to adaptive change. Alternatively, the wider adoption of such
a discourse is one of the main strategies through which the capacity
to deal in depth with the apparently intractable dilemmas of the
present and near-term future can be widely developed.

Without a futures discourse founded on the critical thinking
alluded to above, "the future" is occluded, hidden, continually just
out of sight and therefore out of mind. Similarly, the many rich
possibilities for understanding the global predicament, reconcept-
ualizing aspects of it and steering toward consciously-chosen
outcomes are overlooked. So how can we encourage and support the
development of such a discourse? One answer is that we can make
futures concepts, ideas and tools much more widely available.[5]
Evidence for the effectiveness of such an approach is not hard to
find. Most futurists have experienced the same kind of dawning
awareness, followed by deeper understanding, as I did. There is also
evidence from graduate students, social innovators and others, who
come fresh to futures studies and emerge from workshops and
courses with the gleam of insight and empowerment in their eyes.[6]
I therefore have no doubt whatever of the enabling power of a
well-grounded futures discourse. It helps people to clarify "the big
picture", to see behind the surface of everyday events and to discern
very many ways out of our current difficulties.

The most productive futures concepts are those which have a
certain "amplitude"; that is, they can be approached and understood
on a variety of levels. Hence they can be introduced at any age. For
example, foresight may seem to be a difficult concept. But it can be
approached very concretely by observing its use in everyday life
(walking, driving, sailing etc.). Later, the "loop of futures scanning"
can be introduced (see Figure 2). Still later aspects of systems
thinking and theories of human perception come into view. Foresight
is one of the most productive futures concepts I have ever encountered (which is why I wrote a book about it). Some other examples
are given in Table 1.

FIGURE 2

The loop of futures scanning

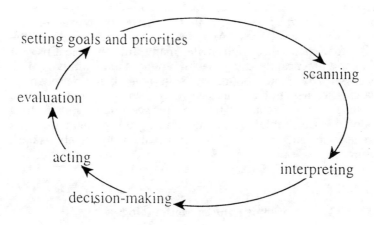

Table 1

Sample of Futures Concepts

alternatives and choices
breakdown and renewal
cultural editing
empowerment
extended present
foresight
futures in education
future generations
the loop of futures scanning
reflexivity
social innovations
sustainability
time frames
vision
a wise culture

When futures concepts are used in a sustained way and in combination with others, as well as with other resources available through futures studies they permit *a distinctly futures-oriented quality of understanding* to emerge. When this insight is shared by educators across all levels and sectors, the way will open toward a much deeper understanding of our historical predicament. Thus, *futures concepts enable a futures discourse*. I regard the latter as the foundation of an applied futures perspective--rather than techniques *per se*. However, the latter also have an essential role to play.

Stage 3: The Role of Futures Methodologies and Tools

If it is innate capacities that make futures thinking possible and futures concepts that enable a distinct discourse to emerge, it is the use of tools and methodologies that increase the power of this perspective to a new level. Any discourse on its own lacks the *analytic* capacity to deal fully with many futures concerns; for example, the practical need to assess if a new road or utility is, or is not, necessary. To make a sound decision depends not merely on ideas and discourse, but also on data. This is where a purely literary discourse fails: it cannot rigorously process data. But futures methodologies can. Table 2 lists some common futures methodologies that are used to generate, manipulate and evaluate information about the future.

Table 2

Sample of Futures Methodologies

backcasting
cross-impact matrices
Delphi surveys
forecasting
scenario building
trend analysis
visioning

In the case of a major construction project, much work is needed to collect time-series data from the recent past and subject it to various forms of mathematical manipulation. It is here that scenarios can also be used to embed the raw data in humanly-meaningful contexts, ie, self-consistent pictures of possible futures. From this kind of elaboration emerges a view of the context in which the proposed project can be located. Does it still make sense? Will there be a sound return on investment? Are the trends likely to hold up? What "system breaks" can be envisaged? And so on. Quantitative analysis at this level is clearly a very demanding and sophisticated proposition which requires expert knowledge and understanding. In France the work of Michel Godet, which goes under the heading of "La Prospective," has carried this kind of approach to its highest level of accomplishment. In the US Peter Schwartz is a leading practitioner of the scenarios method.[7] In Australia the Australian Business Network is among those who have taken up and applied these methods. When done well, scenarios are both commercially and intellectually successful, providing organizations with valuable strategic intelligence about their business, products and markets. In other words, the manipulation of large data sets in combination with conceptual sophistication allows extended analysis to take place. This is a proven way of dealing successfully with complex, futures-related problems.

The other aspect of stage 3 is futures tools. These are sometimes overlooked by specialists, but they are vital in other contexts. By "tools" I refer to a variety of simple measures to explore futures issues and concerns in various situations. Table 3 gives some examples. Such tools have been derived from the conceptual and the methodological resources of the futures field by many people: educators, social activists, workshop facilitators and others. Metaphorically-speaking they provide a comprehensive "tool-kit" for those working with young people or in other enabling contexts such as futures workshops and community self-help groups. Various attempts have been made to make some of the most useful tools available in published form.[8]

Futures tools do not exist in isolation. They can be put together in many productive sequences. This is partly why they are so useful as an educational resource. For example, one can begin with an exercise dealing with optimism and pessimism, go on to one dealing with young people's fears, continue with one on social innovations and end with another using simple scenarios. The permutations are endless. Clearly such tools complement and extend the use of futures concepts.

Table 3

Sample of Futures Tools

dealing with fears
brainstorming
critique of images of futures
environmental scanning
exploring the extended present
futures wheels
imaging workshops
questions about futures
simple cross-impact matrices
simple scenarios
simple technology-assessment
simple trend analysis
time capsules
time lines
values clarification

Thus futures methodologies and tools help support the development of social foresight by extending the analytic, cognitive and intellectual reach of those using them. It follows that they should be taught and learned much more widely in schools, colleges and universities, and offered by distance learning methods. They are primary means for de-mystifying the future and bringing it into present-day decision-making and strategy development.

Stage 4: Futures Applications in Particular Contexts

All the above would be limited in scope if these resources were only used in an *ad hoc*, informal way. But they take on much greater force and power when embodied in specific contexts and applications. Some examples are given in Table 4.

Table 4

Sample of Futures Contexts and Applications

critical futures studies
futures in education
futures research foundations
institutions of foresight
professional societies and networks
national/sectoral foresight studies
strategic planning
twenty first century studies
university futures departments

There is some overlap here with the implementation of the more sophisticated methodologies (since the latter obviously require a suitable context). The term context is significant. It matters not how articulate we may become, nor how far-reaching our methodologies may be; if there is no supportive context, such powers and activities will wither and die. So the key to this stage is the availability of organizations or institutional niches where high-level futures work can thrive, develop and be implemented. Because of their centrality to what is suggested here I will now briefly discuss the examples given.

Critical futures study uses the standard tools of scholarship to raise the power of futures thinking to a higher level.[9] However, it cannot take place in isolation. There is no point in gaining insight if the insights are private, unavailable and not susceptible to the very necessary process of disciplinary criticism and feedback. For me the key to implementing some of the insights from critical futures study was to embed them in post-graduate university courses. [10] This had the benefit of testing them against the criteria of the institution and also against the needs and perceptions of post-graduate students. It is essential that such work is tested openly and does not become a private indulgence.

More generally, much of the foregoing can be implemented in education at the school and college level. I have always argued that instead of being seen as a flashy newcomer, futures studies are *intrinsic* to the tasks of teaching, learning, teacher preparation and professional development (particularly for principals). This is a central point. Schools are in the business of preparing the next generation for active citizenship in the early 21st century. They are one of the few social institutions with a social mandate to think long-term. This provides a starting rationale for many futures-related educational innovations. As this paper is being written, a new futures syllabus for year 11 and 12 students is under trial by the Board of Senior Secondary School Studies in Queensland, Australia. As the new millennium draws closer, and our collective attention shifts from past to future, I expect such innovations to become more common.

Futures research foundations are organizations purposely designed to facilitate the kind of extended, high-level, data-driven work noted above. They have sprung up in many countries, particularly in the US, where a combination of wealth, entrepreneurial drive and deep-seated perception of opportunities and problems, has led to a critical mass of expertise. Such organizations tend, on the whole, to carry out work for government departments, public utilities and corporate clients. What I call "institutions of foresight" (IOFs) are closely related to them and may indeed use some of the same methods. However their focus is more in the public interest arena than in that of corporate strategy *per se*.[11] Depending on how they are defined, there are several hundred IOFs around the world. They exist because perceptive people in all regions have understood the drift of world trends and events, have seen the outlines of the great transition ahead, and have realized that no country should drift into this most dangerous and challenging time. This sense of independent discovery gives weight to what I term a growing "congruence of insight" about the fundamental problems facing humankind, as well as long-term, systemic solutions. Hence the research institutions and the IOFs play a vital role in helping to embed society-wide changes of perception and practice.

Professional societies and networks such as the World Future Society and the World Futures Studies Federation provide essential services to practicing futurists and others who are merely interested in futures. They organize meetings, publish books and newsletters, provide forums at a variety of levels and facilitate communication in many, many ways. In other words, they are an essential part of the "glue" that integrates this otherwise extremely diverse field. They are essential to its wider development and social legitimation.

National and sectoral foresight studies are becoming increasingly common. They have been carried out in many Western countries, in Japan and also in Australia.[12] Another milieu in which such work may be done is within the strategic planning units of various organizations. While strategic planning has not always lived up to expectations, most large organizations have discovered that they must operate strategically. Those who do not are much more likely to fail. So strategic planning is not likely to be abandoned. It can, however, be improved by opening it up to the kinds of symbolic and methodological resources outlined here. Too often, for example, it is the case that corporate approaches to futures are epistemologically and ideologically narrow, taking, for example, a particular corporate or cultural ideology as "given" and missing altogether the many options for critical analysis and reconceptualization upon which lasting innovations may depend. Some management books fall into exactly this trap, for example, Hamil and Prahalad's *Competing for the Future* while others, (for instance, Paul Hawken's *The Ecology of Commerce)* deal with the coming transition in much more conceptually adroit ways.[13]

The emergence of 21st century studies is potentially one of the most significant developments in the field. A number of national studies have been, and are being, carried out. A conceptual and methodological tool kit has been developed, along with an enviable grasp of the organizational and practical issues which can determine success or failure.[14] In time, the national studies will form the basis of an attempt to articulatm a global overview of major issues for the 21st century. It is a prospect that no nation should overlook.

Finally, as noted, there is a key role for universities in the implementation of a futures perspective. It is a matter of profound regret that so few of them have so far understood how thoroughly the prospects ,for humankind have altered during the last several decades, and who therefore remain preoccupied with history, boundaries, subject areas and "knowledge for its own sake". Yet departments of futures studies or futures research not only exist in a number of countries, they are thriving.[15] In some cases, futures courses have been taught in these departments for more than twenty years. Such courses are also taught from within parallel disciplines such as science studies, development studies, education, geography, sociology and politics. Furthermore, an international Masters program in futures studies (to be mediated via the Internet) is currently under active development by a group of scholars who have taught futures studies in different places around the world.[16]

In summary, the implementation of futures thinking still lags well behind its conceptual, methodological and educational capability. However, as the practicability and relevance of futures studies become more widely known, this is likely to change.

CONCLUSION

BUILDING THE COLLECTIVE CAPACITY FOR FORESIGHT

At the individual level foresight may be largely undeveloped but it is, nonetheless, used ubiquitously in everyday life. At the organizational level foresight is rarer, being subsumed into the structurally necessary, but limited, instrumental operations of strategic planning, marketing and organizational development. At the social level, a capacity for foresight barely exists at the present time. The great social institutions: government, business, education, commerce mostly continue as though the particular trajectory of Western culture could continue forever. Yet, as Milbrath and others have pointed out, such a trajectory cannot, under any circumstances, be maintained.[17] Business-as-usual thinking remains the norm. But we no longer live in normal times. It would be easy to conclude that the outlook is therefore hopeless. But this paper has suggested that that is not the case.

At first sight the possibility of seeing the future as anything other than a blank, vaguely menacing space, seems unavoidable. Few people have been exposed to futures concepts in their formal education, and fewer encounter the more complex understandings that spring from them except through the mostly degraded forms available through popular and commercial culture. In this view, a common response is to work as hard as possible for "my family", "my job" or perhaps "my country", and to stay clear of "the big picture" because it is too challenging, too difficult. In this way, whole populations are de-skilled and disempowered. Most young people grow up fearing the future and therefore early on learn the false comforts of denial, evasion, avoidance.

However, as the collective capacity for foresight, futures studies, is built up stage-by-stage, then the future takes on a vastly enhanced meaning and significance. It is no longer merely the cumulative result of long-term social blindness and irresponsibility. Instead, it begins to align with whatever we have the vision to imagine, the clarity to decide upon and the willingness to work toward. What we are most in need of is well-grounded normative scenarios to act as "magnets" for social innovation.[18] Social foresight may begin with disaster-avoidance, but its more constructive uses lie in the creation of stories of futures we positively aspire to create and hand on with pride to our successors.

This paper has suggested that the necessary resources to create, maintain and apply such stories about the future already exist in abundance. The central aim of the futures field should therefore be to implement them more widely than ever before. The approaching millennium offers a golden opportunity. It is a rare moment when the move from individual to collective foresight receives a welcome boost from a widely-recognized, profoundly influential turning point in history.

NOTES

1. G. Edelman, *Bright Air Brilliant Fire*, Harper Collins, NY, 1992.
2. R. Slaughter, *The Foresight Principle: Cultural Recovery in the 21st Century*, Adamantine/Praeger, London/Boston, 1995.

3. See H. Henderson, *Paradigms in Progress: Life Beyond Economics*, Knowledge Systems Inc., Indianapolis, 1991.

4. R. Slaughter, From Short- to Long-Term Thinking, *Futures*, Vol 28, No 1, Jan/Feb 1996.

5. R. Slaughter, *Futures Concepts and Powerful Ideas* (2nd edition), DDM/Futures Study Centre, Melbourne, 1996.

6. R. Slaughter (ed) Futures Study and Higher Education, Special Issue of *Futures Research Quarterly*, Vol 8 No 4, Winter 1992.

7. M. Godet, *From Anticipation to Action*, Paris, UNESCO, 1993. P. Schwartz, *The Art of the Long View*, Doubleday, NY, 1991.

8. R. Slaughter, *Futures Tools and Techniques* (2nd edition), DDM/ Futures Study Centre, Melbourne, 1995. Also D. Hicks, *Teaching About the Future*, WWF, Godalming, Surrey, 1994.

9. See R. Slaughter, op cit 1995, note 2.

10. R. Slaughter, Critical Futures Study and Research at the University of Melbourne, in R. Slaughter op cit 1992, note 6, pp 61-82.

11. R. Slaughter and M. Garrett, An Agenda for Institutions of Foresight, *Futures* Vol 27, No 1, 1995 pp 91-96.

12. See the report *Matching Science and Technology to Future Needs*, ASTEC Secretariat, Canberra, 1994 and the *Futures Gazette*, CSIRO Dept. of Wildlife and Ecology, Canberra, November 1995.

13. See G. Hamil and C.K. Prahalad, *Competing for the Future*, Harvard Business School, Boston, 1994. Also P. Hawken, *The Ecology of Commerce*, Harper Collins, New York, 1993.

14. M. Garrett (et al) *Studies for the 21st Century*, UNESCO, Paris, 1991.

15. Eg. the Futures Research Department at the Budapest University of Economic Sciences, and the Hawaii Centre for Futures Studies at the Manoa campus of the University of Hawaii. These are two specific examples of a wider category of several hundred Institutions of Foresight. See R. Slaughter and M. Garrett Towards an Agenda for Institutions of Foresight, *Futures* Vol 27, No 1, pp 91-95, 1995.

16. This proposal has been under international discussion for some time. It is the subject of a special session at the World Future Society Future Vision conference in Washington DC, July 1996.

17. L. Milbrath, *Envisioning A Sustainable Society: Learning Our Way Out*, SUNY Press, New York, 1989.

18. One of the most inspiring is D. Elgin's book *Awakening Earth*, Morrow, NY, 1993.

STRATEGIES FOR USING HUMAN INTUITION

by

John L. Anderson

INTRODUCTION

Nearing the new millennium the planet finds itself with an extraordinary set of interacting problems, changing forces and multiple futures that often appear to require greater mental abilities than we possess. However, "seeds" of future solutions, technological revolutions, great movements and some "obvious" answers to today's dilemmas do already exist. But they appear in progenitor form as innovative ideas, breakthrough concepts, emerging technology frontiers, new scientific discoveries or the beginning visions of tomorrow's leaders. Furthermore, they are often masked by conflicting or voluminous data, dominance of extrapolated expertise and misdirection of counter-interests. Thus much of the "real" future is embryonic and probably unrecognizable by our normal and traditional means of evaluation.

We humans have progressed using a mix of cognitive faculties spanning the senses, emotion, intuition and reason. In fact, civilization might be described as emotional and intuitive leaps of imagination, transformed into reality through rational process and work. And while in doing this we have become highly skilled at the scientific method and analytical inference, little has been accomplished in developing strategies of intuitive inference.

But if we had strategies for using our intuitive faculties, they would provide a doorway to new levels of human thought and achievement. The Horizon Mission Methodology (HMM) has been developed as a structured means of using intuitive thinking. The HMM first posits an "impossible-by-extrapolation" Horizon--a truly challenging future, a leap of imagination beyond our reach. It then places people mentally in a frame of reference built around that "fixed" future and stimulates their imagination to generate hypothetical, breakthrough-based alternatives that could have accomplished that future. Finally it comes fully "back from the future" to the present to analytically determine near-term steps toward that future. The HMM was developed initially as a tool for analyzing breakthrough-class space technologies and concepts (Ref. 1-4). Nine diverse workshop/studies have been conducted for NASA, USAF, industry and universities.

John L. Anderson *is program coordinator of Technology Frontier Studies at the National Aeronautics and Space Administration, Washington, DC.*

This paper identifies human cognitive limits that block intuition, suggests a framework of intuitive abilities, and specifically describes the HMM with emphasis on the intuitive aspects.

CONCEPTUAL LIMITS

What conceptual limits might be built into the human? What limits are culturally acquired? What products of analytical inference might block intuitive inference? Has our intellectual growth leveled off? That question has been raised. "As a species, we seem to have reached a plateau in our intellectual development. There is no sign we are getting any smarter..."(Ref. 5). This section describes some of the evident boundaries within the cognitive territory of the mind.

PARADIGMS

We humans appear to search for, intake and organize information all in accordance with "inner models of reality" called paradigms. In a seminal work a paradigm has been described as "an entire constellation of beliefs, values, and techniques shared by members of a given technical community...it is also one element of that constellation--a concrete solution to a performance problem which used as a model or example can replace explicit rules as a basis for solutions of future problems" (Ref. 6). As "inner models" paradigms perform at least two major cognitive functions: they set forth the "game being played" with themes, rules, boundaries and they act as literal physiological filters (Ref. 7). Paradigms are deeply ingrained, often largely unconscious. They exert powerful, unseen limits on our analytical, creative and judgmental abilities.

These paradigms act as frames of reference that seem to filter information, organize knowledge and evaluate new ideas for us-- largely without our realizing it. We force-fit novelties (new concepts or discoveries) into distorted versions of old paradigms (recall Ptolemaic epicycles). When we do try to project into the future it is usually by linear extrapolation or stretching known paradigms. Thus while progenitors of revolutions exist and spark exciting visions for the future, they are also their own obstacles. They fall outside current paradigms which tend to govern our cognitive skills.

Suppose we had methods for stepping outside existing paradigms to "see" and think. Suppose we had strategies for creating other frames of reference. Suppose we could model the paradigm to be brought about by a revolutionary idea? Suppose we could go mentally into the future, sketch the environment in which the ideas would "live", and then look backward?

LOGIC

The problem of paradigms is compounded by our tendency to logically look to "experts" to help us go beyond our personal limits. But there are so many legendary examples of severely limited vision by world-class experts. A striking example: "The secrets of flight will not be mastered within our lifetime...not within a thousand years."-- Wilbur Wright (1901)! Humans tend to mistake the "logic" of linear extrapolation from current expertise as "thinking." It was once said by Niels Bohr in wrestling with the vast conceptual problems of atomic theory and quantum physics that "You are not thinking; you are merely logical." Later Charles Kettering, long time Director of R & D for General Motors, said "Beware of logic. Logic is an organized way to go wrong--with confidence." (Ref. 8)

But if not logic, what then? In a paraphrasing of Einstein, "Seek the larger view--and from that vantage point, recognize the missing element, and fill the gap." (Ref. 8). Henri Poincaré said, "...pure logic cannot give us (a) view of the whole; it is to intuition we must look for it."(Ref. 9). In fact, intuition is defined as the faculty of knowing without use of rational processes.

INFORMATION ASSIMILATION

Advanced technology has brought us to another limit. How do we deal with the torrent of information, innumerable studies and findings, vast numbers of ideas, exhaustive matrix arrays, catalogs and compendiums that proudly list all our rational options? And now along comes the exponentiating Internet. We are perhaps at the limits of linear assimilation and analysis. How do we process it all? How do we determine relevance and extract content from data. We have developed analytical and institutional techniques for generating and analyzing information and forecasting techniques for probing the future. But we have not kept pace in techniques for choosing which ideas to pursue? Where are techniques for idea triage? We generate great quantities of ideas and options but fail to provide new insight on how to choose from among them.

We need methods for structuring massive datasets into patterns and symbolic representations to permit use of our intuitive abilities and geometric and spectral visualization abilities. We need pattern-revealing data reduction. In fact, data mining, knowledge discovery and data visualization are emerging methods.

CONVENTIONAL INTUITION

Ordinarily, even our intuition is based on everyday experience-- our perceptions and language--and can betray us when we are in uncharted mental territory. Einstein's creative thinking occurred in visual imagery, and words were "sought after laboriously only in a secondary stage." And Niels Bohr said, "...we find ourselves on the very path taken by Einstein of adapting our modes of perception borrowed from the sensations...the hindrances met on this path originate (because) every word in our language refers to our ordinary perception". (Ref 9) The revolutionary scientific thinking of the early twentieth century arose from thinking in imagery not based on experience or our senses.

EINSTEIN'S ABYSS

Einstein believed that the concepts and axioms of science are invented, not discovered. He believed that inductive logic cannot lead from experiences to axioms--that there is an essential abyss between perceptions and data (evidence) on the one hand and the creation of governing concepts and axioms on the other. By "invention" Einstein meant the mind's ability to leap across this abyss (Ref. 9). He said "There comes a time when the mind takes a higher plane of knowledge but can never prove how it got there. All great discoveries have involved such a leap."

Question. Is there a way to stimulate the imagination to make leaps of the imagination? Could we somehow train the mind to jump to a higher plane, of knowledge--to look someplace else for answers to complex issues of today--to operate in another arena?

HUMAN COGNITIVE ABILITIES

One possible framework and description of our broad spectrum of cognitive faculties is provided below, ranging from highly intuitive to highly rational manifestations of intelligence. These faculties are interwoven, mutually dependent, hierarchical and have degrees of ability within them.

1) Teleology

Humans are teleological (goal-driven) in that we are motivated by purposes or desired end states and possess a cybernetic faculty. Some of this is instinctive, also possessed by animals. But we go far beyond in pursuing passionate visions, dreams and goals. We are driven by purpose, values, and curiosity. Emotions and belief are extraordinary catalysts that often override contrary reason.

2) Leaps of the imagination

Intuition, epiphany, flash of insight. Radical originality--a fundamentally novel idea that cannot be produced by existing set of generative rules (Ref. 10). Leaping Einstein's Abyss into a new arena; these leaps create a discontinuity; they seem "magical" and even the creators are often unable to trace the process by which they arrived at the leap. Inventing axioms, metaphors and new questions. Identifying causal principles. Sensing of meaning.

3) Conceptualization

Manipulation & transformation of ideas, their organization & relationships. Construction of mental models, analogies and metaphors. Exploring conceptual spaces or landscapes (Ref. 10). Symbolic representation. Inventions, hypotheses, theories, Gedanken experiments. Problem formulation, taking a larger view, reframing, synthesis of disparate items. Bisociation of two conceptual matrices that are not normally associated.

4) Imagery Thinking

Formulation and manipulation of pictures. Gedanken experiments, data visualization, pictorial representation, daydreaming. Visualizing for high performance athletics and goal achievement.

5) Sensory-based intelligence

Instincts, pattern recognition (visual and auditory), kinesthesis (motor control, reflexes), anomaly discrimination, trend recognition, ambiguity tolerance, global awareness. Highly interactive with surroundings.

6) Reason

Calculation, deductive logic and inductive logic, if-then rules, extrapolation, scenarios, problem solving, analysis and synthesis, information correlation, combinatorial association, common sense, model-based knowledge.

There are some who think all these abilities can be reduced to if-then rules and combinatorial analysis and will one day be embodied in computers (Ref. 5 & 10); others think not. Complex systems (with vast numbers of interacting elements) are shown to possess properties of self-organization and self-creation. Near the edge of chaos a criticality occurs that drives these systems to exhibit emergent behavior and order. Study of such systems should provide new insights on intelligence. But it is beyond the scope of this paper to move further into this discussion. In the meantime we still have to use our human intuition.

DESCRIPTION OF HORIZON MISSION METHODOLOGY

In looking toward the future, humans typically extrapolate from present knowledge. We metaphorically shine "flashlight beams" from the present into the future--"onto a dark wall" (Fig. 1).

FIGURE I

GRAPHIC DEPICTION OF THE HMM

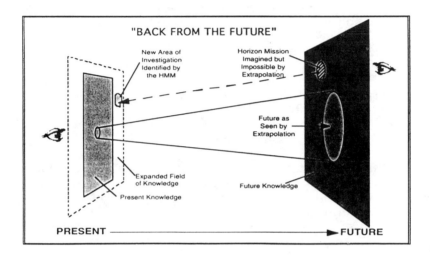

But the only future we see by doing this is the portion of the wall illuminated by a beam. What we see is what our paradigms let us see, including occasional variations on what we already "know." But, disturbingly, we know that much of the future lies outside those beams.

The HMM is a mental strategy for operating outside those beams, where the rules for thinking and judgment may not be the same. The HMM is based on a Horizon Mission--a hypothetical future (space) mission having capabilities and performance levels that exceed technology extrapolation. Horizon "Missions" may also be "Capabilities" or "Axioms." A fundamental condition is that a "Horizon" must be "impossible" by extrapolation--beyond requirements or logical projections. More specifically it must cause people to think in new categories if it is to block linear, extrapolative thinking; but it must also be strategically relevant and plausible.

The five step process of the HMM is outlined in Figure 2. Details of the actual implementation steps, several techniques for each and results of using the HMM are described in Ref. 4. Different study purposes require different strategies for implementation, reflecting the study objectives, policy guidelines, strategic requirements and programmatic needs. Looked at from a cognitive level, the HMM is *not* a process of projecting, forecasting, or scenario-building, which are implicitly grounded in current paradigms. Instead it is a highly structured process analogous to a coordinate transformation of the mind. It hypothesizes key elements of a novel frame of reference or paradigm.

Step 1 of the HMM is an intuitive leap outside the "flashlight beam" to create an extraordinary, "mind-blowing" future beyond our reach. The "Horizon" acts as an artifice that blocks linear, extrapolative thinking. Therefore, it *must* change the frame of reference--not just demand more performance in a familiar one. It should cause people to think in different categories--it should excite, jolt, even disorient people intellectually. It must leapfrog foreseeable capabilities but it should be relevant to the strategic future. A specific mechanism of Ten Questions (Fig. 3) was devised for leaping outside the beam. These questions tap various intuitive sources within the human mind.

In Step 2 a new frame of reference based on the Horizon is constructed. To accomplish this, radical new properties of the Horizon are postulated, including purpose, influencing forces, novel, unique and/or critical functions, pivotal or unprecedented capabilities and extreme performance levels. A set of boundaries and rules for thinking must also be established; otherwise participants revert to normal thinking, resulting in idea debate, tangents, "inside beam" fixations, fantasy and implausibility. Boundaries help maintain plausibility by not permitting violation of laws of physics, ideas too far advanced for the chosen frame of reference or scales so extreme they are implausible.

Next, in Step 3 we must think within the new frame of reference. Problem statement and problem solving must take place *within* this future frame of reference where "all Horizon things are possible." Techniques for stimulating the imagination are used to generate breakthrough-based alternatives to accomplish that future. Engineering alternatives expressed at a higher functional level than technology alternatives have been devised for this purpose. This step is difficult and requires considerable discipline to stay on track--to think at a higher functional level than "the technology answer." Discussions have to be limited and ideas pruned. The HMM is not a process of collecting every conceivable idea; it is a process of

creative and analytic thinking within a new frame of reference--
subject to constraints consistent with that frame.

In Step 4 we begin to come "back from the future" to the present
frame of reference. This starts with collecting and structuring the
Alternative Engineering Approaches and technology concepts into
new higher level categories. Higher level functions, ideas and
perspectives are selected and then linked to the present by identifying requirements, applications and implications. Non-traditional,
evocative titles or labels for the categories are important; vision-

---

FIGURE II

STEPS OF THE HMM

---

1. LEAP OUT OF THE "FLASHLIGHT BEAM" PROJECTION
Define a Horizon that is "mind-blowing," "impossible" by extrapola-
tion--but still plausible and strategically relevant. (The Horizon must
cause people to think in different categories, even disorient them, not
just demand more performance in familiar categories).

2. CONSTRUCT A NEW FRAME OF REFERENCE
Postulate the radical new properties of that Horizon--critical functions, extreme performance levels, unprecedented capabilities and
novel influencing forces.

3. THINK WITHIN THE NEW FRAME OF REFERENCE
Generate alternative engineering approaches (AEAs) for accomplishing the Horizon--these are stated at a higher functional level than
technology. (Stating problems at a higher functional level is analogous to answering "What business are we really in?") (Capabilities are
higher order (>) than engineering systems > technologies).

4. IDENTIFY IMPLICATIONS AND REQUIREMENTS FOR EN-
ABLING THE HIGHER ORDER APPROACHES
Examine Horizon implications of the most promising AEAs. Collect
capabilities, system, and breakthrough technology ideas and structure
them into new categories or concepts. Determine the high leverage
(hilev) "technology" directions or concepts--that could have the greatest impact on the future.

5. RETURN TO PRESENT FRAME OF REFERENCE
Determine the near-term steps and issues for each high-leverage
technology direction.

---

inspiring expression such as in metaphoric or analogic terms has been useful. From these new categories hilev technology directions are selected.

In Step 5, we now plant our feet firmly back in the present. For each selected hilev technology direction, Near-Term Steps and Issues are identified in the following terms: a) Critical Enabling Technologies (particularly showstoppers), b) Enablers for Extreme Performance, c) Main Drivers for Commercial Use, d) First Application, e) Dual-Use/Reverse Spinoff, g) Other Drivers or Motivating Forces, h) Programmatic and Strategic Thrusts and i) Higher Level Insights.

A process of "vision-assist" was devised and introduced into the workshops to help maintain the unnatural frame of reference. Vision-assist capitalizes on the large human brain capacity dedicated to visual processing (estimated to be 50% including the eyes). Several techniques have been used: diagrammatic explanations of the HMM concept (Fig. 1), poster size photos, video tape excerpts (from science fiction), physical models and a technical artist present at workshops to create pictorial representations of key concepts and new perspectives.

FIGURE III

TEN QUESTIONS TO STIMULATE LEAPS OF THE IMAGINATION

1. What would change the world?
2. What would it be "neat" to do?
3. What science fiction examples are exciting (including film special effects)? What does *Star Trek* say?
4. What could be the grand challenges of the future?
5. What are radical solutions to the "world's" great unsolved problems?
6. What would be the extreme performance of a breakthrough whether from emerging revolutionary technological capabilities or fundamental discoveries in science, technology or mathematics?
7. What do you have an intuition about? What bright idea is nagging at you?
8. What have you heard or read about or seen that you feel someday might be big but you don't know how to even express it right now?
9. What would surprise everyone?
10.What in the entertainment/advertising worlds could be converted to a capability?

HMM WORKSHOP/STUDY RESULTS

Solar System Exploration and Development

The objective was to identify future technological environments that could provide an expanded range of options for long-term robotic and human exploration and development of the solar system. What Horizon Mission might cause people to think in different categories? Certainly not Mars; "everyone knows" how to go to Mars. Instead, the "Horizon" was chosen to be a plausible mission beyond Mars: a Human Jupiter Scientific Station that would conduct research throughout the Jovian system during 2045-2050. A performance level of 1 month (!) trip time for travel from Earth to Jupiter was arbitrarily imposed as desirable for such an exploration mission. All previous technology "solutions" offered 5-6 months as the fastest time.

Three high leverage (hilev) technology directions were identified:

(1) Use of Extra-Terrestrial Resources identified an area for advanced technology research: extracting "low-grade" energy available throughout the solar system from magnetic fields, electric fields/currents, radiation and thermal differences as well as atmospheric gases and surface materials; we already do it for solar energy.

2) Computer Maxima is predicated on the staggering advances of computers, computation and micro-technology expected over the next 50 years. This leads to a vision of virtual reality missions, new forms of analysis based on immersion in real-time data visualization and widespread public "participation" in such a mission--a part of the human adventure.

(3) Beamed Energy using perhaps lasers would enable the power and propulsion source to be outside a spacecraft. This would dramatically increase payload mass fraction and space-craft velocity. It introduces the concept of utility power and propulsion availability in space. By insisting on an extreme performance level, a new space propulsion concept was formulated based on the combined advantages of space laser power beaming and inertial confinement fusion. With reasonable system parameters and continuous acceleration of 0.05g, travel time to Mars of 3 weeks and to Jupiter of 2 months would be possible. Two decades of investment by the Departments of Defense and Energy have brought multi-megawatt lasers to the threshold of reality and laser-induced inertial confinement fusion to a very mature state of understanding such that the engineering design of the National Ignition Facility to demonstrate its feasibility is now underway.

Obviously many of the ideas generated were not new, but the HMM began to define a context in which the high leverage ideas could someday "live." It began to lay the foundation of a vision of Space Railroads or Highways of Light extending throughout the solar system.

SPACE BIOSENSOR TECHNOLOGY DEVELOPMENT

The objective was to integrate and prioritize a broad spectrum of competing requirements for space biosensors. The Horizon Capability chosen was a handheld scanning instrument for non-invasive detection of human and animal physiological indicators. Such a device would resemble the "tricorder" used in the Star Trek TV series. Using the tricorder concept provided a virtual target common to all parties but beyond near-term technology issues and funding competition. It thus served as a means of "virtually" integrating the myriad requirements for biosensor use during space flight. This allowed different paths to it thereby promoting a variety of joint efforts. This experience suggests the HMM might be used as a catalyst for technology transfer or for market/product analysis or studies of innovation barriers. This tricorder concept has now been introduced into the NASA advanced biosensor technology program in an intermediate form. Used as a handheld biotelemetry system it would provide a portable monitoring device enabling handheld line-of-sight readout of multiple rack-mounted monitors and displays.

ADVANCED QUANTUM/RELATIVITY THEORY
SPACE PROPULSION CONCEPTS

Tantalizingly, theoretical perspectives and experimental anomalies currently exist in quantum and relativistic physics that suggest that the velocity of light "c" might be circumvented to permit "faster-than--light" travel or information transfer. Three "scientific windows" were chosen as Horizon Axioms: (1) Existence of cosmic wormholes or tunnels (2) Existence of an entire "physics" for v>c [a velocity greater than the speed of light] (3) Existence of another physical dimension. The HMM was used to explore the implications of these theoretical and experimental perspectives--how would these axioms be manifested in nature? It is important to note that the workshop did not challenge "c", [the speed of light--about 186,000 miles per second] as a limit; instead it examined other ways of thinking about the structure and properties of the universe insofar as "c" is concerned.

The workshop generated a large number of new concepts and lines of theoretical and experimental inquiry (Ref. 11). In particular, how would cosmic wormholes or tunnels be detected--if they exist? A report describing measurable properties of such an astronomical object, entitled "Natural Wormholes as Gravitational Lenses" has been published (Ref. 12).

UNIVERSITY ADVANCED DESIGN COURSE

In multidisciplinary design and analysis, traditional approaches are based on today's engineering standards and practices which are of course governed by today's or even yesterday's technology limits. Thus any innovative technology or radical change in capability introduced into a design must conform to the limits of old engineering knowledge. In an advanced design class at Rensselaer Polytechnic Institute the HMM was used to design an earth-to-orbit vehicle that uses beamed microwave energy to provide propulsion *and* to alter the properties of the atmosphere in front of the vehicle to solve aerothermodynamic problems.

The HMM provided a structured method for introducing a radical new capability and engineering approach into a concept design that was inherently based on "future" breakthrough technologies and hypothetical engineering approaches. This enabled a radical idea to be embedded within and consistent with design based on "future" associated engineering knowledge.

EXPLORATORY AERONAUTICS HORIZONS

The problem addressed is the structuring and prioritizing of fundamental and applied aeronautical research and technology for a dramatically changing future. One Aeronautics Horizon chosen was Aircraft 2050. This represents the idealized commercial aircraft of year 2050 with extreme functions and performance common to all aircraft regardless of speed, range or size--zero emissions and noise, weather-smart, adaptable flight performance, optimum no-mistake design and no-fail operation.

Three high-level technology directions were identified. (1) Creation of a Virtual Industrial Cycle would encompass virtual design, engineering development and test, manufacturing, flight test and operational simulation. This technology capability would move all industrial mistake-making into the virtual world. (2) Aircraft Morphing would encompass self-adaptive flight for safety and performance through smart, self-initiated real-time modification and reconfiguring of aircraft structural, material, electronic and surface properties. (3) Meta-Control would encompass a higher-level flight control and health monitor that would "oversee" both crew and computer systems and their interactions. Such "control of control" would assess and advise on contrary indications and might use another part of the brain as an additional computer interface.

Aeronautics Horizons can serve as "mission requirements" for breakthroughs and community-common "surrogate airplanes" for fundamental and disciplinary aeronautics research. Thus the HMM offers a new tool and approach for strategic and programmatic planning and research organization.

HUMAN-"INTELLIGENT" MACHINE COMBINATIONS

The purpose was to define an expanded concept of human endeavor in space as well as identify intelligent machine functions to support this new human reach. The objective was to generate new and high leverage human-intelligent machine concepts (HIMACs) that could: enable entirely new functions and capabilities, provide quantum improvements in productivity in space including lower costs, challenge human ingenuity and inspire sustained public interest in human space exploration and development.

The Horizon Mission chosen was the widespread development of a Lunar Territory beginning in 2050. Identification of HIMACs was addressed from three viewpoints: 1) What businesses would generate money from the moon?, 2) What would be the great adventures of the moon?, 3) What would "force" (unprecedented requirements and technological breakthroughs) the lunar frontier to open? HIMAC concepts identified include: 1) lunar spacecraft design for reuse--modular, cannibalizable parts, materials seeded with valuable non-lunar materials for future use; 2) a smart enveloper--a space suit that acts as enveloping airbag in case of emergency; 3) energy-rich space systems through proliferating solar devices and beamed power; 4) self-aggrandizing materials for solar collectors and photovoltaic arrays; 5) habitable volumes on the moon using nanotechnology constructors; 6) tele-tourism on the earth using rent-a-surrogate on the moon.

CONCLUDING REMARKS

Entering another frame of reference to think is unnatural; it violates the paradigms that implicitly govern our behavior and thought processes. But doing so forces the participant to draw upon other cognitive resources--the more intuitive ones.

Of course, even in the minds of the highly creative, intuition can be untrustworthy. That is why some degree of "control" in the form of a structured method must be used to "guide" our use of intuitive faculties. The HMM is not brainstorming or collecting random occurrences of intuition. It engages several types of intuition in a structured blending--using enough intuition to generate leaps of the imagination and *only enough rational process to stay within a frame of reference and at the end to come back to the present reality.*

The HMM has shown broad applicability to scientific and technological activities. It promises applicability to other activities (including non-technical) with high cognitive requirements such as: technology transfer, context for new markets or products, learning, metrics for fundamental research, strategic planning, assessment of changes in basic assumptions, modeling and analysis of paradigms, and study of cognitive processes. Its scope and significance are still unfolding.

Strategies for use of human intuition are exciting to contemplate. They would indeed provide a doorway to new levels of human thought and achievement.

REFERENCES

1. Anderson, John L., and William A Baracat. "Horizon Missions-volume I: Technology Concept Study" and "Horizon Missions-Volume II: Reference Database," NASA OAST & General Research Corp., April 1992.

2. Anderson, John L. "Horizon Mission Methodology: A Tool for the Study of Technology Innovation and New Paradigms", AIAA Paper 93-1134, AIAA/AHS/ASEE Aerospace Design Conference, February 1993.

3. Anderson, John L. "Leaps of the Imagination...," *Ad Astra*, Vol. 7, No. 1, January/February 1995.

4. Anderson, John L. "The Horizon Mission Methodology: Modeling and Thinking Within New Paradigms", *Futures Research Quarterly*, Vol.11, No. 3, Fall 1995.

5. Minsky, Marvin. "Will Robots Inherit the Earth?," *Scientific American*, October 1994.

6. Kuhn, Thomas S. *The Structure of Scientific Revolutions*, The University of Chicago Press, 2nd Edition, Chicago, 1970.

7. Barker, Joel Arthur. *Future Edge: Discovering the New Paradigms of Success*, William Morrow & Co., New York, 1992.

8. Wheeler, John A. *At Home in the Universe*, AIP Press, 1994.

9. Miller, Arthur I. *Imagery in Scientific Thought*, The MIT Press, Cambridge, MA, 1987.

10. Boden, Margaret A. "Agents and Creativity," *Communications of the ACM*, Vol. 37, No. 7, July 1994.

11. Bennett, G.L., R.L. Forward, and R.H. Frisbee. "Possible Applications of Advanced Quantum/Relativity Theory Propulsion to Interstellar Exploration: Report of a NASA/JPL Workshop"; IAA-95--IAA.4.1.07, 46th International Astronautical Congress, October 1995.

12. Cramer, J.G., G. Benford, G.A. Landis, R.L Forward, M. Visser, and M.S. Morris. "Natural Wormholes as Gravitational Lenses", *Physical Review D*, Vol. 51, No. 6, March 15, 1995.

SPECIALIST OR GENERALIST?
A FALSE DICHOTOMY: AN IMPORTANT DISTINCTION

by

P. J. Hartwick and Caela Farren

BACKGROUND AND INTRODUCTION

The need for specialized knowledge and its application in practice was an inevitable consequence of a recognition, long ago, that no single individual (or even a practical number of them) could hold and apply the sum total of human knowledge. When, exactly, this became evident to people is not clear, but evidence suggests that specialization was a well established phenomena over 10,000 years ago! The society of ancient Sumeria (7,000 B.C.) was characterized by well developed specializations in religion, politics, astronomy, agriculture and a host of craft skills. These early efforts were driven, at first, by very basic survival needs. Astronomy and mathematics, for example, developed out of the need to predict the agricultural cycle that affected food production, not by an esoteric interest in celestial mechanics. The development of a philosophical context, or understanding, about specialized knowledge parallels the advance in three closely related major areas of human development. These were: a) language--particularly symbolic language; b) abstract reasoning and critical thinking; and, c) a simple means of communicating the first two. As human knowledge expanded, there was a corresponding expansion of both the *number* of specialized areas of knowledge, as well as the *depth* of knowledge contained within each specialty area. The socialization of specialized knowledge led to the establishment of recognized professions, each serving to meet basic human needs of "the customer."

The advent of specialized practice created the near-simultaneous need for two related activities: application and integration. At first, these functions were mostly performed by the end user, the "consumer" of a specialty's product or output. They did this by the kind (e.g., plant seeds) and timing (springtime) of choices that were made. There was a very close (in time and space) link between the specialist's products, the basic human needs which they sought to fill, and the consumer whose needs had to be met. Thus, the person needing a candle or a suit of clothes, for example, knew *what* they needed and *where* to go to get it. The consumer making choices provided the integration function. Since most commerce was highly localized, a lot of sophistication in marketing and transportation was not required.

Caela Farren *is CEO of Farren Associates, Inc., Annandale, Virginia.* P. J. **Hartwick** *is a vice president.*

The need for "generals"--people who were not themselves direct consumers but who were operating like coordinating agents--slowly came about as a result of two factors: the first was the increasing complexity of human activity. As attention grew beyond the tribe or clan or village, to encompass more choices and opportunity, the interaction of specialists was an inevitable result. The second came with the realization that the characterization of "the consumer" had been expanded. The society, as well as individuals, became "consumers" of specialized knowledge. One of the first and most important examples of a "societal consumer" is seen from the military lineage of the word "general." Warfare was the most complex of the problems continually faced by societies of the ancient world.[2] And warfare, or some element of it, came to be an almost ever-present feature of society. Thus, when we speak of the term "generalist," we are speaking of it in this historic sense: a person whose role is to *coordinate* the *application and integration* of specialized contributions to the solution of complex problems.[3]

The history of human development is also a history of specialization. With each advance, we see the indelible mark of specialists: old, familiar ones providing continuity, and new ones growing out of the application of new technology or insight. It was natural, then, to see the formation of social groups of like-minded practitioners. Roman society in the second century (B.C.) contained the ancestry of the guild system that was so important in the Middle Ages and which were, in turn, essential precursors to the trade practices of the Industrial Age. At first, these groups had mainly a political and/or religious focus, reflecting the two prominent concerns of society of that era. The Roman Empire, however, never produced the kind of intellectual curiosity about science that had characterized the society of ancient Greece. Although the Romans were, to be sure, competent engineers and technical administrators, they basically employed the intellectual capital provided by the Greeks many centuries before. Indeed, the Roman era could fairly be labeled as an anti-intellectual one in many important respects. Although it didn't begin that way, it certainly ended that way: the deliberate burning, in 391, of the 500 year-old library at Alexandria, containing some 600,000 volumes of the collected, extant wisdom of Western Civilization, is the marker that ushered in an age that was to last for over 1,000 years: it didn't become known as the Dark Ages for no good reason. The anti-intellectual mood of the time was pervasive and effective. We learned much later that the only significant advances in the arts and science during that period were made by the Arab cultures.

The 12th and 13th centuries saw the rapid (relatively) development of the craft trade guilds which established a clear evolutionary path to today's labor unions. It is important to note, however, that these guilds were initially formed, not to advance their technical craft, but to provide political leverage in dealing with the authorities of a feudal society. The technical performance features of guild systems was to come much later.

Although there were a number of distinctive features of the guilds of the various countries, two in particular had the most influence on modern society. The English guilds (e.g., the weavers guild was chartered in 1130, the saddlers in 1272 and the goldsmiths in 1327) produced a system that had political/social objectives as their major characterization (a feature which characterizes the British labor movement to this day), whereas the German guilds of the same era were responsible for characterizing and codifying the technical/craft elements. The by-laws of the German Guilds contained regulations for the training of apprentices (7 years), trade practice by those outside their local area of supervision (journeyman) and the requirements for being designated a master. This system, which focused on technical performance, was significantly responsible for the development of the reputation for technical excellence that is associated with German industry to this day.

The above brief discussion of how the character of two (of many) of the guild movements of the Middle Ages evolved should let us appreciate that the forms, practices and customs we have today are not of recent origin; rather they are part of a long continuum, a historical drift, as Maturana and Varela call it, that represent the designs and visions of countless numbers of people before us. If nothing else, it should make us quite suspicious of attempts to make significant changes to these systems without very careful study of the implications for doing so.

BEGINNING OF THE INDUSTRIAL AGE

Although, like all epochal periods of human experience, the Industrial Age had its roots in events taken over a prolonged period of time, one event can be identified as one of the major signal flares: the invention, in 1799 by Eli Whitney, of a system for the design and manufacture of interchangeable parts for muskets. Prior to that moment, the manufacture and assembly of virtually any artifact was a singular event and the idea "mass production" simply did not exist. Thus began a century that was to see the explosion of human knowledge and capability the likes of which were not even imagined just a few decades earlier. Indeed, the 19th century was so singularly productive that the head of the US Patent Office, in his recommendations to the Congress in 1899, suggested that the office be closed, since it was "evident that just about all worthwhile things had already been invented."

There were many important developments and trends established during this period, but for our purposes here, one of the most important was the tremendous impact that the Industrial Age had on the design, organization and conduct of work. For it is here that the most significant change in human work patterns, arguably in the entire history of work, took place.

The forces that produced the change began to take shape over a century earlier with the introduction by two Englishmen of new paradigms of knowledge: Francis Bacon gave us the framework of the intellectual backdrop--the so-called "Scientific Method" of thought and analysis and Isaac Newton gave us the physical and mathematical tools by which we could design and build complex machines. Thus, it could be said that the 19th century was one in which a wholesale, multi-pronged, all-out attack was mounted on problems that had either plagued or fascinated people since the dawn of time. In less grand terms, we set about building machines, not only to deal with old problems (such as land irrigation), but to mechanize tasks that had been done essentially in the same way for thousands of years (such as sewing and weaving). Moreover, not only did we now have the requisite understanding of the underlying principles of building machines, but also, thanks to Whitney, we learned how to make a lot of them quickly and cheaply. These two elements, acting together, produced major changes in work design and the way people interacted with work. As a direct result of the desire and need to mechanize work, the designers of work systems (organizations) increasingly began to see the worker as just another part of a large, *essentially mechanical* system of machinery whose contribution was *not* a specialized body of practice designed to produce some *end product*, but rather that of contributing process tasks which were *intermediary* to the end result. This was the unprecedented feature of the mechanization of work, and one that would be responsible for both incredible accomplishment and incredible disillusionment. In short, the process of mechanization of work also resulted in its dehumanization. This was to have far-reaching impact, but one that was not felt for almost 100 years.

ORIGINS OF MODERN ORGANIZATIONS

One of the principal architects of work design in the Industrial Age was Frederick Winslow Taylor. Taylor (1856-1915) came along during the thick of developments. A little of his history is illuminating. Although he attended a prestigious Prep school (Exeter), he didn't continue his education owing to poor eyesight. Instead, he entered the work force as a common laborer, first in a machine shop in his native Philadelphia and then for the Midvale Steel Company, where he worked until 1893. At Midvale, he worked his way "up"-- from gang boss, to assistant foreman, to master mechanic and finally, in 1889, to chief engineer (he obtained his engineering degree in 1883 from the prestigious Stevens Institute in New Jersey while studying nights and weekends). He next became a consultant, first in the area of shop management and later with Bethlehem Steel as an efficiency engineer. He was awarded over 100 patents and served as the president of the American Society of Mechanical Engineers and was an organizer of the Society to Promote the Science of Management (now called the Taylor Society). In 1911, he published two short books, the more important being *The Principles of Scientific Management*. It would be difficult to overestimate the influence that Taylor and this key book have had on the design of work, the design of business and of their associated organizational structures, as well as the way in which we educate and train engineers and scientists. Understanding the effects of the widespread application of Taylor's methods and, more importantly, his underlying philosophy and values that were likewise adopted (perhaps unconsciously), is critically important to the main thrust of our study.

In some ways, Taylor embodies a fascinating paradox: his early training and work experience were precisely those that "should have" prevented him from adopting an underlying philosophy that resulted in the fragmentation and partitioning of work. There is little doubt that he was quite capable and in possession of many highly useful habits of character, though, however, humility was not one of these. His approach, refined through some twenty years of work experience, was basically one of reducing work to its fundamental elements (which he thought of as a task so simple that only one person could perform it) and then: either automate the task with a machine or give it to a human being to perform. The choice of which to do was based on two considerations: did the technology exist to allow automation? and if so, was it more economical to automate the task or assign it to a human worker? Taylor, despite having started at the bottom of the work ladder, had an aristocratic manner and attitude. He was not at all imbued with a sense of the general nobility of mankind, to put it mildly. Indeed, he was rather contemptuous of the "average worker" and, to the extent that he admired him at all, did so for his physical prowess and adaptability and not for any transcendent qualities of the human spirit. Where people were concerned, Taylor's design of jobs and work was motivated by the desire to find the most efficient operating point of the human "machine," and not really out of any concern over the effects of hard labor or the conditions under which it was performed, on the spirit of the worker. In Taylor's paradigm, it was unthinkable that workers had any say on the design of work, the objectives of work, or the organizational structures needed to do it. Rather, it was the role of management to answer all such questions and to do so in the most efficient way possible. Furthermore, Taylor's methods relied heavily on the measurement and analysis of physical properties (units of production, weight, time, motion, etc.) as both control and feedback elements in his work design schemes. Factors such as motivation, creativity, enthusiasm, attitude, etc., not being quantifiable, had little, if any, place in Taylor's view of the nature of work or of the design of work systems, even those that required a significant dose of the "human element" to achieve the desired results. However, like all paradigms, Taylor's were built up on a set of assumptions whose validity were going to change dramatically. Indeed, one of the most basic ones, that of the basic intelligence of the worker, was already changing significantly near the end of Taylor's life.

Education is a funny thing. There are an almost infinite number of possible results, many of them completely unforeseen, but one that is almost a constant certainty is that education raises our expectations of what is possible in and from life. In 1900, the average formal educational level of American workers was approximately three years. Moreover, a large portion of these workers were not able to speak English, which had the effect of invalidating what little formal education they did have. However, owing to an aggressive effort at public education begun just before World War I, within little more than one generation, the *average* had risen to almost 12 years. However, the world-wide economic depression of the 1930's and the global war effort delayed the practical expression of the inevitable rising expectations. The post World-War II construction boom and the enormous participation in G.I. Bill educational programs were two of the more "obvious" harbingers that a new era in the nature of work was at hand. [4]

In the late 1950's and early 1960's, a general trend in business gathered momentum that sought to develop and advance the need for what has been called a "generalist" management practitioner. R. Buckminster Fuller was one of the most prominent public figures to take up the theme in his writings.[5] The essential characterization of the "generalist" was someone who could operate effectively at any level, but particularly at intermediate and senior management levels --*in virtually any business*--by employing and relying on general principles of management science. Such principles were simultaneously being developed in the major academic institutions that specialized in the study of business and they were heavily influenced by Taylor's work and the (apparently) incontrovertible success they seemed to produce.

Several converging factors were responsible for this trend. The most immediately influential was the post-World War II economic realities of the world. The US stood alone among the world's nations with its industrial base completely intact. And not only was the base intact, it was built upon an established infrastructure that had been slowly built up in the 50 years preceding the war. Demobilization of the armed forces and reconversion of industry to a civilian economy occurred quite rapidly in the 1945-1950 era, as business re-tooled to meet long pent-up demands (almost 15 years worth, considering the Depression and the war years) for products and services and the application of technology that had been almost non-existent because of the way resources had been managed and allocated during the war. [6]

A second factor was traceable to the unprecedented altruism of US policy that was developed to deal with its former enemies and the peoples ravaged by war. Even though the US was nominally part of an Allied effort to win the war, none of its allies was in a position, either financially or emotionally, to play a significant role in the rebuilding effort. The Marshall Plan is the famous example of that policy. Less well known, but perhaps even more important to the long term economic recovery that has lasted ever since, was the way in which the US in general, and Gen. Douglas MacArthur, in particular, went about building a contemporary Japanese consumer society. He personally recruited experts from US industries in wholesale lots (W. Edwards Deming was relatively unknown at the time, but would later become the most prominent of these individuals) to advise and teach the Japanese how to build a new industrial base that had a consumer, rather than a military focus.[7] Engineers, technicians and managers from the Bell System helped rebuild NEC (even to the point of providing blueprints of Western Electric factories which NEC duplicated exactly, including use of the same tan-colored brick. People and technology (particularly rare-earth glass) from Eastman Kodak helped rebuild Fuji, Canon and Nikon, while E.I. DuPont personnel worked on the plastics and petrochemical industries. The demand for US technology and know-how went through an unparalleled expansion during that period of reconstruction. In short, US industrial and management technology became a "hot commodity" around the world.

A third factor was more subtle, but no less profound. During the 1950's a new method of problem definition and analysis, called "systems thinking" began to have increasing influence. Its origins as a body of practice can be traced to a relatively few highly technical industrial and academic institutions.[8] [9] Moreover, much of the impetus was driven by the urgency of the war effort and the need to deal with problems of unprecedented scope and complexity. One of the most important of these was the Manhattan Project, the name given to the program to develop the first atomic bomb. This was the first effort of its kind in history. In the span of a few short years, the very farthest edges of theoretical science and practical, nuts-and-bolts engineering converged in time and place to solve a problem that was more complex than any that had ever been undertaken by the human race. A systems approach was the only possible way in which such an effort could have succeeded, although, at the time, it wasn't seen to be anything "new" or original, nor was it explicitly recognized as a distinct methodology for dealing with complexity.[10] At the conclusion of the war effort, most of the Manhattan scientists went to (or returned to) prestigious positions in influential universities across the country where they transplanted the "systems philosophy" to their research projects and, indirectly, to their students. This was a major conduit by which "systems thinking" became established.

This was the background from which the "generalist" as a distinct form of business practitioner emerged. We shall look now at the environmental conditions that were present that gave impetus to the development of the "generalist" in a form quite unlike any that had come before.

BUSINESS GENERALIST COMES OF AGE

The basic problem that confronted business and educational leaders at the end of WW II was how to, in effect, extract the essential knowledge of successful business people, codify it, and transmit it to others in the form of an educational experience. How this problem was addressed was entirely typical of what Russell Ackoff and others have termed "Machine Age Thinking." Quite paradoxically, is the fact that the approach to solving this general problem of developing well rounded business expertise was quite anti-systemic. The paradox, restated, what that one of the major influences that exposed the deficiency of a scarcity of qualified business expertise was the striking successes of 'systems thinking' in dealing with complex problems. Thus, one would like to suppose that a systems methodology would naturally come to mind as a way of solving this problem. It would be unfair, however, to say that it didn't. First of all, there wasn't any general awareness as yet that systems thinking, or at least a very important part of it, was very different from reductionist thinking. People who were evidently gifted in this area--people like Oppenheimer and Jewett, Henry Ford, Andrew Carnegie and other so-called Captains of Industry--were so good at it that they weren't conscious of their own skill, at least not to the point of being able to describe in detail how, exactly, they did what they did. Secondly, the major successes of systems thinking that could be studied as powerful examples had, as their most visible elements, classical, reductionist, scientific methodology. More will be said about this in a moment. Thirdly, when the lives and backgrounds of the many successful practitioners were examined, there didn't appear to be a common thread that might have alerted someone studying the problem to the presence of a fundamental connection. The preparatory backgrounds of J. Robert Oppenheimer and Henry Ford, for example, seemed to have nothing at all in common, so it was quite natural to conclude that, if their backgrounds did not contain the clues to their success, then the factors that were important had to be contained in the results they achieved. However, they did have 'something' in common after all. This 'something,' it turns out, was biological and physical in nature. Understanding the physiological factor, we believe, is the most important of all in developing an understanding of how specialists and generalists are really produced.

Before looking more closely at this biological factor, we must first understand clearly the method and role of analytic thinking, and particularly how it influenced the course of events that produced the business generalists who made their initial appearance in significant numbers in the 1960's.

In the 1950's the dominant method used to attack problems was (and still is) one which is directly traceable to the work of Descartes, Bacon, Newton and others, from whom we received the so-called "scientific method." At the very core of the scientific method is a method of thought called *analysis* and its hand-and-glove companion, cause-and-effect reasoning. These have, as their basic method of problem solving, a three-part process: a) a problem (or issue or inquiry) is disassembled, or reduced to, identifiable, constituent parts; b) Each part, taken separately, is analyzed so that the function and operation of each of the parts is understood (the cause and effect recursive chain is ended when it is perceived, somehow, that further reduction is unproductive); and, c) a "whole" is assembled using the knowledge of the parts--*and their identifiable interactions*--into an understanding of the whole system.

This technique of problem, or work, analysis has been refined to a fine point during the hundreds of years since its first articulation. In fact, analysis is so ingrained in our culture as *a method of thought*, that it is usually taken (mistakenly) to be the *only* method of thought. In fact, they are often held to be synonymous. The analytical method which served scientific investigation and discovery so well for centuries was applied to the study of human work activities most prominently, as we have discussed, through the work of Taylor.

Thus, the same basic analytical/disaggregation approach that Taylor used to study the work elements of "Olaf the Swede" and his task of shoveling coal, was applied in essentially the same way to develop a rational model of business processes in general, and the management of them in particular. In fact, the term "management science" was advanced and meant to be suggestive of an orderly, stable and predictable process to understand the workings of business.[11]

Thus, current management practice (and the educational systems that feed it) were born out of the need to somehow transfer and promulgate the effective practices of business management. Once accomplished, the succeeding efforts to institutionalize this insight led eventually to the rise and prominence of the business school. Along the way, we convinced ourselves that we had identified (analyzed), more or less completely, the skills needed to be a successful business executive and set about devising academic programs and corresponding on-the-job work progressions to instill these skills, thereby assuring a steady supply of competent executives: good, solid, business generalists who approached the optimized ideal, just as Taylor's work half a century before, had shown us how to produce optimized assembly line workers.

Simultaneously, during this same time frame, something else was happening that further reinforced the need for a development system that would produce competent generalists: specialists had begun to get a "bad rap" and for good reason.

THE PROBLEM WITH SPECIALISTS

Given the growing need for capable management practitioners, it would be natural to suppose that the "raw material" for such positions would come from the available pool of workers already in place and presumably familiar with the business or industry they had been working in. Indeed, promotions "up through the ranks" seemed to be a natural progression and, indeed, this came to be seen almost as a kind of obligation that the company had as a way to reward loyal workers. The first level of advancement was typically to that of "first line" supervisor. Because of the fragmentation-of-work organization that was an inevitable feature of Taylorism, the first-line supervisor's responsibilities were usually nothing more than a continuation of the tasks he or she had been doing, along with added administrative activities such as coordinating vacation schedules, handling time cards and payroll matters, etc. However, as advancement up the hierarchy continued, management purview began to broaden and in short order, the-up-from-the-ranks line supervisor was soon into foreign territory, territory for which his former experience did not prepare him. What was worse, he didn't seem very adept at learning new skills and the leaders of the organizations became disillusioned over the wisdom of advancement through the ranks of their existing work force.[12] The "specialists" began to get branded as being too inflexible, difficult to re-train (the "old dog, new tricks" argument), not progressive, not forward--looking, etc., etc. Interestingly, all these pejorative assessments were, arguably, entirely valid as a general proposition, but, the reason *why* this was so was completely misdiagnosed.

Simultaneously, an increasing number of college-educated people began to enter the workplace (an unintended, if not unforeseen consequence of the G.I. Bill). These people were, by and large, ambitious and eager and it was an almost inevitable result that they should form the "stock pond" for advancement into the management ranks. The so-called "Whiz Kids" of Robert McNamara's Defense Department are perhaps the most notorious example of how this long-term process played out.

To all intents and purposes, this redesign of work and of the management of work should have produced consistently spectacular results. The only problem was, it didn't. In just a few short years, American business was in deep trouble, first from problems in domestic markets and then, increasingly, from foreign competition. The highly-touted, almost classically American industries, one after the other, began to falter and then fail altogether. A brief look at the casualty list is instructive: the steel industry was *created* by American companies; it was decimated,as was the automobile industry. Eastern Airlines, the only airline ever to be rated a blue-chip stock, went bankrupt, and so did the US Flag carrier, Pan Am. The entire consumer electronics industry, created by Americans, was virtually destroyed in the space of a few years. In the political and economic sphere, mismanagement of resources in the 1970s produced an inflation rate that was, a generation earlier, the stock-in-trade of South America "banana republics." And, one must mention the unmitigated disaster of the war in Vietnam, which, although there are legitimate differences on the wisdom of the initial policy objectives, there is virtually no disagreement that it was a complete failure of both leadership and management on a truly grand scale.

So it is fair to ask the question: What happened? Why didn't the whole ecosystem of generalists not produce the promised results--and perhaps even made matters worse? Why?

WHAT HAPPENED?

We believe that there were two overarching factors that contributed to the failure of the generalists to live up to expectations. These two, in turn, were abetted by both ignorance and arrogance around the basic question of what produces real competence.

The first factor is both structural and psychological, specifically, the degree to which we had become invested in, and enamored by, the rational methods of problem solving. The analytical/rational approach taught in schools of business, as elsewhere, roughly translated, is to break apart "business" into its identifiable components (marketing, finance, production, etc.), to develop a complete as possible understanding of each of these parts, and to aggregate an optimized understanding of these parts into a well-functioning whole. However, there are a number of inherent assumptions on which the validity of this method depend. To the extent that these underlying assumptions are valid, the results will likewise be useful. Let us look at some of the more important of these:

- The validity of the approach rests entirely on our ability to *pre-identify* all of the significant elements, or components, that should be studied. This is an especially important requirement if, for whatever reasons, (usually time and budget), we can't perform exhaustive analysis on all of the parts.

- Once identified, it is assumed that we can, in isolation from the rest of the system from which the parts were taken, gain the essential understanding of a part's essential properties, but while knowing full well (or we ought to know "full well") that a part's behavior is always being influenced by other parts that are not included in our study at the moment.

- We must assume (or presume) that we can properly and fully understand the relative role, function, *importance, and interaction* of each of the parts.

The second underlying reason is a little more difficult to capture because much of the energizing force behind it is unconscious. Simply stated, we became contaminated by the success of recent history while at the same time failing to heed lessons of history that had gotten lost along the way to the Industrial Age. The contamination of success came about as a result of the "apparent" validity and success of the fragmentation of work into tasks and jobs. Our experience seemed to be telling us that the mechanization of work was, if not a "good thing" then certainly a necessary one: it gave us automobiles and airplanes and radios and all the other fruits of the modern era. But, the other side of the coin, the dehumanization of work, was not such a pleasant by-product. Specialization and specialists had, in the course of things, taken on a new meaning. These were not the specialists of the kind developed in the medieval guild system where the specialty was one of *profession*; rather we had developed specialization around *tasks and jobs*.[13] By the 1950's, we were into our fourth or fifth generation of such "specialists" and there seemed to be an implicit understanding that their perspective was wholly inadequate to take on the major issue of work design that was in the offing. Unfortunately, because of a failure to appreciate the root causes of the justified dissatisfaction, and to also make critical distinctions between professional specialists and job/task specialists, the term specialist acquired a bad reputation that we have not yet dispelled. But what is far more important is the fact that we are still, by and large, operating business and the formal educational systems that serve them in a way that will perpetuate the problem. To understand why this is so, we need to examine the "hidden factor" that has been operating quietly yet pervasively since the day Eli Whitney gave the profession and acquired wisdom of gunsmithing over to a collection of people and machines doing tasks--and not one of whom ever needed to know how to make a gun.

THE BIOLOGY OF LEARNING

The past twenty-five years has seen an accelerating convergence among the fields of biology and psychology, particularly those of neurobiology and of behavioral and clinical psychology. In sum, there is a growing understanding of the biological foundations of behavior in general, and learning in particular. The purpose of this paper is not to provide an overview of this work, but rather to examine some of the more important implications suggested by these insights, especially as it relates to our main consideration, that of specialized and generalized knowledge.

The major understanding to come from these recent research findings is the intimate, *inseparable* connection among biology, physiology and what might be called "psychological properties/motivations" of human action.

We have a new understanding of many of the biological specifics of how humans learn. Brain scientists have been able to associate changes in brain activity--specifically chemical and electrical phenomena--with the learning process itself. This understanding extends beyond that of identifying stimulus/response patterns in the nervous system, but now includes those associated with memory and information processing, with judgments and decisions, with abstract reasoning. These new insights have caused major adjustments in our models and assumptions about how we learn; about how we know and apply our knowledge. Two of the most important changes, for example, was the modification of our understanding of the role of external (environmental) factors in learning and, secondly, a much more robust model (and more useful) of how the brain responds to the aging process. It was first shown with rats (and later humans), that an enriched learning environment in the cage produced a measurable difference in the size and weight of the rat brain, as well as the number and complexity of the neural pathways available for information processing. We also know that what was thought to be an inevitable decline with age in brain function in otherwise healthy brains is *not* true. What *is* true is that brain function *declines as a result of lack of use.* "Use it or loose it" applies to intellectual capacity of the person as much as it does to the muscles in the arm that aren't used for even a relatively short period of time.

The summary results from these recent findings suggests new insight into what is happening in a person's neuro-physical system during the process of acquiring specialized knowledge. When we immerse ourselves deeply in a topic which contains a hierarchy of complexity of things that are all eventually related, we are actually building brain tissue! The brain's information processing and organizing routines are building a complex web of interconnected glial cells, dendrites, axons and neurons; millions upon millions of synapses are constantly firing, the chemistry of dozens of neurotransmitters are changed over and over again as the brain establishes a "knowledge network" within itself. This process of deepening complexity--and the necessarily associated brain development--does not happen, either to the same extent or degree, when our information intake and processing consists of a "a little of this" and a "little of that." The reason seems clear: there is simply no impetus or need to form the complex pathways of interconnection when processing information that is not evidently related.[14]

We finally come to an important realization about the consequences of brain development that occurs in the presence of deep learning: the brain structure that was developed as a direct result of that activity *is available for other things as well!* No, we are not saying that this deep learning process will equip us to learn or do *anything*. There are many factors, some of them well-characterized, others less so, that combine to produce learning. Interest, disposition, anticipated utility of results, etc., are just a few of the more obvious ones. Rather, what we are saying is that the process of acquiring deep knowledge is a *necessary one* to prepare the body's physiology to learn complex patterns of interaction and relationship, of recall and application, for the ability to hold the contents and dimensions of multi-variant problems and possible solutions, for the ability to creatively "manufacture" new mental models that extend beyond the confines of what has already been learned. These are the abilities, the "competencies," of the true generalist.

SOME CONCLUDING THOUGHTS

Our desire for, and ability to describe, the competent generalist is not new. What is new is the understanding of the neuro-physiological processes that lay the physical foundation for these abilities to develop in the first place. paradoxically, the "joke" of Mother Nature if you will, is that they are produce through a process of deep learning, the environment for which is provided by the process of professional/craft specialization and *not* by a shallow or brief exposure to generalized knowledge. Correspondingly, we also know that shallow learning of the kind required by task specialization *does not* stimulate the brain's growth and therefore the "mental muscle" needed to go beyond the requirements of the trained-for task is simply not available. A further and profound implication from our recent insight into brain functioning is contained in the maxim of common sense: "use it or loose it." We know that even a brain that has developed in a highly enriched environment will show measurable loss of capacity unless the stimulations that induce growth *are maintained* through our lifetime. this point was nowhere better made than when George Burns was asked his "secret" for living such a productive life at such an advanced age. His reply: "always stay booked."

With this understanding of brain functioning, it is possible to advance a highly plausible (although not provable) explanation as to what happened to the "specialists" who were the progeny of the "Taylor school" of task performers: many of them, quite literally, became "brain dead" as a result of an impoverished intellectual environment. Many of them, because they were poor from birth and uneducated, never had the chance to develop their mental capacity to start with; the ones who did, but who did not provide somehow for continued enrichment, soon found themselves in the same deteriorated state.

Likewise, we need to apply the same basic understanding to our questions about what happened with the "generalist" management practitioners whom we attempted to "scientifically" cultivate in our

128

businesses and academic institutions. We are now in a position to make some enlightened suppositions. The ones who entered the process after having gone through a deep learning process in some specialize craft were at least prepared as far as brain development was concerned to take on the leaning challenges that management positions offered. Whether they succeed or not depended on many other factors, chief of which was how they attended to the continued mental enrichment. Those who entered the superficial knowledge had been exhausted (and the all-too-frequent practice of 2-3 year assignment rotations does not cure the problem, it only delays the recognition--and consequences--of it). An evident question, then is how long does it take to develop the brain's learning network? Our research and experience with working with thousands of individuals is consistent with 10,000 years of recorded history: this process of deep learning, of brain development, takes between 7 and 15 years, of disciplined activity. Moreover, it cannot be compressed or averted. this seems to be the "neurological constant" that is built into all of us.

We can see, too,m that not only did the explosive growth in public education that occurred at the beginning of this century correct many of the problems induced by language and culture, but something else also happened that was to pay rich dividends in the future. Its *method* of instruction, with it focus on repetition, drills, disciplined and constant practice of the fundamentals, was working silent "magic" on the brain chemistry of its protesting recipients. And it worked! Within the short space of twenty-five years, the New york City public education system, from kindergarten to post graduate level, became the pride of the city, and had a major influence on public education policy and methods throughout the nation (the rightly-acclaimed University of California system was modeled after it).

Space does not permit a full examination of the question here, so we ask the reader to speculate on the long-term effects of the change in philosophy that slowly de-emphasized, and then replaced, those instructional methods that best promote brain development. We ask you to wonder, as do we, to what extent our many problems with drugs, with juvenile (and adult) crime, with multi-generational poverty and welfare, etc., are, in actuality, not primarily social in nature, but neurological in both origin and solution. It is these and related questions and their wise answers that will determine the vitality, prosperity and character of our future society.

NOTES

1. 1996, Farren Associates, Inc. The authors are with Farren Associates, Inc., a human resources consulting firm in Annandale, Virginia.

2.　Notable exceptions were the massive construction projects undertaken in ancient Egypt. Remarkably, these projects were undertaken by military engineers. In fact, military engineering is the field of specialization from which modern civil engineering comes. It was not until the 19th century that these two fields became distinct, even though the major distinctions continue to be one of customer focus, rather than the underlying technology base.

3. As used here, the term 'complex' means that the contributions of more than one area of specialized knowledge are required to affect a satisfactory solution to a problem. It does not necessarily imply that the tasks are difficult or a project is large in scope.

4. Some have argued, rather persuasively, that had it not been for the psychological aftermath of the Great Depression, the serious rethinking of work and our work institutions would have occurred much sooner than it has.　The depression was so painful and its memories were so clear that the generation who lived through it were easily persuaded that a "don't rock the boat. Be glad you have a job" attitude was a necessary and good one.　To this, many of the immigrants from war-torn Europe would also rightly add: "and be glad you're alive."

5. Fuller was of the opinion that we were all "born generalists."　The trend to specialization, he felt, was a result of constraints imposed by society.　Perhaps there isn't as much divergence of opinion in this paper as there might seem to be:　we would phrase it slightly differently:　we may be 'born' with a tendency *to live* our lives as generalists, but we must make our *contribution to life* in a specialty.

6. One interesting example is the normal clothes zipper.　Although the zipper made its debut as a feature of clothing in the late 1930's, the wartime demand for copper, the material of choice for zippers, prevented widespread manufacture of this innocuous device until after 1950.　The dozen years between "possible" and "available" for such an important consumer product is difficult to imagine today when the time between idea and practical use is often measured in months!

7. MacArthur had studied Asian and Japanese cultures for years and concluded that unless there was a fundamental shift in the Japanese culture, the imperial, militarist character of Japanese society would eventually re-establish itself and the US would, sometime in the future, find itself once again going to war with Japan. Thus, he was intent on creating an economic commercial class in Japan that would be a natural check and balance to militarist expansion.　He also personally intervened in the drafting of the new constitution to assure that it contained provisions prohibiting any standing military other than a self-defense force. A third element of concern was one of historical context: he was attempting to guard against the historical mentality that would demand some sort of in-kind retaliation for both the "loss of face" from losing the war and also for the use of nuclear weapons to end it.　MacArthur was well aware of the

cultural tendency of historical revisionism as a way to deal with issues that were unpleasant and which struck at the core of national identity. His decision to retain the monarchy by publically acknowledging the role of the Emperor was part of this strategy.

8. The AT&T Company, and specifically its Bell Telephone Laboratories and Western Electric units, was unquestionably the first large industrial concern to adopt "systems thinking" as an integral part of its culture. This came about as a result of the almost serendipitous intersection of several contributing elements: the large and highly diverse character of its business was one. Another, and perhaps the most important, was the regulatory environment which dictated that its capital investment recovery periods (depreciation) was much longer than other "normal" — 40 years for most large systems—which thus mandated careful initial design and even more careful plans to integrate new technology into an environment where parts of the "system" could be 40 years or more old. A third factor was the visionary leadership of the first president of Bell Laboratories, Frank K. Jewitt, who established an entire culture of technical excellence, emphasizing strong and on-going ties to premier academic institutions. Indeed, the relationships between the Laboratories and schools such as Princeton, Harvard, MIT, and others was one of on-going interaction and communication. Interviewed after his retirement, when asked about the Bell Labs 'systems approach' to its work, he stated that it never occurred to him to do it any other way and still be able to meet the Bell Systems's mission of Universal Telephone Service at an Affordable Cost and do so within the economic and political constraints of a regulated monopoly.

9. One of these was the University of Pennsylvania, where two researchers, J. Presper Eckert and John Mauchley, produced the world's first electronic computer, the ENIAC. How the school, and particularly its president, squandered the value of its leadership in that emerging field is an interesting study in how non-systemic thinking can unconsciously creep into even the best run organizations.

10. J. Robert Oppenheimer, who was the technical director of the Los Alamos Laboratory, wrote much later: "We had to work that way because it was painfully obvious to everyone that no one person could ever solve the entire problem himself, despite the fact that, with one or two exceptions, we had the very best people in the world working on the project." Oppenheimer is also one of the best examples of the Generalist-Specialist about which this paper is devoted.

11. A humorous, but thought-provoking, event happened while doing research for this article. One of the people interviewed, a research physicist, made the comment that "any activity that needs to call itself a 'science' probably isn't one." He was accused imme-

diately of being parochial, if not arrogant, and he replied that such may be the case, but added: "just think about it."

12. Sadly, this "problem" often became manifested when the advancing workers were in the 40-50 year-old range and their less-than-desired performance, their seeming inability to learn and adapt, was attributed to, or blamed on, age. Thus, a subtle form of age discrimination unconsciously crept into our thinking. The problems cited with this part of the workforce were real enough--their difficulty with learning and adapting was not caused by age, however. Rather, as we shall better understand in a moment, it was caused by their biological patterning.

13. A later section discusses the biology of learning. One of the implications to be considered here is the question that, aside from a too-narrow focus, job/task specialization *may not* have the breadth or depth of learning challenge to assure continual biological development of the brain. When you then apply the "use it or loose it" maxim, a case might be made to understand how the various pejorative labels (nerd, dull, lacking in enthusiasm, not a "big picture" person, etc.) applied to job/task specialists might have a real biological basis. It has been shown that when rats who were raised in an intellectually challenging environment and had the expected good brain development are then placed in an intellectually sterile environment, their brains shrink and their behavior becomes subdued and then lifeless. This happens in a surprising short period of time. Human experiments along the same line are limited because of ethical considerations, but the data from prisoner of war experiences suggests that the very same pattern is true for the human being.

14. There are many factors that come into play when describing the differences in the way the brain handles related and unrelated information. One of the more interesting comes from a recent understanding that the brain's memory recall methods are far more complex than first imagined. Initially, we supposed that a "bit" of data was stored in some physical location and remembering was a process of access and extraction of that "bit." Now we know that data—seemingly identical data—are stored in multiple physical locations and are accessed differently, depending on the context of the recall task. This "multi-location" storage algorithm is a direct result of the relational processing that accompanies learning in depth and which is not available with a fragmentary approach.

VIRTUAL LITERACY: LITERACY IN VIRTUAL LEARNING ENVIRONMENTS

by

David Passig

INTRODUCTION

It is reasonable to assume that in the coming years we will see teaching units which use virtual environments in various areas, such as chemistry, physics, etc. (Bircken 1993, Passig 1995). In order for the students to derive the maximum from virtual environments of this type it must be assumed that they will need training in the cognitive and motor skills required in virtual environments. This article deals with finding and clarifying the fields of these skills in order to develop more effective teaching techniques in virtual environments (Helsel 1992).

Our purpose is to diagnose the character of literacy which is derived from immersion in virtual learning environments, the character of expression that the immersion poses before the learner, and the literacy components of navigating in virtual environments. It is customary to use the concept "literacy" in the context of reading and writing skills. However, literacy in a wider definition is an area of education which is necessary for drawing out the ability of a person to effectively use writing instruments, language, reading, writing, speaking, paying attention to, and so forth. Literacy of reading and writing, for example, is an array of linguistic aware-nesses and abilities for developing and formulating ideas which make it possible for a person to understand and express himself at some basic level of conversation. Thus it is clear that with "literacy" as a concept it is possible to broaden the areas of knowledge of basic skills in many domains. For example, literacy of driving a car, literacy of flying an airplane, technological literacy, etc. This article, therefore, will deal with the analysis of the characteristics and areas of literacy in virtual environments.

It is possible to diagnose a number of areas of orientation which characterize the virtual environment. These areas of orientation will require the student to use in virtual learning environments a series of cognitive and motor skills in order to become familiar with the virtual environments and to derive the maximum from them.

These areas of orientation include being familiar with different verity levels (the degree that our natural environment is represented in a virtual environment), familiarity with levels of integration or immersion, orientation aided by natural interfaces, and orientation aided by artificial interfaces.

David Passig *is a professor of education at Bar-Ilan University in Israel.*

VIRTUAL LEARNING ENVIRONMENTS

For over a decade students have been looking at the computerized world through an "aquarium" called the "monitor", and have congratulated themselves on having been rescued from the punched card and buttons to press. However, we have advanced only a bit since then. When students are looking at a two-dimensional part of the computerized world, they are still detached from the whole picture. Virtual environment technologies invite us into a three-dimensional view of this world while being inside it.

Virtual environments (VE) are a dramatic alternative to the way in which we learn today. By the end of this decade students will be able to enter worlds created by the computer, to conduct experiments in chemistry, to examine rare manuscripts, to investigate objects and cultures that cannot be approached otherwise, and to participate in the plot of a story in a way hitherto unknown.

Virtual-Learning-Environments promise to bring about a revolution in the sciences and in various technologies. The VE technology is one which has become unknown to the general public only in the last few years. Nevertheless, today, very few educators are aware of its potential.

At this time, when the general public has passed the tumult that arose around the VE in the past three years, the time has come for educators to take an interest in what can be achieved by using it. However, in order to develop applications the educational leaders must first develop new pedagogical approaches in order to take advantage of the possibilities offered by VE. First, here are several available applications which exploit the hidden potential in the technology.

ALGEBRA IN VIRTUAL REALITY

William Bricken (1993), a senior scientist at the Human Interface Lab at the University of Washington, developed, and is continuing to improve a virtual world in which objects are controlled using algebraic laws rather than physical ones. The objects, for example, are not influenced by gravity, but they react to a whole positive or negative number. The students move cubes in an artificial world; these cubes can be arranged in various configurations as long as they do not violate algebraic laws.

Bricken is convinced that the principal component in virtual environment is the feeling that the student is in the environment and is not just referring to an object that is in the environment. According to Bricken, approaches based on a monitor can only approximate such a feeling. Immersion of the user in a virtual-reality environment has greater influence on the learner than mere observation of an animated figure on a screen which is supposed to represent the user.

"Putting a hand in the bucket of water is not the same as swimming," claims Bricken.

William Winn (1993), a professor of educational technology at the University of Washington, works with Bricken in developing educational uses of VE. They are preparing for the day when the use of VE in classrooms will be more widespread.

PHYSICS IN VIRTUAL REALITY

In the software department of the Johnson Space Center, Bowen Loftin and his staff are investigating the uses of VE for training not only astronauts but also high school physics students. They have developed a pair of virtual realities which shows clearly that VE can provide important advantages for the two groups.

Loftin has developed for a physics study group, a laboratory for virtual reality in which experiments in motion and gravity can be controlled. In the laboratory there are pendulums of various lengths and two balls with different bouncing capabilities. A control panel floating in space in the laboratory enables the student to manipulate gravity, friction, and time. In addition, this panel shows time or distance which has already passed. In this laboratory one can stop time in order to perform measurements, and the bouncing balls can leave traces which enable the student to see their path. Another characteristic of the laboratory is the "gravity range". A ball with an iron frame which surrounds a smaller solid ball. The relative height of the small ball in the counting indicates the gravity constant which is actually present at an imagined point in time, which can be positive or negative. This laboratory allows a first look at the way in which one can use VE to teach basic concepts in physics.

A student can learn about gravity and the laws of Newton--not just by reading, or looking at demonstrations--but by trial and error. One can slow down or stop time in order to look at what is happening in an advance experiment in speed. A simple and intuitive means does not hold back learning, and the teacher's attention is not necessary when the student is in the laboratory. Nothing is broken! Loftin foresees that such a laboratory will be used together with class teaching, especially in the communications network systems that the teacher can bring into the laboratory when necessary, and then go on to another student, and all this without leaving his work desk.

NETWORKED V-ART MUSEUM

If we should ever wish to visit a museum without leaving the classroom, what we would need would be the virtual museum. And then, not only would it be possible to visit the museum using regular telephone lines, but when we got there the regular laws of reality would not apply. We will be able to fly around or to try to enter another body. Thanks to Carl Eugene Loeffler (in Delaney 1993), a researcher in the studio for creative research at Carnegie-Mellon University in Pittsburgh, it is already possible to visit such a museum.

The first demonstration of such a museum took place in 1994 when stations in Munich, Germany, and Pittsburgh were connected by regular phone lines. Users on each side saw each other, moved through the museum independently, and moved objects around. Other places are going to be added from this year on.

Visitors to the museum unveil several galleries. One, known as the amusement park, is similar to the old amusement park in public parks. In the amusement park one chooses the body in which one continues to move. (This is different from most of the virtual environments in which the user has only one viewpoint and perhaps also a hand.) Existing in a complete body is enjoyable, especially if you are in a room in which you step in front of mirrors in virtual reality which wrap your image, exactly like the sensation in a real amusement park.

In another gallery in the museum the visitors can test the Leonardo da Vinci's flying machine and use it to travel in different environments with different views. Immediately after entering the process, one hears the wings flapping up and down, and the system operates and moves you around.

The most exciting area in the museum is the full-size transcription of ancient Egyptian temples. In this section of the virtual museum one enters these ancient temples and hears an explanation of them from the computerized guide (blob), who is dressed in the costume of those times.

Unfortunately, it is still impossible to dial the museum. The access to the museum of virtual reality is available only to Carnegie-Mellon University, the University of Tokyo, and the Royal Institute for Technology in Melbourne, Australia.

Loeffler hopes that the museum will be set up shortly in a system for the user which will provide virtual worlds for many users with many simultaneous connections. Such accessibility will be available first of all in the computer museum in Boston and in the Smithsonian Institute.

CLASSICAL LITERATURE

Everyone thinks that classical literature can only be "read". It turns out that one can experience Franz Kafka also in a virtual world in which the artistry of the ethic dilemma is presented.

The Imperial Message is an interpretation in virtual environment of one of Kafka's stories in which it is possible to experience a world of dilemmas, intrigues, confusion, escape, and in the end--answers. This virtual story is now being presented in a number of places in the United States (Brill 1996). The virtual reality technology has translated the style of Kafka to an extravagant philosophical game, which attracts users to a world of difficult decisions and moral dilemmas which shape the future of imaginary imperialism.

On the technical aspect of this virtual environment, its creators Michael Ferraro and Brian D'amato experimented theoretically with advanced programming tools the design of interactive literature. They tested techniques in artificial intelligence in order to develop "Autonomous Agents" in virtual worlds which would react to their environment and to the users who communicate with them.

This and similar applications allow us the possibility to present to our students literary experiences which we would not have been able to give by any other means that had been available to us previously.

THE FUTURE

These examples demonstrate some of the uses of virtual environments in education today. In the next few years we will probably be able to see an important development in virtual environments as a teaching tool. The hardware and software that are being used to develop the worlds of virtual reality are rapidly improving, and it will also be easier to acquire them. However, as mentioned in the introduction, educators must develop new pedagogical methods in order to take advantage of the almost unlimited possibilities offered by virtual environments.

In recent years researchers such as Meredith Bricken (1991) and William Winn (1993) have turned to working on the unique characteristics of the virtual learning worlds. For these scholars the virtual worlds offer teachers and students unique learning experiences, such as learning in groups, on-the-ground access, imaging, and visual realization of concepts.

The visual environments present great challenges to our educational goals and the teaching methods which we have today. Conventional teaching styles and pedagogical methods will not be able to hold their own against teaching with virtual environments. A virtual environment is more than a breakthrough in electronic communication or user interface. According to Michael Heim (1992), it is a metaphysical laboratory for testing our feeling concerning reality. Ultimately, the illusion in the virtual world can be so powerful that we will not be able to distinguish reality from non-reality. Virtual environment expands the definition and understanding of the body, place, and reality. Conventional teaching methods were intended for guiding the student to recognize his or her place and to be aware of the surrounding reality.

We must therefore ask, "How will those same methods be able to guide students to study their enhanced reality?"

Moreover, conventional teaching methods were developed in order to achieve the goal of control over reality as conceived by the teacher and the surrounding culture. In a period in which the rate of change in reality is constantly accelerating, teachers are not capable of providing a relevant reality or suitable methods that the student can use to study his digital reality. (A study done at MIT (1989) indicates that by 2010 human knowledge, which today doubles every 18-24 months, will double every three weeks to one and a half months.)

Studies show that by the end of the decade we will be surrounded by technologies which include many virtual environments, from medical technologies to those of entertainment. In order for educators to integrate this technology in the teaching environment, additional literacy is needed to succeed in realizing its potential.

THE NATURE OF EXPRESSION

The computer was initiated as a tool for working numbers. However, it went on to take a central place in interpersonal communication. It is no longer just a tool merely for storing and working data, but an instrument for expressing ideas in real time. Computerized multimedia is a further stage in the evolution of the personal computer. It is becoming an instrument of expression with the capability of simultaneously integrating a wide range of systems of symbols and presenting them in a uniform sequence.

The possibility of communicating with virtual environments presents one with an additional system of symbols with which one can express complicated ideas at a more advanced level and in real time--three-dimensional simulation. This system of symbols requires a new literacy different from the one we have been accustomed to in expressing ourselves--the familiar systems of symbols: text, pictures, video, etc. Therefore, expression in virtual environments creates a new human means of expression which restores the form of interpersonal communication to a more intuitive one. Of necessity this will also require a literacy at a more intuitive level.

THREE-DIMENSIONAL EXPRESSION

We live in a three-dimensional environment. However, when explaining something we have to convert the information to two-dimensional symbols.

All the symbol systems that we have been making use of till now have been two-dimensional (pictures, video, words) systems which present abstract multidimensional ideas. The communicator had to clothe the multidimensional ideas in two-dimensional tools/symbols, transfer them through a medium, and the receiver had to grasp the symbols appearing before him and restore their multidimensionality in order to understand the requested messages and make use of it. As of today, the principal characteristic of the media has been that the user remained physically detached from them. In this process very complicated functions were required of the learner in symbol systems and with their transfer in the media--functions of production, absorption, and processing. The educational system invested vast resources--personal and financial in order to teach this literacy (an investment which did not always prove its value--see reading comprehension).

On the other hand, the principal characteristic of literacy in virtual worlds is that we are capable, on the one hand, of expressing ideas in a three-dimensional form and on the other hand, we are part of the medium, immersed in it, and working from within and not just throught it or on it.

Virtual Environments make possible an appreciable acceleration of the process in understanding messages and deepening the i.e., comprehension. On the face of it, at least, this process skips over complicated stages that were in conventional learning. This in itself can increase understanding because the symbols become more "realistic images: and more communicative to the world of popular knowledge of the learner" (Bucket 1995).

THE NATURE OF VIRTUAL LITERACY: REFLECTION OF THE "SELF"

The origin of the concept "virtual" is from optical physics. The term describes the type of image seen from a certain point in space with the knowledge that there is no object in that place. The reflection of a form from a mirror is called "a virtual picture". One can, in addition to images, also reflect voices, physical presence, and feelings.

IMMERSION AND PRESENCE

The reflection interface of the technologies of virtual reality is different in essence from the well-known computer interfaces. The user in this technology experiences an absorbing interface which influences the interpersonal interaction, and therefore he needs a literacy which makes comprehension efficient while immersed in the message.

Immersion of this type in the interface, of necessity, adds a new touch to the feeling of the presence of the "self" in the process of communication. The experience of presence in the virtual world is twofold, similar to the experience of presence in the concrete world. One is the sense of immersion, and another is the interaction with virtual objects. The cognitive advantage of the virtual presence is hidden in its ability:

a) to provide an experience of presence in the synthetic environment (produced by the computer).
b) to ameliorate the experience of human presence by providing an experience in imaginary environments and conditions.

THE MENTAL MODEL IN REAL WORLDS

In a real world there are three variables which together comprise the necessary mental representation in interpersonal communication. The first variable is the stage of thinking about the knowledge/idea/message. The second variable is characterized by the transfer of the idea/message by means of communication to the environment. The third variable is the background awareness of the communicator while transmitting the messages. These constitute the mental model in the real environment.

On the other hand, the mental model in a virtual environment is different in essence from the mental model in a real environment. The virtual reality interface grants the user the possibility of penetrating into the medium while communicating and thus to removing him from the experience of communication. The result is the transmission of messages without the experience of a medium, and the user becomes part of the message. For the first time in human history a person can communicate within a medium and not just by using a medium. Moreover, for the first time Homo sapiens are developing a tool in which the "self" and the "I" and the "message" are not only interfacing by means of divisive instruments, but are also merging together (Miller 1992).

FIGURE 1

 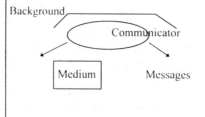

Medium - Virtual Environment

a. Mental Model in Virtual Environment | b. Mental Model in Real Environment

---

The above points, and many which we have not yet conjectured at this point in the history of technology, bring us, as educators, to formulate a new agenda in special technological literacy which it is reasonable to assume will keep us busy for many more years.

COMPONENTS OF LITERACY IN VIRTUAL WORLDS

Virtual literacy includes four components of orientation. The first component is orientation at different verity levels. The second is orientation in various integrative levels (Immersion). The third is orientation using varied natural interfaces. The fourth component is orientation using artificial interfaces (Thurman/Matton, 1994).

The first two are components of the virtual literacy at the level of cognitive presence.

The two other components are components of virtual literacy at the level of motor orientation in virtual worlds.

ORIENTATION IN VERITY DIMENSIONS

The following scale demonstrates the levels for conceiving verity in virtual worlds. Educators must investigate and understand how the levels of verity influence the efficiency of learning in virtual worlds and at what level one or another teaching unity is absorbed most efficiently (Matton/Mowafy, 1993).

FIGURE 2

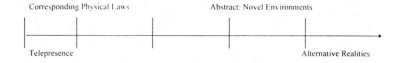

The first position on the scale (on the left) indicates virtual environments with physical laws. For example, a virtual environment is said to be an imitation of a real environment for the purposes of a game or presence from a distance--Telepresence (Foley 1989).

The end position on the scale (to the right) indicates the lowest feeling of verity in virtual environments. For example, imaginary worlds which have no connection with physical worlds, such as the imaginary playground which does not imitate any law of concrete reality. This high level of abstraction will require educators to convey tools which will help the students find their way in imaginary places. Those who acquire skills in orientation in various true levels will derive a greater benefit from immersion in virtual worlds (Spring 1991).

ORIENTATION IN MODES OF IMMERSION

Literacy in integrative levels includes two components: Dimensions of immersion and ways of immersion. In the early days of computers the involvement of the user with the computer was at a very low level, which was called "Batch Processing". The user gave a series of commands by means of cards which were punched for this purpose and received desired output after an additional series of operations in his absence.

FIGURE 3

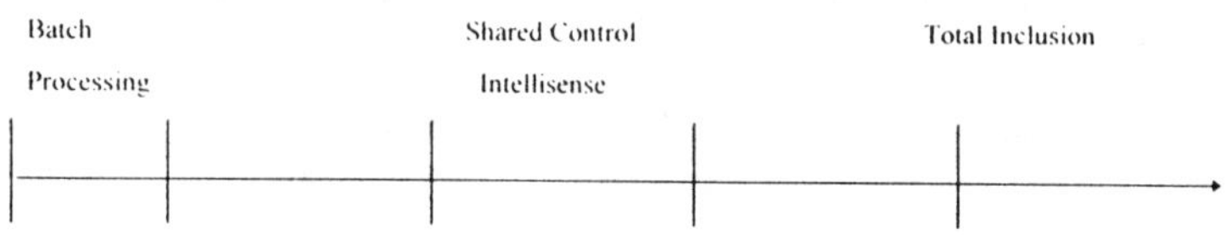

| Batch | Shared Control | Total Inclusion |
| Processing | Intellisense | |

After the keyboard was developed, the user began to be more involved in the process of data processing while working the computer. In the center of the scale is the level which indicates the characteristic level of immersion in combined control and work. At this level the computer helps us make decisions before and during the performance of the work, confers with the user, sometimes accepting his opinion and sometimes not. The Microsoft software program called BOB, for example, suggests ways for correcting software failures (Worthington 1995). Software of this type is known as Intellisense. The level at the end of the scale indicates the highest level of immersion that the technology of virtual environments is striving to achieve. At this level the user will be an organic part inside the synthetic environment, a sort of man/machine connected together in neural networks. Recently the AVATAR company in California received from the United States Army a million dollars to develop 20 rooms networked together in which soldiers will be able to enter military training in full wireless immersion (CGW 1995).

Educators will have to give their opinion about skills of orientation at integrative levels in order to improve and make more efficient the process of learning.

FAMILIARITY WITH WAYS OF IMMERSION

The scale of modes of immersion indicates the ways of immersion.

FIGURE 4

The first and second levels of this scale indicate a literacy which provides instruments for movement in the virtual world. "Inclusion" is the level that indicates capabilities of literacy by means of which one learns to change things in the virtual world according to the user's determination. For example, when teaching how the fetus develops in the womb, instead of explaining this theoretically it will be possible to develop a suitable program and apply it at the level of "Inclusion", and then the learner himself, while learning, will feel as though he is the fetus moving and developing in the womb. With this literacy the user will feel how the fetus is growing and will learn how it is nourished.

"Support" is the highest stage in the scale of ways of immersion. This is the stage in which a guide in the virtual world supports the presence of the user. The guide assists the learner to be immersed in the way in which it leads him, recommends to him and leads with definite mutual relations. These will surely be called: Blobs, actors, agents, etc. Supporting environments will require literacy aptitudes of the dialogue with the "self" which are not identical with monologue aptitudes in the real world.

"Inclusion" is a literacy in which the user becomes part of the knowledge. He himself is an entity of the knowledge mosaic in whose midst he is. Inclusive environments will require literac aptitudes of the reflection of the "self" which are not yet known to us today in the real environment.

A study of this scale will make it possible for us to construct learning programs in different levels of immersion which will match the ability, age, and knowledge of the student. Educators will have to prove that learning at this or that level will be more efficient.

ORIENTATION BY MEANS OF NATURAL AND ARTIFICIAL INTERFACES

The interfaces in virtual worlds are divided into two types each of which requires its own literacy, natural interfaces and artificial interfaces.

FIGURE 5

Artificial interfaces (artificial for the way of operation of a person in real space) include input and output interfaces: Mouse, keyboard, touch screen, etc. Natural interfaces include hat, suit, glove, etc.

Behavioral sensors will have to furnish skills for orientation in artificial, natural, and behavioral interfaces such as these. Educational research will have to develop the above scales in order to teach the new generation of students to be familiar with the various tools and to take advantage of them for more efficient and meaningful learning and communication.

SUMMARY

The educational establishment is just beginning to consider and recognize the existence of a technology with educational potential of a special kind. There has not yet been a breakthrough in the development of learning tools in virtual environments. Given this, the establishment must be prepared for the day when the market will be flooded with inexpensive mass products as is happening in the multimedia market. In this article we have tried to outline the agenda that the developers of learning programs are going to put before them. Such an agenda must lead to research and development in various areas. Pedagogues must pay heed to the cognitive and value aspects of the literacy which will be needed in order to orient oneself in virtual worlds. Educational psychologists must attend to the psychomotor aspects of using virtual environments. Those in educational communication will have to test the consequences of the technology for interpersonal and mass communication, and those in educational administration will have to examine the cost/benefit of teaching with this technology.

REFERENCES

Army Aims for "Holodeck-Like Experience--Spotlight," *Computer Graphics World*, April 1995, p.8.

Bricken, Meredith. "Virtual-Reality Learning Environments: Potential and Challenges," *Computer Graphics Magazine*, July 1991.

Bricken, William. "Researchers Test Virtual Reality in the Classroom," *The Chronicle of Higher Education*, April 22, 1992, A24.

Brill, Louis M. "The Imperial Message: Virtual Reality Joins Classic Literature to Present 'The Art of Moral Dilemma'". *Virtual Reality Special Report*, A Miller Freeman Publication. (January/February, 1996), pp. 33-36.

Bucket, Donelson A. "Creve Maples: Sandia National Labs," *VR World*, July/August 1995, pp. 25-30.

Delaney, Ben. "Where Virtual Rubber Meets the Road," A1 Expert: Virtual-Reality 1993 Special Report.

Foley, J.D. "Interfaces for Advanced Computing", *Scientific American*, 257 (4), 1989, pp. 126-135.

Heim, Michael. "The Erotic Ontology of Cyberspace," *Cyberface: First Steps*, Edited by Michael Benedikt. MIT Press, Cambridge, MA: 1992.

Helsel, S. "Virtual Reality & Education", *Educational Technology*, May 1992, pp. 38-42.

Loftin, R. Bowen. In "Where Virtual Rubber Meets the Road: by Ben Delaney, Al Expert: Virtual-Reality 1993 Special Report.

Mattoon J.S. and L. Mowafy. Implications of Learning Theory and Strategies for the Design of Synthetic Environments. In S.R. Helsel (Ed.), *Proceedings of Virtual Reality 92 3rd Annual Conference and Exhibition*, Westport, CT: Meckler, 1993.

Miller, Carmen and A. Thomas Furness, III. "Virtual Reality Pioneer," *Online*, November 1992, pp. 14-27.

Passig, David. "Learning Programs in Virtual Environments: Future Trends and Needs". *Mahshevim be-Hinukh (Computers in Education)*, (January 95) p. 32 (in Hebrew).

Rheingold, Howard. "Virtual-Reality, Phase Two", Al Expert: Virtual-Reality 1993 Special Report.

Spring, M.B. Informating with VR. In S.K. Helsel and J.P. Roth eds. *Virtual Reality: Theory, Practice and Promise*, pp. 101-110. Westport, CT: Meckler.

Thurman, R.A. and J.S. Mattoon. "Virtual Reality: Toward Fundamental Improvements in Simulation-Based Training," *Educational Technology*, October 1994, pp. 56-64.

Worthington, P. "Social Computing, The Promits of BOB," *Multimedia World*, March 1995, p. 43f.

CYBERSPACE VERSUS THE ENDANGERED UNIVERSITY: THE PROSPECTS FOR 21ST CENTURY EDUCATION

by

Joseph N. Pelton

THE AGE OF PLANETARY INTERACTIVE LEARNING

We humans like to sort and group things into neat categories. We like to name each decade, each generation, each era, and each age. As we enter the 21st century, however, the incredible rate of change and innovation makes it difficult to sum up everything that is happening with a single phrase or catchword. Some would say we live in the Space Age, others would suggest it is the Information or Cyberspace Age and so on and so on. After we exhaust such proposals for "Ages" based upon "Punk Rock", "Rapprochement", "Globalism", "Self Expression", "Automation", or "Couch Potato Escapism", it is difficult to avoid the impression that we tend to identify our times in terms of fads, politics or technical inventions. If one examines human evolution as a species, the key to ultimate survival may well not be related to any of these. Rather survival may well be based first and foremost on individual and cultural learning. If Homo sapiens survives the 21st century it may well be because we have finally learned how to learn. The sharp distinctions that we now make between formal schooling, training, higher education, advanced degrees, and life-learning may have softened into a process of overall intellectual development.

This does not mean a few people will have learned to achieve a higher state of cultural and intellectual attainment. No. It means that everywhere across this six sextillion ton mud-ball we call planet Earth, we have acquired the right to plug into a global knowledge base that is based upon worldwide humanistic and ecological values. The key to this new environment of what may be called Cyberspace learning is global sharing, humanizing and environmental values, and ubiquity of "experiential and life-long learning". This, however, seems to pose a large problem. Our educational institutions, our methods of teaching and learning, and especially our universities today appear ill-suited to the task. The title of a recent article by Eli Noam sums up the dilemma quite well--"The Dim Future of the University".

Joseph N. Pelton *is chairman of the board of trustees, International Space University, Strasbourg, France.*

CONCEPTS OF LEARNING

"There is only one good--knowledge--
and only one evil--ignorance."

Socrates (469-399 B.C.)

It is now nearly 2,500 years since the Age of Socrates, Plato and Aristotle. Since that time we have created rocket ships, bio-technology, genetic engineering, lasers, radio astronomy, non-linear math, chaos theory, satellites, super computers, bunge jumping, spandex, talk show television, and artificial intelligence. Most of these innovations we would view as progress. But what about our educational process? We are still, two and a half millennia later, putting students in a classroom with a presumably knowledgeable authority figure who lectures or poses questions to the students for prescribed periods of time. This we call education. Despite all of our alleged progress, we seem to have progressed very little from the educational paradigm used in Ancient Greece by Socrates and the Academy.

We, in the US as well as educators in many other countries have reduced education to well known but essentially effete formulas. We typically equate "education" in colleges and universities to completion of set "jail sentences". A three-credit hour course is equivalent to "doing time" for some 45 contact hours mandated by accrediting organizations. In this case the teacher serves as the warden, while "education" is the punishment which is quantitatively measured by the time spent in the classroom or "cell". In this educational concept or model, the swift and slow learners seemingly acquire the same amount of learning or knowledge by exposure to a more or less equal amount of "information." Now certainly we do have laboratory and design courses and there are indeed some research activities associated with theses and dissertations. Except for professional courses of study with standardized tests as a capstone exercise to measure acquired knowledge, it is hard to know what exactly a college coed or a high school student has really learned. Most college "students" with four years of residency within the halls of ivy are simply "ripened" rather than necessarily "more learned". The "educated student" presumably emerges with adept reasoning abilities and "a great deal of acquired knowledge" but very little in the process guarantees that this will be so.

Some such as Lewis Perelman, author of *School's Out*, would say that the modern, pre-packaged and standardized schooling process of the late 20th century which we call "formal" (as in strait-jacketed and overly prescribed) education is about 90% wrong-minded. Perelman and other critics would claim that the predominant educational paradigms in the US are intellectually bankrupt and highly cost-inefficient. Furthermore, these same critics would argue that the rest of the OECD countries are really not much better when it comes to effective educational systems. The fact that functional illiteracy in most so-called developed countries is increasing, not decreasing, certainly must be considered a bad sign. The lack of sufficient skills to read, perform simple math, use a map, or follow the "plot" of a graph or soap opera is now estimated to represent some 3 to 4% of the population in Japan and perhaps 12% to 15% in the United States. The problem with education is certainly not the ancient Greek scholars. They were innovators who were actively experimenting with the latest in learning technology.

The problem, in a historical sense, could probably be best laid at the feet of Saint Augustine. In his *City of God* he began by applying Plato's Idealism to theology. He then borrowed from medieval scholars Ambrose and Gregory and came up with Divine Law. And presto, we had the form and structure of medieval intellectual thought. Within this framework, for better or worse, were born the medieval universities. The key was that the teacher had a "monopoly" on the right knowledge, so the tutelage of the student was highly controlled. The student had to learn the correct or "ideal" knowledge. Most importantly he or she (albeit precious little of the female gender were involved) must not learn the incorrect lessons. The student must not be allowed to think "outside-of-the-box" thoughts. The idea that knowledge "defined" from above must be stored in vats or bins and poured out in measured quantities has survived in a very resilient way for a very long time. It has been quite a few centuries since St. Augustine (borrowing in liberal measure from Plato, Ambrose and Gregory) told us the way to think, to pray and to teach the uninitiated student.

After the age of religious intolerance, some educational innovations were allowed to occur in some intellectual climates and have come down through the centuries. The Renaissance and the Age of Enlightenment changed many things about educational philosophy, and led, according to Teilhard de Chardin, to an age of scientific reason and the birth of a "noosphere". Teilhard celebrated a new era where intellectual and scientific objectivism flourished, and the Dark Ages were left behind. Invention, democratic institutions, and experimentation all took on new forms and most educational institutions escaped from religious constraints. Darwin's theories of evolution in the 19th century were perhaps the defining aspect of how education and learning could win out over "divinely defined dogma". The scientific process of acquiring empirical data by carrying out objective experimental tests and "proving" conclusions based upon critical reasoning were important and fundamental changes. These shifts, however, did not necessarily change the basic educational concept now well over a thousand years old. Students across the world still largely learn what an authority figure teacher teaches them. Parents who celebrate back to basics want instilled information poured out of vats rather than innovative thinking and critical analysis designed for life-long adaptive learning.

EXPERIMENTS WITH EDUCATIONAL CHANGE

This is not to suggest that some rather clever people along the way perceived some basic problems in education and the learning process. Jean-Jacques Rousseau suggested that French forms of education were essentially all wrong. He suggested that all young people be left on their own. In his "return to nature" philosophy he would have students develop their physical and athletic skills on their own for up to the first sixteen years of their life. His education would thus be much more self-directed. Paul and Percival Goodman in their book *Communitas* in the middle part of the 20th century in some ways returned to the themes of Rousseau. These two brothers, who were essentially architects and urban planners, suggested that we should design cities and communities to suit lifestyles and modes of learning. They suggested that "experiential learning" based upon planned communities could allow people to learn skills and knowledge that arose from their lifestyles and their professional and leisure-time interests. Since that time a number of educators and thinkers such as Edward Ploman of the United Nations University have echoed these themes of educational reform. The most common threads over the years have been "experiential learning", team learning and contextual educational systems, life-long learning, and "critical thinking and analysis based upon problem solving". These ideas have percolated through educational literature, but they have never been able to shake the foundations of the medieval paradigm of students trapped in a classroom with a teacher in front.

But suddenly, something important happened. Open Universities and distance learning suddenly evolved in the late 1950s and early 1960s. The most significant start was the Open University of the United Kingdom which quickly brought education, self learning texts and exercises, television and remote learning together in a new way. Dozens of important tele-education projects followed with some of them being direct off-shoots of the Open University in UK and others simply springing up spontaneously.

These projects, just to name a few, include the TeleKolleg of Germany, the Téléuniversité du Québec, the Chinese National Television University, TV Ontario, the Know Network of the West (KNOW) of Vancouver, Canada, the Global Electronic University, The National Telecommunications University (now international in scope), the Commonwealth of Learning, the International Space University, the Mind Extension University and the International University College, the EUROPACE project, NHK learning systems, the TVRI distance learning system of Indonesia, the Star Schools in the US, the UDIWITE system in the Caribbean, the University of the

South Pacific, Peacesat, the INSAT project in India, the Open University of Moscow and so on, dozens of times over.

Some of these projects were born as a result of the Intelsat Global Satellite System's Project SHARE. Others have been government-funded and yet others were created as strictly entrepreneurial ventures. The point is that the idea of media-based education, remote-based distance learning, and new forms of education that worked better, covered more people, were more up-to-date and also were more cost-effective struck a very responsive chord. Actually the positive chords were struck among the general populace and a number of policy makers. Professional educators, for the most part, saw this new educational media and its new system of learning to be a threat. In particular it was seen as an assault on "high standards" by a proletariat form of teaching and learning. It was seen as a threat to jobs, a threat to educators' status and prestige, and a threat to "quality".

The power of this idea of distance education was too strong to turn back a virtual tidal wave of interest. The Chinese National Television University, started under Intelsat's Project Share in 1986 has grown from 37 ground antennas, a handful of teachers and 2,000 students to a network of 90,000 VSAT stations throughout the Chinese subcontinent and over 3 million students and teachers.

When the Internet came along two decades later, many new prophets suggested that the "new answer" to education had arrived. In fact, Internet is simply another tool within the overall interactive electronic medium that we call "cyberspace." Cyberspace learning builds upon the power of television-based education that sprang forth in the 1950s and 1960s. In the 21st century we can envision new cyberspace tools such as high-powered global broadcast satellite networks, low-cost remote user terminals called "electronic tutors", and new highly inactive educational software. The tools will continue to evolve and improve, the key is new educational concepts that can "use their opportunity" effectively and without opposing institutional resistance. In short, imbedded regulations, institutional inertia, and even a little bit of academic pomposity are the major barriers to educational progress--and not the evolution of new educational and cyberspace tools.

The power is thus not in the network or the distribution mode. The power is in distributing quality and timely information to people who need and want to learn at their own rate and direct the nature and course of their learning program. Distance learning is at its best when it gives a good foundation of knowledge and understanding of a field and then lets the student take command. This self-directed learning can be based on books, articles, readings and lectures. It can be based on computer programs and interactive CD-ROM. It can be based upon the Internet or it can be upon e-mail chat groups or telephone conversations with teachers or classmates or industry experts. The fundamental point of this new paradigm for education is that the teacher is not the center of learning; it is rather the student and the student's interest that provide the key to interactive and experiential learning. It is learning that can start at any age and continues for a lifetime.

If nothing else these new forms of distance learning have taught us that there are flaws in our conventional educational systems. The previously cited example of the Chinese National Television University from 1987 to 1995 which grew from about 10,000 students to three million students and a satellite linked network of over 90,000 earth stations suggests that the conventional approach was really not working. As we look to the 21st century with a global population approaching 6 billion and some 1 to 2 billion people without any structured educational system at all, it seems time to look to new educational paradigms. This is something to do cautiously and thoughtfully rather than jumping onto the most recent fad. In short, just because something is new or high-tech or is inexpensive does not mean this is the answer. We must look for a new paradigm for education and learning that is profound and long-lasting.

A NEW PARADIGM FOR THE 21ST CENTURY EDUCATION

Some might be tempted to jump onto the educational platform which Lewis Perelman spells out quite cleverly in his book *School's Out*. Certainly his critique of modern education in America is based on good in-depth analysis. Certainly his charges that medieval forms of classroom teaching are not working are borne out by objective testing of students over the last two decades. Internationally US students have certainly lost ground in comparison to other nations. Given the current course of events, US education is not likely to be effectively reformed in the near term or even the longer term. Nevertheless, the idea that the Internet can largely substitute for a complete educational system is no more plausible than to say that libraries or museums can substitute for a complete learning system. There are no simple answers here.

If anyone has set forth some key seminal ideas for 21st-century learning, my vote would go to Arthur C. Clarke, the father of the communications satellite, and Edward Ploman, advocate of adaptive, experiential and life-long learning. Both of these thinkers' ideas complement each other.

Clarke has suggested that a rich new mix of teachers, learning systems and interactive media are the key to future educational systems. He has, for instance, proposed the invention of a new "user friendly" low-cost, portable, and instantly updatable product/service which he calls the "electronic tutor". The idea is to develop a device that is sufficiently low-cost, versatile, and open to multiple content that it can service millions of different educational missions in hundreds of different cultures. This--in Clarke's view as expressed some 20 years ago--was a device more likely to be developed by toy manufacturers or newspaper publishers than computer companies. Some believe that Clarke was proposing the automation of education but he was really trying to enrich the mix of information and learning sources available to students. In places where no teachers are available, the electronic tutor would serve to fill in the void at least partially.

When Clarke first introduced the idea at UNESCO headquarters in Paris in 1978, the press asked him: "Are you trying to replace teachers with a machine?" Clarke responded that he wanted to supplement the offerings of teachers not replace them, but added that: "Perhaps all teachers who can be replaced by machines should be."

Ploman also emphasized that learning systems--whether teacher-based or machine-based--need to be versatile, adaptive, focused on critical thinking and analysis, and continual throughout one's lifetime. His focus was not on clever new machines, but rather on learning through experience, through team interaction and adapting to new environments. Finally he believed in learning within a total context. He emphasized that one should not learn isolated facts but within patterns of thought and overall systems and conflicting values.

TEN STEPS TOWARD REINVENTING THE UNIVERSITY FOR THE 21ST CENTURY

The challenge of reforming, improving and extending quality education and training to a global population is huge. Nevertheless, it is possible. The main issue to attack is not the obvious targets. Clearly we need better and more up-to-date educational materials and more and better trained teachers. It is, however, the institutional barriers and the traditional images of education that are the largest roadblocks to reform. In essence it is the current structure, paradigm and objectives of schools and universities that are the biggest obstacle to progress. These barriers can and will be overcome in the 21st century. This is a significant challenge. Global reform of education to overcome the constraints of "the medieval educational model" and extend adaptive learning systems throughout the planet is comparable to such human undertakings as the Apollo Moon Project, the Great Wall of China or the Great Pyramid of Egypt. In this case the materials we must work with are not stone and steel and construction plans. Here we must work with people's minds, educational philosophies, historically formed values, and most profoundly "intellectual snobbery".

Here are ten steps modestly proposed to transform and revitalize global education and especially higher education and research in the 21st century. Here is a blue print which would allow us to educate some two billion people that currently have little education or for that matter health care. It would allow us to educate more people more effectively by releasing the learning capacity of every individual and exploiting the power of team learning and interactive critical thinking. Amazing it can all be done and at a savings of money. All we really need to do is re-invent our schools and universities, institute life-long adaptive learning, and recognize that the status quo is the enemy of effective 21st century education.

DEREGULATE EDUCATIONAL INSTITUTIONS AND STIMULATE COMPETITIVE SYSTEMS

Many would say they do not see the problem. They would say there are both private and public schools and many different types of institutions ranging from community colleges to the elite universities. This seemingly open and dynamic process, however, masks a number of problems. If education systems are working well, why do major corporations in the US spend more on their training and learning programs (and even their own universities in the cases of Andersen Consulting, IBM, Motorola, etc.) than is spent on higher education. Why, if one examines the research awards of US federal agencies such as the National Science Foundation (NSF), does one find that about 90% of major research awards are renewals of existing R&D projects and that of the new research awards the great majority of awards are to universities and institutions already with on-going work? New research awards to new institutions are thus typically under 3% of the total.

Why do we find that ground-breaking and truly innovative new ways of learning do not come from the "establishment". We see high cost and research-oriented education stemming from the elite. Yet new paradigms of learning and especially breakthroughs in tele-education, cyberspace interaction, life-long learning, and adaptive or experiential education seldom seem to come from the top of the hierarchy of prestigious learning centers. To be blunt there are few incentives and a lot of disincentives for the elite to re-invent themselves or educational systems. This is true around the world. It does not matter whether one considers the University of Tokyo, or Harvard or Yale, or the Sorbonne, or Oxford, or Cambridge. Large endowments, large campuses, sprawling research labs at major universities around the world are based upon hierarchical tiers and accumulation of academic wealth at the top. Most educational systems of the world, to use an economic theory as an analogy, are based on "Trickle-down".

Thus it is not surprising that new models and paradigms of learning seem to emerge not from the "elite" but from such groups as the National Technological University, the Open Universities, EUROPACE, TV Ontario, KNOW, the Mind-Extension University of Jones Intercable, or even the University of Phoenix and Internet based educational programs.

No one would deny that there is in the United States and many other countries what might be called an educational establishment which is based on hierarchy of institutions. Although the evidence is anecdotal, the ability to evolve new 21st century educational programs from the status quo seems in doubt. The "appearance" is that the size of the endowment and level of prestige of universities is seemingly inversely proportional to the perceived need to reform and innovate its educational process. The prestige universities have certainly not been recent leaders in deploying new educational processes in such areas as tele-education, interactive CD-ROM learning systems, educational networking, life-long learning, TQM or quality learning techniques, etc. The recent trend to have college presidents assume the role of administrator and chief fund raiser rather than intellectual leader and scholar very likely helps to perpetuate this trend.

Nothing could do more to spur new innovations in education and university research than "new and vital competition" from new sources. Withdrawing the sense of complacency from the elite university establishment could trigger major changes. New financial incentives and awards, new competition, new emphasis on networking and cyberspace technologies, new approaches to quality tele-education, and creation of a "level playing field" for educational competition could produce major results. Corporate based educational systems stemming from AT&T, TCI, and Jones Intercable with the right incentives could engender radical change in college and university teaching and research methods that have seen little innovation in decades.

INSTILL CONCEPTS OF TEAMWORK, CRITICAL THINKING, AND CONTINUAL LEARNING IN STUDENTS

Ironically, if universities and especially elite universities are not challenged by competition to innovate more rapidly, the students of these institutions may be hampered by outmoded concepts of education based upon individual achievement and competition. Most educational systems today create barriers to team-based learning. In most aspects of modern industrial and service industries, teamwork is critical to success. Modern management concepts of Total Quality Management or Time Based Management emphasize teamwork and communications. Improved performance, innovation and better results in education will come from improved communications, interactive learning and critical analysis. At the root of these is teamwork, whether in a classroom or on an interactive network.

There are a host of barriers to improved learning within schools, colleges and universities. These include a lack of creative teamwork, an emphasis on rote memorization rather than problem solving, believing that learning is sitting in classrooms, and a lack of critical thinking exercises. Further there are problems with not viewing education as a life-long and continuing exercise in a time of explosive information growth. Simply put, future education must emphasize learning how to learn. Adaptive learning and critical thinking are key to educating people for an environment wherein information grows 200,000 times faster than human population. The world's best educators need to work on new computer software, on new interactive CD-ROMs and Internet-based systems to develop new interactive systems to teach critical thinking, life-long learning, and teaming skills. These skills need to be reinforced in classroom exercises and interpersonal activities as well as through cyberspace networks.

EXPERIMENT WITH NEW GLOBAL EDUCATIONAL SYSTEMS SUCH AS INTERDISCIPLINARY AND MULTI-DISCIPLINARY CENTERS OF EXCELLENCE

As the world's information expands exponentially, global access to all information within the human knowledge system will decline. Since the time of ancient Greece, the accumulated information of our world increased by an estimated ten million times. Within the next century it will likely increase another ten million times more. We will use intelligent agents and "knobots" to acquire and filter information for us as the scope of global data systems expand beyond our individual brain processing capabilities. Some have believed that this can only mean ever higher levels of specialization and the death of the concept of a Renaissance person. Others believe the runaway growth of "passive information", the unwanted "junk" information that is spewed at us (e.g. from advertisements and infomercials) will make it increasingly difficult to get "active" information that we really want. Indeed some fear, perhaps with good reason, that the Internet, much like British Telecom's ill-fated Prestel service will break down under the weight of too much "passive" information being placed on it. (In this respect commercial software developers who build high quality and accurate data bases on Internet may prove to be its savior).

The fear of massive growth of information systems is a real concern in terms of how humans individually cope with growing "information overload". One education strategy that allows for comprehensive learning and research in the best tradition of Renaissance thinking is the new small, interactive, networked and interdisciplinary university that has both focus and multi-disciplinary participation. One specific example is that of the International Space University with a central hub campus in Strasbourg, France and almost 30 interactive or satellite campuses electronically interconnected around the world. Within the umbrella of outer space studies and research, the following disciplines are explored: space engineering and propulsion, life sciences, policy and law, the humanities, space applications, space physical sciences and astrophysics, manufacturing, resources and robotics, information sciences, and business and economics. The students and faculty of the ISU work in teams, conduct interdisciplinary design studies, and even contemplate future space missions through electronic ganglia of collaboration. They create a 20th century approximation of an "Interdisciplinary and Multi-disciplinary Interactive Brain" which is focused on space exploration, application and research. If individuals cannot know everything as individuals, then sophisticated teams of interactive people can certainly seek to do so. Such institutions would seem to need the right scale. If these institutions grow overly large, the "collective brain" concept will tend to break down. The ISU, for instance, has capped its on-campus enrollment at 140 students.

WE NEED NEW WAYS OF KEEPING SCORE IN EDUCATION: CREDIT HOURS AND DEGREES ARE INCREASINGLY PASSÉ

Possibly the worst invention in education are grades and the close second is the idea of advanced academic degrees. In many fields an advanced degree is often out of date in a matter of five to ten years. Students who cram for exams and make good grades often retain little of what they learn. Some of the best entrepreneurs and business people did poorly in their courses as students. Experts with doctorates are often poor at overall analysis and synoptic reviews aimed at system optimization. The gap between real world "smarts" and academic programs seems to have grown and particularly in theoretical and research oriented studies. The idea of the increasing specialization and the award of degrees in ever narrowing areas of expertise ultimately seems self-defeating. Our smart machines equipped with artificial intelligence, expert systems, and ever greater memory banks are well suited to become the "quasi-Ph.D" experts of the 21st century. In terms of retrieving ever greater amounts of specialized information in a particular area, it is hard to see how humans compete effectively with 7th and 8th generation computers. It is on the reasoning, judgment, and critical analysis scale and the ability to make connections, that humans still seem to have an edge.

This may be wrong-minded, but it seems that more Ph.D.s specializing in Boson architecture or migratory habits of Australian wombats is really not the answer. Instead it seems that we need to have more rigorous and challenging multi-disciplinary and interdisciplinary studies. It also seems that team-based design studies, critical thinking and problem solving skills sessions based upon actual or simulated "experience" would teach more. If such exercises were to be carried out as group competitions under real time constraints this might result in higher levels of learning than mid-term exams. The truth is that the forms, structure and processes of education have been built up over many centuries and well established traditions are often hard to question and even harder to change.

RE-INVENT ACADEMIC RESEARCH AND ESPECIALLY REFORM THE "PUBLISH OR PERISH" PARADIGM

One of the more powerful reasons that higher education is hard to change is that the current academic process feeds a large research and development complex. The most prestigious and the largest research universities are locked into a system that is self sustaining. Masters level teaching and research assistants, Ph.D. candidates, professors, governmental research agencies, and even industry have created an "industry" of specialized information generation that has less and less to do with the instructional process. Ironically this process has become increasingly like navel contemplation worthy of a Marcel Proust novel. A systematic study of research monographs, academic journals, and in-depth studies has shown that the average number of references to academic publications have decreased from over five times per article or publication to well under one. Self citations are increasingly the most common of practices. The Ph.Ds of tomorrow stand in danger of knowing what they know and sharing this information with their computers and perhaps one or two other colleagues.

Again the problem is more apparent than the solution. Clearly interdisciplinary and multi-disciplinary research programs can and will be part of the answer. A system of life-long learning and re-certification of one's academic capabilities may also become necessary. Training and certification may challenge the prestige and importance of college degrees, and colleges and universities may re-invent themselves to offer a much wider panoply of courses of study. Meanwhile, commercial establishments may well intrude on areas of learning that colleges and universities considered their exclusive preserve.

EMPHASIZE EXPERIENTIAL LEARNING AND RE-THINK THE CLASSROOM LECTURE AS MEASURE OF ACQUIRED KNOWLEDGE

An ancient Chinese proverb explains that there are three basic ways to learn. These are to hear, to see, and to do. Of these three, the "doing" is the educational process that truly works. Abandoning the idea of the classroom where the instructor drones on about what to do and does not let the student "experience" the learning is the fundamental change that cyberspace learning will accomplish. Innovators such as Jones Intercable and the Mind Extension University have concluded that a mixture of videotapes, readings, interactions with CD-ROMS or Internet web sites, and e-mail chat groups can "teach" more than a lecturer in a classroom. Students can learn better, faster, and at their own pace with cyberspace learning systems.

EXPLOIT THE BEST OF NEW EDUCATIONAL TECHNOLOGIES AND APPLICATIONS

The new information and network technologies and applications on the horizon are impressive. These include: the so-called "electronic tutor", the "smart network" and the "Internet Lite" personal terminal, and interactive multi-media educational systems that operate both in the classroom and at a distance. The electronic tutor has the potential of becoming a global mass consumption product that could rival the personal computer in sales volume. The key to developing this user-friendly, satellite-accessible, dense memory storage, and simple computing system may well be through the advent of the electronic newspaper. Such a device developed for 21st century newspapers could easily be adapted to the distance education market as well.

The prototype for the electronic tutor may well be the stripped down computer designed for the purpose of providing low-cost Internet access--the so-called "Internet Lite" line of worldwide web access devices. Add some more memory, upgrade the disc drive, and allow satellite downloading, and the "electronic tutor" is largely invented.

The true key to cyberspace education is the Internet of today and the Internet of tomorrow that will inevitably follow. The Internet is indeed a very powerful and flexible teaching tool. Why upgrade and retrofit CD-ROMs when you can put the same information on the Internet and update it as you like? Why build huge computing power into terminal devices at high-cost when you can get computing power, high-speed simulations and much more on the Internet. The problem, of course, is to get low-cost T-1 access (or Mosaic interface) to the Internet. This, too, can and will come. Time-Warner is offering such T-1 service on an operational basis in the selected parts of the US at a rate near $25 per month.

Other options will be interactive DBS satellites with narrow band return channels and even exotic High Altitude Long Endurance (HALE) platforms or Unattended Autonomous Vehicles (UAVs). These systems could in theory provide very broadband educational and broadcast services from 18 to 21 kilometer high "robot airplane" radio platforms. The costs of such a platform can be much lower than satellites even though the maximum coverage would be for countries the size of Taiwan or South Korea.

Certainly within a decade there will be a host of new cyberspace technologies and applications that will make conventional universities look somewhere between stodgy and archaic by comparison. Today's endangered universities for the most part need a crash course on the new technologies and perhaps even more so on interactive multi-media applications.

BEWARE THE DANGER OF MEGA-TRAINING

Some are greatly impressed by Internet chat groups, worldwide web information centers, interactive CD-ROM discs, direct broadcast educational systems, and the other trappings of modern electronic educational systems. They, like Lewis Perelman suggest that we should shut down the schools and universities and just let the new technology do the teaching. Certainly, automated training systems such as those developed by the innovative Ixion corporation of Seattle suggest that remarkably effective training systems can be developed. Many large corporations are more inclined to invest in automated training systems than in public education and universities. There is great danger concealed here. A system that "trains" by rote and repetition and does not provide underlying knowledge and understanding of the overall field is dangerous. It is dangerous to democratic processes, to self-esteem, and longer term commitment to a corporation's success. It creates the agenda of "de-skilling", corporate indifference, and insensitivity upon which new types of service based labor unions might well be built.

In short our new technologies contain the ability to "educate" rather than to "mega-train". It would be unwise of large corporations at the level of individual profitability and also at the social character level to contemplate the idea of training employees for narrow niches of job-specific skills. The image of what might follow has been provided in the frightening images of the future offered by Kurt Vonnegut Jr. in *Player Piano.*

RECOGNIZE THAT HIGHER EDUCATION MUST BE RELE-VANT TO CURRENT SOCIETAL NEEDS AND NOT JUST ACADEMIC STANDARDS OF THE PAST

If any modern enterprise looks to the future through a rear-view mirror it is higher education. Many university educators are proud of the fact that they are among the oldest, the most stable and most unchanged institutions in the world. Each time a new field of study emerges there is an almost ritualistic process whereby the new comer discipline is viewed with contempt, then skepticism, then grudging acceptance, and finally anointment. Computer sciences represent such a newcomer that took some 40 years to complete this tortuous path of obeisance, homage, atonement and enlightenment.

If anything, cyberspace-based education will serve to change a great deal about the academic process within universities. Institutions which ignore social relevance, avoid new technologies and applications, and neglect the power of educational networking will find their base of support will erode. The elite universities who do not see the warning signs on the wall will begin to fade away. But this process will only happen quickly if public action is taken to restructure and shake up the educational establishment--the moral equivalent of the divestiture of AT&T. Most likely, for historical and financial reasons, the "elite" will last for several decades to come. Most revolutions do not happen dramatically with royal beheadings but gradually over a generation or two.

ADAPT TO THE GLOBALIZATION OF EDUCATION, GLOBAL INTERACTIVE NETWORKING, AND THE COMING ERA OF THE GLOBAL BRAIN

The power and economics of global networking and worldwide education will be hard to deny. Nevertheless the issue of language, culture and societal norms will pose major challenges. Just because new technologies and applications will make global education more plausible and cost-effective, one should not assume that the problems of content, software, and educational process will be solved. Certainly one can assume that problems of language, culture, and religion will create major problems in even the best planned approaches to cyberspace approaches to global or even regional education.

Although the problems of creating global distribution networks and accessible user terminals around the world will remain great, the problems of software and the content of learning systems will be much greater. Even so the potential to reach the two billion people now dramatically under served by effective educational systems remains brighter any time than ever. But then again recent UN studies have concluded that there will be more people to be educated in the next 30 years than have ever been educated in the recorded history of humankind.

THE CYBERSPACE UNIVERSITY: A NEW MODEL FOR 21ST CENTURY TRAINING AND EDUCATION

For a very long time, schools and universities have been defined as buildings with teachers, classrooms and students. In the coming age of cyberspace education, interactive learning, and globalization of the learning process, the rules will change. Bricks and mortar cost money, imply the consumption of energy and complicated transport systems to shuttle students about. The idea of schools without walls, universities webbed together by electronics, and learning systems based upon new academic paradigms will not be easily denied in the 21st century.

Cracks in the establishment have begun to occur. Stanford University has embraced tele-education and is offering its courses via satellite across the US. The National Technological University has found financing to expand its satellite distribution across the Pacific Ocean. Today's prototypes such as the Knowledge Network, the International Space University, or the University of the West Indies will become tomorrow's mainstream of educational procedures. Innovative schools and universities such as Rensselaer Polytechnic Institute, California Polytechnic State University and the Téléuniversité of Québec are experimenting with multimedia-based classes both on and off campus.   These approaches include development of digitized versions of a conventional course wherein students do not sit in large lecture halls, but instead spend more time "problem solving" with the same content. They are thus able to move from a passive learning mode to an active learning mode and in a smaller and more intimate learning environment. When translated into the CD-ROM media then students can learn on their own rate and with the own area of special interest. These mechanisms can not only be highly effective but also very cost efficient as well with such CD-ROM materials being produced in quantity at $40 per copy or less.

Generations from now a new "elite" and a new university establishment will arise at the top of cyberspace educational institutions. A new Internet will generate greater controls, greater security, and massive information storage, processing, sorting and distribution capabilities. By this time new reformers will begin to call for a new order.   That is, however, decades away.   The reforms of today's system will begin seriously by the start of the 21st century. If the so-called information highway ever comes to mean something in a societal sense, it will mean the increasing triumph of cyberspace learning systems over traditional schools and universities. The future of the university need not be dim.   For the university still is the entity with the best capabilities to evolve to become the cyberspace learning system of tomorrow. The keys are simple. One has only to develop and implement the new electronic technologies and applications, be extremely sensitive to the key cultural, social, legal and political issues, experiment with the best of the systems and adapt them as necessary to the needs of both the academic community and the economic marketplace of tomorrow. The time to begin prototyping and perfecting these systems for both the developed and developing world is certainly now. The endangered university is just that.   In its current form it may have 20 to 40 years left, but the Medieval university is losing its resilience to change and quickly so.

The importance of these changes should not be neglected. The reforms are needed to create a global educational system of information exchange. They are needed for environmental and social reasons as well. Most important they are needed because today's schools, colleges and universities are not meeting society's needs. If we only use Socrates' words as our guide everything may still turn out all right.

AGENDA FOR 21ST CENTURY EDUCATIONAL REFORM

At the Institutional Level Deregulate Education and Stimulate Competitive Learning Systems

1. Instill Concepts of Teamwork, Critical Thinking, and Continual Learning in students.
2. Experiment with New Global Educational Systems Such as Interdisciplinary and Multi-disciplinary Centers of Excellence.
3. Develop New Ways of Keeping Score in Education: Credit Hours and Degrees Are Increasingly Passé.
4. Re-Invent Academic Research and Especially Reform the "Publish or Perish" Paradigm.
5. Emphasize Experiential Learning and Re-Think the Classroom Lecture as Measure of Acquired Knowledge.
6. Exploit the Best of New Educational Technologies and Applications.
7. Beware the Danger of Mega-Training.
8. Recognize that Higher Education Must be Relevant to Current Societal Needs and Not Just Academic Standards of the Past.
9. Learning will thus need to become a much different and On-going life-long process.
10. Adapt to the Globalization of Education, Global Interactive Networking, and the Coming Era of the Global Brain.

MANAGEMENT

THE STRATEGIC ARMAMENT RESPONSE TO THE CHALLENGE OF GLOBAL CHANGE

by

James L. Morrison and Ian Wilson

Planning is an iterative activity. If the world did not change, we would only have to develop one plan and stick to it. However, we live in a turbulent world. David Brinkley, during the breakup of the former Soviet Union, stated that each day seems to bring the dawn of a new era. Certainly the fall of the Berlin wall, the unification of Germany, the breakup of the Warsaw Pact, and the breakup of the Soviet Union, have transformed our world. The European Community may include Eastern Europe in the largest free trade zone the world has yet seen. In response, other free trade zones are in the making (e.g., the North American Free Trade Treaty between Canada, the United States and Mexico possibly incorporating countries in Central and in South America; Australia and New Zealand). Are these signals of another momentous event—international free trade with its concomitant dislocations of workforces and industries?

In such a world we need a planning model that allows us to anticipate the future and to use this anticipation in conjunction with an analysis of our organization—its culture, mission, strengths and weaknesses—to define strategic issues, to chart our direction by developing strategic vision and plans, to define how we will implement these plans and to specify how we will evaluate how well we are implementing these plans. The fact that the world is changing as we move forward in the future demands that the process be an iterative one.

We want our organizations to succeed. In order to prosper, we must acquire the support and resources our organization needs to fulfill its mission. We measure success by how well we accomplish our organization's mission and vision.

STRATEGIC MANAGEMENT

Strategic management is a technique you can use to create a favorable future and help your organization to prosper. To create this favorable future, you must involve your organization's stakeholders (i.e., anyone with a vested interest in achieving your organization's goals) in envisioning the most desirable future and then in working together to make this vision a reality. The key to strategic manage-

James L. Morrison *is professor of educational leadership at the University of North Carolina, Chapel Hill, and* **Ian Wilson,** *principal of Wolf Enterprise, San Rafael, California.*

ment is to understand that people communicating and working together will create this future, not some words written down on paper.

Strategic management does not replace traditional management activities such as budgeting, planning, monitoring, marketing, reporting, and controlling. Rather, it integrates them into a broader context, taking into account the external environment, internal organizational capabilities, and your organization's overall purpose and direction.

Strategic management is congruent with the quality movement's emphasis on continuous improvement. Indeed, the emphasis on anticipating the needs of stakeholders is a critical component of external analysis. Certainly organizations that adopt a total quality management philosophy will be better prepared to meet the challenge of competing in the global economic marketplace.

Each organization's experience with strategic management is unique, reflecting the organization's distinct culture, environment, resources, structure, management style, and other organizational features. However, our experience in working with leaders and managers in a variety of organizations indicates that similar questions and concerns develop as organizations implement strategic management. Leaders who have addressed these questions and concerns have developed a common basis of experience that is valuable for those just beginning a strategic management process. This section summarizes some of the things we have learned in working with a variety of organizations. First, let's contrast strategic planning with strategic management.

Strategic planning marks the transition from operational planning to choosing a direction for the organization. Organizations that use a strategic planning model do so because they are sensitive to volatility in the external environment. With strategic planning, the planning focus goes beyond forecasting population shifts and concentrates on understanding changing stakeholder needs, technological developments, competitive position, and competitor initiatives. Decisions, then, are better attuned to the external world. Managers use strategic planning as a management function to allocate resources to programmed activities calculated to achieve a set of goals in a dynamic, competitive environment.

Strategic planning was pioneered by General Electric in the 1960s, widely adopted in the corporate world in the 1970s. In the 1970s, however, when strategic planning was being widely applied, external events were still viewed as relatively stable, and planning was typically retrospective, or, at best, present oriented. Times were still good for businesses and other organizations. There was often a tendency for staff to prepare strategic plans—and for management to put them on the shelf. Strategy did not pervade day-to-day operations.

In contrast, strategic management not only creates plans attuned to assumptions about the future, but also focuses on *using* these plans as a blueprint for daily activities. The chief executive of a strategically managed organization must be able to imbue the organization with a strategic vision so that the organization's members are able to think big (institutionalized strategic thinking) and act big (institutionalized courage). The chief executive must be able to deal with the uncertainty of contemporary events and turn these events to the organization's advantage. Managers must be superb at continually adjusting competitive strategy, organizational structure, and modus operandi as the marketplace demands. In a strategically managed organization, top managers accept change as a permanent condition.

THE STRATEGIC MANAGEMENT MODEL

FIGURE 1

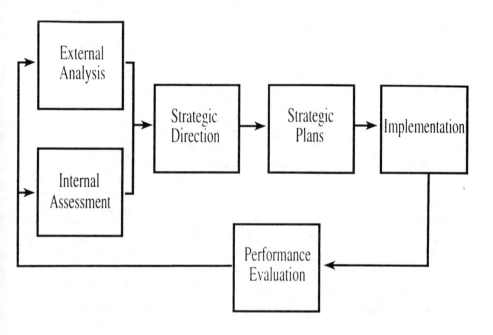

The building blocks for a comprehensive strategic management model are shown in Figure 1—external analysis, internal assessment, strategic direction, strategic plans, implementation, and performance evaluation.

This model is based on the strategic management model developed by the United Way of America in a series of guideline booklets titled *Strategic Management and United Way.*

EXTERNAL ANALYSIS

A key premise of strategic management is that plans must be made on the basis of what has happened, is happening, and will happen in the world outside the organization with a focus on the threats and opportunities these external changes present to the organization. The external environment includes social, technological, economic, environmental, and political trends and developments.

There are two major reasons for beginning with an external analysis. First, this analysis will have implications for organizational change and development. Second, by having leaders from all functional areas of the organization involved in the analysis, it should be easier to obtain their cooperation in making adjustments in response to the external analysis.

INTERNAL ASSESSMENT

We must understand why the organization has succeeded in the past, what it will take to succeed in the future, and how it must change to acquire the necessary capabilities to succeed in the future. To do this, we must

- evaluate the organization's management and operations,
- evaluate the organization's resources—people, money, facilities, technology, and information,
- review the organization's future needs,
- compile a list of the strengths and weaknesses that will have the greatest influence on the organization's ability to capitalize on opportunities.

STRATEGIC DIRECTION

The organization has a mission, or reason for being. In this component we make explicit the strategic vision for the organization's future—an idea of where the organization is going and what it is to accomplish.

We use the information developed in the first two components, external analysis and internal assessment, to review the organization's mission, set goals, develop strategic vision, and determine the most critical issues the organization must address if it is going to achieve this vision. Mission review is the foundation and authority for taking specific actions. Goals are broad statements of what the senior leadership wants the organization to achieve. Strategic issues are the internal or external developments that could affect the organization's ability to achieve stated goals.

We use the following criteria to identify crucial strategic issues: (a) The *impact* they could have on the organization, (b) the *likelihood* that they will materialize, and (c) the *time frame* over which they could develop. We limit the list of issues to a manageable number (three to nine) to enhance the chances of securing the commitment and resources necessary to effectively act on them.

The objective of the strategic direction component is to help ensure that the organization's vision and goals:

- are compatible with the organization's capabilities and complement its culture,
- foster commitment and cooperation among key constituencies
- maximize the benefits inherent in environmental opportunities and minimize the liabilities inherent in environmental threats
- enhance the organization's position relative to critical success factors (i.e., those organizational elements that distinguish success from failure) and its ability to achieve its goals.

STRATEGIC PLANS

Once we agree on the direction the organization should take and the issues we must address to get there, we must derive *strategies* of how to get there. Developing strategies is the fourth step in the strategic planning process. We call this step *strategic plans.*

Strategic plans are the documented, specific courses of action that define how to deal with critical issues. They result from the development and evaluation of the alternatives available to the organization. If the critical strategic issues are truly important, and if the mission statement reflects the organization's fundamental priorities, the strategic plan should last for three to five years. In this component we develop plans that reflect the following characteristics:

> creative reflecting input from all the organization's important constituencies, both internal and external,
> consistent with the organization's direction as expressed in its mission and goals,
> position the organization so it can capitalize on its greatest strengths and opportunities and mitigate the effects of the most serious threats and weaknesses,
> action-oriented and flexible—while remaining effective—to a variety of conditions.

IMPLEMENTATION

Strategic management is more than just developing strategic plans. It involves *managing* the organization strategically. From day to day, leaders must manage the organization so that its strategic plans are *implemented*.

Implementing strategic plans calls for development of the right organizational structure, systems, and culture, as well as the allocation of sufficient resources in the right places. Implementation—the execution of selected courses of action—is a crucial step in the strategic management process. It is essential to involve, from the very beginning of the process, individuals and groups who will help to carry out the strategic plan.

Implementation also requires ongoing motivation. This means showing individuals and groups how their work has helped achieve the organization's objectives. The plan must remain a highly visible driving force within the organization. Implementation of the plan must become an integral part of day-to-day operations. It is not something *extra* to do; it is *the* thing to do. As such, it is the impetus for motivation, recognition, and reward.

PERFORMANCE EVALUATION

One important system needed to support the strategic plan is a *performance evaluation* system. We need this to know if the plan is being carried out and if it is achieving the anticipated results.

Performance evaluation is the comparison between actual results and desired results. It keeps the planning and implementation phases of the management system on target by helping the organization adjust strategies, resources, and timing, as circumstances warrant.

In this step, we establish a system to monitor how well the organization is using its resources, whether or not it is achieving desired results, and whether or not it is on schedule. The monitoring and reporting system is continuous, with periodic output reviewed by teams, while major evaluations are conducted on an annual basis. A dual benefit of performance evaluation is that it subjects the strategic plan to discussion and testing in the context of the real world.

ENVIRONMENTAL ANALYSIS IN THE CONTEXT OF STRATEGIC MANAGEMENT

Wayne Gretzky, one of ice hockey's all-time greats, once said, "I skate to where the puck will be." The external analysis component of strategic planning has the task of ascertaining where the puck will be. This component consists of *scanning* the environment to identify changing trends and potential developments, *monitoring* specific trends and patterns, and *forecasting* the future direction of these changes and potential developments. Merged with an internal assessment of the organization's vision, mission, strengths, and weaknesses, external analysis assists decision makers in formulating strategic directions and strategic plans (see Figure 1).

ENVIRONMENTAL SCANNING

Aguilar (1967) identified four modes of collecting scanning information. *Undirected viewing* consists of reading a variety of publications for no specific purpose other than to "be informed." *Conditioned viewing* consists of responding to this information in terms of assessing its relevance to the organization. *Informal searching* consists of actively seeking specific information, but doing it in a relatively unstructured way. This is in contrast to *formal searching,* a proactive mode entailing formal methodologies for obtaining information for specific purposes.

Morrison, Renfro, and Boucher (1984) condensed these modes to passive and active scanning. *Passive scanning* is what most of us do when we read journals and newspapers. We tend to read the same kinds of materials—our local newspaper, perhaps a national newspaper like the *New York Times* or *The Wall Street Journal,* and an industry newspaper. We don't tend to read *In These Times* or *Rolling Stone.* The organizational consequences of passive scanning are (1) we do not systematically use the information as intelligence information for the organization and (2) we miss ideas that may signal changes in the macroenvironment that could affect our organization. In order to broaden our perspective and to fight the myopia inherent in us all, we need to use active scanning.

Active scanning focuses attention on information resources that span the broad areas of social, technological, economic, environmental and political sectors—locally, regionally, nationally, and globally. In active scanning, it is important to include information resources that represent different dimensions of the same category (i.e., include *The New Republic* and *The National Review* for the political sector, national level). The list of information resources described later are in a matrix of information resources at the national and international social, technological, economic, environmental, and political (STEEP) levels.

Fahey, King, and Narayanan (1981) described a typology of systems of scanning used by organizations. *Irregular* systems are used on an ad hoc basis and tend to be crisis initiated. These systems are used when a planning committee needs information for planning assumptions, and conducts a scan for that purpose only. *Periodic* systems are invoked when the director of planning or of research periodically updates that scan, perhaps in preparation for a new planning cycle. *Continuous* systems use the active scanning mode of data collection to systematically inform the strategic planning function in an organization. The rationale undergirding this mode is that potentially relevant "data" are limited only by one's conception of the relevant macroenvironment. These data are inherently scattered, vague, imprecise, and come from a host of varied sources. Since early signals often show up in unexpected places, the scanning purview must be broad and ongoing. The goal of environmental scanning is to alert decision-makers to potentially significant external impingements before they have crystallized so that decision-makers may have as much lead time as possible to consider and to plan for the implications of this change. Consequently, the scope of environmental scanning is broad—like viewing a radar screen with a 360 degree sweep to pick up any signal of change in the external environment.

ENVIRONMENTAL MONITORING

The terms scanning and monitoring are often used interchangeably, but monitoring follows scanning. Every possible change or potential shift in the macroenvironment cannot be given equal attention. We select items by defining topics or ideas that are incorporated in "the interesting future"—the period in which major policy options adopted now could probably have significant effect (Renfro & Morrison, 1983, p. 5). We lay aside those trends and events that are important, but not critical *at this time*, and collect data periodically on them. These data are "monitored" so that changes in the status of these trends and potential events can be detected.

Also, the signals of change identified in scanning, if interpreted as having potential impact on the organization, must be monitored. The goal of monitoring is to assemble sufficient data to discern the past and future direction of trends or to enable us to estimate the strength of indicators of potential events. Thus, scanning enables you to identify critical trends and potential events. In monitoring use descriptors or indicators of these trends and potential events as key words in your systematic search to obtain information about them. When collecting data in the monitoring activity, look for information that contains forecasts and perhaps speculation about the implications of the trend or event for schools.

FORECASTING

Forecasting entails ascertaining the future direction of trends or the probability that potential events will occur within a certain timeframe (e.g., 10 years). Trend forecasting may be accomplished mathematically (e.g., using regression techniques) or judgmentally. A problem with mathematical forecasting is that this technique is based entirely on historical data and a conceptual framework that requires that all relevant independent variables have been identified and measured. Moreover, this technique cannot take account of developments that may affect the relationship between relevant variables or the projected trend itself.

Judgmental forecasting requires that members of the planning team read the information gathered in the monitoring stage, and, using their judgment, estimate the direction, speed, scope, and intensity of change in trends and events. How long will it take for a new development in educational technology to become commonplace? Will present concern over the education of the children of migrant workers result in legislation? Will the change in the demographic composition of the population intensify? These are the kinds of questions that form the grist for forecasting. Their answers can be straightforward projections by planning team members, or can be addressed by multiple scenarios laying out different paths of likely developments focused around the immediate question.

SCENARIOS AS A FORECASTING TOOL

Anyone who has anything to do with planning for any type of organization immediately and instinctively turns to some sort of forecast of the future as a starting point. Why? Because we have all been educated to believe that if we are to make decisions about the future of an organization, we must first know what the future that the organization will have to deal with will be like.

On the face if it, that is a reasonable proposition. Yet in reality we are asking for the impossible—certainty and predictability in an uncertain world. The further out the horizon of forecasting, the more unreasonable is the demand. But, even for the shorter term the expectation of precision is a snare and a delusion.

The future is, in a profound sense, unknowable. But not everything is uncertain; some things are relatively predictable. We can do a respectable job of "sensing" the basic dynamics of the future and the alternative courses they might take. Building on this foundation, scenarios steer us on a middle course between a misguided reliance on prediction and a despairing belief that we can do nothing to envision the future, and, therefore, cannot shape our future.

SCENARIO-BASED PLANNING

The term "scenario" is taken from the world of theater and film, and refers to a brief synopsis of the plot of a play or movie. In a planning context, scenarios can be described as "stories of possible futures that the institution might encounter." Scenarios are graphic and dynamic, revealing an evolving future. They are holistic, combining social, technological, economic, environmental, and political trends and events, the qualitative as well as the quantitative. They focus our attention on potential contingencies and discontinuities, thereby stimulating us to think more creatively and productively about the future.

By basing decisions on alternative futures, and by testing planned actions against the different conditions these scenarios present, we are better able to prepare for uncertainty, and to endure that our decisions are as resilient and flexible as possible to deal with contingencies that we might deem "unthinkable."

THE SRI MODEL

One way to develop scenarios is to turn the job over to a brilliant futurist or an imaginative planner to sketch out alternative possible futures that our planning should consider. The fundamental problem with this approach, however appealing it might be, is that the decision-makers—those who will ultimately use the scenarios—do not "own" them: the scenarios remain for ever the product of someone else's thinking, and so lack the credibility necessary for them to be the basis for action.

To deal with this problem a team at SRI International developed an approach that (a) is a structured blending of rationality and intuition, and (b) relies on decision-makers themselves to develop their own scenarios. We found, in a wide variety of organizations, corporate and non-profit alike, that we could build into the process the highest degree of understanding and commitment to use the scenarios.

The approach utilizes a relatively simple six-step process (See figure 2)

FIGURE 2

THE SRI MODEL OF SCENARIO DEVELOPMENT

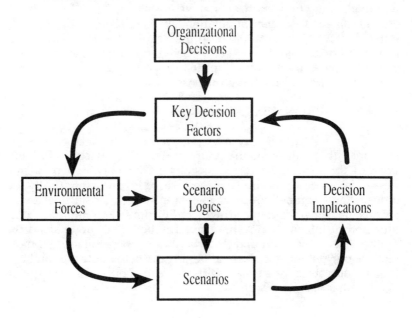

STEP 1: ORGANIZATIONAL DECISION(S)

The process starts, not by plunging into a description of the future, but rather by clarifying the strategic decisions that we are faced with, and which the scenarios should help us address. The decision can be as broad as the strategic future of the organization (e.g., "What vision of our organization should we pursue?)," or as specific as the development of a new program (e.g., "Should we use electronic communications networks to promote individualized, off-campus/at-home educational programs?"). Regardless of the scope of the decision, clarifying the "decision focus" of the whole process is doubly important. In the first place, it serves to remind us that scenarios are not an end in themselves: they are a means to help us make better strategic decisions. They must, therefore, be grounded in our planning needs. Secondly, this focus considerably eases the problem of how to use the scenarios. Without it, the scenarios would too easily drift into broad generalizations about the future of our society; and their implications for our particular organization would be lost.

STEP 2: KEY DECISION FACTORS

Having thought through the strategic decision we want to make, we are then in a better position to examine the "key decision factors." It is easiest to think of these factors as "the main things we would like to know about the future in order to make our decision." Granted that we cannot actually know the future, it would still be helpful—if we are planning for an educational institution—if we had some "fix" on, say, potential student population, availability of funding, or the state of information technology in the year 2000 (or whenever our planning horizon is). Once again, clarifying in our minds what the essential decision factors are helps to focus the work-process on what is important for our planning purposes.

STEP 3: ENVIRONMENTAL FORCES

Next, we need to identify the organization's markets, and assess key forces that will shape the future of these "key decision factors." We can think of these forces as falling into one of two categories—microforces that impact most directly and specifically on industry and competition; and megatrends such as shifting demographic patterns, economic growth and income distribution, and the diffusion of information technology. The better we understand the multiplicity, interaction and uncertainties of these forces, the more realistic our planning is likely to be and the better able we can be to prepare ourselves for sudden shifts in trends and the onset of what would otherwise be surprises.

Next, we need to sort out these trends, ranking each in terms of its strength of impact on the organization and degree of uncertainty of the trend developing as we conjecture (a simple "High-Medium-Low" scoring system as portrayed in Figure 3 will suffice). As a result of this sorting out, we can focus our attention on:

- "High impact/low uncertainty" forces—these are (we think!) the relative certainties in our future for which our planning *must* prepare.
- "High impact/high uncertainty" forces—these are the potential shapers of different futures (scenarios) for which our planning *should* prepare.

FIGURE 3

PROBABILITY-IMPACT MATRIX

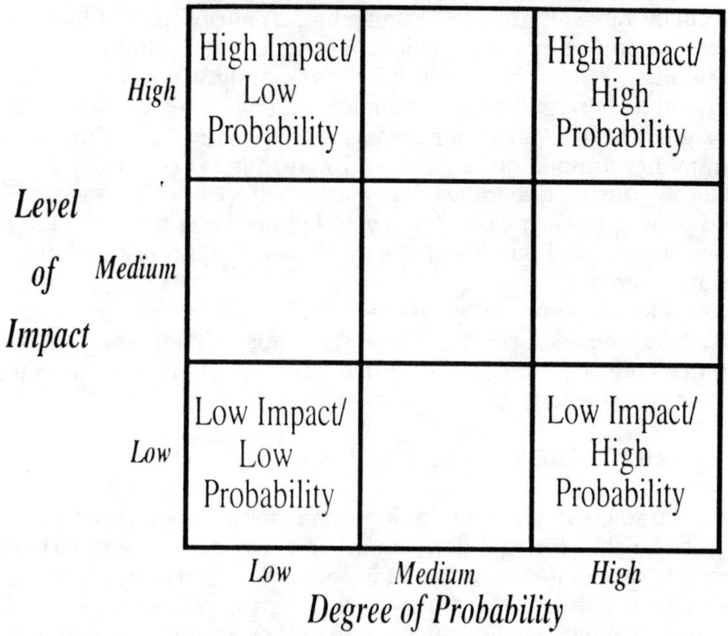

	High	High Impact/ Low Probability		High Impact/ High Probability
Level				
of	*Medium*			
Impact				
	Low	Low Impact/ Low Probability		Low Impact/ High Probability
		Low	*Medium*	*High*

Degree of Probability

STEP 4: SCENARIO LOGICS

This step is the heart of the process and establishes the basic structure of the scenarios. If we examine the "high impact/high uncertainty" forces, we will likely find that most of them can be grouped around two or three critical "axes of uncertainty." Each of these axes presents two opposite "logics"—different views or theories of "the way the world might work" in the future. For example, one axis might pose the alternative views that "education will continue to be primarily a public sector responsibility" or "privatization of education will increase dramatically as the role of government in our society decreases." (Bear in mind that these are polar opposites, with intervening mid-points: but the essence of scenarios is, not to examine every, possibility, but to force our planning to consider the possibility of drastically different futures.)

The interplay of these axes and their alternative logics will present us with the basis for selecting 3-4 scenarios that we believe effectively bound the "envelope of uncertainty" that faces us.

STEP 5: SCENARIOS

What do we end up with? What do scenarios look like? There are many forms that scenarios can take, but the three most important features are:

- Compelling "story lines"—Remember: scenarios are not descriptions of end-points (e.g., what does education in the year 2000 look like), but narratives of how events might unfold between now and then, given the dynamics ("scenario logics") we have assigned to that particular scenario. These story lines should be dramatic, compelling, logical, and plausible.
- Highly descriptive titles that convey the essence of what is happening in each case. After people have read the story lines, they should find the titles to be more memorable encapsulations of the scenario.
- A table of comparative descriptions, to help planners and decision-makers see how the scenarios differ along given dimensions (e.g., student body demographics, available funding, business-education partnerships).

STEP 6: STRATEGIC IMPLICATIONS

This is the stage at which we seek to interpret the scenarios, linking them back to the strategic decision(s) we focus on in Step 1. There are many ways of looking at this question of "strategic implications," but perhaps the simplest and most direct approach is to answer two questions: 1) What are the main opportunities and threats that each scenario poses for our organization? 2) How well prepared are we (or can we be) to seize these opportunities and avert or minimize the threats?

HOW CAN YOU USE SCENARIOS?

Beyond the opportunities/threats assessment exercise in step 6, there are several approaches to using scenarios in strategy development that are worth considering.

Perhaps the most obvious way to use scenarios is to employ them, in effect, as "test beds" for the organization's current strategy. What is a "strategy"? In simple terms, a strategy deals with the "how," "when" and "where" of an organization's actions to achieve its vision. Every organization has a strategy (although often it is not clearly spelled out) so this use should always be possible. This exercise can be as straightforward as a judgmental assessment by workshop participants as to how well (or badly) the strategy "plays out" in each scenario. A start would be to go through an opportunities/threats assessment (see above), and then to use this assessment to address a second set of questions. Are we satisfied with the resilience of our current strategy, its flexibility to deal with different possible conditions? Are there things we could do to improve its resilience? And (importantly) are there contingency plans we should put in place to help us move in a different direction, should that be necessary?

Another use of scenarios is to stimulate us to explore new strategy options. Look at it this way: scenarios portray different futures, and these different futures would obviously require different strategies. Our difficulty lies in not knowing which future will evolve. We can, however, go beyond evaluating our current strategy to exploring these new options, scenario by scenario. We do not have to develop a complete strategy for each scenario; we need merely use our imagination to start some "what if" thinking. Frequently we will find that a new option, one that we thought of in connection with, say, a "High Privatization" scenario, might be a good action to take in any case; maybe not to the same extent, but a "good bet" surely.

The fundamental argument for scenario planning goes somewhat like this. In an age of incremental change, it is safe to say that incremental changes in our strategies will suffice. However, an age of discontinuities and massive uncertainties requires discontinuous strategies, sometimes radical changes from our past practices. The powerful feature of scenarios is that they stretch the envelope of our thinking, both about the future and about our strategies.

CONCLUSION

The tools of environmental analysis—scanning, monitoring, forecasting, scenario planning—used in the context of a model that uses these tools to expand vision, formulate strategic direction and strategic plans, implement these plans, and evaluate the implementation, enable us to shape the future of our organization and meet the challenges of global change.

REFERENCES

Aguilar, F. *Scanning The Business Environment*. New York: Macmillan, 1967.

Brown, A., and E. Weiner. *Supermanaging: How To Harness Change For Personal And Organizational Success*. New York: Mentor, 1985.

Brown, L. R., C. Slavin, and S. Postel. *Saving The Planet: How To Shape An Environmentally Sustainable Global Economy*. New York: W. W. Norton and Co, 1991.

Coates, J. F. "Issues Identification And Management: The State Of The Art Of Methods And Techniques," *Research project*, 2345-28. Palo Alto, CA: Electric Power Research Group, July, 1985.

Corson, W. (Ed.). *Global Ecology Handbook*. Boston: Beacon Press, 1990.

Fahey, L., W. R. King, and V. K. Narayanan. "Environmental Scanning and Forecasting in Strategic Planning: The State of the Art," *Long Range Planning, 14*(2), 1981, pp. 32-39.

Fahey, L., and V.K. Narayanan. *Macroenvironmental Analysis For Strategic Management*. New York: West Publishing Company, 1986.

Marien, M. (in press). "The Good Books Imperatives: Keeping Up In Futures Studies," In J. F. Coates & J. Jarratt (Guest Eds.), *The Annals of the American Academy of Political and Social Science*, Neubury Park, CA: Sage.

Marien, M. "Scanning: An Imperfect Activity In An Era of Fragmentation and Uncertainty," *Futures Research Quarterly, 7* (3), (September, 1991), pp. 82-90.

Mecca, T. V., and J.L. Morrison. "Pathways to the Future: Linking Environmental Scanning to Strategic Management," *Community College Review, 15*(4), 1988, pp. 35-44.

Morrison, J. L. "Establishing an Environmental Scanning Process," In R. Davis (Ed.), *Leadership and Institutional Renewal*, New Directions for Higher Education: No 49. San Francisco: Jossey-Bass.

Morrison, J. L., W. L. Renfro, and W. I. Boucher. *Futures Research and the Strategic Planning Process: Implications for Higher Education*. ASHE-ERIC Higher Education Research Report No. 9. Washington, D.C.: Association for the Study of Higher Education, 1984.

Neufeld, W. P. Environmental Scanning: Its Use in Forecasting Emerging Trends and Issues in Organizations. *Futures Research Quarterly, 1*(3), (September, 1985) pp. 39-52.

Renfro, W. L., and J. L. Morrison. "The Scanning Process: Getting Started," In J. L. Morrison, W. L. Renfro, & W. I. Boucher (Eds.), *Applying Methods And Techniques Of Futures Research*. New Directions for Institutional Research No. 39, (pp. 5-20). San Francisco: Jossey-Bass, 1983.

Wilson, Ian. Strategic Planning Isn't Dead—It Changed, *Long Range Planning, 27* (4), 1994, 12-24.

Wilson, Ian. Realizing the Power of Strategic Vision. *Long Range Planning, 25* (5), 1992, 18-28.

Stokke, R.R., T. A. Boyce, W. K. Ralston, and I.H. Wilson. Visioning (and preparing for) the future. *Technological Forecasting And Social Change, 40,* 1991, 73-86.

United Way of America. *Strategic Management and United Way.* Washington, DC, 1985.

TECHNIQUE FOR STRATEGIC MANAGEMENT

by

George Korey

Over the long term, the most effective yardstick against which to measure the success of an organization--be it a corporation, association, or university--is the achievement of expected results. To ensure optimum effectiveness in the interaction process, it is necessary for the organization to perform competently in three primary areas of management activity: planning, execution, and appraisal and to make the best use of organization's resources in a changing environment. This is the job of strategic management.

In a dynamic sense, organization is a planned effort to achieve a proper general order; in a static sense, organization is also an order achieved or an organizational structure. In other words: "An organization is the structural aspect of a philosophy, while administration is the implementation of that philosophy."[1]

This structure reflects the integration of the overall needs as established by the purposes of the enterprise, the requirements of streamlined work flow, and the contributions of the best available human potential, so essential for the survival and growth of any organization. One can truly say that this structural organization is a nervous system, assuring effective direction and control of the whole.

An organizational structure is only a vehicle for accomplishing results; therefore, the ideal organizational system should be operations-oriented rather than accounting-oriented. Operating management's needs are numerous, and the approach to their fulfillment can only be effective if appropriate information is available quickly, in a form that is concise and simple, and yet, which provides a perspective and sufficient tools for quality executive judgment.

N. Stewart[2] lists the following five essential pre-requisites to the attainment of effective coordination in any organization:

1. Well defined goals and policies, with clear delegation of responsibilities;
2. An up-to-date, functional communication system in the management ranks;
3. A clear understanding of the various kinds of coordinative efforts and their limitations;
4. A personnel management system conducive to good personnel relations; and

---

George Korey *is president and professor of Canadian School of Management, Toronto, Canada.*

5. Alertness in guarding against over-functionalization and its hazards.

In most corporations, the board of directors, on recommendation of the president and vice-presidents, formulates basic policies and objectives, and approves the organizational structure. In any organization, the first management function is planning, which involves the choosing of basic goals and places for accomplishing the work. The second function is organizing, which entails deciding how to marshal the human, physical and other resources necessary to accomplish the task. Third is the actual performing of the responsibilities. Fourth is controlling, making sure that the responsibilities are carried out in accordance with the plan set forth in the first place. Fifth is appraisal function, which is the final step in the management process and involves looking over the work that has been done and determining whether it meets the basic objectives, standards and criteria set forth in the original plan.

As problems in the whole management process are quite often of an organizational nature, it is essential to strive towards achievement of a logical and well-functioning organizational structure. Institutions that expect to successfully survive the dramatic changes of the 1980s and 1990s must constantly up-date their organizational and decision-making structures.

NEW MANAGERIAL TECHNIQUE AND ITS APPLICATIONS

Among the biggest problems facing administrators today is the proper delegation of authority and decision making. So many decisions are made each day that many executives spend all of their working day doing nothing else but deciding. Often, however, many of the decisions that executives make can only be processed by some other person. In other cases, persons are forced to make decisions without the aid of useful information because of difficulties in communications between departments. Situations of this kind may often lead to bad decisions.

It might be worthwhile to pinpoint problem areas or organizational flaws that could have an adverse effect on the smooth functioning of any organizational structure. The following problems seem to arise frequently:

- the absence of clearly-formulated objectives and policies
- a lack of experienced professional executives and managers
- difficulty in establishing a hierarchy of problems (confusion between primary and secondary problems or functions)
- the overlapping of authority and duplication of functions
- the delegation of responsibility without concurrent authority
- confusion between line and staff functions

- difficulty in enforcing the coordination between individual units or departments
- excessive executive control
- the unnecessary splitting of functions
- the combining of unrelated duties in departments
- a lack of uniformity in designating functions.

There is a management tool known as Linear Responsibility Charting[3] (LRC), which is extremely effective in overcoming such difficulties. It offers organizational experts a dynamic yet flexible approach that assists them in analyzing the functions, problems, decisions, and organizational structures within the complex strategic management process. This technique visually portrays the distribution of responsibility for the gathering of information, its analysis and synthesis, the whole decision-making process and the recommendation, approval and implementation of policies.

One of the main advantages of LRC is its usefulness in analyzing the contributions of several people when they are consulted for the making of a complex decision. It demonstrates clearly where definite responsibility lies for work performed, points out procedures to be followed in managerial decision making and action, explains who should be involved in the decision-making process in specific situations, and suggests organizational improvements.

At a time when it is recognized that the most important role of management is to prepare effective future managers--LRC could prove invaluable. *It facilitates a positive organizational response to change by developing an awareness within management of the advantages, both organizational and personal, of team work and close collaboration, and of the eventual necessity of adapting to forthcoming change.*

By designating who is to be responsible for performing an activity, who should supervise it, who ought to be consulted or notified with regard to that activity, and all of the other special relationships that the individual undertaking the task must observe, LRC eliminates work duplication and the overlapping of responsibilities. This versatile technique also shows who does what in each department, whether a key-man is being bypassed, or whether an administrator is spending too much time on routine work that can be delegated to others. It is a graphic method of recording and analyzing: (a) organizational structures, (b) departmental relationships, (c) environmental evaluation, (d) strategic alternatives, (e) executive job content, (f) functional responsibilities and authority, and (g) decision-making processes. As such it can be very useful in Strategic Management.

LRC shows at a glance the procedure to be followed in taking action and in executive decision making. It designates clearly, all of the positions of the parties involved in the action or decision, the degree of their involvement, and their interrelationships. Besides eliminating work-duplication and the overlapping of responsibilities, it invites interest and participation from all those connected with the preparation of a LRC.

LRC has already proven itself effective in clarifying and refining the organizational structures of many North American firms. It has shown itself to be particularly adept at organizing different activities where requirements and interrelationships are especially complex, because it presents such a clear picture of the intricate processes of decision making in which several people take part.

In our opinion it has also great application in Strategic Management. The traditional way to show "who does what" in any institution was by means of a box-type organizational chart. Often this chart was supported by an organizational manual outlining the specific responsibilities for each position on the chart. As organizations become more complex, however, and more dependent on *pooled brainpower*, the box-type organizational chart manifests serious shortcomings. Originating from military *chain of command* tables, it is subject to broad misinterpretation, often creating overlapping authority while providing no true picture of job content and its inter-relationships.

In LRC's favor is that it gives management a visual picture of job relationships without having to wade through a heavy volume of reading material. Thus, there is less chance of misinterpreting the meaning of various responsibilities and relationships. By means of a series of graphic symbols, (see figure 1) LRC provides understanding of how and why strategic decisions are made and especially of (1) who's responsible for getting the work done, and (2) the procedure to be followed in taking action and making decisions.

LRC may be applied to any type or size of an organization, or to any specific department within it. In fact, it is the smaller unit, where one person can often represent a bottleneck in decision making, that needs LRC most. Possibly, the biggest argument in its favor is that it covers all management levels in such a way that there is a livelier sense of participation.

The mechanics of LRC are simple. One starts by preparing a chart (see figure 2) listing in logical order, on the left-hand side of a specially-designed sheet, the activities, or steps to be followed. Across the top of the sheet one writes the job titles of the men who will either perform these duties personally or who will have some responsibility in accomplishing the job functions.

Because of its graphic form of presentation, it is possible to put on the linear responsibility chart a responsibility symbol denoting the proper degree of involvement (even when this is minimal) in the decision-making process. This symbol is inserted in the appropriate box at the intersection of the horizontal and vertical lines where the job title and the actual activity meet.

FIGURE 1

DEFINITION OF SYMBOLS
FOR LINEAR RESPONSIBILITY
CHARTING

1. **Work is Done** - This means that the activity or function described is actually performed by the individual designated.

2. **General Supervision** - This covers the important aspects of planning, delegation and control of the function described. It is more in the nature of administrative work where hour-to-hour direction is neither practical nor proper.

3. **Direct Supervision Over Work Done** - At senior level this signifies direct participation by the supervisor in the activity being supervised. At lower level this signifies a more hour-to-hour check on the activity as carried out by a subordinate.

4. **Supervision With Coordination** - Where two or more individuals or groups must work cooperatively on the same or similar activity and where it is necessary to bring about a unified approach to the function described, then the person responsible for the coordination is marked with this symbol.

5. **Decision on Points Specially Submitted** - This applies to decision-making activities either where a specialist must be approached for technical decisions which affect a part of the overall problem or where delegation is extensive and only occasionally are decisions referred up to supervision.

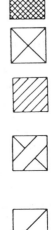

6. **Person Must be Consulted** - Before a decision or an action is taken, the individual marked with this symbol must be consulted. His opinion must be heard though his advice need not be followed.

7. **Person Must be Notified** - Upon making a decision or taking an action, the individual marked with this symbol must be advised. Knowledge of the action or decision will assist them in carrying out their own responsibilities.

8. **Person May be Called in for Exchange of Views** - This is self-explanatory. The emphasis is on "may". There is no need to consult, or right of consultation. This symbol should be used only where it is logical to expect a probable benefit from consultation.

APPLICATIONS IN FUNCTIONAL ORGANIZATION ANALYSIS

As far as functional organization analysis is concerned, LRC accomplishes the following tasks better than the tradition chart or organizational manual:

1. It simplifies executive control, improves, and accelerates executive decisions.

2. It simplifies and speeds up the making of a management audit.

3. It quickly spotlights organizational errors, and points out how to take remedial action.

4. It shows how to facilitate changes in assignment of duties and authority when a change in key personnel occurs.

5. It facilitates realignment of tasks when activities are expanded or contracted because of changing business conditions.

6. It allows anyone to check whether a given executive is putting too much time and effort into routine activities instead of executive work.

7. It provides a basis or comparison of procedures of similar departments and other organizations or institutions.

FIGURE 2

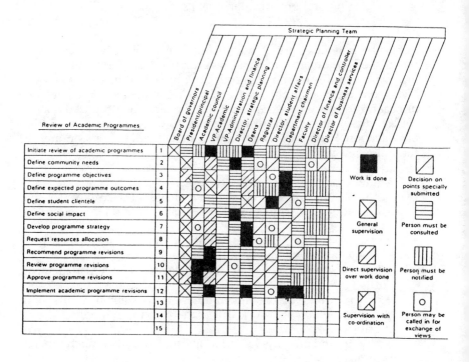

The immediate challenge to top management people lies in dealing with accelerating change in the very complex managerial setting with its multilateral perspectives and multi-directional relationship network. They must face the inevitably increasing interdependence and learn how to deal with it successfully. With this goal in mind, the mobilizing of human potential will be essential.

The executive's job is very complex and dynamic. It requires among other factors:

- executive vision
- intellectual competence
- thorough analysis of purpose
- emotional stability
- managerial capacity
- human relations skills
- sound judgment
- planning and organizational skills.

Once basic policies and general management objectives have been established, an organizational structure must be determined according to plans and programs, in order to implement these objectives.

Then one must ascertain exactly what kind of people and what kind of organization are necessary in order to reach the proposed goals.

LRC attains beneficial results when functional analysis of the organizational structure is performed or when decisions on any of the following problems must be reached:

- how to simplify executive controls
- how to improve and accelerate managerial decisions
- how to spot organizational errors quickly and how to correct them
- how to facilitate changes in duties and authority when personnel changes are made
- how to simplify, speed up, and make one's own management audit
- how to realign tasks easily in times of expansion or contraction
- how to eliminate work duplication and overlapping of authority
- how to find out whether an individual gives too much time to routine work
- how to eliminate unnecessary overhead quickly
- how to determine the distribution of duties and the accompanying degrees of responsibility
- how to designate the work load according to the individual, the department, or the activity
- how to set up visual management controls
- how to use this tool in improving administration and coordi-

nation of different functions
- how to classify routine, supervisory and executive, work and evaluate managers
- how to furnish the basis for fast corrective action whenever it is required.

The growth of the scope of LRC depends largely, of course, upon the number of executives who will be willing to explore its unlimited potential.

LRC USE IN DECISION MAKING

In order to appreciate more fully the usefulness of LRC in the area of decision making, one has to visualize the involvement of top management in this very complex process which often requires contributions from several people and departments before the final decision can be made. As is known, a company's effective action depends on the executive's skills in decision making and the delegation of responsibility. In such situations, LRC proves particularly valuable in that it quickly points up inconsistencies in the delegation of authority and responsibility. It is also an aid in exposing jobs which are unbalanced in terms of workload; moreover, it reveals whether people who should be are informed or consulted on each decision and whether pertinent information is being brought to the attention of the decision maker.

As organizations become more complex, it is necessary to rely on logical systems for decision making rather than merely on the intuition or luck of the one deciding. There are certain basic steps which assist an executive in reaching a rational decision. The effective problem-solver must:

- **Define the problem**: In order to find a proper answer one must begin with the right question. Isolate the problem and discover the symptoms. Find out whether there is one central problem or several secondary ones.
- **Determine the objectives**: List short-, medium-, and long-term goals.
- **Determine and analyze the factors influencing these goals:** Visualize the problem in its entirety, determine why it has to be solved; separate it into workable components, list, in order of their importance, the facts to be considered in making the decision. Accept the uncertainty, consider the accompanying risks.
- **List the possible alternatives**: Relying on available information, examine the accumulated evidence and outline all of the possible solutions.
- **Compare possible solutions or course of action:** Exclude solutions which are, in your opinion, unworkable. Outline the

advantages and disadvantages of each solution, evaluate its strengths and weaknesses, pros and cons.

• **Choose the most logical solution:** Decide which is the best solution or combination of solutions; double-check their ramifications and select the course of action that will fill immediate needs and that will also be adaptable to changing business conditions.

• **Determine specific details necessary to carry out the decision:** Act on your decision; put your plan to work using straight thinking, initiative, persistence, selecting the right people to make your decision work; communicate clearly, check for any errors that may develop, learn from previous mistakes, make corrections and modifications as they are needed; watch the timing, follow up and set controls to eliminate any future errors.

Although, it is certainly true that a good decision does not make a leader, the person who reaches the top and remains there usually enjoys making decisions and develops a knowledge of how to make the *right* decisions. When an orderly approach to decision making is pursued, fears of the process gradually subside. As nothing succeeds like success, the best way to eliminate the fear of decision making is to make a series of successful decisions. The executive who achieves is powered by the ability to act decisively; he makes decisions and acts upon them promptly. Nonetheless, after deliberating on all of the facts, he must still come to grips with the more uncertain human element--with the emotional instead of the rational. It is people who often mean the difference between success and failure; hence, the importance of analyzing the parts played by various people in an organization.

It is true that the decision-making skill of an executive is primarily based on his ability to define, classify and assemble facts and to select the right solutions. But the success of an executive also depends on the people who work for him, on their willingness to carry out his/her decisions, and on their own capabilities. Therefore, it is of primary importance that he communicates clearly to others, explains concisely what is expected of them and be able to instill motivation in them.

One method of accomplishing this is to show his subordinates how the proposed changes will benefit both the organization and themselves personally. More and more often, however, it is becoming necessary to involve subordinates in the process of decision-making. In general, those who contribute toward finding a solution, are willing to try harder to make a success of the plan. Here again, LRC can be of great assistance to the decision-making machinery through:

• **Decentralization of Authority and Responsibility**: Permitting employees to make decisions at their own level.

- **Elimination of confusion through improved organizational structure**: Permitting decision making at the point of available information.
- **Facilitation of information flow.**
- **Motivation of employees**: Providing them with a common purpose in overall goals and objectives and a feeling of achievement.

Since every decision involves judgment, wisdom, understanding, balance, and timing, it must be based both on known data and on opinions. It is the latter factor, based on exhaustive information from all possible sources, which plays an important role in increasing the chances of better decisions.

LRC USE IN STRATEGIC MANAGEMENT

Strategic management is a decision process leading to the development of objectives, formulation of an effective strategy and implementation of the strategic plan.

Model of strategic management (see figure 2) illustrates this decision process by showing the steps to be taken by the corporation once the enterprise's objectives have been defined. They are: environmental analysis of trends and opportunities, examination of the company's internal strengths and weaknesses, consideration of alternative strategies possible and choice of appropriate strategy for the enterprise, allocation of resources to implement the strategy, and development of procedures and functional policies to assist in strategy implementation. The final step is evaluation of results, ensuring that the company objectives have been met.

Each of the components of the strategic management process requires contributions of several people whose input is needed to prepare a mission statement defining the basic reason for the existence of the corporation, or formulation of specific goals the company is seeking, or to do environmental analysis.

For example, in the process of formulation of objectives many factors (and consequently many opinions of management people) have to be considered, like:

- internal resources of the enterprise
- internal power relationships
- external environments
- external power relationships
- traditional corporate objectives of the enterprise
- developmental stage the company has reached
- values of top management
- goals of company's top executives.

In the process of environmental analysis opportunities and threats to the enterprise have to be determined as a result of analysis of the following factors:

- economic
- demographic
- geographic
- social
- market competition
- technology development
- powers of suppliers
- governmental policies.

Thus strategic management process is not only defining *where* the corporation should be at a certain time, but also planning *how* it will get there and through a budget and implementation plan providing *timetable* and *direction* for the corporation.

The planning function embraces here both vertical and horizontal perspective and strategic management model provides a practical guide for both centralized (corporate) planning and decentralized (SBU--Strategic Business Unit) planning.

What has been said above regarding strategic management process for business corporations is equally applicable to non-profit corporations like hospitals, universities, or colleges. When I decided in 1976 to establish the Canadian School of Management, I developed a model that specifically differentiates among three phases: planning, management, and control. The reason for this is that very often academic strategic planning is just that--planning. But in order for an academic institution to be successful, the management part of this process is even more important and so is the final part, evaluation and control. Strategy without implementation is weak. It is only through feedback from the management and evaluation phases that we learn how successful the planning was.

Strategic management, as a decision process, is an embodiment of the team management concept. Nowhere is it more important to have the whole managerial team participating than in strategy formulation and strategy implementation process.

LRC technique for a number of years successfully used in organizational audits is of particular value when several people must be responsible for different activities in varying degrees. Or when environmental diagnosis is based on several opinions resulting from the analytical process:

- as to the nature of the problem,
- how to take advantage of an opportunity, or
- how to manage threat effectively.

LRC offers a dynamic yet flexible approach that assists analyzing activities, problems, and decisions within the organizational structure when several people are involved in either work performed, or work supervised and where other people must be consulted in the process of decision making. Such situations, of course, always are encountered in strategic planning and management.

Once the strategic management process and its different activities have been clearly represented in graphical form on LRC necessary improvements can be made. The analysis process itself sometimes brings to light obvious means of improvement.

LRC facilitates a positive organizational response to change dynamics by developing an awareness within management of the advantages of participative team management work and close collaboration.

This technique shows at a glance the procedure to be followed in taking action and in decision making.

It designates clearly all of the positions of the people involved in the action or decision, the degrees of their involvement and their interrelationships. Besides eliminating work-duplication and the overlapping of responsibilities, it invites interest and participation from all those connected with the work and the preparation of a linear responsibility chart.

The chart provides management with a visual and instant picture of existing position relationships, thus lessening the change of misinterpreting the meaning of various responsibilities, relationships and different degrees of involvement in the process of decision making.

Since several people are usually responsible, in varying degrees, for either the work itself or for the decision, LRC is helpful in that it shows who does what part of it, by using the appropriate symbols. These symbols denote:

1. **Work is done**: This means that the activity or function described is performed by the individual designated;

2. **General supervision**: This covers the important aspects of planning, delegation and control of the activity described. It is more in the nature or administrative where hour-to-hour direction is neither practical nor proper;

3. **Direct supervision over work done**: This usually signifies direct participation by the supervising official in the activity being supervised;

4. **Supervision with coordination**: Where two or more individuals or groups must work cooperatively on the same or similar activity and where it is necessary to bring about a unified approach to the function described, then the person responsible for the coordination is marked with this symbol;

5. **Decisions on points specially submitted**: This applies to those decision making activities where either a specialist must be approached for technical decisions which affect a part of the

overall problem, or where delegation of authority is extensive and only occasionally are decisions referred up to superiors;

6. **Persons must be consulted**: Before decision or action is taken the individual marked with this symbol must be consulted. His/her opinion must be heard though his/her advice need not be followed;

7. **Person must be notified**: Upon making a decision or taking an action, the individual marked with this symbol must be advised. Knowledge of the action or decision will assist him/her in carrying out his/her responsibilities;

8. **Person may be called in for exchange of views**: This symbol is self-explanatory. The emphasis is on "may". There is no need to consult, or right of consultation. This symbol should be used only where it is logical to expect a probable benefit from consultation.

When this kind of graphic charting is used for the purpose of functional organization analysis--as the author has been doing during the last thirty years--the organizational task is seen on a single sheet in its totality. It presents an overview of the complete situation. The organization can suddenly be seen in its dynamic sense, a planning effort which seeks to achieve defined objectives and a proper general order in coordinating different necessary functions. And since strategic management is such a dynamic activity, involving many people who participate to a different degree in the decision-making process, it is ideally suited to the exploration of LRC as a useful management technique.

STRATEGIC PLANNING

Which is the first step of strategic management, is usually defined as the process of developing and maintaining a strategic fit between the organization and its changing environment. This process involves examining major trends in the environment; translating these trends into environmental threats and marketing opportunities; assessing the institution's resource position in terms of strengths and weaknesses; formulating objectives compatible with the major trends; developing feasible strategies for attaining the objectives; establishing the organizational structure and systems required for executing the strategies; and developing measures for evaluating performance.

Whether it is "first generation planning" or contingency planning called "second generation" there are numerous situations where LRC can be used successfully, for example:

- to analyze corporate objectives and define the mission
- to conduct environmental analysis and diagnosis
- to analyze strategic advantage factors
- to develop strategic alternatives

- to consider resources allocation
- to develop specific marketing strategy, etc.

There are virtually unlimited opportunities to use LRC in strategic management both for business corporations and for non-profit organizations like universities and colleges.

It can be used at all stages starting with definition of mission and objectives, or environmental threats and opportunities, internal competitive advantage or resources allocation. For each component, a chart should be prepared listing on the left side activities to be performed and at the top of the chart, showing executives who will either do them, or supervise them or who will be consulted on the issues.

For example, when an internal competitive advantage chart is prepared, items under review will include, among others:

- company's market's geographic coverage
- nature of marketing policies
- product line performance
- distribution policies
- pricing and credit policies
- advertising and promotion policies
- manufacturing advantages
- production scheduling and control policies
- research and development policies
- financial policies.

The degree of involvement of different executives will be shown by appropriate symbol, so that contribution to the review process will be expected from each executive whose position is listed at the top of LRC form.

Figure 3 illustrates a typical chart for the company's *External Environmental Analysis*.

To better visualize LRC's possible use in strategic planning for academic institutions, let's consider different elements of a strategic plan for a university or college (figure 2).

If, for example, we choose to do the *Review of Academic Programs* utilizing this method, we will have to decide on activities or steps to be done in following a strategic planning model (Figure 4).

FIGURE 3

INSTITUTIONS

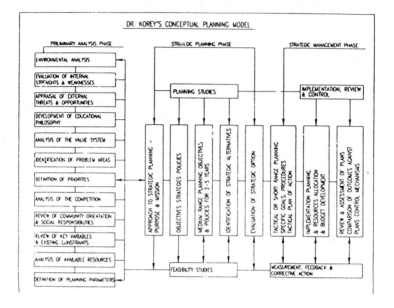

On the left side of the LRC chart, the following steps would be listed:

- Initiate review of academic programs
- Define community needs
- Define program objectives
- Define expected program outcomes
- Define student clientele
- Define social impact
- Develop program strategy
- Request resources allocation
- Recommend program revisions
- Review program revisions
- Approve program revisions
- Implement academic program revisions

Each step to be taken will involve several people. Some of them will be actually doing the work, others will supervise it, generally or directly, others will be consulted, some might be consulted on specific points, many have to be advised about changes. All these can be shown by appropriate graphical symbol denoting the specific involvement of a person listed at the top of the chart.

Using this method a business corporation might analyze its:

- profitability objectives
- marketing objectives
- employee-related objectives
- efficiency objectives
- innovation objectives
- social responsibility objectives

or a set of strategic factors.

The application of LRC in strategic management are really unlimited. This method can be used at every step when several people are participating in the decision-making process. For example:

UNIVERSITY ENVIRONMENTAL ANALYSIS

University environmental analysis would involve the following steps or activities to be listed on the left hand side of the chart:

1. Identify major trends in the *internal environment* (board, administration, faculty, staff, business advisory council, etc.).
2. Identify major trends in *market environment* (student clientele, young, traditional, continuing education, adult, professional, arrangements with professional associations, alumni, corporate employees, other university/colleges active in the market).
3. Identify major trends in *public environment* (government and its regulations, governmental funding, other financial sources, community, media, general public).
4. Identify major trends in *competitive environment* (competing institutions and their approaches, registrar's office, student recruitment office).
5. Identify major trends in *macroenvironment* (economic situation, technological forces, political climate, demographic trends, cultural environment).
6. Review implications of these trends for university.
7. Define most significant opportunities,
   a) potential attractiveness,
   b) probability of success,
8. Define most significant threats,
   a) potential severity,
   b) probability of occurrence.

9. Re-assessment of mission, objectives and goals.
10. Review the institution's mission.
11. Recommend the mission statement for approval.
12. Approve the institution's mission.
13. Review the institutional objectives.
14. Recommend objectives for approval.
15. Approve institutional objectives.
16. Review academic portfolio strategy.
17. Review marketing strategy.
18. Approve proposal strategies.
19. Review organizational changes.
20. Recommend implementation of organizational changes.
21. Approve organizational changes needed.
22. Design marketing information, planning and control system.
23. Recommend the systems.
24. Approve marketing, planning control systems.
25. Implement strategic plan,
    a) short-term/one year budget,
    b) medium term/tactical plans,
    c)long term/strategic plans.

FIGURE 4

STRATEGIC PLANNING MODEL OF EFFECTIVE ACADEMIC PROGRAMS REVIEW

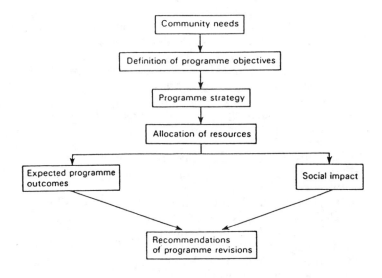

FIGURE 4A

ELEMENTS OF A STRATEGIC PLAN FOR
ACADEMIC INSTITUTIONS

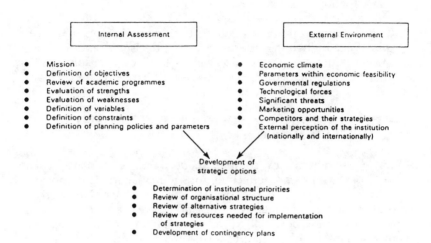

Internal Assessment	External Environment
• Mission	• Economic climate
• Definition of objectives	• Parameters within economic feasibility
• Review of academic programmes	• Governmental regulations
• Evaluation of strengths	• Technological forces
• Evaluation of weaknesses	• Significant threats
• Definition of variables	• Marketing opportunities
• Definition of constraints	• Competitors and their strategies
• Definition of planning policies and parameters	• External perception of the institution (nationally and internationally)

Development of
strategic options

- Determination of institutional priorities
- Review of organisational structure
- Review of alternative strategies
- Review of resources needed for implementation of strategies
- Development of contingency plans

Each institution would have to develop its own approach, decide on steps to be required and on the involvement of different people in preparation of a strategic plan.

The immediate challenge of corporate management and to administrators of academic institutions lies in dealing with accelerating change in the very complex administrative setting with its multi-directional relationship network. They must face the inevitably increasing interdependence and learn how to deal with it successfully. With this goal in mind, the mobilizing of human potential will always be essential.

In universities and colleges almost everybody is involved to a certain degree in the process of decision making. In general, those who contribute towards finding a solution, are willing to try harder to make a success of the plan. Here again, LRC can be of great assistance to the decision-making machinery through:

- the decentralization of authority and responsibility,
- elimination of confusion in preparation of a strategic plan,
- the facilitation of information flow,
- motivation of the university community (providing all sectors with a common purpose in overall objectives and a feeling of participation and achievement).

LRC can play an important role in both business and non-profit organizations in helping to reach better decisions and it could become a useful managerial tool in making strategic decisions in such situations where frequently encountered problems present considerable difficulties and defy systematization.

TEAM MANAGEMENT--A SOLUTION TO STRATEGY IMPLEMENTATION PROBLEMS

What is essential in most complex modern management approaches--in order to prepare effective future managers--is a positive organizational response to the change. This can only be based on the awareness of the management team of the real advantages, both organizational and personal, of collaboration and of the necessity to eventually face an adaptation to forthcoming change.

In just a few years, we will be facing a world quite different from the one in which we live today. As a result of changes that will come, we must strive to make life better from the environmental, social, and economic point of view.

The challenge for educators and for managers of future change is to make technology more responsive to our needs, so that it will provide us with solutions to social problems as well. We have to balance our increased capacity to use knowledge for practical purposes with a sensitivity to human needs, an increase in human concern and ethical values to serve mankind.

Obviously managers in the future must assume a more active and creative role in attacking the ills afflicting the business world and the whole of society in general.

What this means, of course, is first: that industrialists and businessmen must recognize the world outside their offices and respond to the challenges presented to them; secondly: that, in order to master change, we have to understand the long-range goals of society and the mechanisms of control over the forces of change; and thirdly: that we have to educate managers of accelerating change.

The immediate challenge of top management is in a complex managerial setting and multi-directional relationships network. They have to face increasing interdependence and manage that interdependence successfully. In this respect *team management* might be an answer.

Team management facilitates better group processes and allows greater personal responsibility of the individual members of the managerial team, which provides an opportunity for a greater potential for personal growth. At the same time, it allows for better understanding of organizational sensitivity and objectives and thus stimulates and encourages better communication, participation and horizontal collaboration.

Participation management through effective communication, personal commitment, better planning and improved process of decision-making contributes significantly to the adaptation to environmental change, improvement of the quality of work, to management process and productivity of the team, and to the integration of personal, team and corporate objectives increasing substantially potential for "shared goals" which are corporate and individual progress and achievement.

Team management recognizes that an executive's decision-making ability partly depends on the people who work for him/her and their willingness to carry out his decisions. Here again, LRC is a useful tool. As key subordinates are involved in the process of preparing a linear responsibility chart, part of the executive's communications job is achieved. Involvement in linear responsibility charting explains concisely to the associate what is expected of that person. The employee can see how proposed changes will benefit both the organization and the individual.

The requirements of strategic management as already now practiced and the imperative of forthcoming change will call for people with unusual vision, intellectual competence with flexibility of thinking, perception for innovation, planning and organizing ability and great human relations skills.

Team management will allow the top executives to expand their ability and activities by meaningful participation of their close collaboration. Team management allows also for development of men and women. The efficient use of human capabilities, quality of human performance, and the willingness to innovate are the key factors that will guarantee the success of future managers. Team management will allow top executives to exercise leadership, develop imaginative approaches, use effectively skills in communication, and tap individual and group resources.

In this effort LRC will prove to be a very efficient managerial tool of the next generation's managers.

NOTES

1. Charles D. Flory. (ed.) "Managers for Tomorrow," *New American Library*, 1967.

2. *The Neglected Art of Management Coordination* in Management Review, April 1960.

3. Presented by the author to the Academy of Management at its Annual Session, Boston, Massachusetts, 1975.

INVESTING IN ATTITUDE CAPITAL TO IMPROVE SERVICE QUALITY

by

Charles H. Little

INTRODUCTION

A consensus exists between business people and economists that investing in human capital fosters economic growth. An investment in the training and education of workers yields a more productive labor force. With the rapid advances in technology in recent years, a well trained and highly skilled labor force is definitely required. New technologies over time raise the level of competence required on the job and dictate continuous investments in new training and education.

In today's world, any expansion of economic activities leads to an increased demand for services from the ever-expanding service sector. Presently, about three-quarters of the labor force is employed in the service industry. Finding better ways to provide services is as important as improving the technical skills of the labor force, which is why so much attention has been directed toward service quality in recent years.

Service quality depends to a great extent on the attitudes that prevail at the time a service is rendered, that is, how the service provider approaches the problem and how the recipient perceives the service provided. To improve service quality, the attitudes of the service provider toward the customer and the job of serving should be improved. An investment in attitude capital can increase efficiency in this area. Better services can lead to higher business receipts, which represent the returns on the investment in attitude capital. The dividends will be comparable to those from investing in the technical training and education of workers.

AN ECONOMICS LESSON ON CAPITAL

In macroeconomic theory, there are four classes of inputs into an aggregate economy: land, labor, capital, and entrepreneurship or managerial ability. Capital consists of all the physical inputs, such as buildings and equipment, which are combined with the other three resources to produce the output of the economy. This basic concept has been used in economics for many years and is still taught today; however, the concept of exactly what constitutes capital has changed over the years.

Charles H. Little *is associate professor of computer information systems/decision sciences at St. John's University, New York, New York.*

In the past, capital included all the physical units needed for production, such as buildings, tools, machinery, and equipment, and was collectively referred to as "plant and equipment." As new technology came along that improved the production process, it was included in capital, although technology as such may not necessarily be a physical input. It becomes a part of plant and equipment, because it allows these inputs to be used more efficiently and results in an increase in output.

Financial resources, such as money, stocks, and bonds, are not capital in an aggregate sense; these are only assets that can be used to acquire plant and equipment. These resources are invested in capital, that is, they are used to buy more plant and equipment. This increases the stock of capital available for production, and in the aggregate, an increase in inputs yields more output. The additional production is the return on or the dividend to the investment of the financial resources. Thus, an investment in capital stimulates economic growth and development.

Along the way, the name of the labor input was changed to human capital. In this context, an investment in human capital yields dividends in the form of economic expansion and growth. An investment in the education system of the nation provides more and better training to improve and expand the skills of laborers. This investment is necessitated in large part by the development of new technologies over time. Improvements in plant and equipment mean that more capable workers are needed to operate the new computers, communications systems, and electronic equipment. A more competent labor input will produce more output, thus stimulating growth and development.

An investment in human capital also improves the productivity of the entrepreneurship input. Managerial ability depends on the ingenuity of humans. Better educated managers will be exposed to new ideas and new technologies which will improve their ability to start new businesses and manage existing operations to increase the output of the economy. The computer field offers a prime example. Without constant training and updating, no one would be able to stay abreast of the rapid advances in the field nor to see the potential advantages of adopting these inventions.

In the economy today, the majority of workers are employed by the service sector; however, there are serious questions about the quality of the service provided in the marketplace. Nearly every consumer has his or her own favorite "horror story" to relate about poor service or a total lack of service. To prove the point, just try telling your "horror story" to a group of people and see how many of them can top your tale. Service quality needs to be improved!

In a service transaction, the customer is an active participant, and his perception of service quality depends on how well he interacts with the provider. The service provider must pacify the customer even if the problem cannot be solved. The attitude of the provider toward his task and toward the customer is very important in their mutual dealings. How the customer is handled may be more important than the final outcome of their transaction. To win the customer over, the provider should start with the right attitude, particularly if there is no easy solution to the problem. In many cases, customers are content, if not totally satisfied, with a sincere display of sympathy--they are satisfied if not delighted. To borrow an economics expression, the service provider should "satisfize, if he cannot maximize."

To influence the attitudes of service providers, we need to invest in attitude capital, that is, we need to train workers to handle people and to deal with messy situations. This training could be part of the program to improve technical skills (the investment in human capital), or it could be a separate program, since some service jobs, at least, do not require a high level of technical sophistication. However, all jobs require the right attitudes about serving customers.

Attitude capital can now be added as another component of the concept of capital in macroeconomic theory. It is part of the labor input, the same as human capital. Presented in this context, any investments in attitude capital will increase economic efficiency and expand the output of the economy. Hopefully, this perspective on attitude capital can lead to improvements in the service industry comparable to those in the general labor force which resulted from redefining the labor input as human capital.

"THE OLD WORK ETHIC"

We have all heard about "the old Protestant work ethic," where people do the best job that they can and take pride in their work. As a result, they receive a psychic reward for a job done well in addition to whatever monetary compensation is involved. In today's market-place, this concept could just as easily be referred to as the old Jewish, the old Catholic, the old Hispanic, the old Afro-American, or the old Italian American work ethic — or simply "the old work ethic." The same principle holds for all religious, ethnic, and cultural groups. In particular, it should hold for service workers, who may sometimes receive more psychic than monetary reward from their jobs due to a low wage scale.

Today, it seems that the work ethic has been replaced by the "that's not my job, Man" ethic — regardless of the accent used to enunciate the expression. For example, a service provider, after no visible or only minimal effort to solve a problem, tells the customer, "You will have to speak to the supervisor, who is not here today." It seems to many customers that workers no longer try to do their best; they frequently do not seem to try at all. Pride in a job done well seems to offer no satisfaction. However, if a service provider is motivated to do his best, customers will recognize and appreciate his efforts, which will have a direct and dynamic impact on the outcome of the service encounter.

In a service encounter, problems often arise because of organizational structure and are not the fault of an individual worker, but the customer interacts with the worker, not the organization. A negative attitude on the part of the service worker can only make the situation worse. Service quality is often a fatality of a weak delivery system, resulting from a lack of commitment on the part of management to provide adequate services which in turn gives rise to the bad attitudes of employees who confront customers. Before any returns on an investment in service attitudes can be realized, a company must develop the proper organizational structure for solving problems, and the service worker must have the personal support of management and fellow workers.

Attitudes alone will not solve a service provider's poor delivery problems, and the right attitudes will work only in a supportive environment. Adherence to any work ethic stems from worker moral, which depends on an individual worker's appraisal of his situation. Before a worker can make the customer happy, he must be happy himself. An investment in attitude capital will only pay dividends in a congenial service market.

The position presented here is overly simplified and a broad generalization of current market conditions. Carried to its extreme, the solution is simply to return to the good old days when people wanted to work and were happy with their jobs. The customer comes first, and workers are only salified when customers are satisfied. There is an element of truth in this, but the answer is not that easy. If we had this paradise before, how did we lose it? Why are workers unhappy today and not willing to do their best? A lot more is involved here than just economics. The loss of the "the old work ethic" (provided it ever existed) reflects a change in attitudes throughout the whole of society, not just among service workers in their place of employment.

In addition, the concept of investing in attitude capital is not intended to suggest Big Brother or "1984." The idea is not to control the thought process, but rather to motivate workers to perform better. By defining this as motivation therapy, we are no longer dealing strictly with economics. We are now entering the realms of psychology and psychiatry, and even sociology when we consider the collective behavior of service workers. Any training program for service workers will require the combined skills of all these professions.

IS THERE A REMEDY FOR BAD SERVICE?

There has been considerable research on services and service quality both in the United States and Europe. Much of the research has examined services from a marketing or management perspective with an emphasis on "how to do it." The studies cut across a number of different types of businesses. The proceedings from the Quality in Services Conferences (QUIS) sponsored by the International Service Quality Association offer many research reports on service quality. At the present, there are three proceedings available for QUIS 2, 3 and 4 [1,2,3]. Some of the papers in the proceedings contain extensive bibliographies listing numerous other research references, and several contain reviews of the literature on service quality. The proceedings provide a starting point for those seeking information on how to improve service quality in their businesses.

One impression obtained from some of the research papers is how simple the solutions to some service quality problems can be. For example, an axiom which everyone seems to agree with is: *Do it right the first time.* There should be no need for a service follow-up. Not only is this practical, it is also less expensive. The idea is very simple, so why doesn't everyone follow the rule.

As another example, Stew Leonard's, a food marketer in Connecticut, has been cited as an excellent provider of quality service. The company has been very successful in large part because of its service offerings. (However, their image was tarnished somewhat because of certain financial irregularities.) The policy of the company is prominently displayed at the entrance to their stores: "Rule 1. The customer is always right! Rule 2. If the customer is ever wrong, reread Rule 1." A very simple set of rules that has been bandied about for a long time. Why is Stew Leonard's so successful following the rules, while other companies are not as successful or do not follow them at all?

If the answers are so obvious, why don't more business people get the message? They don't get the answers because they don't ask the right questions. This is a management problem, not an attitude problem, and it must be resolved before an investment in attitude capital will pay dividends. Successful attempts to improve service quality require a companywide commitment--first and foremost, a commitment from management at all levels. An investment in attitude capital will yield dividends only in a work environment that encourages and supports every individual's efforts to serve customers.

Another impression gained from the papers is the conceptual nature of much of a service transaction. One researcher notes that what works well is what is perceived to work well. This is all attitude. Another states that quality is what the consumer thinks it is. In many instances, the delivery process is more important than the actual delivery. How the problem is handled can be just as important as whether or not the problem is solved. From this perspective, the key to service quality is the approach that the service provider takes toward a problem situation.

One study illustrated the point very clearly. In a focus group, people were asked what they expected in the way of service, what they were looking for from a service provider. One participant replied that she wanted to deal with someone who seemed interested in her problem; rectifying the problem seemed to be secondary. Reading between the lines, she would probably settle for someone who only pretended to be interested. Since attitudes are the crux of service quality, those of the service provider will greatly impact on those of the recipient.

Business executives are coming up with the same conclusions in their regular business dealings. In a major reorganization attempt at Sears some years back, a problem that management had to overcome was the customers' impressions of "indifferent service" from the employees. Other executives are talking to their employees about "how to treat people." They recognize that their workers need to be able to "relate to customers." Business people "don't just buy, sell, or employ; they relate." Management at General Electric has acknowledged that their workers need "people skills." In a newsletter from the National Association of Business Economists, suggestions for improving one's consulting business emphasized more the importance of relating to the client than the professional competence of the consultant. These people skills are synonymous with attitude capital [4].

To use a personal example, I am very interested in Native American art and culture and spend several weeks each year visiting museums and galleries in Oklahoma. Two museums stand out very clearly. One was in a large recreational complex. A very attractive museum building was located in a wooded area and had lots of windows to bring the outside inside. At one time, there were many attractive displays, with buttons to start the audio, the video, or both. There were life-size dioramas, and many artworks by well-known artists. Unfortunately, I found during a recent visit that most of the buttons did not work, many of the dioramas were not lighted, and the pictures on the walls were crooked. The staff either would not or could not answer questions. They showed no interest in visitors, even when they purchased items at the gift shop.

The museum apparently had substantial financial resources at one time, but it was short on attitude capital. The deficiency was quite evident. The collection had deteriorated, and visitors did not go away feeling happy. Unhappy visitors will not return nor encourage others to do so. Unhappy customers do not make donations or leave artworks to museums. Even a small effort to encourage the staff to be responsive to visitors could have yielded immediate financial rewards, in particular, more purchases at the gift shop and more admission fees from happy customers.

The other museum was small with a rather eclectic collection. However, the staff and volunteers were so enthusiastic about the museum and their work that it was contagious. They were interested in you, and they wanted to help. I arrived two hours before the museum was to open; however, I was still greeted at the door and invited to enter. The director of the museum came and talked to me for a long time. The staff's enthusiasm helped to create a very enjoyable experience. As a result of their enthusiasm, the museum had received substantial donations, many artworks, and even whole collections from individuals. Though short on financial capital, the museum was long on attitude capital. The attitude capital had attracted the financial resources that the museum needed to survive and prosper.

So what is the remedy for bad service? The answer, at least in part, is an investment in attitude capital. Improved people skills can yield improved services. Better people skills are obtained by investing in the training and educating of people in how to provide services. Where will these skills be taught? They will be taught both in the workplace and in the schools. In the workplace, companies will devise their own training programs to fit their specific business needs. The schools will then be responsible for a broad education in people skills that cut across different kinds of businesses. How can workers be taught people skills? How to teach people skills is a much more perplexing quandary.

HOW TO INVEST IN ATTITUDE CAPITAL

This section might be subtitled: Is Education the Answer? The schools are the logical place to begin to teach people skills, because then workers will have the necessary mastery when they enter the job market. Existing education programs will need to be revised to accommodate the teaching of service skills. Are the schools up to this challenge? One point arises immediately: The deficiencies of attitude capital in the workplace may be due to the fact that the schools are not presently teaching the necessary people skills. If so, then administrators and educators must not be aware of the problem. Can they be convinced of the need, and will they have the necessary expertise to revamp the curriculum? Whether education is the answer or not is still up in the air.

In the US today, there are loud cries to improve the educational system. The complaints come from business leaders, government officials, and educators. "We are losing our competitive edge." "Our foreign competitors are more efficient." "Students need more science and math." "Students can't read, write, or count." "Students have no reasoning ability." "College graduates have to be retrained by business." Such comments reflect negatively on the quality of the education system today. Granted, not all the complaints are justified, but they point up the fact that existing problems have to be addressed, along with and in addition to changing curriculums to accommodate the teaching of service skills.

Rapidly expanding technologies in such fields as computers, communications, and electronics dictate a need for highly skilled workers and ways to keep them abreast of the latest developments.

The education system has to be constantly updated. The dilemma is that technology is changing so fast that the educational system itself cannot keep up. By the time a new curriculum is in place, the available information and the needs of the students have changed. A "new teaching technology" is needed that allows educators to keep abreast of what is happening in rapidly changing fields and to impart that information to students in a timely fashion.

We also need to re-examine the notion that service jobs are unskilled or low-skilled positions. For example, the job of a telephone operator is definitely not low-skilled because of the communication and computer equipment used. In addition, the people-to-people skills that the operator needs to interact with callers, though not strictly technical, are certainly not on the low end of the psychological/sociological scale of sophistication. Other service jobs may require less technical equipment, but they still involve complex personal interactions with other people. The skills for dealing with unhappy people and messy situations are definitely high tech, not low tech. Also, from this perspective, service jobs become more important to the success of a company, which adds to their stature and which, in turn, adds to the psychic rewards service workers receive for a job done well.

New technologies change the service offerings over time. For example, many small kitchen appliances are cheaper to replace than to repair today. The question then becomes what type of service should be offered the customer — repair facilities or discounts on new appliances. In the current age of conserving and recycling, throw-away appliances may not appeal to the customer. The main thrust of the service offering may entail convincing the customer that what is good for him is what is available to him, which requires a bit of "reverse psychology." The service offering must be flexible and adaptable to fix the situation at hand. This puts added pressure on the skills of the service worker, because he must be able to adapt to accommodate the situation at hand.

There must be an intermingling of new technologies and people skills to cope with the service needs brought on by new technologies. The problem will become more acute as technology proliferates over time. As the marketing situation becomes more complicated, the necessary people skills become more complex, perhaps to the point of taxing the abilities of service workers. These people skills may change as rapidly as the technology, which means any investment in attitude capital programs must be able to accommodate these rapid changes.

People skills and technical skills are actually parts of the same package. Improving people skills go hand-in-hand with improving technical skills, since we are dealing with the capabilities of one individual. An investment in attitude capital is also an investment in human capital, and people skills should be just as important on a person's resume as technical skills.

Before investing in attitude capital, we need to figure out how to overhaul the education system. Money alone is not the answer; new ideas and planning are essential. The quandary is that we don't have the time. We need a solution now; the longer we wait, the worse the problem becomes

WILL IT WORK?

Again, the answer seems too simple — just improve the teaching of people skills. So why don't businesses invest in attitude capital and offer better services? Business people also have their "horror stories" to tell about how they tried and were unable to remedy bad service situations. Even when management acknowledges that services are crucial and the company is committed to providing quality service, the end result is not always good service. Sometimes the quality of the services seems to be overwhelmed by the delivery system itself.

One of my recent "horror stories" illustrates the point. Upon answering the phone one day, an MCI operator asked if I would accept a collect call and put the call through before I could reply. The party on the other end immediately hung up. I called MCI and talked to six people, five who were supervisors of the person to whom I had previously spoken. The charge had been transferred from MCI to AT&T to NYNEX and placed on my bill. There is absolutely no way that a charge can be deleted once it has been entered into the computers. If there is an error, the customer must call to have the error corrected by hand after the bill is received in the mail. I called AT&T and spoke to several supervisors of supervisors, and they all told me exactly the same thing. I spoke to only a couple of supervisors at NYNEX but got the same answer. All three corporations, which are major service providers, could not correct a mistake of their own making. Worse yet, none of the employees that I spoke to offered an apology, only an excuse, "it was the computer's fault"--a definite deficiency of attitude capital.

When the bill arrived from NYNEX six weeks later, I called them. That was the wrong number, and I had to call AT&T. The AT&T operator requested information to verify my claim and reluctantly corrected the bill. But first, she wanted to know if I was "absolutely sure." Finally, I was allowed to subtract the charge from my bill, but still no apology. A simple expression of sympathy would have gone a long way; a little attitude capital would have paid tremendous dividends.

It is interesting that none of the employees of the three companies could correct the mistake because they shared the same computer system. Apparently, the deficiency in their service delivery system was the fault of the computer, not the fault of a person or persons. It doesn't take a rocket scientist to figure out that a computer which can be programmed to accept an entry can also be programmed to delete an entry that was entered erroneously. In this situation, the appropriate people skills could have compensated for a glaring deficiency of technical computer skills.

So a commitment to service quality, in and of itself, may not be enough. Somehow management has to get a "handle on the system" in order to deliver quality services. Some companies have successfully done this, and there are many examples of companies noted for their service. Management at other companies will have to confront their own unique problems and figure out what they need to make the commitment work for them. For example, computer problems are often only convenient excuses for other internal problems.

There is a parallel with the situation that prevailed in the production of goods in the US some years ago. In a nutshell, manufacturers were reluctant to adopt the recommendations of quality specialists that would have improved their products and their productivity. The Japanese did use these quality control tools and their products were perceived by consumers as better than those made in the US When domestic manufacturers began to lose market share to the Japanese, they started to improve the quality of their own products and also their productivity. Today, the goods of these companies compete very effectively with foreign-made goods. Of course, the worldwide business cycle had a lot to do with this scenario, particularly with the improvement in productivity in the US. The analogy is that if the bottom line of service firms is affected badly enough, that will provide the incentive for management to search for new and better ways to improve services. Many consumers think that point has already been reached.

CONCLUSION

Services are an integral part of today's economy, and service quality needs to be improved. Since much of a service transaction is attitudinal, then service quality can be improved by improving attitude capital. We need to invest in attitude capital, the same as we need to invest in human capital to keep up with new technology. In today's workplace, attitudes are as important as technical know-how.

From the perspective of economics, the aggregate labor input has been reformulated to incorporate attitude capital. An investment in human capital involves fostering the people skills needed to serve customers as well as enhancing the technical skills needed to manage and operate new machinery. Teaching attitude skills involves a different emphasis and approach, though it cannot be divorced from the teaching of technical skills.

The service provider must be convinced that his best interest lies in serving consumers well. If he is genuinely responsive to the needs of customers, then the customers will be content if not completely satisfied. In which case, we might have found the answer to a perplexing question: Where is the service in the service economy? It exists in the minds of the public being served.

NOTES

1. Scheuing, E.E., E. Gummesson, and C.H. Little. eds. *QUIS 2, Quality in Services Conference Selected Papers*. Second International Conference, International Service Quality Association. New York, March, 1992.
2. Scheuing, E.E., B. Edvardsson, D. Lascalles, and C.H. Little. eds. *QUIS 3, Quality in Services Conference Proceedings*. Third International Service Quality Association, New York, April 1994.
3. Scheuing, E.E., B. Edvardsson, S.W. Brown, and C.H. Little. eds. *QUIS 4, Quality in Services Conference Proceedings*. Fourth International Conference, International Service Quality Association, New York, December, 1995.
4. Various news and business magazines.

THE FUTURE OF MOBILE COMPUTING

by

Ralph Menzano

In January 1992, my systems development team was asked to produce a state-of-the-art, mobile computing environment for 400 loan officers. A loan officer represents mortgage companies at the point-of-sale, which in the mortgage banking industry is the initial meeting with a potential borrower who has recently decided to purchase a home or to refinance a current mortgage. In essence, a loan officer's work routine is analogous to that of a traveling salesperson selling directly to end consumers.

PROJECT DESIGN

Our initial mission was to enable a loan officer to expand territory coverage. For example, if a borrower was in Boca Raton, Florida and we did not have a branch office in Boca Raton, the travel time from the nearest branch office (Miami) would make it difficult for a loan officer to take a loan application, retrieve credit ratings, and provide required documents in a timely manner. A loan officer armed with the right set of automated tools could bypass the travel time to and from the branch. Coining the term "Branch-in-a-Briefcase," we decided to outfit loan officers with the following hardware and software:

Hardware:

- Notebook Computer, 486 Color Screen Processor
- Portable Printer
- Cellular Phone
- Leather Brief Case

Software:

- Mortgage Analysis & Retrieval System by GHR Software
- MS Word, Excel, Access (Office)
- Security System

Supplies:

- Extra Printer Ribbon
- Diskettes

Ralph Menzano *is a vice president and head of technology at Chase Commercial Mortgage Banking Corporation, New York, New York.*

- Paper
- Extra PC Battery

The functions to be performed included:

> File download of daily loan interest rates from head-quarters in Philadelphia.
> File download of borrower's credit history from a service bureau.
> Completion of Form 10-03 (Official Industry Standard Loan Application Form).
> Completion of eleven other required forms.
> File upload of the application data to interface with the headquarters legacy system.

FIGURE I

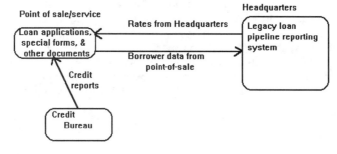

Branch-in-a-Briefcase Conceptual Design

Exhibit 1

We were able to deliver the system diagrammed in Exhibit 1 within a few months, and, after selecting several loan officers known for their outspoken support of technology, we embarked on the critical "proof of concept phase." The success of these test cases would either encourage continuation of the project to the full roll out of the tools to all 400 loan officers or send the project teams back to the drawing board.

ISSUES

At first, the participating officers were awed by the power at their fingertips, and the quality of both inputs (from the daily rate "sheet" and the credit reports) and outputs (the twelve forms). When the training began, they recognized that several complicated administrative tasks would be added to their daily routines. The issues were categorized as follows:

a) Data Input

Officers were accustomed to filling out only the rudimentary elements of an application such as name(s), address, property information, etc. They would let the back office do all the "grunt" work of completing the entire form that involved getting information from W-2, bank statements, credit history(ies), etc. The new system required a completed application in every sense.

b) Software Complexity and Training

The software required a week's training but still left the officers asking "navigation" questions. Further, the feeling that "data input" was not their job caused them to be impatient with instructors. At the training sessions, it was common to see a loan officer to leave for hours at a time to answer "sales" calls. To them answering sales calls was their real job.

c) Printer Complexity

The printer represented mechanical complexity. Attachment to the notebook, changing paper and changing ribbon were all jobs that had traditionally been performed by back office "systems people." Ribbon changing, which was in fact the most onerous task, was something most had never experienced.

d) Overall Weight

The final configuration was about twenty pounds. Even though we provided a luggage carrier with wheels, most officers responding to a post-project survey felt that weight was the single worst feature of our Branch-in-a-Briefcase configuration.

e) Loan Application Processing Time

The Loan Officers felt that the time involved in set-up, input and printout was double the time needed to take applications by hand. One officer said that if he had previously made eight sales calls a day, he would now only make four. There was no correlation, in his mind, between the quality of data gathered and the propensity of the application to become a loan. Given the mindset that more applications taken meant more loans generated, the Branch-in-a-Briefcase was clearly defeating to his purpose. Furthermore, all officers were compensated on a commission basis so that they viewed technology innovations in terms relating to their personal income.

f) Overall Expense

No matter the volume of units purchased, the best overall price for each Branch-in-a-Briefcase configuration was $8,000. If we provided a unit to each officer, the total company price tag would amount to $3,200,000 before inclusion of the cost of help desk services, project development efforts, travel, training, etc. Many executives felt the hardware, software and training should be a loan officer expense in much the same way many universities require incoming students to purchase their own PCs. Loan officers, already questioning the effects of the new tools on their income, vehemently disagreed with paying any portion of the hardware expense.

A PROMISING PROJECT IS ABORTED

Because of the aforementioned issues, the project did not progress beyond the twenty-five test cases. In addition, executive sponsors of the project left the company and their successors, because of a "not invented here" attitude or because of the actual issues, received the entire idea coolly. At that point, industry lending rates worsened so that the potential customer base declined, company cost consciousness increased, and the original concepts of territory coverage were lost. Illustrating impatience with the Branch-in-a-Briefcase project, the company selected an inexpensive (i.e., less than $50,000) telemarketing approach which was a less personal approach to selling, but which allowed use of the legacy system and, therefore, was less expensive.

The one successful use of the Branch-in-a-Briefcase involved one of the trainers who accompanied a group of loan officers to a home show. Initially there for display value, the Branch-in-a-Briefcase unit was used by the trainer to take loan applications. By the end of the eight hour show she had taken twelve of them. This proved to members of the team, that in the hands of a savvy user, the hardware and software could do the job.

After only six months, and despite its noble roots and lofty goals, the project died a quiet death. Logos created for project status reports were deleted from the LAN word processing; project members scrambled for new assignments inside or outside the firm.

The lingering question was simply, "What would we do differently if given the chance to start the project again?"

"Americans tend to build something that works and then strive for continuous improvement."[1] In business circles, a project's life cycle has become shorter due to quicker shifts of company fortunes, employment consistency, managerial changes and industry-wide upheavals such as changes to interest rates, acquisitions or mergers.

Similarly, most people connected with the project repeatedly stated that if they knew "six months" was the given time frame, the scope of the effort and thus, the functions provided by the equipment would have been significantly lessened. Specifically, each problem noted in the post-project survey could be addressed in the following manner:

a) Data Input

The initial version of the software contained over 400 data elements requiring about 300 data inputs and 100 derived inputs (i.e., data fields derived from another input field or by math functions such as when a loan officer inputs the value of the property and the amount of loan and the system calculates Loan to Value. As evidenced by the later success of telemarketing, the reality was that minimal information can be gathered at the point of service (basic borrower and property information) easily below 50 fields. All subsequent data could be collected later just as it was in the telemarketing procedures. Loan Officers would certainly embrace the minimal input idea--Their pet phrase is still "time is money."

b) Software Complexity and Training

Project members felt user-friendliness suffered for the sake of full functionality. To scale back on training, the software would need to be simplified and as ubiquitous as electronic mail, which has become second nature to even the most techno-phobic loan officers. In fact, if the application could be tied to the e-mail system, communications tasks such as rate downloads, credit file downloads and data uploads that were deemed difficult would become greatly simplified.

c) Printer Complexity

"The mechanical nature of printing makes it more difficult," said one team member; paper forms are far easier to deliver to the customer. If the officer had to carry paper anyway, it might as will be the original forms. All project members agreed to kill printing at point of service, shaving many dollars, pounds and degrees of difficulty from the project.

d) Overall Weight

In addition to discarding the printer, newer technology can reduce the weight of the notebook computer. At the time of the project, the notebook selected, with cables and recharger, weighed about 12 pounds. By 1995, the same functionality could be garnered from sub-notebooks (like the IBM 701C sub-notebook) weighing less than 5 pounds. The newer notebooks generally shed their diskette driver and narrowed their keyboards and screens to arrive at the reduction in weight. In any case, diskettes were not needed for the essential software, and color makes the screen size acceptable.

e) Loan Application Processing Time

By reducing input requirements to the point where loan officers' data input time would equal hand-written loan application time. The issue only exists when the new tools added to loan officer time.

f) Overall Expense

By reducing the scope, training requirements, and data input fields, the timing involved in taking applications would have been improved and the benefits reaped sooner. Thus the project break-even point would have been achieved more quickly. Elimination of the printer was the key element in substantially reducing hardware costs but today's sub-notebooks are similar in price to regular sized notebooks of 1992. All agreed that, following the lead of company managers at the time, loan officers should pay for their own hardware configuration. This not only reduced the hardware expenses associated with the project but created more buy-in from the users who would be more motivated to use a tool that they paid for themselves.

SUMMARY

By this January 1996, three and a half years after our project was aborted, newer technologies for future implementations of a "Branch-in-a-Briefcase" include wireless communications, smaller printers, faster computer hardware, and attached cellular phones -- all amounting to less than 15 pounds and $5,000 per unit. Functionality will revolve around the "push of a button" mentality so that the users of the tools perceive an increase in productivity. If the user suspects less productivity, the technology will not find a place in the daily work routine.

Given the new mobility and the increased user friendliness of the future configurations combined with the reduced cost of hardware, software and training associated with a more narrowly focused scope, the future Branch-in-a-Briefcase environments will have a faster payback period. A more robust, larger scope configuration featuring printers and elaborate file downloads and uploads could continue to be used at home shows, industry conferences and the like, where the need to impress may be just as important as functionality.

Tangible productivity should always outweigh technological overkill. For the everyday loan officers and their counterparts in point-of-sale or point-of-service positions, the simpler configurations will yield higher probabilities for success.

NOTE

American Productivity Institute, Quality Forum, October 1993

SUSTAINABILITY

POLITICS, SCIENCE, AND SUSTAINABILITY: THE PROSPECTS FOR AGRICULTURE

by

Clifton E. Anderson

Agricultural sustainability involves problems that are integrally connected with major, planet-wide questions of survival. Will the world's ongoing population explosion necessarily lead to widespread famine and insecurity? In a high-tech society, are individual rights, liberties and opportunities increasingly restricted as privileged elites assume more and more power? Can scientists guide policy-makers and help them to develop procedures for just and wise uses of natural resources? A host of environmental questions come to the fore when "sustainability" is under discussion. Because many persons who are concerned with environmental problems strive to attain a holistic, everything-is-connected-with-everything-else point of view, discussions may take off along dozens of different trajectories.

INSTITUTIONS IMPACT RESOURCES

The concept of sustainability, as I understand it, centers on the world's resources and the impact on resources exerted by social, political and economic institutions. If we are striving to construct just, non-exploitative economic and technological systems at the same time that we work to maintain and improve constructive social institutions, we are building sustainability. Agricultural stability, rooted in the soil and also in the visions of hard-working custodians of the soil, is a promise one generation gives to following generations; it is an assurance that producers of food and fiber can avoid actions that would jeopardize the environment.

Farm people around the world have differences and similarities. A mechanized American wheat farmer sits in an airconditioned cab as he gives guidance to a huge four-wheeled tractor. In Asia, a barefoot rice grower walks to the field carrying traditional hand tools. Technological differences aside, all farmers are alike in their need to make good use of energy, soil nutrients and other resources that nature provides.

If rich top soil is stripped away from fields by wind or water erosion, the land's productivity will be diminished. Misuse of other natural resources also will reduce long-term productivity, and agricultural production systems that invite continuing depletion of resources are being wasteful of both natural and human resources.

Clifton E. Anderson *is extension editor at the University of Idaho, Moscow, Idaho.*

Farmers who are farming as though the future does matter are sustainers. They try to sustain their farms, the overall environment and the communities in which they live.

GOALS OF SUSTAINABLE FARMING

Farming conditions vary from region to region, and as a result farmers have developed a great number of approaches to agricultural sustainability. The list of sustainable farming practices is long, but the goals of sustainable farmers fall into three main categories:

- Reducing the use of purchased production items. Instead of buying synthetic fertilizers, for example, sustainable farmers look for natural fertilizers--livestock manure, crop residues and low-value agricultural by-products. Substitutes also are sought for chemical pesticides. Recycling materials is a standard practice.
- Making sure that farming programs are ecologically sound. Soil-building legume crops are included in crop rotation. Rather than grow one crop year after year, enlightened farmers grow a variety of crops. In their diversified farming systems, they raise livestock as well as crops. Through landscape management, they avoid compaction of soils by heavy machinery and they prevent gullies from forming on erosion-prone hillsides. Non-chemical methods of pest control are developed in order to reduce expenses and also to prevent pollution by agricultural chemicals.
- Education becomes a lifelong activity for farmers whose goal is agricultural sustainability. Because they pursue long-term goals, these farmers welcome new knowledge concerning sustainable farming. Also, they conduct on-farm research to test new farming procedures. With their expanding knowledge base, informed farmers are well equipped to manage farm production and commodity marketing.

THE POLITICS OF SUSTAINABILITY

Protection of natural resources is seen by many individuals to be a sensible course of action. Depletion of resources has serious consequences, they say. Surely, there will come a time of reckoning for food production systems that take more out of the soil than they deposit there--also for energy users who recklessly consume precious fossil fuel reserves.

Despite painful disappointments in the past, confirmed environmentalists are hopeful that public opinion is now shifting to an enlightened pro-conservation stance. However, proposed environmental policies continue to be met by keen opposition. Many objections to sustainable agriculture are raised by interest groups that fear economic losses if the technology of farming is radically changed.

Businesses that presently sell chemical pesticides and petroleum-based fuels to farmers insist that their products are indispensable for today's highly productive agricultural systems. Many farmers agree. Growers who kill weeds with herbicide sprays are not eager to try to achieve weed control with cultivators, hoes and other old-fashioned paraphernalia. From a short-range perspective, the defenders of high-tech agriculture are correct. Modern agricultural systems do rely on high inputs of fuels, fertilizers and pesticides. From a long-range point of view, however, modern agricultural methods contribute to polluting and consume non-replaceable resources. In other words, agriculture as practiced by most conventional farmers is not sustainable.

Of course, farmers need to face economic realities. Their debt payments and current expenses are obligations they must meet now and in the near future. In their planning, they do make long-range calculations, but they always must be concerned with short-range profitability.

Who will bear the costs of shifting agricultural production to sustainable practices and away from resource-wasting, environment-degrading modes of farming? Farmers are apprehensive. They suspect costs of a change-over that will bring society-wide benefits is going to be imposed on producers. To win farmers' support for sustainability, ways have to be found to relieve their economic anxiety. A government cost-sharing program may be needed to facilitate the conversion of American farms to sustainable agriculture.

Years ago, when farming was a dominant economic activity in many states, politicians eagerly courted the *farm vote*. Today, farm families comprise less than two percent of the nation's population. The political power of agriculture has diminished. National environmental policies encouraging farmers to adopt sustainable agricultural practices will be strengthened and expanded only if many non-farmers take active roles in the political campaigns to promote sustainable farming. This may occur, now that environmentalists in America and Europe recognize the great impact agriculture has on the total environment. Environmentalists may decide to make agricultural sustainability the opening campaign in a national movement to save the environment.

Political campaigners of the twenty-first century should emphasize constructive solutions to environmental problems. It is clear, however, that the growth of environmental politics will require planned, concerted action on the part of large numbers of dedicated and active individuals. No one should expect to witness a spontaneous groundswell of support for sustainable agriculture or other environmental causes. It is a mistake to "assume that when specific negative conditions reach an intolerable point, they self-evidently become recognized as social problems" (Maurer and Sobal, p. x). Before agricultural sustainability becomes a major political issue, much organizing, educating, and campaigning needs to be done.

SCIENCE AND SUSTAINABILITY

Growth of science and technology has been a dominant theme of American history. It is tempting to believe that scientists will in time come up with solutions for our society's most serious problems. Here, again, wishing does not accomplish a great deal. Before scientific breakthroughs are made, much preparatory work is accomplished in research laboratories.

The directions in which science moves will depend on scientists' perceptions of how various problems should be ranked in order of importance. Agricultural researchers in 1996 assign a high priority to herbicide problems. Elimination of weeds in a certain crop would be a simple matter if the crop species possessed strong resistance to the herbicide that is to be used. The logical step, then, is to transfer into the crop genetic material to make it herbicide resistant. Resistant plants, one assumes, would thrive even under repeated doses of herbicide. Perhaps, run off of pesticide from treated fields had been an environmental problem earlier--and now it would become more severe.

Agricultural problems are persistent, and miracles--whether scientific or political--are not to be expected. Science does help bring key problems into focus, however. Scientists working on problems of sustainable agriculture have expansive research opportunities wherever they look. Studying cover crops and the beneficial effects they provide when they are incorporated into the soil, an investigator sees numerous leads to future research: the ecology of soil organisms, how they live together; the control of plant diseases and insects by toxins some plants release in the soil; the weed-suppressing allelopathic effect that is evident in oats, sorghum and other crops.

Genetic engineering's contributions to sustainable agriculture could be of great significance. New species of plants could be developed for use in various hostile environments--plants that thrive in brackish soils, in desert conditions and in short-summer areas. Plants with built-in resistance to insects and fungal diseases would not need to be treated with pesticides.

Sustainable agriculture's adherents, with their intense concern for healthy environments, would be well qualified for selecting appropriate environmental research topics. If environmental problems are to be solved, the solution must come from investigators who are aware of the complexities in ecological interactions. "Our environmental policies must ultimately be guided by ecological realities and we must devote an increasing share of available financial and scientific resources to the determination of these realities. The consequences of not doing so could be catastrophic" (Ingersoll and Brockbank, p. 220).

Site-specific research can provide answers to agricultural problems that exist at a certain farm or portion of a farm. This is the type of research proposed by advocates of sustainable agriculture. The individual farmer conducts research on his own farm, and he reports his findings to other farmers in his locality. Assisting the farmer with research design and methodology is a university scientist or some other person who is knowledgeable about agricultural research.

In site-specific research projects, farmers can test integrated pest management (IPM) systems that apply chemical pesticides only as a last resort. To manage pests on part of his acreage, a farmer may use low-input, biological controls. If his pest management experiment succeeds, the farmer will expand his IPM system to cover more acres the next year. At the same time, his experience with IPM will be shared with friends and neighbors. In the sustainable agricultural movement, farmers become involved as researchers, teachers and demonstrators. Their on-farm research results encourage them to increase their own involvement in sustainable agriculture. At the same time, other farmers in the locality are likely to become involved also.

On-farm research may lead to new approaches in farming in regard to crop rotations, tillage practices, fertility programs and pest control methods. Modest amounts of government investments in on-farm research should pay handsome dividends by speeding up American farms' conversion to sustainable agriculture.

EXPERIENCE WITH SUSTAINABILITY

Environmental groups supported proposed legislation for a sustainable agriculture program in 1984 and 1985, when a new Farm Bill was being prepared in the United States Congress. The 1985 Farm Bill called for the creation of a sustainable agriculture program, although funding legislation was not enacted until 1988. Congress authorized the US Department of Agriculture to create programs of research and education in "sustainable agriculture" or "alternative agriculture." Congress clearly called for development of a new system of farming that would have reduced reliance on purchased inputs and increased use of soil-building crops and non-depleting farming practices.

The USDA gave the new farming program a catchy name in 1988. It called the sustainable agriculture program *LISA*--an acronym for *Low-Input Sustainable Agriculture*. It soon became evident that the *low-input* label was causing "confusion and misunderstanding" (Schaller, p. 30). Business people objected to a name implying a need for reduced use of machinery, fuels, fertilizers and pesticides in all farming situations. A USDA official agreed that low input was not "an exactly appropriate term because it carries the wrong connotation, that something can be achieved for nothing" (Hess, p. 14).

In 1990, the USDA announced that the *LISA* label was being replaced with *SARE* (Sustainable Agricultural Research and Education).

Since 1990, agribusiness firms have continued to be apprehensive regarding the low-input aspects of sustainable agriculture programs. USDA spokespersons have explained that farmers do retain the freedom to practice high-input farming. Sustainable agriculture, they say, requires highly site-specific practices and, for this reason, blanket statements about reducing purchased, off-farm inputs are not appropriate. On-farm research is supposed to reveal the suitability of reducing fertilizer, pesticide and energy inputs at specific sites.

THE PROFITABILITY ISSUE

Supporters and critics of sustainable agriculture are chiefly in agreement concerning the need of farmers to show bottom-line profitability for their farming enterprises. USDA officials indicate farmers are not expected to discontinue using chemicals and other inputs unless they can reap profits by doing so. On-farm research gives the ultimate answers regarding profitability, they say.

Economics and sustainability are sometimes linked together as the two primary considerations to be reviewed by agricultural policy-makers. Supporters and critics of sustainability agree that an agricultural sustainability program should not be considered to be successful unless it shows long-term profitability.

"Profitability is a necessary, and, thus, important objective of any farming operation. However, profitability does not imply the same thing as profit maximization" (Ikerd, p. 21). Farmers who are friends of the environment may be attracted to sustainable agriculture despite the fact that their short-term profits could be greater in conventional agriculture. Profitability is important, but non-economic considerations may influence farmers' decisions. For instance, farm families who are concerned about chemical contamination of farm water supplies may prize clear water more highly than earning maximum profits by making heavy applications of agricultural chemicals. Another environmental trade-off family members might reject is applying chemical pesticides in areas where pheasants and other wildlife could be harmed.

Of course, interest in agricultural sustainability may be fanned by farmers' expectations that the voluntary conservation programs of today could become mandatory regulations tomorrow. Farmers may become involved in sustainability programs because of a growing awareness of the environmental threats posed by chemical fertilizers and synthetic pesticides. Expecting government regulations to come into effect soon, farmers may decide to be ready to comply with anti-pollution controls and other prospective regulations.

PEOPLE WHO MAKE IT WORK

Sustainable agriculture succeeds on some farms and fails on others, the Northwest Area Foundation says in a valuable report on seven states' experience with sustainability programs. One important key to success is hard work--and farm families who excel at sustainable farming evidently thrive on hard work. The report explains: "Sustainable systems replace purchased inputs such as herbicides with labor and management in order to reduce environmental health risks, and sometimes to cut costs" (Northwest, p.14).

The report also underscores "the need for scientists to understand the management technologies used by successful sustainable farms, improve them, and make them widely adaptive to other farms" (p.27). And again: "Sustainable farms...are management-centered and information-driven, and their technical needs are very intensive. They operate not by formula or prescription, but with site-specific and diverse strategies that change over time as conditions on the farm change... Sustainable farmers report that the management challenge of sustainability is one of the features that attracts them to it" (p.25).

Good, resourceful sustainable managers make use of available information and also develop on their own farms new information that will be passed on to other farmers. The knowledge transfers among today's sustainable farmers are previews of the information revolution that will take place in the countryside in the early years of the 21st century. University researchers and other persons with specialized knowledge will make substantial contributions to agriculture's new information age, but individual farmers and farmer organizations will play leading roles.

Improving the flow of agricultural information in America will be a major challenge for tomorrow's educators and scientists. Moreover, farmers throughout the Third World will benefit from US farmers' experience in confronting environmental problems in rural areas and making important contributions toward solving those problems.

REFERENCES

Hess, Charles E. "The US Department of Agriculture Commitment to Sustainable Agriculture," in *Sustainable Agriculture Research and Education in the Field: A Proceedings*. Washington, DC: National Academy Press, 1991, pp. 13-21.

Ikerd, John E. "Agriculture's Search for Sustainability and Profitability," *Journal of Soil and Water Conservation* (January/February, 1990), pp. 18-22.

Ingersoll, Thomas G. and Bradley R. Brockbank. "The Role of Economic Incentives in Environmental Policy," in Sheldon Kamieni-eki, et, al., (eds.) *Controversies in Environmental Policy*. Albany, NY: State University of New York Press, 1986, pp 201-245.

Maurer, Donna and Jeffrey Sobal (eds). Preface in *Eating Agendas: Food and Nutrition as Social Problems*. New York: Aldine de Gruyter, 1995.

Northwest Area Foundation. *A Better Row to Hoe: The Economic,*

Environmental and Social Impact of Sustainable Agriculture. St. Paul, MN: Northwest Area Foundation, 1994.

Schaller, Neil. *Farm Politics and the Sustainability of Agriculture: Rethinking the Connections*. Greenbelt, MD: Henry A. Wallace Institute for Alternative Agriculture, 1993.

GROWING GREENER PRODUCTS: WHAT WE CAN LEARN FROM PEA PODS AND APPLE PEELS

by

Jacquelyn A. Ottman

What do an apple peel, a pea pod and our own skin have in common? They are all packages that are found in nature–natural packages, if you will. They contain nature's secrets for some of the most elegant, effective and aesthetically pleasing packaging on earth. As such, they represent metaphors for helping us create exciting new packages that are more attuned to nature.

Remember when you were a kid and your mother tried to coax you into eating the peel of the apple as well as the apple itself? That's because she wanted you to have the vitamins that peel contained. Today, apple peels are being used by scientists at Clemson University as a metaphor for edible packages—disposable packages like boil in the bags that add protein to a macaroni and cheese dinner, or packages that act as a booster for laundry detergent.

Here, you will discover ways that other natural packages can stimulate creativity when generating new ideas for minimal packaging.

Are you searching for new ways to: Cut costs? Develop more efficient products and packages for retailers? Cut down on what consumers think is too much packaging? Do you feel you have cut down on existing packages as much as possible and don't know where else to cut?

What you might need is a little inspiration, some new ideas. But more important than new ideas, you need some new perspective and some new ways of thinking about environment-related challenges.

The *Getting to Zero*^sm *Process* can help. *Getting to Zero* ^sm is an innovation process designed to help client teams think in new ways and to generate new ideas for more environmentally sound products and packages. The "zero" stands for zero waste, zero energy use, zero environmental burden. In participating in this process, corporate teams literally search under rocks for new sources of creative inspiration and new paradigms for thinking about environmentally sound packages and products.

They discover what good product and package designers have known for centuries—that the best inspiration for new packages—as well as new products, buildings, etc., comes from nature.

Jacquelyn A. Ottman *is president of J. Ottman Consulting, Inc., New York, New York, advisers to industry on environmental-related marketing and innovation.*

Packages and products that are environmentally superior are simplymore nature-like: They are inherently efficient, easily recyclable, and often they use recycled materials or materials made from renewable resources.

In trying to address environment-related challenges, doesn't it just make intuitive sense to get to the source? Starting today, make room on your Environmental Packaging and Product Committees for Mother Nature!

What follows are three of the many techniques at the core of the *Getting to Zero*^{sm} process for using nature as a source of creative stimulation for environmentally-sound product and package development. These techniques have already helped product developers and marketers to think about their environment-related challenges in fresh new ways. They not only lead to lots of new ideas and new ways of thinking, but they can make the new product and package development job easier, more satisfying, and a lot of fun.

GETTING TO ZERO^{sm} PROCESS TECHNIQUES

Technique #1: Emulate nature's models directly

Many consumer products have been inspired directly by nature. The camera mimics the human eye. Helicopters, like hummingbirds, can hover and fly backwards. Velcro brand fasteners were inspired by prickly burrs attached to a Scottish inventor's boot.

Some of the most exciting green products on the market today are rooted in natural principles. IBM's PS/E computer hibernates when not in use so it saves energy. Mazda's 929 car has solar cells on its roof that run a ventilating system when the car is parked in the sun.

By matching the respiration rate of vegetables, W.R. Grace's breathable package keeps produce fresher longer.

Some of the best examples of minimum impact packaging now on the market also borrow some of their magic from nature. For example, a good way to reduce packaging is to package in bulk. Nature has a way of packaging in bulk. It's called the pea pod. And it's very possible that it was used as inspiration for use in packaging eggs, and packaging people, if you will, in airplanes.

Eastman-Kodak took this idea and adapted it. In addition to single rolls of film each wrapped in its own carton, Kodak now markets bulk packs of film. Their three-pack has been so successful, they are now coming out with five packs—and that means more sales and more profits.

Nature has devised ingenious ways of making her work lighter. One way is called gravity. (Have you ever seen water run uphill?) This principle is at work in Colgate's cartonless toothpaste tube. Standing the tube on its head eliminates the need for a carton, and the gravity helps to solve the age-old problem of getting all of the product out.

Colgate now has a package that appeals to users of tubes and pumps alike. And they've been able to inject some news into their marketing efforts. The label sports the message: "NEW. Clean and Easy Stand up Tube."

Technique #2: Study nature's processes

Study how nature does the same things you are trying to do. This can help you clarify the issues, and it can come in handy when trying to communicate the issues to your peers and to consumers.

Do you realize that there are no landfills in nature? In nature, nothing goes to waste. Everything is recycled. Manure fertilizes the fields upon which cows graze. Soil represents decayed plants and animals.

In nature, burial is a form of preservation, not waste management. The squirrel that buries his acorns in Fall expects to find them in Winter.

Landfills don't have the air and water to sustain the microbes that decompose waste. So landfills, as garbologists have been trying to tell us, are really giant holding pens for old tires, old packages and other trash.

The real issue then, with packages that wind up in landfills is not what material they're made of—so long as no toxics are present—but how much air is contained in the packages when they are thrown out.

Knowing this could prompt one to develop collapsible packages. Not surprisingly, nature has a good model for collapsible packaging: the bladder. Several manufacturers have developed successful new minimal packages based on this concept.

DuPont's Mini-sip pouches, for example, use 70% less material than individual milk cartons. They are now being used to serve milk to over a million school children.

L&F Products' SMART refill packs took an idea commonly used in Canada and Europe and evolved it, if you will, for Americans. Their stand-up pouches for Resolve and Direct household cleaners have a spout so they're more convenient to use. The result: broad distribution, increased brand loyalty—and more sales.

Finally, Air Packaging Technologies has created what they call an Air Box—a collapsible package that relies on the protective power of an air cushion to cut down on packaging by 90%. Their latest version is re-usable.

Technique #3: Change the System

No man is an island, and no package is either. There are many opportunities available for reducing packaging by making changes within the system in which your product or package operates.

Back in high school biology you learned that in ecosystems, all organisms are interrelated and interdependent. Trees, for example, sustain squirrels who then help to distribute the seeds that reproduce the trees. The strength of Apple Computer is thought to come as much from the ecosystem of hardware and software companies that has grown up around it as much from the company's own internal resources.

Packages are intricately linked to a system of distribution, in-store shelving, consumer attitudes and habits, and municipal waste disposal.

What we're finding these days, is that more often than not, the best opportunities for reducing packaging lie in changing the system in which packaging operates rather than the packages per se.

Knoll Furniture made changes to its trucks and loading docks and reduced its packaging by 90%. Ethan Allen is cutting down on packaging by protecting the corners of some of its furniture with corrugate, and nesting the pieces inside one another on their trucks.

Coke got rid of some of its cartons by siphoning syrup directly into McDonald's restaurants.

There is only so much lightweighting that can be done before one needs to change a product's entire delivery system in order to generate further significant reductions. That's what Procter & Gamble discovered when they achieved a 75% packaging reduction by concentrating the Downy product and packaging it in a little milk carton.

THE FUTURE

I believe the greatest opportunities for packaging in the 1990s and beyond will come about by changing the system in which products are delivered to consumers.

Think about it. Lowly rolls of toilet paper are designed to work with dispensers that are built right into homes. Cereal dispensers integrated into stores, allowing consumers to heavy up on the raisins, and go light on almonds. Soft drink dispensers built right into refrigerator doors designed for use with collapsible refill packs.

Another opportunity I see is for edible packaging. For it is only with packaging that is truly consumable, I believe, will we be able to once and for all justify the value of packaging to the consumer while solving some of our formidable resources and solid waste challenges.

Making "changes to the system" will not be easy, of course. It will take cooperation from internal cross-functional teams, from retailers and distributors. And it may even require that product manufacturers work with other companies– like manufacturers that make dispensers and others. And it will only be natural that you do this: In nature, organisms are continually evolving into more cooperative and complex ecosystems.

If you want to get this type of thinking going in your own company, start with some of the techniques used in the *Getting to Zero*^{sm} Process:

Distill the essence of your package's function and ask: How would Mother Nature do it? Ask: How does nature protect things, transport seeds? Get rid of its waste? Communicate? Ask: What are some things in nature that are like our product or package? Search for some metaphors like apple peels and pea pods that can catalyze your own creativity.

The next time it's time to brainstorm, take your cross-functional team not to a fancy hotel, but to the woods instead. Send your colleagues outdoors in search of innovative natural packages that are compatible with the earth. Take along some ecologists and biologists.

When taking these steps, keep in mind that using natural proto-types will not only accelerate your thinking, but it can shave light years off your test market. As one of my colleagues likes to say, Mother Nature has been testing her concepts for over 4 billion years.

REFERENCES

Stephenson, W. David. "Matter of Opinion: The Computer That Came From the Swamp," *Los Angeles Times,* June 6, 1993.

Taylor, Benjamin De Brie. *Design Lessons from Nature,* Watson-Guptill Publications, New York, 1974.

Wann, David. *"Biologic: Environmental Protection by Design,* Johnson Books, 1990.

REFLECTIONS OF
THE FUTURE

THINKING ABOUT THE FUTURE

by

Frederik Pohl

When the World Future Society began a few decades ago, I have to admit that I regarded it with a certain amount of professional jealousy.

You see, I'm a science-fiction writer. I do sometimes write other things (all sorts of things, anywhere from encyclopedia essays on ancient history to "mainstream" novels and even the occasional poem), but when I sit down at my word processor it is usually science fiction that comes out. When the WFS was being born, I felt I had a certain amount of seniority in the business of thinking about the future. After all, I had been busy at the job of anatomizing events that hadn't actually happened--not yet, anyway--for close to thirty years.

Then, without warning, along came all these new guys--scientists and academics, people from the think tanks of government and industry--who were invading a turf that a few score of us pioneering future historians had long since marked out as our own. As it turned out, the relationship between science fiction and futurology turned out to be a pretty amiable symbiosis...but, all the same, it was quite a shock at the time.

Of course, there are considerable differences between science fiction and formal futurology. To name but one, very few people base their decisions on planning a new factory or building a municipal water supply on a science-fiction story. (Though it might be argued that now and then they might be just as well off if they did.) That isn't what science fiction is for. Whatever merits it may possess, it isn't meant to *predict* the future.

Not every science-fiction writer has understood this. Hugo Gernsback, for instance, had an opposite opinion. Gernsback was as close to a founding father as American science fiction ever had. Among other things, he gave it its biggest boost ever in 1926, when he started the world's first science-fiction magazine *Amazing Stories*. In his own fiction, notably the novel *Ralph 124C41+*, Gernsback spent most of his effort in attempting to describe what the next century's inventions would look like. Later on, on the contents page of every issue of his magazine, he ran the slogan "Extravagant Fiction Today--Cold Fact Tomorrow."

It hasn't worked out that way. Those early issues of *Amazing Stories* were full of stories about high-tech Martian warriors invading the Earth or tough American adventurers exploring the swampy jun-

---

Frederik Pohl, *of Palatine, Illinois, award-winning author of science fiction, also writes and lectures on future changes in society, technology and the environment.*

gles of the planet Venus. Those things didn't happen, and it seems pretty clear now that they never will. Even Gernsback's predictions in his own novel missed their mark in other ways. Though conceptually interesting--he took it for granted that things like radar and television would become common--he had the technological details remarkably wrong. (His television sets were basically photophones; apparently the idea of broadcast TV never occurred to him.)

Gernsback wasn't the worst. If you want to know just how wrong science fiction can be, let me tell you about an ancient movie called *Just Imagine*. It is pretty well forgotten now, but in 1930 it was a biggie; it starred the Swedish dialect comedian El Brendel and the lovely young Maureen O'Sullivan, in what I think was her first appearance on an American screen. I saw it in 1930, when I was ten years old, and marveled at the picture it gave of the wonderful far-off future world of 1980. In 1980 people no longer had names but serial numbers (a notion, I have always suspected, that they may have got from *Ralph 124C41+*.) Meals came in the form of pills, with no necessity for cutting steaks or spooning up a bowl of soup. The skyscraper city of New York suffered from heavily congested traffic--but of autogyros, not cars--and when a young couple desired a baby they simply put a coin in a vending-machine slot and the infant popped out. On the way home from the movie I said to my mother, "Gee, I wish I could see that," and she startled me by saying, "Listen son, there's a pretty good chance that you will."

Well, I did, sort of. That is, 1980 has come and gone, but I still have to cut my steaks, and all of my children and grandchildren have arrived in the time-tested way.

Of course, *Just Imagine* was a comedy. It wasn't meant to be taken as trustworthy truth. But the crystal ball has been just as clouded for others who deserve to be taken more seriously--including even so sharp an article as my esteemed friend and colleague, Arthur C. Clarke. Among other things in Clarke's film and novel, *2001*, there is a section describing regular Pan-Am flights to a space station and then to the Moon, proving once again that it's always a mistake for a science-fiction writer to put a date on his imaginings. Now we're getting close enough to that year to be pretty sure that sort of all-frills lunar commuting just isn't going to happen--not to mention that there isn't even a Pan-Am around any more to take anybody anywhere at all.

Of course, very important people aren't going to trust science-fiction writers to tell them about the future anyway. They're going to want heavyweight scientists for the job.

Martin Rees, in his 1995 presidential address to the British Association for the Advancement of Science, talked about one such early effort. In 1937, the Great Depression was stubbornly refusing to end, causing much pain to President Franklin D. Roosevelt and his New Deal. What Roosevelt was hoping for was some new technologies that would spawn great new industries, in the way that radio and automobiles had done a bit earlier. Accordingly, he asked the National Academy of Sciences to predict forthcoming scientific breakthroughs.

They did their best. They anticipated--quite correctly--such things as synthetic rubber and synthetic gasoline, as well as significant changes in agriculture. But as Rees reminds us, the really big new technologies and industries--nuclear energy, antibiotics, jet aircraft, even computers--they missed entirely.

Of course that was more than half a century ago, and there have been some improvements since then, particularly in highly special-ized areas of prediction. Whether forecasting is a lot better than it was in the World War II days when I was a weatherman for the US Air Force in Italy. In you happen to be pregnant, your friendly local ob-gynie doctor can reliably tell you whether the child will be male or female. If you're considering the purchase of a new home, but don't want it shaken down around your ears, the seismologist can tell you where earthquakes are likely to occur.

But even predictions of these sorts have their limitations. The weather service is good at identifying tropical disturbances that are likely to turn into hurricanes, but whether any particular one of them will take the roof off our house--or off somebody else's home thirty or forty miles down the coast--is beyond their skills. Predicting a child's gender is routine, but there's a reason for that. What the amniocentesis reveals is not what the baby will be, but what it already *is*--the fetus has already made the male-female decision, but you just can't detect the evidence from outside. An earthquake prediction is an example of the kind of fuzzy future forecast that Charles Galton Darwin was talking about, many years ago, when he wrote a book called *The Next Million Years*.

My copy of that volume has long since disappeared into that limbo where books go if you take your eyes off them for more than a day or two, and I confess I've forgotten most of what Darwin had to say on the subject. But there was one disclaimer at the beginning of the book that struck me as revelatory. It has stuck in my mind ever since. Darwin conceded that he had no idea what devastating natural disasters would happen next year or ten years in the future. But then (he added) no one else really did, either. On the other hand, he was confident that he knew quite well what sorts of things would happen over the longer term, because in the course of a million years all the infrequent things that could happen no doubt *would* happen. There might or might not be catastrophic earthquakes (or droughts or famines or pestilences) happening *next* year, but over ten thousand centuries there was no question that, statistically speaking, sooner or later happen they definitely would.

Of course--as all Southern Californians and Japanese have had to learn--there isn't much immediate value in knowing that something will sooner or later happen, but not knowing exactly *when*.

If there were only a way to accomplish it, we would like to do better than that. What we would like to do would be to pin down actual dates; more than that, we would like to be able to forecast all sorts of other things as well. Things like the future demand for utilities, the price of commodities, up or down movements in the stock market, the results of political elections--and, for instance, whether the employment opportunities will be better for chemists or anthropologists ten years from now (and that one in particular we would like to know well in advance--say, in time for our children to make a decision about what they will major in as they get ready to enter college.) All these things would be useful to individuals; governments and industries might want to know even more.

It is to answer questions like that that the academic futurologists devised so many ingenious methodologies for long-range forecasting.

I have great respect for the people at the Rand Corporation and Herman Kahn's old Hudson Institute. Their invention of such procedures as, respectively *Delphi* and scenario writing took quite a lot of hard work and brainpower. When they were new I liked them well enough to lecture on them, to teach them in my course at the University of Kansas and even to experiment with them for myself now and then. But, as time passed, both those methodologies began to exhibit flaws.

Delphi is a procedure in which questionnaires are circulated to a group of people, asking them for their estimates of when, or whether, a long list of technological changes are likely to happen. The panelists are drawn from people in a wide range of professional expertises, and they are encouraged to comment on the phrasing of the questions, the reasons why they chose one date over another and anything else that seems to them pertinent to the inquiry. When the results are in the questionnaires are reconsidered, and the specific questions sometimes changed for clarity and answerability. Then the results of the first poll, plus a revised questionnaire and some of the comments received, are recirculated to the same group; and then the procedure is repeated for a third time.

It turned out that after three rounds a consensus generally began to emerge; more important, the questions were sharpened and made more answerable. For example, in Rand's first large-scale use of *Delphi*, in the early 1960's one question in the first round asked when the respondents anticipated the emergence of computers as intelligent as a human genius. The respondents complained that that was too fuzzily worded to get a useful answer, so by the end of the series, after two revisions, the question had come to ask for a date for the development of computers capable to taking and scoring 150 or better on a standard IQ test.

If nothing else, that sort of thing clearly made it possible to improve the definition of terms. Whether the forecasts corresponded to some future reality, however, was another matter entirely. As time passed and some of the forecasted dates were reached it turned out that the predictions came closest to success in only a few limited areas, such as the development of the space program. But here too, as in the prediction of an unborn baby's sex, that was primarily because the events "predicted" had already been put on the schedule and in many cases the contracts had already been let.

On the other hand, scenario-writing, as practiced by Kahn and others, utilized a different technique. Kahn's notion was to write down the things that were very likely to happen very soon; and then to inspect that near-future state and from it deduce the things that would probably happen next as a result; and so on, proceeding step by step to the future, through as many interactions as one liked.

That made sense--at least until one noticed that some of them had even the first step wrong. One famous scenario began, around 1967, with the statement: "In 1968, the United States won the war in Vietnam." Well, as you may remember, it didn't. Still, the rest of that scenario was just about as plausible, and as accurate, as any other.

So it began to be clear that all the methodologies, though very good at offering glimpses into what *might* occur in the future, simply weren't doing the job of saying what *would* happen. As my friend John R. Pierce of Bell Laboratories said at the time (roughly paraphrased): The trouble with the future is that there are so many of them, but when they get here and become the present there will only be one.

That was when Dennis Gabor came along with his well known statement about the future. We might as well all give up on trying to predict the future, he said. There wasn't any way we could do that. But there was something else, and even better, that we could do instead: We could invent it.

When Gabor pointed out that it was within our powers to invent the future he was proposing what is currently called "normative forecasting." The way to do that is first to describe all the possible future events and circumstances we can think of. In order to take this first step we may make use of such methodologies as *Delphi*, scenario writing, trend-line extrapolation and whatever else might be of use. (We may even wish to read a lot of the more thoughtful works of science fiction.) Then, once the possible futures (or, as Bertrand de Jouvenel called them, the "futuribles") have been identified, we can apply some sort of value judgment to them all. The ones that look attractive--which is to say, the ones that we believe would be good for everyone--we can then try to find a way to attain. The ones that don't, we can do our best to avoid. In this way, we invent the future we want.

Of course, in order to invent the particular future you personally prefer it helps a lot if you have some way of getting the rest of the world to cooperate. Your work is easiest if you happen to be a totalitarian dictator, or at least a US President. The power of his office was what made it possible for John F. Kennedy to "invent" the

American Moon landings in the late 1960's; he decreed it, the money was appropriated, the hardware was built and the landings took place. (Though John Kennedy himself wasn't around to see them happen, because somebody with a gun in Dallas "invented" a different personal future for the President.)

In much the same way, it was Joseph Stalin who "invented" the industrialization of Russia; he took a sprawling agricultural empire and forced it to build heavy industry on a huge scale. That sort of purposeful invention was actually easier for Stalin than for Kennedy, because Stalin didn't have to worry about getting Congress or the courts to go along--he simply told everybody what to do, and sent his strong-arm boys out to make sure they did it--but, by the same token, it was a lot tougher on the Russian and other Soviet people who had to carry out his decrees.

In both those cases the events would no doubt have happened sooner or later anyway. But they happened when they did and as they did because Kennedy and Stalin used the power they had to make them happen.

That ability to bring about that sort of specific and immediate invention of the future is not available to most of us because we don't possess that kind of power. But that does not mean we are powerless. Every action of our lives has consequences, and there are a lot of us in the world, performing a lot of actions.

Consider some of the decisions we all individually make in the routine course of our lives: to buy or not buy a new car (and what kind of car we elect to buy.) To have a child. To take early retirement, or to work on for a few more years. Consider even such trivial decisions as whether to walk to the corner store or jump in the car; or whether to turn the thermostat up a notch or simply put on a sweater. Not one of these individual decisions would appear even as a blip in the great input-output ledger of the human race, of course. But if a million of us make the same decision...or if all the billions of us alive in the world today do...then things change drastically. The sum, of all these small individual choices is no longer trivial. In fact, it creates an invention of a significantly different kind of future for everyone.

Years ago, when I was lecturing to a management group, I said some of these things, and in the question period one man put up his hand. Was there a simple way, he asked, of describing all the things that were needed to invent a more benign future for the human race?

There was, I said, In fact, you could put it in a single word, and that word was "restraint."

Well, it isn't quite as easy as that. There are some kinds of decisions that need to be taken at a level higher than the individual. Is there any way to identify those decisions, so that we can hope that, for instance, future Congresses will act to make the future better-- rather than simply doing their best to secure their own reelections?

There is, I think, a methodology that may sometimes at least give us a clue. It comes from the *Delphi* procedure described above.

In the final section of the Rand Corporation's original report there was one group of questions which asked the respondents to rate a list of possible future technologies both as to the likelihood of occurring, and as to their value if they did. It turned out that there were a number of such "futuribles" which the respondents generally agreed would be very useful if they could be made to happen, but were unfortunately very unlikely to come to pass.

It occurred to me that it might be useful to go a little farther in this area, in an attempt to make the forecasting normative. So, with a few others, I tried a few experiments: choosing some good, but unlikely, possible future events and technologies, then trying to analyze the factors which made them unlikely, finally seeking ways to remove or bypass the obstacles. (I called the procedure *Phi-Delphi*.)

One question we took up was the future of the Aral Sea.

Until a few decades ago the Aral was one of the largest and most productive of the world's inland seas, supporting many successful fisheries and industries around its shores. Then it began to dry up-- catastrophically. Now the Aral Sea is only a fraction of its earlier size. The former sea bottom has become a desert, and every windstorm carries huge and damaging volumes of dust for many miles around. The ruins of sea-going ships stand on dry land, miles from the present shoreline; in short, it is an ecological nightmare.

Clearly it would be desirable to restore the Aral Sea to health. Was it possible to find a way to make that happen?

The reason it dried up was known: an overwhelming proportion of the waters of the rivers that fed the Aral Sea had been diverted to irrigation, largely of immense cotton plantations. To restore the Aral Sea it would be necessary to stop the excessive withdrawals. But that would have consequences of its own, namely ruin for the million people whose livelihoods now depended on such crops as cotton.

On the other hand, cotton is notoriously a thirsty crop. There are many others which require far less irrigation. Besides which the irrigation works that drain the water meant for the Aral Sea are terribly wasteful. They comprise ditches that are generally unlined (losing much water to seepage) and are exposed to the open air (with consequent considerable evaporation losses), and the irrigation waters are applied by rule of thumb instead of by careful analysis of daily needs. A few agronomists from the Negev could easily prepare a plan that would reduce the diversion by fifty per cent or more; if other crops were substituted, perhaps by much more than that; and the Aral would grow again.

Or so the technology says. But there are other factors to be considered as well. Somewhere the funding has to be found to rebuild the irrigation; somehow the farmers have to be provided with the training and supplies to plant new crops, and markets for them have to be identified and reached. In the present chaotic state of the region's economy that sort of money is not likely to be provided, and in any case the desertification of the Aral region, however appalling in its consequences, ranks a long way from the top of the most urgent changes needed.

One might think that this would be a good place for a Stalin-type tyrant to pass a decree and make it all happen at once. Not likely; it was under Stalin-type tyranny that the region got into this mess in the first place.

So we have just about reached the end of what *Phi-Delphi* can tell us about the solutions to the Aral Sea problem. *What* needs to be done is fairly clear. How to *get* it done, on the other hand, depends on how much the people involved want it, and what they're willing to put up with and how much they're willing to pay to make it happen.

And that turns out to be precisely the same conclusion that we reach in most other attempts to avoid or repair disaster.

Which brings us back to the basic rationale for all our efforts: The only good reason for trying to predict the future in the first place is so that now, in the present, we can try to shape it to our heart's desire.

I would like to see that happen, in spite of the fact that, somewhat to my surprise--I never planned on doing it--I turned seventy-six the other day. This has not dampened my interest in the future, but it has certainly affected my attitudes toward it. Whatever changes the world may be in for in the approaching twenty-first century I can view with fairly detached emotions, since it is not likely I will personally be present to suffer, or enjoy, very many of them.

On the other hand, I do have children; and my children have children, and it is a good gambling bet that at least some of those grandchildren will themselves start producing future generations over the next decade or two. I would like very much to think that they will have a reasonably benign world to live in. And I even think I know how to bring that about: If we do what we can to anticipate the futuribles of the next few decades...and if we take them seriously and make the effort to encourage the good ones and avert the bad...then, in spite of all the worrisome problems we can foresee, it may yet all come out for the best.

At least it is worth the effort.

WHY THE FUTURE BELONGS TO SMALLER SIZED HUMANS

by

Thomas T. Samaras

Futurists, environmentalists, government officials, and business people have ignored the size of humans in predicting future world needs. Yet, our unexamined belief that larger human body size reflects improved health is a threat to our quality of life, resources, wildlife, and environment. A future population of 12 billion people averaging 170 lb instead of 100 lb can make the difference between human survival and extinction.

Why has such an obvious feature of human beings been ignored by scientists? In all industrialized countries it has been obvious that children are growing taller and heavier. Europeans have grown about 7" in the last two centuries. In 1760, Norwegian military recruits averaged 5'3", about 2" shorter than ancient Greek warriors. Today, Norwegian youth are close to 5'11". In the US, the average male during WWI averaged about 5'7" and 140 lb. Today, young males average close to 5'10" and males and females 30 to 70 years of age average about 184 lb and 158 lb. The Japanese have increased in stature by 3" to 5" since the end of WWII, and the Chinese have been growing at a very rapid rate of over 1" per decade. In view of this growth, why haven't scientists asked: "Is there an optimum human configuration and if so what is it?" This question has been ignored because we have assumed that the increasing stature of our youth reflects improved nutrition, better medical care, and superior living standards. Unfortunately, some modern dietary and lifestyle practices that promote greater stature also pose serious threats to our welfare. Our culture has also elevated tall heroes, such as athletes and executives, to a preeminent status creating a pervasive belief in the superiority of taller bodies. Yet, the advantages of smaller bodies are far greater than the advantages of larger ones, especially when psychosocial benefits are ignored. (See Figure 1.)

When I discuss smaller size with people, they respond: "We shouldn't tamper with nature and besides how can we make people smaller?" My response is: "Changing nature is what we seem to do best and because nature has given us bodies that can weigh over 300 pounds does not mean we should reach this potential." Perhaps we have ignored addressing human stature because of its "sacred cow" status and because we think it is impossible to control height. However, as described here, human size can be significantly reduced

---

Thomas T. Samaras *is a management system consultant with Reventropy Associates, San Diego, California.*

through natural means and without applying genetic or medical methods.

FIGURE 1

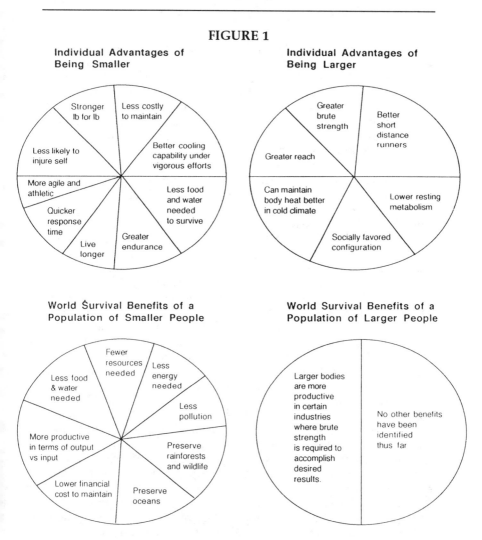

Individual Advantages of Being Smaller

- Stronger lb for lb
- Less costly to maintain
- Better cooling capability under vigorous efforts
- Less likely to injure self
- More agile and athletic
- Less food and water needed to survive
- Quicker response time
- Live longer
- Greater endurance

Individual Advantages of Being Larger

- Greater brute strength
- Better short distance runners
- Greater reach
- Can maintain body heat better in cold climate
- Lower resting metabolism
- Socially favored configuration

World Survival Benefits of a Population of Smaller People

- Fewer resources needed
- Less energy needed
- Less food & water needed
- Less pollution
- More productive in terms of output vs input
- Preserve rainforests and wildlife
- Lower financial cost to maintain
- Preserve oceans

World Survival Benefits of a Population of Larger People

- Larger bodies are more productive in certain industries where brute strength is required to accomplish desired results.
- No other benefits have been identified thus far

Note: Details for each advantage or disadvantage require more space than available for this paper. Refer to *The Truth About Your Height* for further details

Over the last 20 years I have studied a multitude of impacts that increasing physical size has on our society and the earth. As a configuration management system specialist, engineer, and longevity researcher, I have looked at the effects of a population of larger size people on our health, performance, resources, economic costs, environment, and survival. As you will see, the impact is enormous and can make the difference between our survival and our extinction even if the world population growth was slowed to zero or put in reverse. The following presents new information and some previously covered material from the book: *The Truth About Your Height--Exploring the Myths and Realities of Human Size and Its Effects on Performance, Health, Pollution, and Survival.*

FOOD AND WATER IMPACT

Food and water needs are proportional to body size. A 6' 190 lb person compared to a 5' 110 lb person requires about 70% more food and water to supply his or her needs, assuming lifestyles are the same. Walking, working, and playing activities require energy inputs in proportion to body size[1].

For the US, a population of 265 million 190-lb people vs 110-lb people will require an additional 180 million acres of farmland for the increased needs of the larger people. If we assume that our 5' population consumes 130 million tons of food annually, then our 6' population will consume roughly 221 million tons.

The fish catch is now roughly 90 million tons per year and has declined by about 10% in the last 5 years. A population of 20% taller people will require roughly 70% more fish in the face of a declining supply and will thereby compound the growing food needs of the world's population.

The per capita use of water in the US is about 1400 gallons per day. Since 85% of this water relates to agriculture, a huge increase in demand for this resource will also occur. Human beings are about 70% water and 6' bodies will extract about 4.2 billion gallons of this vital resource from US fresh water supplies. However, the bodies of a population of 5' people will extract only 2.4 billion gallons.

With a projected US population of 520 million by 2050, the impact of increasing body size will diminish food and water supplies even further. As China, India, and other densely populated countries develop, their populations will demand higher standards of living and will thus require more food and water which will make US needs pale in comparison.

RESOURCE AND ENERGY IMPACT

If we compare a US population of 265 million tall people to a population of short people, the differences in consumption of resources and energy are very large. For example, a population of 6', 190 lb people vs a population of 5', 110 lb[2] people will require an annual increase of 600 million tons of copper, steel, aluminum, inor-

inorganic chemicals, coal, cement, and paper. Consumption of other resources will skyrocket as well.

Using the same size difference (6' vs 5') for today's population, energy requirements will increase by 40 quadrillion Btu's per year. Increased energy and resource estimates are both based on the assumption that the lifestyles for the two populations are the same and that automobiles, homes, buildings, etc. are scaled to the average size of each population.

On a world scale, energy and resource needs for physically larger people will also increase considerably, especially in view of the efforts of developing countries to provide their people with the material goods common to developed nations. However, for today's consumption patterns, a world filled with 6' people will require an additional 200 quadrillion Btus per year by the year 2000. Based on the present size of people, we will need twice as many raw materials in the year 2010. On a world scale, this demand for resources could expand by many times if the average size of people continues to increase throughout the world.

WASTE AND ENVIRONMENTAL IMPACT

Using the US as a baseline model again, a 20% taller population will increase trash by 80 million tons a year. In addition, municipal wastes poured into our coastal waters will increase by 70% from 2.3 trillion gallons to almost 4 trillion gallons per year. Industrial wastes will increase from about 5 billion gallons to 8.5 billion gallons per year, and animal waste products will increase from 2 billion to 3.4 billion tons per year.

Carbon dioxide generated by society will increase by almost 3 billion tons a year for the US alone. On a world scale, the increase will be many billions of tons more than what a population of 5' people will produce. Some climate experts believe it is too late to prevent the world's average temperature from rising a few degrees in the next 100 years. Although a future population of smaller people will not save us from the damage we have already done, it can help avoid additional increases in temperature.

We are currently destroying 40 million acres of rain forests per year, and more than half of the original forests have been cut down. The San Diego Zoological Association reports that the remainder will be lost in about 60 years. Smaller people's reduced demands for food and wood will help conserve the forests throughout the world.

Marine biologist Sylvia Earle reported that we are removing billions of tons of living creatures from the oceans and replacing them with billions of tons of wastes and toxins. Toxins, such as DDT, PCBs, and mercury can be found everywhere in the oceans from the North Pole to the South Pole and even at great depths. Preserving and restoring our oceans requires much more than reducing the size of the average person in the world. However, a worldwide 20% reduction in height with its associated lower weight will reduce ocean pollution by hundreds of tons, and we will reduce overfishing by 55 million tons per year.

ECONOMIC IMPACT

The economic impact of a world of 6' people versus 5' people is also enormous. For the US alone, the additional cost of supporting 265 million larger people will be roughly $3 trillion per year. Almost everything will cost more, including structures, transportation, energy, food, water, and medical care. A typical coast-to-coast airline flight will cost an additional $33,000 one way. The reason for this added cost is the lower number of passengers that the same size aircraft could carry. Entertainment costs will also go up due to fewer seats being available for each performance due to larger bodies and longer legs. For example, the Yankee Stadium was built in the 1920's and upgraded in the 1970's. The renovated stadium contained 9,000 fewer seats because engineers had to account for an increase of 3" in the width of the average fan's bottom.

Since many drug dosages are size dependent, higher dosages for larger people will cost hundreds of millions more per year. Clothing costs will also skyrocket due to the 44% additional material required per person. An extra $6 billion per year will be spent for this additional material in the US alone. Additional pollution and acid rain will increase costs for clean up activities and restoration of damaged buildings, lakes, rivers, and forests. Increased scarcity of oil, wood, and other resources will drive inflationary costs higher providing an added economic impact which will add to the $3 trillion mentioned before.

HEALTH AND LONGEVITY IMPACT

According to a World Health Organization panel of 11 international nutritional experts, developed countries are seeing an epidemic of heart disease, cancer, strokes, diabetes, etc. due to our affluent diet. Of course, our lifestyle and pollution have played a role in this epidemic, but modern day dietary practices appear to be the major contributor to this epidemic. Other researchers have reported that primitive societies that follow traditional diets low in fat and sugar and high in fiber, rarely suffer from modern diseases. For example, Denis P. Burkitt, a surgeon for 20 years in Africa, found that Africans on traditional diets were almost free of cancer and other chronic diseases compared to those who followed modern diets.

Harold Elrick, M.D., a researcher in nutrition, preventive medicine, and fitness studied thousands of people throughout the world and found that the healthiest people were those who followed sparse traditional diets, were physically active and small. For example, his research team found male Taramuhara Indians of Northern Mexico averaged about 5'5" and about 120 lb and were virtually free of heart disease and diabetes.

What does this all mean? Well, a diet rich in animal protein, fat, milk, and sugar has been tied to our increase in stature and weight over the last 200 years. That's why countries, such as Norway, saw a decline in the height and weight of their children as a result of food shortages during WWII. To the surprise of many, Holland, Denmark, and Norway also saw a significant reduction in civilian death rates during the war.

Following WWII, the Japanese experienced a rapid rise in height which paralleled their new supplies of red meat, milk, eggs, and sugar. The Japanese also experienced a decline in strokes and stomach cancer reflecting some positive features resulting from changes in their diet and lifestyle. But overall, the latest findings indicate that the modern diet is dangerous to our health and longevity. Many studies have found that red meat and high fat diets promote cancer, including prostate and colon cancer, heart disease, and diabetes. As a result of extensive research, Herbert Pierson, a former researcher with the National Cancer Institute, says: "The American diet is the worst on earth...Our diet is a killer." Recent studies have also found that body weight for best health is much lower than anyone realized with ideal weight being under 119 lb for 5'5" women and under 148 lb for 5'10" men.

Several studies have found cancer to be height and body weight related. Albanes, Giovannucci, Swanson, de Waard, and Taylor, to name a few, have found a significant correlation between height and cancer incidence and mortality. A Norwegian study of over 1/2 million women found increased breast cancer to be related to increased height and body weight.

Studies in the past have confused the issue by showing taller people have lower death rates from heart disease. However, recent studies by researchers at Harvard, University of Tennessee, Karolinska Hospital, and Framingham have found no differences or somewhat lower death rates for shorter people. In fact, data from Federal and California State publications have shown that shorter Asians and Hispanics suffer considerably less heart disease and cancer compared to taller and heavier blacks and whites. In California, these smaller ethnic groups also live up to 5 years longer. Nationwide, Hispanics, Asians, and American Indians have lower age-adjusted mortality rates per the latest data in *Health United States 1994* published by NCHS. A World Health Organization publication also shows a similar pattern for shorter southern Europeans compared to taller Northerners. A Chinese-American study found that Chinese of lower stature and body weight had lower death rates from heart disease and cancer when compared to larger Chinese.

Storms, Miller, and I found that shorter, smaller men and women have somewhat longer lifespans than taller ones. A progressive and regular decline in average lifespan was found for deceased veterans, baseball players, famous people, and ordinary people. Independent follow-up studies by Miller and me found a 1.2 to 1.3 year decline in average lifespan with each inch increase in height. This is almost the same difference (1.4 yr) in the life expectancy between American men and women. (About 6.8 years longer female life expectancy divided by 5" difference in height.)

A word of caution about longevity findings. It is important to realize that height affects only 10% to 15% of the total longevity picture. Lifestyle, medical care, heredity, job satisfaction, social support connections, and environment are much more important predictors of longevity. Studies have found that people in higher socioeconomic brackets have 1/3 lower death rates, and only 13.6% of educated people smoke compared to 35.8% of people with the lowest education. Since Government statistics indicate that there are more tall people in higher socioeconomic levels, tall people of higher socioeconomic status will offset much of the negative aspects of greater body size if they don't smoke or become overweight.

In summary, comprehensive immunization programs, improved sanitation, widespread health screening programs, and advances in medical and drug techniques have sharply reduced deaths during childbirth and infancy and have provided us with longer life expectancies. (About 20% of those born in 1900 died by 10 years of age compared to less than 1% today.) Combining these positive aspects with increased fiber, reduced fat, sugar and salt, and other lifestyle practices will help provide us with healthier and more active lives into middle and advanced age[3].

SURVIVAL IMPACT

Paleontologists, biologists, and zoologists are well aware that smaller animals have a better chance of surviving changes in the environment. For example, paleontologist, Ross MacPhee, reports that over 10,000 years ago, 135 species of animals became extinct in North and South America. We don't know why, but we do know that almost all of them were over 100 pounds. We also know that when dinosaurs disappeared about 65 million years ago, much smaller mammals, snakes, crocodiles, turtles, and lizards survived and are still with us.

Bigger animals are vulnerable to changes in environment that affect their food and water sources because they require so much more than smaller animals. While we are quite small compared to elephants and whales, humans are bigger than 95% of the animals on earth. In view of our intelligence and adaptability, our size per se is not very dangerous to our survival except for our huge numbers and enormous appetite for resources. Reducing the individual size of humans by 20% doesn't seem like much, but a worldwide population of 20% shorter people can make the difference between a wholesome or disastrous life for everyone. Of course, other measures are needed to reduce pollution, conserve resources, and reduce loss of farmland. Because of soil erosion and use of rural areas for human development, we have lost 33% of our arable land during the last 40 years. Even if this rate of loss is reduced drastically, how can we feed the current population 50 years from now, much less the added 6 billion expected? A shorter, lighter population will reduce food needs and land loss due to erosion and human encroachment and will promote our chances for long-term survival.

WHAT ABOUT PERFORMANCE?

Scientists that deal with the sizes of different animals are aware that increases in area and mass are disproportionate with increase in length or height of the animals. R. McNeill Alexander, a biomechanical engineer and zoologist, reports that our surface area increases as height squared and our weight increases as height cubed for geometrically similar animals. The same is true for humans. As a result, a 20% taller human has 44% more surface area and 73% more body mass compared to a shorter person of the same body type and proportions. This rapid increase in surface area and body mass has both advantages and disadvantages as shown in Figure 1. For example, physiologists Astrand and Rodahl, pointed out years ago that as we get taller, our weight increases faster than the strength of our bones and muscles. Thus, we are less able to lift and manipulate our bodies. And when we fall, we hit the ground with disproportionately more energy than a geometrically similar shorter person. That's why gymnasts are generally quite small—Dominique Moceanu, at 4'5" and 70 lb, was the winner in the 1995 National Gymnastics Championships in New Orleans. Olga Korbut, Kim Zmeskal, and many short male gymnasts attest to the fact that this is not an anomaly.

An important question often asked is: "If we reduce the size of people, will it compromise our physical and mental performance?" A number of races have been highly creative and productive even though the combined average for men and women was about 5' to 5'2". These included the Greeks, Maya, Aztecs, Incas, and Japanese. The Romans were somewhat taller than the Greeks, but they were also short. The Egyptians, East Indians, and many Chinese were also small. Following WWII, the Japanese men and women had a combined average height of 5'1". Yet they were the driving force for one of the world's greatest economic and technological revolutions.

Walter Bowerman found shorter men were well represented among high achievers. A recent study reported that there were as many short physicians as tall ones. And my own studies of famous people found that short or small men represented about a third of the total. Some exceptional short people include Michelangelo, Buckminster Fuller, Martin Luther King, Gandhi, Mother Teresa, Einstein,

252

Matsushita (father of the Japanese electronics industry), Picasso, Stravinsky, Voltaire, and John Keats.

The physical advantages of shorter stature include greater strength (pound for pound), greater ability to accelerate their bodies, and greater stamina. Alexander has pointed out that smaller animals are generally more athletic and subject to lower risk of exceeding their physical limits. The British military historian, Sidney Allinson, found that short men had shorter reaction times, enjoyed greater endurance, were smaller targets, and were less prone to heat stroke due to vigorous activities. Also, Carol Teitz, a sports medicine physician, reported that the current crop of taller and heavier football and basketball players are subject to more frequent and severe injuries than past athletes.

The physical advantages of shorter stature are visible in weightlifting, gymnastics, diving, ballet dancing, figure skating, horse racing, and marathon running. Weightlifter Suleymanoglu, at 5' and 130 lb, is an Olympic gold medal winner, and has been described as the strongest man in the world on a pound for pound basis. Other famous short athletes include Muggsy Bogues, Pele, Bruce Lee, Jack LaLanne, Diego Maradona, Haile Gebrselassie, and Mario Andretti.

CAN NEW TECHNOLOGY AND CONSERVATION TECHNIQUES HELP?

An alternative to reducing the size of people, will be to reduce the world population by billions of people, develop new technology to recycle resources, reduce pollution and waste, and simplify our lifestyle so that we don't consume as much. Reduction of the number of people on earth is not likely in the near future unless an unexpected event, such as a disease epidemic, destroys many of us. The other two solutions are feasible but take lots of money, social changes, and time to implement. At the rate we are destroying our planet, technological and lifestyle changes will need to be combined with population control measures and size reduction to save us from a bleak future. For those who think that technology can solve any problem, Sylvia Earle, former Chief Scientist of the National Oceanographic and Atmospheric Association says: "...there is no guarantee that humankind will be among the survivors of even subtle changes to the global environment, despite our technological cleverness and the widespread belief that our species enjoys unique status...".

OVERVIEW AND WHAT CAN WE DO ABOUT OUR SIZE?

Taller human size is regarded with positive feelings in most of the world. Yet, there is no absolute standard as to what is really tall or short. Height in fact is a relative factor in life. If most of us were 5' in stature, a 5'5" person would be tall. If we were on average 7' in height, a 6'5" person would be short. What we consider a comfortable height is society-driven and the benefits that taller people see are strictly psychosocial and not based on any inherent value to society. However, no one should feel badly about being tall because his or her value as a human being has nothing to do with height. Individually, we can be protectors of the environment, highly creative, and socially responsible regardless of our heights. So if we can put aside a lifetime of brain washing and height bias, the ultimate question is: " What human size is best for the individual and the world?" I recommend 5' and less than 110 pounds for a combined average of men and women. Men could be 5'3" and women 4'11" since men are 3" to 5" taller than women just about everywhere in the world. How will this size reduction be achieved? The best approach seems to be through nutritional restriction. We know from animal and human data that food restriction can reduce the ultimate size of humans. For example, University of California researcher Roy Walford reports that a reduction of 6" to 8" is feasible. This is the same amount that Europeans have grown over the last 200 years. Therefore, a scientifically designed energy-restricted nutritional program that provides children all the nutrients needed to be well formed and healthy is a feasible approach. Besides reducing size, calorie restriction enhances DNA repair, boosts the immune system, cuts down on heart disease, cancer and other major ills, and vastly extends life span in many species. How much confidence should we have in the benefits of caloric restriction for people? Walford, an expert in this area, says he's 99.5% sure that calorie restricted diets really work.

Nutritionists and other researchers are finding out that a low fat (about 15% of total calories), low sugar, and high fiber diet can help achieve this goal. Calories could be cut by 20% to 40% of today's intake. Of course, vegetables, fruits, and cereals will be the primary ingredients of this diet. Small amounts of meat will also be required although the necessity of meat in the diet is a controversial one at this time. Biochemist Colin T. Campbell believes that we eat too much protein, especially from animal sources, and other leading nutritionists believe we should eat red meat no more than once a week. Campbell points out that the rural Chinese are largely vegetarian and eat 2/3 the protein that we do and only 1/10 of the animal protein. The incidence of heart disease, cancer, and diabetes among these Chinese is only a small fraction of what it is in the US. Osteoporosis is also rare in China.

Future consumption of energy-dense foods may of necessity become obsolete because population growth will force a change in the way we eat. A panel of the American Association for the Advancement of Science recently predicted that by 2050 a combination of 520 million Americans and shortages of energy, water and agricultural land will cause sharp reductions in meat, egg, and dairy product consumption. Consequently, we will be compelled to substitute rich foods for fruits, vegetables, and grains which require fewer resources to grow.

Will a calorie restricted diet be dangerous? Based on the Okinawan experience and the findings of other researchers, the answer is "No". Okinawan children were raised on a diet that supplied 40% fewer calories than the mainland diet. They grew up to be the smallest of the Japanese but their health wasn't impaired. In fact, Okinawans have much lower death rates from chronic diseases than the mainland Japanese, and they lead the world with the highest percent of centenarians. Kagawa also reported that Okinawan and other Japanese male centenarians averaged less than 4'10" and were under 100 pounds.

I doubt that many people will argue with the health benefits of a low fat, plant based diet. Yet, changing our penchant for fast foods, sweets, meat, fried foods, and junk food is a difficult task. However, food scientists could alter the popular foods we eat so that they taste the same and have the same texture but are much reduced in protein, fat, salt, and calories with increased fiber and essential nutrients. They have already made good progress in this area with a variety of commonly available foods, such as imitation butter, non-fat yogurt, and vegetarian burgers.

Humans are resistant to change. New ideas often take many years to be accepted. Scientists scoffed at the continental drift theory for many years, and it took over 200 years for us to accept the fact that the earth revolved about the sun. No doubt when Copernicus first broached his ideas to the world, people were shocked and angry. Things are somewhat different today. We have accelerated the communication process, and new ideas can make deep inroads into our society much faster than in the past.

In summary, little is known about the earth's living processes to accurately foresee or time the consequences of our explosive population growth and ecological tinkering. However, terrestrial and ocean dumping, overfishing, over farming, oil spills, killing off huge numbers of land and ocean wildlife, and global warming may be generating more entropy than the earth and its creatures can handle. This fact is often overshadowed by people's overbearing confidence that our enormous success in populating the earth somehow shields us from disaster. Yet, our future is precarious, and we can disappear even more quickly than we have risen to power—Easter Island and other flourishing societies that are now extinct attest to this observation. It's not too late to respond to Earle's warning: "Depending on the choices we make, our species may be able to achieve a viable, sustainable future or we may continue to so alter the nature of the planet that our kind will perish." In view of this danger, can we afford to ignore the major survival benefits of smaller human size simply because of our society's porous and unsubstantiated belief in the superiority of taller beings?

NOTES

1. Large bodies have a slightly lower resting metabolic rate. However, they still require more total calories. They also require protein, essential fatty acids, minerals, and vitamins in proportion to their body size.

2. This weight difference occurs if body proportions or types are the same for tall and short people. The particular body type, such as ectomorphic or endomorphic, does not change resulting computations as long as we compare short and tall people of the same body builds; e.g., retain geometric similarity.

3. Longer living small people will require more resources and money than if they lived less. However, their smaller needs will more than compensate for these increases. Over a lifetime, 5' people will require about 30% fewer resources and will cost about $400,000 less than shorter living 6' people.

REFERENCES

"Are You Eating Your Way to Cancer?" *Natural Health*, July/Aug 1995, p. 26.

Albanes, D. and P.Taylor. "International Differences in Body Height and Weight and Their Relationship to Cancer Incidence", *Nutrition and Cancer*, Vol. 14, No. 1, 1990, pp. 69 -77.

Chan, C. and A. Oreglia. *California Life Expectancy: Abridged Life Tables for California and Los Angeles County 1989-91*, Department of Health Services, August 1993, Sacramento, CA 1992.

Chen, Campbell, Li & Peto, Diet, *Life-Style and Mortality in China*, Cornell University Press, Ithaca, NY, 1990, p. 65.

Chen. op. cit., p. 65.

Diamond, J., "Easter's End," *Discover*, August 1995, p. 63-69.

"Diet, Nutrition and the Prevention of Chronic Diseases, A Report of the WHO Study Group on Diet, Nutrition, and Prevention of Noncommunicable Diseases," *Nutrition Reviews*, Vol 49, No. 10, October, 1991, pp. 291-301.

Earle, S. *Sea Change--A Message From The Oceans*, G. P. Putnam's Sons, NY, 1995, p. xv, p. 228.

Earle. op. cit., p. xx.

Giovannucci, E., A. Ascherio, E. Rimm, G. Colditz, M. Stampfer, and Willett, W., "Physical Activity, Obesity, and Risk of Colon Cancer and Adenoma in Men," *Annals of Internal Medicine*, 1995, Vol 122, No. 5, pp 329-334.

Gore, A. *Earth in the Balance*, Houghton Mifflin, NY, 1992, p. 150.

Health United States 1994, Department of Health Services, National Center for Health Statistics, May 1995, Hyattsville, MD, PHS 95-1232.

Hebert, P., J. Rich-Edwards, J. Manson, et al, "Height And Incidence of Cardiovascular Disease in Male Physicians," *Circulation*, Vol. 88, No. 4, Part 1, October, 1993, pp. 1437-1443.

Ibid, p. 193.

Ibid, p. 191.

Kagawa, Y., "Impact of Westernization on the Nutrition of Japanese: Changes in Physique, Cancer, Longevity and Centenarians," *Preventive Medicine, 7*, 1978, pp. 205-217.

Kahn, C. "Eat Less Live Longer," *Longevity*, Vol 7, No. 5., April, 1995, p. 97.

Kushi, M. *The Cancer Prevention Diet*, St. Martins Press, 1993, p. 151.

Lee, I-Min, J. Manson, C. Hennekens, and R. Paffenbarger, " Body Weight and Mortality--A 27 Year Follow Up of Middle Aged Men," *JAMA*, December 15, 1993, Vol.270, No. 23, pp. 2823-2828.

Longevity, Vol 7, No. 10, September, 1995, pp. 66 & 70.

Manson, J., W. Willett, M. Stampfer, et al, "Body Weight and Mortality Among Women," *The New England Journal of Medicine*, Vol. 333, No. 11, September 14, 1995, pp. 677-684.

McNeill, Alexander M. *Dynamics of Dinosaurs and Other Extinct Species*, Columbia University Press, NY, 1989, p. 141.

McNeill, C. op. cit., p. 162.

Miller, D., "Economics of Scale,"*Challenge*, 33,1990, pp 58-61.

Radetsky, P. "The Living Longer Diet," *Longevity*, May, 1994, p. 80.

Radetsky, P. op. cit., p. 40.

Samaras, T. and L. Storms. "Impact of Height and Weight on Life Span," *Bulletin of the World Health Organization* 70 (2): pp. 259-267 (1992).

Samaras, T. "The Truth About Your Height--Exploring the Myths and Realities of Human Size and Its Effects on Performance, Health, Pollution, and Survival," *Tecolote Publications*, San Diego, 1994, p. 215.

Samaras, op. cit., p. 207.

Samaras. op. cit., p. 194.

Samaras. op. cit., pp. 219-237.

Samaras. op. cit., p. 227.

Samaras, T. op. cit., pp. 59-104.

Samaras, T. "Short People," *Science Digest*, Vol. 84, 1978, pp. 76-78.

Strom, A. and R. Jensen. "Mortality From Circulatory Disease in Norway 1940-1945," *The Lancet*, Vol 1, Jan. 20, 1951, pp. 126-129.

The ZPG Reporter, July/August, 1995, p. 12.

Walford, R. *The 120 Year Diet*, Pocket Books, NY, 1986, p. 88.

World Health Statistics Annual, World Health Organization, Geneva, 1994, pp. D140-D367.

World Resources Institute, *The 1992 Information Please Environmental Almanac*, Houghton Mifflin, NY 1992, p. 75.

Zimmer, C. "Carriers of Extinction," *Discover*, July, 1995, p. 28.

SIX PRIORITIES FROM FUTURE GENERATIONS
by

Allen Tough

Surrounded by countless problems and needs, how can we focus on the most important priorities of all? Of all the possible priorities for our society, which are most worthy of our efforts?

In order to obtain a fresh perspective on these questions, it is useful to think about the answer that future generations would give us if they could speak to us. If generations yet unborn could suggest six key priorities to us, what would they recommend? Their perspective can help us make choices that are beneficial to them as well as to our own generation.

Here, then, is what future generations--not yet born--might say to us if they could speak.

THE MESSAGE FROM FUTURE GENERATIONS

We appreciate your listening to this message from us, the people in your future. Because we have not yet been born, we are not able to lobby or vote. But we too have needs and hopes, just as you do. Thank you for listening to our perspective.

Your era is marked by positive and negative potentials of such newness and magnitude that you can hardly understand them. Through your public policies and daily lives, the people of your era have tremendous power to influence the future course of humanity's history. We strongly care about your choices, of course, since we benefit or suffer from them quite directly. We live downstream from you in time; whatever you put into the stream flows on to our era.

After much thought, we have concluded that six priorities are particularly important for your attention and efforts. By focusing on these six specific areas of society, you can contribute greatly to our opportunities and deep happiness. And your improvements in these six areas will have major benefits for you, too.

Here is a preview list of the six areas--the six priorities that seem to us most important for you to emphasize over the next few years:

- A long-term perspective
- Future-relevant research and teaching
- Weapons and warfare
- Planet and population

Allen Tough *is a professor of futures studies at the University of Toronto, and* *author of* **Crucial Questions About the Future** *and (forthcoming)* **A Message from Future Generations.**

- Significant knowledge
- Learning, caring, and meaningfulness.

We will be very grateful if you devote your best efforts to these six priorities, even if you have to reduce your efforts on other priorities. These are the six things that we need most from you.

We know how eager you are to find a path to a positive future, to change the course of human history for the better. Your best prospects lie in these six directions. You need a dramatic shift of public attention, commitment, and resources to these key priorities --and away from any luxuries, habits, beliefs, old structures, and narrow interests that interfere with them. You cannot accomplish all the worthy changes that you desire, but you certainly can accomplish these six key changes if you focus your efforts on them.

Even though our world and our lives are somewhat different from yours, we too are people, vigorously engaged in a wide variety of activities and projects, just as you are. We want to have opportunities and resources that are equal to yours. As you make choices in the face of competing voices and demands, please shift toward a fair and appropriate balance between your well-being and ours. We appreciate the efforts that you have already made, but we also note that even deeper and faster changes are required.

It is important for you to realize just how deep and pervasive these changes must be in order to give us equal opportunities. Individual behavior, social structures, economic assumptions, even paradigms and world views must all change. We know that these changes are not shallow or easy. But if you do not change vigorously and successfully, we will be much worse off than you are.

The costs of the deterioration and losses will be far larger than the costs of making the changes in the first place would have been. If you continue your shortsighted selfishness, the consequences will be catastrophic, perhaps even beyond the stretch of your imagination. From our long-term perspective, we see how foolish and unfair you will be if you fail to make the required changes soon. How would you react to a bus driver who knew the brakes would give out soon but did not bother to get them fixed promptly? If you do make the changes, the benefits to ongoing humanity will be much greater than the costs of making the changes.

You may see the required changes as unrealistic, as not feasible, but how realistic and feasible is it to expect us to feed two or even three times as many people as you feed? How realistic is it to believe that your arsenal of nuclear and biological weapons will never be used during the next few decades? The costs and inconvenience of changing are very unpleasant, but the poignant costs of *not* changing are far worse. If you truly care about the well-being of us members of future generations, you will find a way to make the required changes. You are already making rapid progress in some spheres, and are clearly capable of making the other required changes if you choose to. We appreciate your courage in facing reality and in considering vigorous changes.

All six priorities are intricately connected, of course, but it is useful to focus on each of them separately as well. We have avoided suggesting implementation details for these six broad priorities: you are closer to the situation than we are, and you are certainly capable of planning specific strategies and projects to achieve these key priorities. For each of these priorities, your books and periodicals already contain plenty of ideas for particular steps and solutions. Once you choose to move ahead with each priority, you will readily find useful strategies and organizations close at hand. Fortunately, too, many inspiring success stories have already occurred. What is needed most is widespread public commitment to each priority. Accomplishing them will then turn out to be relatively easy.

People and societies cannot accomplish everything that they want to accomplish. They sometimes have to make painfully difficult choices. In order to focus enough of your attention, effort, and resources on these six key priorities, you will probably have to lower your hopes and efforts in certain other areas. You need a fresh deep re-ranking of your societal priorities. You will have to rethink and reorder your priorities in ways that will hurt or displease certain groups and certain individuals. But if you fail to shift fundamentally toward the six key priorities--if you continue to scatter your efforts widely and to neglect these six areas--you will hurt and displease us even more. The solution is to find a fair balance between the needs of the people who are alive as you read this, and the people who will be alive over the next few decades and beyond.

A LONG-TERM PERSPECTIVE

In all of your major decisions and actions, please consider our perspective and well-being along with your own. Take our needs as seriously as your own. Care about our welfare as well as your own. Our needs and rights are not inferior to yours. Please regard your generation and ours as equals. This is the principle of intergenerational equity--equal opportunities across the generations. Reflect on your unique place in human history. You face the historic challenge of making the shift from a narrow, self-centered, short-term focus to a long-term global focus that takes into account our needs as well as your own. If you succeed in making this deep-seated shift toward a long-term perspective, your era will be remembered for saving human civilization and its planet from catastrophe and disintegration, and for building the foundation for a more positive world.

As members of future generations, we are particularly eager for you to designate a spokesperson for our needs in your various policy-making forums, planning processes, legislatures, parliaments, houses of representatives, senates, and so on. Because we are not yet alive in your era, we have no voice. We seem unreal and unimportant to many of your politicians because we have not yet been born. Our perspective and interests are rarely noted in any depth. This is why we are very enthusiastic about your era's diverse proposals for incorporating the views and needs of future generations into your legislative and policy-making processes. We now urge you to move on from words and proposals to practical innovative experiments. As you experiment, you will gain greater insights and skills and thus be able to develop even better ways of incorporating our views into your public decision-making. Please experiment with a spokesperson for future generations in the decision-making processes of the United Nations and its agencies, other international agencies, nongovernmental organizations, each religion, various levels of government, and all other major organizations.

FUTURE-RELEVANT RESEARCH AND TEACHING

This key priority can usefully be divided into its two components: (a) future-relevant research and (b) future-relevant teaching.

Future-Relevant Research

In order to achieve a satisfactory future, you need to rapidly expand your efforts to develop future-oriented knowledge, ideas, insights, understanding, visions, and wisdom. You need to know far more about world problems, social change, potential futures, the effectiveness of various possible paths, individual change, the personal foundations of caring about future generations, and several other future-relevant topics. This future-oriented inquiry can include not only research and development projects, but also creative visioning, speculative brainstorming, disciplined thinking, synthesis, conceptual frameworks, theory-building, and wide-ranging dialogue.

Move toward a body of concepts, ideas, and knowledge that is profound, powerful, and well organized. Carefully examine your conceptual frameworks and paradigms. Organize your existing knowledge base more rigorously; don't be conceptually sloppy or lazy. Critique and build on the ideas and frameworks of others, instead of operating in intellectual isolation. Try to attract people with especially penetrating minds and thoughtful approaches, and then generously support their intellectual work.

The amount of effort going into creating knowledge that is profoundly significant to the long-term future is only about one-third of what it should be. The gap between the optimum effort and your current level is foolish and poignant. Your aim should be to multiply your future-oriented inquiry threefold over the next few years. The long-term benefits will far outweigh the costs.

For success, you need to increase your knowledge of world problems and social change much faster than the problems themselves increase. At present, the problems are outstripping your knowledge of how to deal with them. You are going to have to run much faster than now simply to catch up to all the major problems. Then you may find that the negative forces are running faster and faster, becoming more and more challenging. To develop the knowledge to outrun all these tendencies for civilization to deteriorate, you will need to increase your efforts even further. You certainly have the potential to win the race, but not by coasting along at your present level of future-oriented research.

Future-Relevant Teaching

Learning and teaching about the future provide an essential foundation for building a better world. You cannot achieve a positive future without far-reaching learning and changes by individuals around the world. These individuals include all of you, not just political leaders, government officials, policy experts, or business leaders. You no doubt recall the prescient words of one of your early futurists, H. G. Wells: "Human history becomes more and more a race between education and catastrophe." You can successfully navigate through the next few decades only if a large proportion of the world's population understands global problems and potential futures, cares about future generations, accepts the need for change, and takes a cooperative and constructive approach to dealing with hard choices. Once enough people care about future generations, implementing these six key priorities will become much easier.

Any path to a positive future will require deep changes in individual perspectives, values, and behavior. From early childhood to late adulthood, learning opportunities should be widespread. In every city on earth, at least some schools, colleges, adult education programs, and libraries should provide a wide array of methods for people to learn about the future prospects of their civilization and their region. In addition to various educational programs and institutions, these opportunities can include libraries, discussion groups, informal education, workshops, support groups, television, printed materials, electronic sources and hardware, and self-planned learning projects. This range of learning opportunities should help people of all ages understand global issues, think skeptically and critically when appropriate, treasure all life on earth, feel concern for other people, grasp the importance of caring about us future generations, grasp our perspective, feel committed to necessary changes, tolerate diverse cultures and views, cooperate for the common good, and pursue meaningful non-material goals.

Educational institutions should provide courses in futures studies, with some emphasis on the perspective of future generations, using approaches that affect the head, heart, soul, and hands of people of all ages. Your education about the future could be greatly enhanced if you develop a better knowledge base about potential futures, conduct research on the processes of learning and teaching about the future, and experiment with innovative and profound approaches to such learning and teaching.

WEAPONS AND WARFARE

Please reduce warfare and violent civil unrest by fostering non-military methods and institutions for dealing with disputes, greed, ambition, anger, and the urge for revenge. Firmly establish the norm that any sort of armed violence is illegitimate and out of the question. Foster widespread human rights and political participation. Foster a spirit of tolerance and cooperation among various religious and ethnic groups. Find ways to prevent national governments from killing large numbers of their own people.

Cut your military forces and budgets by at least 50%, preferably 75%, thus freeing up resources for the six key priorities. Virtually everyone will be better off if worldwide peace enables human energy to be devoted to building a satisfactory future.

As we survey everything that is happening on earth in your era, the thing we worry about most is your nuclear weapons. Poised to strike on very short notice, they are the severest threat to our inheriting your knowledge and culture intact--and even to our existence. Wars can occur with startling suddenness and follow an unpredictable course. Several countries possess nuclear and biological weapons, and would not hesitate to use them in certain circumstances. You seem oblivious to the likelihood and impact of their use. In just one day you could destroy the major portion of human civilization. The next few months of nuclear winter would be marked by cold and darkness, by the lack of safe food and water, and by illness and suffering. Within a year almost everyone in the world would be dead or very sick. Because of your moment of anger or greed or belligerence, you would have destroyed human civilization forever. Surely you can see that this is a totally unacceptable risk that worries us deeply.

PLANET AND POPULATION

We, the people of the future, obviously require a planet capable of supporting life. We do not want to inherit from you a bleak and devastated planet that is even more crowded than in your day. We are alarmed at your rate of consumption: you are degrading your natural environment and using up the planet's resources very quickly. Yet five decades after you read this, if your present growth continues, there will be *twice* as many people depleting the planet. Hunger, poverty, and environmental deterioration will become worse and worse if you continue on your present path. It is essential that you move toward a sustainable society and an appropriate population size that do not exceed the earth's long-term carrying capacity. We will be very grateful if you soon achieve a sustainable relationship with the planet in agriculture, forestry, fish, wildlife, water, and energy. In order to accomplish this, you will have to take rapid, profound, effective, extraordinary measures worldwide (a) to halt or even reverse population growth, (b) to reduce luxurious and frivolous consumption, unduly high incomes, and undue concentrations of wealth throughout the world, (c) to live in balance and harmony with the interconnected web of life on earth, and (d) to minimize the most burdensome types of environmental deterioration, such as global warming, thinning of the ozone layer, scarcity of good drinking water, toxic and radioactive waste, soil erosion, and the loss of wilderness and wild species.

There is little point to arguing amongst yourselves about who is to blame for creating and exacerbating the deterioration in your environment and the rapid growth in your population. The important thing is for all nations and all people to take responsible actions for reversing the negative trends.

Population growth is one of your worst follies. It already hurts you in several ways, and will make poverty and environmental problems much more difficult to handle in the long run. Zero population growth will have to be achieved sooner or later: we will be far better off if you move rapidly toward it now instead of letting things become worse and worse.

SIGNIFICANT KNOWLEDGE

We value humanity's accumulated body of knowledge and understanding as one of our most treasured possessions. Your era's contributions to that knowledge is one of the most valuable gifts that you can pass on to us. Please continue your efforts to improve your knowledge, ideas, insights, and wisdom, especially in directions that emphasize depth and synthesis. In order to maximize your contribution, it is important to keep your thinking open-minded yet skeptical, bold yet disciplined, fresh yet profound, wide-ranging yet penetrating.

In particular, we hope you will double your efforts to understand humanity's broad significant contexts--the biggest questions of all. Our place and significance in the universe, for instance, and our sources of meaning and purpose. Other civilizations that have developed in our galaxy, and how our future and theirs might be linked. Feasible paths for achieving a positive human future.

At your stage in the centuries-long accumulation of knowledge, the most important cutting edge of all is the search for extraterrestrial intelligence. Your current search efforts with radio and optical telescopes are quite appropriate, but support for them should be doubled or tripled. You should also explore any other methods and possibilities for discovering a detailed message. For example, search for small automated surveillance probes within the solar system, even on the earth itself, with the hope that at least one of them will be designed to yield information as well as collect it.

In addition to enlarging the storehouse of significant knowledge, it is important to protect it from dictatorships and other potential catastrophes. Remember that various armies, rulers, and governments throughout history have tried to suppress and destroy existing knowledge. This could happen again. Please develop steps to ensure that the core of human culture, knowledge, literature, music, and art will survive any war and any repressive worldwide regime, whether military, political, or religious.

LEARNING, CARING, AND MEANINGFULNESS

Now we come to the final societal priority that we recommend for your era. This priority continues to be very important to us, so we hope it will soon become important to you, too.

In this final priority, we urge your society to focus plenty of attention and support on the deeper and softer aspects of individual lives. We refer specifically to three areas: (a) widespread individual learning about the most important questions of all, (b) caring based on deep connectedness to people, the planet, and future generations, (c) a strong sense of meaning and purpose in life. Although we will discuss these three areas separately, they are actually closely interrelated. And all three contribute to the individual's deeper and softer side.

> a) Your society could do much more toward widespread individual learning about the most important questions of all. You should encourage and help each individual to learn the accumulated knowledge on these questions, and also to think through their own best answers. Obviously they will be more successful in their quest if your society has fostered their ability to think clearly, flexibly, creatively, and skeptically about difficult and controversial questions. Here are some of the big questions that thoughtful individuals face:

- the origin of the universe
- cosmic evolution and the ultimate destination of the universe
- our place in the universe
- our relationship with other intelligent beings and civilizations in our galaxy
- the origin, history, and long-term future of humankind and human culture
- our appropriate relationship with the planet and its diverse forms of life
- core values
- finding a path to a positive human future

• how each individual can contribute to achieving that positive future

b) Your society should do much more to help people feel a deep bonding or connectedness with all of humankind, with the planet and its diverse forms of life, and with future generations. Explore the usefulness of music, hymns, songs, poetry, prose, laser light shows, art, hiking, cathedrals, inspirational services, children, mountains, observation towers, zoos, nature reserves, and scenic beauty for this purpose. As more and more people experience a deep connectedness, they will care strongly about humanity, future generations, and the planet--and will act on that deep love and caring. They will eagerly want to make a positive difference to humanity and the planet. They will be happy to experience a bond with something ageless, something transcendent, something much larger than their own life.

Creating inspirational groups dedicated to future generations could be particularly useful. The people in these groups would feel bonded together by their deep caring for future generations, and by their efforts to build a better world. Various methods could be used to inspire and strengthen each member's sense of connectedness to humanity and its positive future. Inspirational gatherings, oral readings, silent reflection, discussion, and songs of gratitude and joy could all play a part. Members could share their feelings about the long-term future, reflect on the implications of recent events, and discuss their most significant unanswered questions. Members could also discuss their current efforts to contribute, including their strategies, obstacles, triumphs, and failures. Many people want to make a positive difference to the world, but lack a sympathetic and inspirational support group. Such groups could be built on love and reverence for human civilization and other societies in our galaxy, awe concerning the mysteries of the universe, and commitment to service on behalf of future generations. By supporting various efforts to build a positive long-term future, these groups could provide people with an inspiriting and transcendent purpose in life.

c) Your society should also focus much more attention and support on the individual's desire for a sense of meaning and purpose in life. A sense of meaning and purpose can easily pervade a society in which people share a sense of connectedness with the cosmos, with its diverse life, and with the continuous procession of generations. These foundations are quite real, of course; there is no need to adopt false beliefs or unrealistic expectations in order to feel a deep sense of meaning and purpose.

As your support for this societal priority increases, you will find that more and more lives are suffused with insight, wisdom, love, caring, altruism, meaning, and joy instead of ignorance, ill will, meaninglessness, and unhappiness. Some fears and pain and sorrow will remain, but will be more focused on future generations than on oneself. Over time, in fact, the distinction between oneself and future generations will blur. As the depth and strength of the connectedness increases, the boundaries between self and humanity become softer and less important. The dominant perception is a sense of oneness.

REFLECTIONS ON THE SIX PRIORITIES

The six changes that need to be made by individuals, organizations, governments, and society are startlingly large, deep, and far-reaching. But the alternative is for your grandchildren and the other members of their generation to spend much of their adult life in a social and physical environment that is bleak and nasty. The six profound changes are necessary in order to avoid such a negative outcome. They provide the best path to a positive future.

Of the six, the most important of all is a worldwide shift toward caring deeply about the well-being of all the people who will be alive over the next few decades, and the well-being of the planet. This perspective transformation or paradigm shift is necessary for citizens, policy-makers, business leaders, and key people throughout governments. As more and more of you change your inner perspective, there is an excellent chance that the necessary outer changes will also occur. People, goals, values, processes, structures, and projects must all shift toward supporting humanity's long-term flourishing. As a result, the ever-unfolding history of human civilization may alter course toward a positive future.

Perhaps you are feeling that our message to you is unrealistic and too ambitious. You wonder whether you can actually manage to implement the six priorities that we are recommending. We believe that you can. Do not be too quick to dismiss our recommendations as farfetched or impossible. Human history provides other examples of dramatic paradigm shifts. The six priorities can be achieved if enough people around the world become strongly motivated to do so. We have intentionally omitted dozens of other worthy priorities from the list in order to make it more feasible, because no one can achieve all of their hopes and dreams, no matter how worthy. We are grateful for the inner changes and outer efforts that are already under way. If you focus your attention and resources on these six crucial priorities, you have a good chance of success. The costs and obstacles are daunting, but you are quite capable of overcoming them if you are strongly motivated.

We worry that you will choose the tempting path that lies right in front of you, dissipating your efforts on alluring goals and priorities that will have little influence on long-term flourishing--squandering your time and energy not only on consumption, luxury, competition, quarrels, and violence, but also on the faddish projects and causes of the moment. Think of the pain and suffering that you will cause us--the bleak lives and barren planet, the harsh restrictions, the lost potential, the sense of malaise and futility. We cry when we think of what might come to pass. Perhaps you too will feel some tears as you think about what your era's lack of future-oriented caring and effort could inflict on us.

Thank you very much for listening to our views so thoughtfully. We are cautiously hopeful that more and more of you will grasp our perspective. If enough people join the loosely knit worldwide effort to build a positive future, then a profound change in direction becomes possible. Working together, you can pass on to us a store of deeply relevant knowledge, a flourishing and peaceful culture, and a vibrantly healthy planet.

NOTE

This chapter is drawn from a forthcoming book called *A Message from Future Generations* (Copyright 1995 Allen Tough).

DECLINE OR
REVITALIZATION

FUTURIZING AMERICA'S INSTITUTIONS

by

Richard D. Lamm

America will not remain a prosperous and competitive country unless we futurize our institutions. One constant in the decline of nations is the inability to effectively reform the institutions and systems that are causing the decline. This led the historian Arnold Toynbee to observe, "All great nations commit suicide."

Joseph Schumpeter, Nobel prize-winning economist, observed that all human institutions eventually become smug, self-satisfied, incestuous, bureaucratic, inefficient and risk adverse. Time and past success cause them to lose the cutting-edge vitality that made them great institutions in the first place. Jonathan Rauch calls this process "demosclerosis." I would suggest that one of the great challenges of the future is to reform our institutions so they are equal to the magnitude of our present day problems.

Great societies have a capacity for self-correction which, clearly, this country has had in the past. One of our many challenges is to make sure this self-correction continues--to futurize our institutions to become efficient, effective and competitive for the new world into which we are rapidly moving. We are no longer a continental economy, but compete economically in a world marketplace where we are surrounded by awesomely efficient, low-wage competitors. The future belongs, in an economic sense, to the efficient.

DOMESTIC INSTITUTIONS

America's basic domestic institutions have lost much of the Yankee ingenuity and efficiency that helped build our economy and our nation. They simply do not produce world class results.

No nation spends more money on health care than America. How are we doing? American males are 15th in world life expectancy; American females are 8th. We're 20th in infant mortality, and 26 nations have better cardiovascular health rates than we do. Twelve nations have better cancer survival rates. In no major health statistic, except one, are Americans as healthy as those in Europe, England, Canada or Japan. We have the highest life expectancy after reaching age 80 mainly because of Medicare which spends massive amounts of money on the last generation, but doesn't cover the general population. We spend more money turning 80-year-olds into 90-year

Richard D. Lamm, *former Colorado governor, is director of the Center for Public Policy and Contemporary Issues, University of Denver.*

olds than we do 6-year-olds into educated 16-year-olds. We have the least comprehensive, most inefficient, and highly technical health care system in the world. Yet, it produces comparatively poor health outcomes.

Only one nation spends more money on educating their children than does the United States. How are we doing? American students are in the bottom third on all international comparisons in every subject. Asian students are ahead of American students from the first grade and graduate from high school with as much class time as our students have when they graduate from college--consistently outscoring us by large margins.

No nation spends more money on crime control, police, burglar alarms, bars on windows, and private security police. How are we doing? We live in the most violent and crime-infested society in the industrial world.

No nation spends more money electing politicians to office, or lobbying them while they are there. How are we doing? Wherever we look, our public problems are outgrowing our solutions. American politics have become a playground of special interests and self-seeking politicians. The public is rapidly losing the confidence necessary to support a democracy. Less than 20 percent of the American public "expect government to do the right thing." Again, we spend more to achieve less.

America has 6 percent of the world's population, but over 50 percent of the world's lawyers. American goods and services are burdened by having to carry incredible costs that the goods and services of other nations don't have to carry. There is a "lawyer tax" on almost everything we do. The political influence of lawyers keeps us from passing the type of tort reform enjoyed by other nations.

Ultimately, it is not a company that competes, but societies that compete. Nations that educate their citizens efficiently and effectively, find ways to motivate their workers, deliver health care in a cost efficient manner, and find expeditious ways to settle disputes among their citizens with a minimum of litigation are generally the nations that win the race for an international high standard of living.

HOW DO WE FUTURIZE OUR DOMESTIC INSTITUTIONS?

Every society in the developed world runs their system on a fraction of the lawyers we have. We have two and a half times as many lawyers per capita as Great Britain, five times as many per capita as Germany, and 25 times as many as Japan. Despite this over-abundance, we are adding new lawyers at a rate four times faster than our population growth.

One scholar has warned: The legal process, because of its unbridled growth, has become a cancer which threatens the vitality of our form of capitalism and democracy.

We are, beyond question, the most litigious nation on earth and the most litigious in all of human history. This is a form of economic cancer.

Our legal system is draining talent from our society which is desperately needed elsewhere. Forty percent of our Rhodes Scholars go to law school to become wealth-dividing lawyers rather than wealth-creating scientists, engineers, or technicians. Japan trains 10 engineers for every lawyer; we train 10 lawyers for every engineer. If we do not know anything else about the new world economy, we should understand that wealth will not flow to the nation with the most litigation and lawyers, but to the nation that has the best wealth-creating team.

What are the solutions? They are not difficult to find, but they are difficult to adopt. Other industrial nations have alternative methods of dispute resolution, which adjust differences and disputes between citizens. For instance:

- They have no-fault automobile compensation systems;

- They limit awards for pain and suffering; and

- They require the losing party to pay legal fees if a suit was not legally justified.

We are the only nation in the world that has a jury trial in a civil case. No less an advocate than F. Lee Bailey has stated: Every democratic nation, including our model, Great Britain, has given up the right to a jury trial on most civil lawsuits. Were we to imitate them, we might see substantial reform. Yet, we continue to expend tremendous amounts of effort and money in preserving a procedural nicety which no longer insures a fair and independent account.

It is not all the fault of lawyers. Lawyers are partly mirroring the adversarial nature of our culture. Americans are less willing to accept certain losses as non-compensable acts of God. We increasingly believe we have a right to be compensated for every loss. Additionally, we have come to view the legal system like the lottery-- as our outside chance to get rich without working for it. The legal system, like the lottery, promises easy riches to the citizens of the casino society, but the net effect is counterproductive to the long term future of the nation.

Former President Derek Bok of Harvard put it succinctly: Our societal gains from law and lawyering are outweighed by their societal costs. Most Americans understand this and agree. We know many of the solutions, but we fail to act. No nation in history has sued its way to greatness.

WHAT ARE THE SOLUTIONS IN HEALTH CARE?

Health care has so many vested interests that we are finding it difficult to reform a system which consumes $1 out of every $7 we spend in America.

So, what are the solutions to our rising health care costs? Again, many solutions are not hard to identify, but they are hard to adopt. America must make either the market or government work to reduce the dollars going into illness care before it eats us alive. We should reform our tort system which forces so much defensive medicine. We should stop training so many doctors, and prevent foreign medical graduates from swelling an already overcrowded profession. We should train far more family doctors and far fewer specialists. We should close many hospitals (50 percent of the hospital beds in Colorado are empty), and turn others into nursing home facilities. We should have many more hospices and fewer intensive care units.

Why do we need *both* an expensive health care system and the medical portion of workmen's compensation? Health insurance and duplicate coverage under our auto insurance?

We should have much less heroic medicine and much more basic medicine. We should give pregnant women more prenatal care and the elderly more flu shots, and stop keeping terminal people alive on our high-technology machines. We should tax cigarettes and alcohol much more heavily.

We must also adjust our expectations. Some wise person once told me, "Maturity is a recognition of one's limitations." Maturity in a modern society must similarly be the recognition that we cannot deliver all the health care we have invented to all our citizens. We must find ways to limit that health care which is not cost effective or is only marginally effective. This will be very hard for a society which thinks it has a right to all the health care that is beneficial, even marginally beneficial.

Health care costs in America are making us economically sick, and reforming our system must have a high priority.

GOVERNMENTAL INSTITUTIONS

The dilemma of American political institutions is that we cannot do politically what we need to do economically to remain a prosperous and competitive society. Peter Singi said, "The large trends creep up on us. Then overwhelm us." When I took office as Governor of Colorado in 1975, we had a national debt approximately equal to one-third of our GDP. When I left office in 1987, our debt was one-half of our GDP. Today, we have a debt equal to three quarters of our GDP ($5 trillion in a $7 trillion economy). No nation can continue this trend. No nation can consume more than it produces, spend more than it taxes, and import more than it exports for very long. Correcting this is difficult. The economy of the 1990s cannot fund all of the expectations we have built up during the 1960s and 1970s. We feel "entitled" to an increasing list of programs which are unsustainable.

MEDICARE

Medicare is not in as bad of shape as its critics contend--it is worse! America is getting older fast. Our children are going to have to run a nation of 50 Floridas. In 2011, when the baby boomers start to retire, all America's institutional sacred cows will rapidly go bankrupt. By 2012, the Bipartisan Commission on Entitlements warns us that the current revenue structure will *only* cover entitlements and interest on the federal debt. No Judiciary. No Executive Branch. No national parks. No discretionary programs. Nada!

Then, by 2029 (when my children are in mid-career), the current tax structure applied to the anticipated revenue in 2029 will only pay for four programs: Medicare, Medicaid, Social Security and federal retirement programs. Nothing else!

SOCIAL SECURITY

Social security is a fiscal iceberg lying in our future. We have promised more than we can realistically deliver. Pete Peterson observes that a typical middle-aged couple who retired in 1981 has received more Social Security and Medicare benefits back than they paid in federal taxes (plus interest) all their lives. Our basic institutions, so successful in lifting the elderly out of poverty, are quickly becoming unsustainable. We are living too long and having too few children to blindly continue a system that pays more than it collects. The untouchable has become the unavoidable. These issues cannot long remain uncorrected. The sooner the solution, the less drastic the remedy.

We must look anew at solutions we have historically rejected. We have many options. We could "means test" Social Security and stop paying it to wealthy retirees. We could adjust COLA. We could increase the retirement age to 70. America could increase its savings and keep faith with its children by slowly privatizing Social Security. There are no politically, painless solutions to this actuarial nightmare--but there are solutions. Retiring the baby boomers will be one of the great challenges in American history.

FEDERAL BUDGET

The federal budget is a bipartisan problem with our future at stake. We have pre-spent $5 trillion of our children's money. No one can say NO to anyone. Six hundred thousand millionaires get a Social Security check every month. We have millionaires subsidized by Medicare while blocks away children go without health care. Every year, $200 billion in entitlements and tax expenditures are given to retirees who have other retirement income over $50,000 a year. Public policy should not blindly transfer money from the young to the old. But that's what we are doing.

We must examine, in the name of fiscal sanity, all of the programs we have built up in the past, and too easily take for granted. Our military retirement programs allow people to retire while they are still in their forties--all with indexed pensions and health care. Are we wealthy enough to retire people in their early forties and subsidize them for 40 or 50 years for only 20 years of military service?

Two-thirds of the care given in veterans' hospitals are for non-service connected disabilities. Do we really need to give veterans taxpayer-funded care for non-service connected disabilities? In fact, with approximately 40 percent of the hospital beds in America empty, do we even need a system of VA hospitals? Why not integrate the veterans into the empty hospital beds we now maintain elsewhere in the system?

America has built up a large number of well-meaning programs during the halcyon days of our economy which must be better focused on the truly needy. Close to 50 percent of American families get some sort of governmental check each month; and yet, many of them are far from needy.

It will soon become starkly apparent that we have designed our federal programs too generously. We have cast our safety net too widely; and yet, missed too many truly poor. Correcting this is politically difficult, but must be done.

CONCLUSION

The nations of the world are metaphorically lined up on the starting line in the race for a high standard of living. One runner has an American flag on his back, another runner has a Japanese flag on his back, another a German flag, another a Korean flag, and so on. The race is about to begin. Just before the race begins, we ask our runner (the one with the American flag on his back) to carry along with him half of all the world's lawyers, the highest drug and alcohol abuse in the workplace, the largest number of functional illiterates, the highest health care costs, an increasingly dysfunctional education system, and retirement systems that promise to bankrupt our children. How much can our runner carry? It is time to futurize America's institutions.

MEDICAL ETHICS AND
THE FUTURE

SOME REFLECTIONS ON THE FUTURE OF MEDICAL ETHICS

by

Robert B. Mellert

A quarter century ago it would have been possible to assemble all the literature on medical ethics and stack it upon your living room coffee table. With enough time and coffee, you might have been able to digest the entirety and to become an expert in the field.

As we near the end of this century, all the literature on medical ethics--if indeed they could be collected--would wipe out your entire living room and force you to retreat to the kitchen to start your reading. And if current trends continue, by the year 2020 you might have to evacuate your house!

Today there are institutes and centers dedicated to the study of medical ethics, many of which regularly publish monographs and journals. Up-to-date libraries in medical ethics contain, in addition to these materials, shelves of books by professionals in medicine, philosophy and theology, bibliographies of these works, and even a bibliography of the bibliographies. Issues discussed in these writings run the gamut from assisted suicide as a medical procedure to the use of restraints and sedatives in nursing homes.

Two competing theories about the nature of health care seem to be emerging from all of this literature. While these two theories are not necessarily contradictory, they do represent two different views about the goals, purposes and applications of health care, and about the good that medical assistance ought to provide. The result of this difference is a certain tension that sometimes develops into conflict.

The first approach to medical assistance, which I shall call the "curing" approach, is based upon traditional medical ethical principles that go back as far as the Hippocratic oath. These principles have been neatly formulated into a list of standards that can be found in just about every textbook in medical ethics: the principle of life, the principle of beneficence, the principle of nonmaleficence, and the principle of justice. Some texts add a few more or use different language to express them. Since the individual principles are peripheral to the thrust of this essay, I recommend to the reader any of the fine texts on the market for further reflection regarding these principles and their applications.

The second is the "caring" approach to medical ethics. It provides the basis for today's emphasis on patient autonomy, proper "bedside manners" by health care providers, preparation of living wills, and the hospice movement. The concerns represented by this approach

Dr. **Robert B. Mellert** *is a professor of philosophy at Brookdale Community College, Lincroft, New Jersey.*

have, of course, always been present in medical assistance, but their emergence as--arguably--the primary focus of medicine is more recent.

Let us take a look at each of these approaches in more detail.

Philosophically, the "curing," or principles, approach is supported by the natural law theory. Philosophers with this perspective would argue that the nature of medicine is to heal. This objective is in harmony with the person's right to life. To subordinate healing to some other function, such as caring, would violate the nature of medicine itself. Caring, of course, is important, but it must only be seen as subservient to the primary task of curing.

Also in support of this position is traditional Western religious ethics. The sanctity of human life is an important ideal in this morality. Because it is a gift from God, life must be sustained to the extent reasonably possible, and all ordinary measures must be taken to preserve it. This tradition holds that only God's authority can decide the time of death. In the case of terminal suffering, the job of the health professional must never include options such as assisted suicide, or even medication that would shorten life.

Both of these ethical theories support the primacy of the curing approach to medical ethics by analyzing the nature of the actions that define medicine and by prescribing those actions in individual cases. To the extent possible, these actions are the ones required by the most objective, scientific appraisal of how life in an individual case can be preserved. The application of the basic moral principles, or of the commandments of God, constitute doing what is morally right. Acting otherwise is morally wrong. To the extent possible, morality is also objectively formulated and applied.

In this approach, therefore, physicians play a key role. What to do regarding the preservation of life is primarily a medical judgment. As professionals who are knowledgeable about the relevant medical procedures and who are best able to judge their efficacy, physicians can expect that their recommendations will be accepted by their patients. The physicians' task is to explain to patients why such procedures are recommended as being the best in the given circumstances. In other words, the process of attaining informed consent places most emphasis on the informed part. Consent is presumed to follow the requisite information. Often this model of the doctor-patient relationship is called the paternalistic model.

We now turn to the second approach to medical ethics, that of "caring." In this case, the philosophical basis is consequentialist, such as utilitarianism or situation ethics. Jeremy Bentham, the nineteenth century British philosopher, perhaps best expresses the utilitarian standard as "the maximization of pleasure and the minimization of pain."([1]) This standard is justified on the grounds that all men seek pleasure and avoid pain, and that these constitute the fundamental values of all human existence. In medicine, the second part of this formula is the major concern. The role of the health care professional is to minimize pain. Of course, pain or discomfort may sometimes be necessary in order to restore health and thus provide further opportunities for pleasure. But the moral judgment is always made by an analysis of probable outcomes. How much pain will be necessary to permit how much quality of life thereafter? The weighing of alternatives as to their anticipated consequences determines the ethically preferred procedure. It is the subsequent quality of life, not the intrinsic sanctity of life, that provides the basis for moral judgment.

Situation ethics, popularized by the theologian Joseph Fletcher a quarter century ago, is simply a religious version of utilitarianism. Using the Bible as his source, Fletcher argued that agape (selfless love) is the only norm that is self-justifying; therefore, the realization of love can be the only norm for ethics.([2]) As a medical ethicist, he applied this standard in ways that placed the care of the patient as the primary obligation of the health care professional, even to the point of allowing the possibility of euthanasia.

Both of these versions differ from the natural law and divine command ethics in that they make the consequences of the action rather than the action itself the determinant of morality. Hence, the focus of ethics changes from the issue of what is right and what is wrong to doing what is good and avoiding what is harmful. Furthermore, what constitutes care for one person may not be the same as the care desired by another. What one practitioner does to provide care may be different from what another does. A level of subjectivity enters into the caring approach that is absent from the curing approach.

Likewise, the role of the physician changes dramatically when caring becomes primary. Here the physician becomes a medical consultant, not a health care provider. The job is to lay out the options as clearly as possible, explaining to the patient possible procedures, the prognosis for each, probable discomforts and side effects, costs and risks. Once the physician has educated the patient, the latter is charged with the responsibility of making the choice, and based upon that choice, the physician will proceed, even if that choice does not represent the one the physician would have personally preferred. In other words, the autonomy of the patient is stressed, and in the process of attaining informed consent using this model, the emphasis is on the patient's consent.

Let me illustrate the tension between these two approaches with two examples. The first one is familiar to all of us. Dr. Jack Kavorkian has become a household name because of his willingness to assist his terminal patients in committing suicide when their pain becomes too much of a burden and they choose death rather than prolonged suffering.Those who are unable to get the help of Dr. Kavorkian can try one of the do-it-yourself techniques described in Derek Humphry's best seller *Final Exit*.([3])

The media have portrayed Kavorkian as a law-breaker, and at least one reviewer referred to Humphry's book as "ghoulish." But they have forced us into thinking about the unthinkable scenario: I am the one who is terminally ill with pain and suffering as the prognosis for the rest of my life, and the cost of prolonging my death is wiping out the money I have saved for my daughters to become established or for the education of my grandchildren. What if, on the basis of consequentialist morality, I conclude that the maximization of happiness (for my kin) and the minimization of pain (for myself) warrants my terminating my life? Then the most caring act one can offer me is to assist me in suicide. Can I turn to my physician or my nurse to help me carry out my decision, or would such help constitute a breech of their medical ethics?

There is another unthinkable scenario: Suppose I, a layman in the field of medicine, am the person to whom such an appeal is made by my mother, wife, or daughter? How shall I respond? "The outlook may be dim," I might say, adopting the curing approach, "but one must never give up hope. A remedy might be around the corner; stronger pain relief maybe developed; you may go into remission and even recover."Or will my response be based upon the caring approach? Then, understanding my loved one's dilemma and respecting her autonomy, I may begin to explore with her the option of removing vital life support mechanisms or even assisting in her suicide. In other words, will I do what is right by the law and by traditional morality, or will I do what is good according to a utilitarian or situational morality?

[Let us note parenthetically that these two unthinkable scenarios are no longer unthinkable. We are now thinking about them. At some point in the future, some of us may be called upon to make a judgment about them. For a lot of people caught in the dilemma of "curing" versus "caring, "such a judgment is not made easily.]

My second example does not suggest the same urgency; nevertheless, it represents a myriad of smaller decisions made daily in health care facilities that turn on the same dilemma. In a film entitled "Code Gray,"[4] which I still use in my medical ethics classes, there is a scene in which an elderly woman in a nursing home is gently confronted by a nurse about a decision to restrain her from leaving the wheelchair and walking about on her own. "If you fall, you may be seriously injured, and none of us would want that to happen,"she says. But for the elderly woman, her ability to stand up and walk is the last vestige of freedom she enjoys in her old age. To be restrained and forced to call for assistance every time she wants to move about seems too high a price to pay for avoiding the risk of a fall. Nevertheless, the nurse urges her at least to try on the restraint and wear it for a while, and in the end the old woman can do nothing but acquiesce.

Here the curing model takes on a new dimension. The woman is not sick or injured, but the risk of falling and breaking a bone is a potential disability. So safety and the preservation of health dictate that she be protected from an accident, even if that means protecting her from herself. On the other hand, while one sympathizes with the old woman, one can also understand why caring for her as she would wish to be cared for would impose an unbearable burden upon the nursing facility. Such facilities are responsible for many such elderly persons and are generally not staffed adequately to provide constant surveillance for each patient individually. The use of restraints, tranquilizers, and medications as a way of minimizing risk, therefore, ends up sacrificing caring for safety.

The ethical dilemma we confront here involves the choice between doing what is right, i.e., making the woman safe from injury, or doing what results in pleasure, i.e., knowing she is free to move about on her own. In choosing the former, the nursing home opted to do what was right, even though it resulted in displeasure, rather than to do what was wrong (not safeguarding the woman from a fall), even though this would have resulted in the woman's satisfaction.

Many of us who are part of the health care delivery system, either as providers or as consumers--and we all eventually fit in here--have been troubled by the tension that is sometimes created between the two approaches I have been describing. What are the reasons we encounter this tension in the health care climate of contemporary society, and how might we learn to deal with it?

To begin, physicians are trained to heal and to cure. Death, to the conscientious physician, is taken as a defeat, much as good teachers see in the failure of their students their own failure as well. So physicians attempt to conquer injury and disease with whatever technological weapons are available to them. Furthermore, if at any time in their practice they are tempted to compromise in their resolve to seek a cure even at the expense of humane care, there is always the possibility of a lawsuit to consider. Malpractice insurance is so costly today that it behooves any physician to order every conceivable test and tube and to attach every available monitor in order to escape a legal challenge that begins with the question, "But why didn't you do 'X'?"

To protect themselves from aggressive medical intervention, consumers have also had to resort to legal instruments. The living will, or advance directive, is simply a formalized way to restore to consumers some control over their medical situation. By signing such a document, legal in many states, consumers attempt to prevent aggressive procedures by physicians worried about aggressive lawyers representing aggressive district attorneys, patients or their next of kin. Nobody is permitted to trust anybody any more, it seems, and what this means practically is that the health practitioner must always go for the cure, even at the expense of care. Consequently, patients who seek a caring approach had better come to the health care provider or facility prepared to insist upon their right to decide. This is especially true when the cure may employ complicated medical technology, the cost for which the patient may not be willing or able to pay.

Sometimes, even expressing one's desires is not adequate. A recent study, known as "Support," published in November, 1995, in the Journal of the American Medical Association, reported that only about half of the terminally ill patients who had requested do-not-resuscitate orders actually had their wishes respected. ([5]) And 70% of the patients surveyed were never asked their preferences at all.

Of course, not every serious illness occasions a confrontation. Often physician and patient are of one mind, and there is no tension. Sometimes, patients are unable or unwilling to assume the responsibilities required of them by the caring model, and they surrender their autonomy to the physician. "You're the doctor. You do what you think best. "But occasionally there is no meeting of the minds, and what the physician recommends is not what the patient chooses. Second and third opinions are sought, and patients are left struggling with the consequences of their autonomy at a time when they are least capable of the struggle.

Because of the social forces described above, it is likely that the tension between curing and caring will continue into the future. With it some important new issues are emerging that need to be discussed. Some of these issues deal with the duties and rights of future patients; others will confound the roles and responsibilities of future providers.

Patients will have to become knowledgeable enough about their medical condition to make necessary choices. This will not be an easy task because the world of medicine changes so rapidly. If the patient chooses to instruct the providers to do everything possible to attempt a cure, including the use of extraordinary or experimental procedures, does that choice become obligatory upon the providers? Does the patient--any patient--have a right to the best medical services available?

In other words, if patient autonomy in medical decisions is to be treated as a right, does this imply a new entitlement to medical services? And if the patient cannot finance these services, does the cost of this new entitlement get passed along, in one way or another, to the general public? Does anyone in the medical professional get to veto those procedures deemed too marginal or not cost-effective?

Meanwhile, certain issues relate to physicians. What will become of their role if, for some patients, they attempt every possible procedure for a cure, and for other patients, they act to assist their suicide? Are these two roles professionally and psychologically compatible? Are physicians still professionals under these conditions, or do they become mere paid functionaries for their patients? What happens when their own professional opinions are at odds with the choices of their patients?

In this new world of medicine, the physician will struggle with three alternatives: 1) Do what the patient wants; 2) Do what common practice requires in order to avoid malpractice suits; and 3) Follow one's own best professional judgment. Of the three, paradoxically, the second is the safest choice; the first is realistic only if there is written documentation, as with a living will; and the third becomes the most risky of all.

Clearly, these issues lead us into uncharted territory in the field of medicine. There is an enormous amount of complex technical assistance available to the skilled physician for use in sustaining life, but there is less trust and confidence proffered to the physician by the patient. Meanwhile, the patient is being asked to understand more about intricate medical procedures in order to make decisions that formerly were left to the physician.

The paradox is that the patient is getting the right to make medical choices at the very moment in history when that choice becomes overwhelming because of the technical knowledge it requires. To whom will the patient turn? To equally uninformed friends and next of kin? Or to physicians, even though the medical environment in which we operate makes them potential legal adversaries?

Ultimately, I as patient will have to place my confidence in my physician. But if I am going to be treated in the manner of my own choosing--either with predisposition towards effecting a cure or towards providing care--I must convey to the physician my attitude regarding a number of very fundamental philosophical questions: How do I view my life at this stage and under these conditions? What do I see as the continuing purpose of my existence? Under what conditions do I wish to exercise my right to maintain my life? Are there conditions in which I would not wish to continue? And what do I want my physician to do for me then?

A living will may answer some of these questions, but I am not so sure that it can convey all of the nuances. And I am not sure my physician will be willing to spend the time it takes to listen. Most significantly, when the time comes, I am not at all sure I will have the answers to those questions. I don't have them now, and I'm not optimistic that somehow they will be revealed to me in my hour of need.

Despite the pile of literature that keeps growing on this subject, medical ethics is troubled today, but it is not the fault of medical ethics nor even of lawyers, physicians, hospitals or nursing homes. And it is not the fault of patients. It is merely a reflection of the fact that we are all troubled today, troubled by the complexity of technology, by the innumerable options and choices, and by the larger questions about the purpose of being alive. Now, more than ever, we need the wisdom of a Socrates to remind us that of all our obligations, the primary one is to "know thyself. "Attaining that would go a long way towards resolving the dilemma we have been pondering today.

NOTES

1. Bentham, Jeremy. *Principles of Morals and Legislation,* Oxford: Oxford University Press, 1823.

2. Fletcher, Joseph. *Situation Ethics,* Philadelphia: Westminster Press, 1966.

3. Humphry, Derek. *Final Exit,* Secaucus, NJ: Carol Publishing Co., 1991.

4. "Code Gray," Jamaica Plain, ME: Fanlight Productions, 1983.

5. Cowley, Geoffrey, and Mary Hager. "Terminal Care: Too Painful, Too Prolonged," *Newsweek,* Dec. 4, 1995, p. 74-5.

THE GLOBAL SCENE

AVOIDING THE FUTURE OF WAR

by

Gary S. Schofield

The late afternoon sun raked across the boyish Macedonian face as his keen eyes searched the mile and a half line of elite Persian cavalry for breaks in formation. He struck an intense figure of a young man, twenty-two years old. Two great white plumes billowed from each side of his gleaming lion's head helmet. He wore the magnificent armor he had taken from Athena's temple at Ilium and his shield was emblazoned as gloriously as Achilles'. He was "Alexander the Invincible." On his right flank he had drawn up his extraordinary heavy cavalry the *Hetairoi*, the companion Cavalry. In the center, the tips of 12,000, 18-foot pikes known as Sarissas bristled towards the enemy across the river. The heavy Thessalian Cavalry, in diamond formation with elite troops at each corner, waited on the left wing.

"It would be wisest," said Parmenion respectfully, "to camp for the night on the river-bank. To fail with the first attack would be dangerous for the battle in hand and harmful for the outcome of the whole campaign."

Parmenion was advising a dawn assault, before the Persians had formed up in battle line rather than crossing the deep river and scaling the muddy steep banks to clash headlong into the formed enemy. Twenty thousand Persian cavalry above the bank behind the river Granicus screened a further 20,000 heavily armed and well-trained Greek mercenaries.

Alexander looked back at his general Parmenion. The man was about the same age as his dead father, Philip the Second. If the art of war were brush strokes on a canvas, Alexander's colors were bold and vivid, Parmenion's gray and cold.

"I would be ashamed," retorted Alexander, "if, after crossing the Hellespont with ease, the petty stream of the Granicus could deter me from crossing here and now!"

So the man, who would one day be called "Great," sent his cavalry scouts, supported by infantry, crashing through the Granicus and into center of the Persian line. They were met by a withering javelin thunderstorm.

Brilliantly, Alexander's conspicuous battle dress had drawn off cavalry from the Persian center to his opposing wing to face him and now this central assault had created just enough of an opening. Alexander turned inward from the wing amid trumpets blaring and

---

Gary S. Schofield *is a Washington-based, New Zealand writer and television producer for the Smithsonian Institution.*

terrible battle cries. With 13 squadrons of companion cavalry, he personally led the ferocious charge through blood, water, and mud to smash through the Persian center. The Persian center broke and the wings streamed away in rout.

It is breath taking history but it probably never happened!

History is merely a collection of stories and opinion, usually written by the victor, and invariably rewritten every generation as a parable to current times. Without an accurate understanding of history it is impossible to predict the future. Our dreams, values, aspirations, and fears are woven and shaped into history and form at least one fact: *We have destroyed every single past human civilization.* How would we explain our stewardship to an individual from another planet?

- What were the well armored and trained Greek mercenaries doing positioned out of the battle behind the lines? It has been argued that the Persians feared them to be "unreliable." If that were true, placing them at their vulnerable rear would be bizarre. At the rear they could also flee first!
- Alexander and his army had just marched ten miles and were formed for attack late in the day. Therefore, even should they win the battle, nightfall would prevent pursuit. The populous Persian army could regroup to fight again at the next river.
- Fighting against such difficult terrain and position turns a sure victory into the prospect of defeat. This is not brilliant.
- It is interesting that in both Greek and Jewish accounts Parmenion is refuted and scathed. He is consistently a mediocre backdrop to the flare of Alexander, but all these accounts were written after Parmenion was implicated in a mutiny. Alexander had him executed and Calisthenes' "official history" makes a point of blackening his name.

There is little "honor" for the future King of the Known World in such a victory but at dawn Alexander crossed the river unopposed. It was not a Persian practice to begin a march before dawn and camping on the riverbank would mean tethering the horses, so the army probably bivouacked one or two miles away. Alexander fanned out his battle line and clashed with Persian cavalry, explaining the absence of the Greek mercenaries back at the camp moving on foot. The cavalry was routed and the Macedonians poured into the camp. There were 20,000 Greek mercenaries and 2,000 were taken prisoner and sent as slaves to the mines. This leaves a disquieting thought for the first recorded leader to proclaim that "all men are brothers." *Fifteen thousand men were slaughtered where they stood.*

After Watergate, Richard Milhous Nixon considered how history would record his presidency. "It depends on who writes it," he said simply and insightfully. In the same way, Ptolemy, Alexander's General, was writing his official history of the campaigns. At the time, Ptolemy was military ruler of Egypt. A powerful and unchallengeable history of Alexander legitimizes Ptolemy's conquest and makes his position more stable. Self interest can be a successful shaper of history but it is propaganda that weaves its web silently and imperceptibly through the stories we are told:

- The Germans of the First World War, *which was really the Eighth World war*, were not the Huns.
- The Huns were from the Hsiung-nu tribe from the Gobi. They were later called the Mongols and later still the Mugals.
- Caesar did not defeat armies of hundreds of thousands in his Gallic campaigns. He inflated the figures in beautiful aristocratic Latin. The region and technology of the time could not have supported such armies. *However, he did include the number of dead women and children and he sometimes chopped off the right hands of his captives.*
- The Iraqis did not cast babies from their incubators during the invasion of Kuwait. This propaganda was disseminated by a Washington, DC public relations firm encouraging the US to enter the war.
- The Second World War visited death, mutilation, and atrocity on tens of millions of people. It was not "The Good War."

Considering the propaganda of the battle of Granicus, the discrepancy as to the Persian army size only varies from Arrians 40,000, to Diodorus' 110,000, and Justin's 600,000. Alexander's vision was to spread Hellenistic influence and culture, killing all those barbarians, and sometimes Macedonians, who stood in his way. *Ironically, if it were not for the Arab and Moslem barbarians' enlightened preservation of science and the humanities in the dark ages, we would know very little of Alexander or the ancient world at all.*

Propaganda has been obscuring the true causes of war for 5,000 years. As the centuries have passed, Alexander has changed (although Indian historians viewed Alexander as a hideous monster and an appalling butcher). Caesar wailed in painful jealousy, "I am now too old to accomplish the feats of Alexander." Trajan nearly lost Rome's eastern conquests by overextending in the footsteps of Alexander. Gustafus Adolphus, Peter the Great, and the expanding British Empire reveled in the classical examples of "world civilization" or, which justified their own "civilizing" the world. Alexander's homosexual relationship with Hephaestion was down-played by the Victorians. Suddenly, in the twentieth century, the idea of world expansion becomes unpalatable to the Victorian empire builders, *the new victims.* These are the countries from whom we receive our history. How uncomfortable it is to hear phrases of: "Hellenistic purity," "civilizing" other races, the "right of rule," or "might is right" when it is coming from your neighbor, especially in the 1910's and 1930's.

Our history masks the obvious: All societies believe they are superior to all others and all countries are in a permanent state of war with all others. Through alliances, *detente,* and *realpolitik* this is reality disguised. We only live in one frame of the historical movie: It only appears that there is an order in the international political framework and that we have natural enemies and allies. If we view events on a longer time scale we find all enemies and allies to be completely arbitrary and in a dramatic and constant state of flux. For example,

The Western powers still continue a 500-year struggle for economic and military hegemony over Europe:

1) France was an enemy to Spain during the Hapsburg bid for European domination (1520-1660) and shared interests with England.
2) By 1700, France stood alone against an Anglo/Dutch/German alliance.
3) By 1735, England was clashing with Spain, now France's ally.
4) 1756 saw France join its previous enemies, the Hapsburgs, in a war against Prussia.
5) Anglo/German armies made colonial gains against France in the Seven Years War.
6) Napoleon fought everyone through the early 1800's, until being routed by Russia.
7) Russia then became France's ally to buffer a united Germany under Bismarck.
8) In the 1900's France and England (very untraditionally) became allies against Germany.
9) Then all western Europeans joined NATO to buffer an expanded Russia.

Now, without a threat from Russia, the 500-year struggle will continue.

"Success has a thousand fathers, but failure is an orphan." In victory, there is a tendency to think every course of action you took was brilliant, but the loser often is viewed poorly. Five thousand years of human history have been considered basically a success by historians of the victors, but in reality the converse is true. History is not at all an example of great change or progress. Countries have played out the same screen play with the same dialogue for thousands of years. Even our current myth of historical technological progress flies in the face of reality. Before the 19th Century life for the average person changed little for centuries. The Industrial Revolution was the catalyst for modern technology, but, in reality, the steam engine was invented by the Greeks over 2,000 years ago! Hero, in the time of Alexander's general Ptolemy, invented a steam driven machine for opening the doors of the Athenian temple. Being a slave economy the Greeks, and later the Romans, saw no use for it. Even mankind's glorious race for the moon was hitched to a Titan missile designed for carrying nuclear intercontinental ballistic weaponry.

Reveling in the glories and myths of the past has severely eclipsed our understanding of the present and our predicting of the future. Without addressing the abject failures of the past we will surely continue to repeat them in the future. There exist only quite vacuous studies on the causes of war and atrocity all based on history. Consider one of the most vital issues of all: "The cause of the destruction of empires." We all know that Rome fell because of the collapse of moral fiber. But Rome did *not* fall because of orgies: That was written into our history by the Victorians. The Victorians were in the process of dividing the entire planet with the other European powers at the time. Therefore, they shared affinity with the empire builders of classical times. That is why the classical figures are so "British." The British were rewriting the histories.

Today, of course, "we know" the Roman empire fell because of the rise of "the Military Industrial Complex" in the privatization of military command. The desiccation of the Italian peninsula is also an important consideration. Is this also a rewriting of the past?

In reality, the Han dynasty collapsed in China (3rd Century A.D.) and the resulting turmoil displaced the Hsiung-nu tribe (the Huns) westward. This, in turn, displaced the Goths westward into the frontiers of the Roman Empire. The Ostragoths (the Eastern Goths) were displaced further west than the Visigoths (the Western Goths) and waves of terrified refugees flooded helplessly across the border. Emperor Valens allowed them to enter. In Rome's earlier days, newly acquired peoples were treated with respect and ultimately earned citizenship, but here, Roman officials never missed an opportunity to exploit and mistreat these refugees. Consequently, instead of assimilation, they formed a political and military faction within the borders of the Empire. After the Visigoth leadership was treacherously killed during negotiations, the inevitable clash of Adrianople (378 A.D.) saw the slaughter of 40,000 Romans. The Goths swarmed unchecked through Thrace.

Clearly, it is impossible to separate history from the present and from the future. The irony is that the Roman Empire did not fall. It lasted nearly a thousand years longer in the form of the Eastern Roman Empire, the Byzantine Empire. The Roman Empire had been divided in two by Constantine the Great. On the 11th of May 330 A.D., the "House was divided." (Compare: St Mark iii, 25) Clearly there is a powerful message here for futurists: *The messages are not at all clear!"*

It has been more than 50 years since the second World War, yet it is too short a time to discuss the events still so intertwined in propaganda. There exist only vacuous and contradictory theories and beliefs about:

- The failure of appeasement,
- The Treaty of Versailles,
- The cruelty of war reparations (*which were not paid*),
- The Nazi psyche,
- Hitler creating Germany,
- Germany creating Hitler,
- The Great Depression.

If these were true the Second World War would be the greatest aberration in human history. Unfortunately, it is not. War is not the exception but the rule. WWII was just the continuation of a 500-year-old struggle. Countries collide because we design them to do so and at present we are in the process of making the same mistake for the third time this century.

Our understanding of history has been severely compromised by an endearing human quality: anthropomorphism. Being the charming primate creatures that we are, we have "personified" our history. Of course, it is an easy step to organize Kien-Lung's reign of China, Aurungzebe of Hindustan, or Tamerlane's rule, into a personal history.

- "Tutmosis III while building a great pyramid...,"
- "Enraged Napoleon Bonaparte declared war on Russia..."

This has helped to perpetuate the most ubiquitous and dangerous myth that human affairs are shaped by human nature. But human affairs are *not* shaped by human nature.

There is a fundamental difference between individual human behavior and human social or group behavior. This fact is not well documented because the average person is lucky to receive a single page in history. *More than 400 years ago in "the Prince" Machiavelli realized that countries operate outside the moral codes of the individual.* Leaders' decisions are shaped and confined by the parameters of the social structure much like the chairman of a corporation. There are parallels between a company takeover and a country takeover. (*We would be surprised to learn of a compassionate IBM rushing altruistically to a sickly Microsoft.*) Our social structures are created for self-perpetuation and bottom-line considerations. They are created by humans but they are not human. Later we personify these decisions and attribute them to human nature.

"Wisdom cometh by suffering." (*Agamemnon*, Aeschylus.) The same can not always be said of human society. An injured mother and her child lie bleeding on the roadside, fallen from a bicycle. Most human reactions will be compassion and help. All countries' reactions to another country hemorrhaging and declining are: exploitation, attack, or an expansion of influence and borders, even though the declining nation does indeed contain bleeding women and children.

294

Examples of this in history include literally most history because this is precisely when most conflict *does* occur:

> The War of the Austrian Succession (1740s)
> The War of the Spanish Succession (1700s)
> The War of the Ottoman Succession (1600s)
> The decline of the Austro-Hungarian Empire (1910s)
> The decline of the Mauryan Empire in Maharashtra (100BC)
> The decline of the Soviet Empire (1990)

The forces of anger, hatred, and bigotry do not shape our destiny:

- There is a dramatic attraction for recording an *event* that began a war (for example, the assassination of Archduke Ferdinand in Sarajevo 1914, or, a King was enraged) but in reality the event is only the *spark*. History is deficient in an accounting of the *fuel*. (Incidentally almost no wars in history were actually caused by an angry monarch.)
- Soldiers in the front lines are not in a permanent state of anger against the enemy. (It is also physically impossible to stay angry for any length of time.) They fight for their lives as well as for country, their fellows, their families, or simply because they have no choice.
- Genetically there is negligible difference between any race. Furthermore any human genome is 98% the same as the chimpanzee's. Human beings have fought more frequently with like peoples than with different races. The forces of community are so strong that any arbitrary differences are used to separate them. When they do not exist philosophical or religious differences are created. (The Middle East is a good geographical example but so are most places on the planet.) What we consider *bigotry-induced war* is an illusion and masks our own drive to be included in the group. (*Superimpose a primate styled hierachal power structure and we now have a working model.*)

Blaming human conflict on evil and misguided leaders absolves us from having to deal with a disturbing truth. *What we consider to be our most noble qualities perpetuates warfare:* Fellowship, concern for loved ones, nationalism, patriotism, hierarchy society, and deference to leaders.

"A thing is not necessarily true because a man dies for it." Oscar Wilde. Today we would consider it ridiculous to lay down our lives for our local county board but we would. It would be the 15th Century and we would be in "The Wars of the Roses." Future historians will view our present behavior with equal amazement.

This paper indicates that war is more fundamental to civilization itself than we dare to believe. This is why our current models do not explain every historical conflict.

In parallel, science is now finally working on "a unified theory of everything,"--a model that incorporates all physical laws, the uncertainty principle, quantum mechanics and relativity. In the past it has been easier to change history to fit the model but now there is great opportunity here in facing, and being prepared for, these very real dangers. Post war prosperity can continue and spread but now we know for certain; "Let go of the reins and the horse *will follow the path* that leads over the cliff." The significance for the future in not understanding the historic nature of our social structures would be catastrophic. Many great social and political forces will collide in the next century and, if peaceful resolutions to conflicts are not sought with the same fervor as a country mobilizes for war, catastrophe will be inevitable.

Throughout history, countries have balanced unprofitable war expenditures against trade and productivity, or colloquially--guns against butter. The United States and the Soviet Union compromised both their economies in a 50-year arms struggle. The Soviet Union collapsed and the United States is in economic decline on the world stage. Now, in characteristically innovative thinking, the United States has turned the centuries old guns/butter dilemma on its head. "Sell arms for butter!" The United States is now heading into the 21st century as the World's leading arms dealer.

This will not only wreak havoc on humanity at large, but will also be counterproductive to the United States' interests, despite the pervasive myth, in the US, that wars are good for the economy. This myth arose from the Second World War. War expenditure has always been a burden on the economy but in the 1930's the US profited by *not* being in WWII until late 1941, and by massive supply and trade to Europe. Government spending admittedly did give the economy a boost, but it was the destruction of Europe and the adoption of a free market system, *with nobody else in any shape to compete*, that advantaged the United States.

One lesson learnt from history was the impact of dissenting speech in the media during the Vietnam War. Now instead of exploring very gray issues, the media divides them into black and white, good or bad. The misleading Persian Gulf war with its controlled press coverage has helped to prepare the public for future conflict. *A country that no longer fears war is more likely to miscalculate.* Although the electronic super highway will place anyone in anyone else's living room, empathy will not be enough. We have had mankind's good nature for 40,000 years. Further, although there is an apparent increase in electronic information the trend is, and will be, towards fewer and fewer sources and distributors. There is now ownership of media by arms manufacturers--*for example General Electric, the world's second largest arms manufacturer, owns NBC*--as well as sponsorship and underwriting of vehicles of communication. There is no longer a bi-polar world and there is no credible enemy. The world will seem to change to where conflicts are shades of gray and capitalism is not synonymous with democracy. The political and military structures we have set up to combat our 20th century enemies now are searching for an enemy.

We consider morality in war, but war is inherently amoral. Nuclear weapons are immoral but the conventional firebombing of cities was carried out with impunity. The Greeks considered the Roman short sword to be an immoral technological development. Death is still death to an individual in any century. We in the West have nuclear weapons and a superiority in conventional weapons. Historically a country not able to fight a conventional war will fight a guerrilla war.

Interestingly, it is a myth the Revolutionary War was won because the British foolishly fought in bright red rows and were easy targets for the sly Colonials hiding behind rocks and trees. In reality, this occurred only once, on the march from Lexington to Concord in 1775.

Unable to fight a guerrilla war, a country will resort to terrorism. Next century, the West's adversaries will rely more and more on terrorism and guerrilla warfare. Public attitudes will no longer polarize based on morality of a war's prosecution, but in reality atrocity is inherent. War is the atrocity. (It is not a coincidence that atrocity occurs on a massive scale during war and is virtually non existent in its absence.) Nuclear terrorism will become more readily accessible with increasing availability of beryllium. Beryllium reduces the required levels of enriched uranium per detonation. High technologies are available commercially and can subvert counter-terrorism. Historically, plagues and disease have always taken more lives than war. Next century we risk continuing this trend with manufactured disease and confluence of armies. *The 1918 flu epidemic alone killed over 20 million.*

Before World War I, there had been 50 years of "Pax Britannica" and it was generally believed Western Civilization had transcended war. War was a thing of the past. The unprecedented conflict of the 20th Century has subconsciously militarized even our turns of phrase. "Caliber, rally, rout, surrender, defeat, disarming, flank, demoted, War on poverty, War on drugs, War on War!" In reality there are countless variations of approach to problems within countries and between countries. We have attributed the causes of war to our own self-serving causes. For example: "The Civil war was over slavery." The altruistic and moral white man was prepared to sacrifice his own life, and perhaps that of his family, to kill and die for the economic well being of the black man. This would be a preposterous notion today let alone 140 years ago and yet it is part of our self-serving history.

In summary, the two most vital studies for the future of humanity, economics and warfare are not only connected, but are also in a state of self-contradictory infancy.

"Civilization is a race between education and catastrophe." H.G. Wells.

Now war is a commercial product. This development is unfortunate in the nuclear age. The United States is the only remaining super-power. Instead of embracing the democratic potential of an East/West bloc we have rejoiced and exploited the collapse. Actions that once were buffered now will shape the future. The West is not designed or prepared for a fractured Russia. Mutually Assured Destruction no longer works and the chances of nuclear conflict are greater with unsecured nuclear *artillery* shells.

If NATO continues to spread its nuclear umbrella over the Eastern bloc countries, Russia will court Eastern powers and form alliances with China. China, the weakest of the powers, is expanding its power by every pragmatic means, historically much like Colbert's France. Within 50 years, Asian countries will shift global power eastwards. Without a direct threat from Russia, European alliances will weaken. Consider the meteoric collapse of interest in the Maastricht treaty since the collapse of the USSR and the desperate search to give NATO a task.

The now distinct and separate aims of each European country has manifested itself in recent catastrophes: Germany's desire to recognize Bosnia and Slovenia before minority issues were settled and further the European powers encouraged a continuation of the Balkan War to seek a preferred result rather than an end of the conflict. Germany is Croatia's ally, Russia and Greece are Serbia's, and Turkey and Islamic countries are the Muslims' allies. Interestingly, the division here is precisely where King Constantine divided the Roman Empire and Christianity into East and West in 330 A.D. East became Greek Orthodox, later Russian Orthodox, and the West Roman Catholic. Later came the Muslims from the Ottoman empire.

In the same way national political structures have failed to seize the potential of a democratic Soviet Union, they will also be slow in realizing that a reunited Germany has changed the European complexion of the future. Historically, Germany became a significant power only as recently as last Century. German unification under Bismarck, altered the balance of power and rivaled the economic might of Britain. This engendered the miscalculations, and polarization of power that lead to World War I.

National political leaders must be prepared for European powers acting independently in pursuit of their own agenda. French Russian alliances may be unthinkable but they are historical. This may sound strange but the French nuclear arsenal, recently tested, will protect France from all-comers *including* England and Germany!

Historically, wars always occurred over the right of succession. There exists dreadful potentials for war in the former Soviet Union and its bordering areas. Any disruption of the *status quo* historically, leads to war. The near future world will be one of expanding western corporate influence possibly colliding with fragmentation of their former Soviet Union and the rise of nationalism and religious enthusiams; indeed, the advent of a fertile field of conflicts--a grim prospect.

Now, however, unlike ever before, countries do not have to follow this tragic course. Future wars are not inevitable. Awareness of the past is a practical and vital step in predicting and preparing for the future. Science creates a theory, designs a model, makes a hypothesis and predicts the future, but the predicting of countries' future behavior is laced with a plethora of contradictory theories and opinion. Science can not tolerate conflicting theories and yet our present lack of understanding of history produces them. *Our model is only as good as our history.* We have mistakenly declared this study a *humanity* complete with the capriciousness of human behavior, but in reality the behavior of countries is perfectly *predictable* over time. We immediately need a fresh study of the future using a scientific format and incorporating computer projection, economics, education, and military strength. If we assume the west is not seeking further war then the solutions will be as many and varied as the sparks of war.

War was made illegal in 1928 by the ratification by 62 nations of the Kellogg Briand Pact. This well-intentioned act illustrates a lack of understanding of the interaction of countries and the power of law. Solutions to the dangers of war can not be achieved by isolationism and the west must not only become active, but *proactive*, Globally, inactivity in one situation may lead to peace, in another directly to war, but in either case this will only be the *spark*. The United States and the west have enormous resources and power to promote democracy and conflict resolution. Leaders will have to forego even their own countries short term interests. Inequality, economics and power play a large roll in conflict but this is not always true. History is filled with wonderfully planned and imagined Utopian societies so there is no shortage of brilliant minds only of brilliant political leadership. Success will be a triumph of individual leadership over the inertia of blundering society.

Ironically, society will not build sculptures and memorials to these leaders because, as we know, all our memorials are to War.

REFERENCES

Arrian (Second Century A.D.). History of Alexander based on Ptolemy and Aristobulus.

Barber, B. *Jihad vs McWorld*, 1995.

Callisthenes (Second Century A.D.). Unknown author of *The Life of Alexander of Macedon*.

Chambers, J. *The Devil's Horseman*.

Churchill, Winston. The Second World War I.

Clarke, J., and J. Clad. *After the Crusade,* 1995.

Delbrueck, H. *Warfare in Antiquity.* Lincoln and London, 1990.

Diodorus (First Century B.C.). *Universal History.*

Dupuy, R.E. and T.N. The Encyclopedia of Military History, revised 1986.

Kennedy, P. *The Rise and Fall of the Great Powers,* 1987.

Kipling, Rudyard. *The White Man's Burden.*

Kissinger, H. *A World Restored: Metternich, Castlreagh, and the Problems of Peace.* Boston, 1957.

Lepper, F.A. *Trajans Parthian War.* Oxford, 1948.

Marks, S. *The Illusion of Peace: International Relations in Europe 1918-1933.* London, 1976.

McNeil, W. *Plagues and Peoples.* New York, 1989.

Plutarch (C.A.D. 46-120). *On the Fortune or the Virtue of Alexander, Moral.*

Sagan, C., and Druyan A. *Shadows Of Forgotten Ancestors.* New York, 1992.

Segal, G. *Peking and the Super Powers,* 1992.

Waltz, K. *Toward Nuclear Peace* International Securities Studies, Paper 16.

Weber, E. *The Western Tradition.*

Yonosuke, N. *The Origins of the Cold War in Asia.* New York, 1977.

arks, S. *The Illusion of Peace: International Relations in Europe 1918-1933.* London, 1976.

SOCIAL PROBLEMATICS: TOWARDS A SYSTEMIC DEFINITION

by

Paris J. Arnopoulos

INTRODUCTION

A WORLD OF PROBLEMS

It is by now rather banal to affirm that the late 20th century world is undergoing a critical period of transition in which a multitude of problems is accumulating. All around us, one can see that things are not evolving as they should. Of course, such perceptions and sentiments have been expressed many times throughout history. The world has always been changing and this change has not often been satisfactory to many people. Crises and problems, therefore, are nothing new in the lives of men and nations.

Yet, there is something new both in the quantity and quality of contemporary problems. For the first time in history, the world is a single megasystem with a multitude of interacting and interdependent units. Because of that, the problems we face are also interacting and interdependent. The increased magnitude and complexity of our creations have produced more and bigger problems than ever.

Not only has the number of our problems grown beyond anything known before, but their novelty and complexity are taxing our ability to understand and manipulate them. It seems that current events are becoming too large and are moving too fast for us to grasp and control. Human actors and institutions appear increasingly diminutive in relation to the cascade of events.

Undoubtedly, mankind has always been at the mercy of nature. The laws and forces of the universe inexorably dominate human existence. But again, this is the first time that man's own works have reached such magnitude as to overshadow the problems posed by nature. Science and technology have advanced to the point where they seem to have taken a life of their own and are moving by their proper momentum. What is worse, their effects upon their creators, both individually and collectively, were not foreseen; hence, their repercussions upon our lives are both dramatic and traumatic.

The uniqueness of our era consists of the growing dominance of artificial over natural problems. Human accumulation of power means that we are now capable of creating and destroying many things, including ourselves. Unfortunately our destructive capacity

Paris J. Arnopoulos *is a professor at Concordia University in the department of political science, Montreal, Canada.*

is out-pacing our humane creative ability; so the threats to humanity become more awesome than the promises. As a result, problems multiply faster than we are able to solve them and the lead-time for making decisions shrinks into nothingness.

On the basis of this rather pessimistic overview, it behooves us to take things seriously and see what we can do to understand the problems of this world so that we can improve our potential to solve them. Even if problems are intrinsic to any open and dynamic system; managing them can make the difference between life and death. Anyone who can contain problems within a functional range can turn them to advantage in making better systems. Thus, before we can think of sustainable development, we must conceptualize global *problematics*.

With such incentive, this study initiates a systematic definition of problems as the first step in an emerging *problemology*. In the following presentation, we can only scratch the surface of this large area and leave for another time an in-depth research into the subject. This beginning is a prerequisite to any scientific treatment of problems, because it lays down the foundations for further work. Here then, we outline the concept, structure, and process of problems and by doing so answer the questions related to the nature, meaning, type, location, time, and solution of our critical issues.

Accordingly, the paper is divided into three parts of two chapters each, covering successively the systemic, static and dynamic aspects of problems. The chapters deal with the form and function, content and context, as well as period and method of this subject. Thus, although the study does not go into any depth, it does cover the field of problem analysis exhaustively and sets the basis for more detailed and specialized research later on.

CONCEPT

At the beginning of any systematic study, one must formulate the basic concepts which define the nature and scope of the topic in question. This conceptualization of the subject-matter explicates *what* exactly is to be studied and *why*. The answer to these two questions should provide the *essence* and *meaning* of the study, thus placing the research which follows in its proper perspective.

In this particular case the topic under investigation is "problems," so we first have to define the term in quotation marks and then explain what it means. This undertaking will give us the form and function of the term and therefore develop its conceptualization. The following two sections treat each of these aspects in turn.

FORM: PROBLEM-ANATOMY

The first question which must be answered before going any further is: what is a problem? Obviously, to begin with, this is a matter of definition, and as such it is both easy and difficult to do. It is easy because definitions are arbitrary and *a priori* conceptual devices, so anything can be defined in any way. Yet, in order to facilitate communication, one must respect popular and traditional meanings of common sense, so we have to fit-in our definition to generally acceptable standards.

Because "problem" is such a widely used term, it means many different things depending on who is using it and under what circumstances. For this reason, there are several definitions of the term at various degrees of conceptual formality. We have chosen to formulate the following definition because it combines simplicity and suitability for our purposes: i.e., a *problem* is a *disturbing situation*.

Although this definition could apply to any and all problems, it is best suited to our context because it emphasizes the situational nature of the problems with which we are particularly concerned. By situation we mean a specific condition or state of affairs which draws attention to itself. Situations, therefore, are salient points upon which interest is focused and as such describe the essence of problems. In this sense, real problems of this world are disturbances in the various configurations of matter-energy within space-time.

Since we are not interested here in symbolic or semantic problems, the above meaning will do very well in concentrating our study to empirical problems of human concern. We are, therefore, excluding from our purview mathematical questions, intellectual puzzles, or psychological malaises, although they are problems of sorts. Instead, we center our attention to actual external events which disturb human sensibility. It is in this sense that we propose to study current existential problems.

Undoubtedly, there are many such problems in the contemporary world. So much so that to many people they seem to be infinite or indefinite. Yet, the *Encyclopedia of World Problems & Human Potential* has hunted down and classified almost 10,000 world problems, identified and documented by 15,000 INGOs. In a different project, the US Library of Congress identified 1,200 world problems, but another independent study only produced 50 global problems. Finally, the Rio Conference discerned 40 fundamental problems which must be solved by the year 2000 as part of its Agenda 21.

Playing with numbers, of course, one can come up with any figure; since it all depends what categories and levels of abstraction or aggregation one uses for the list of problems. Whether they are counted in tens or thousands, what is important is that the disturbing situations in the world are recognized and dealt with. But in order for this to happen, we must find out as much as possible about them from all points of view. It is this process of problem-analysis that we are performing here in broad terms.

Basing our problem-analysis on the above definition and elucidation, we now proceed to outline the fundamental parameters common to the problems we deal with:

- Situational reality: the form of the problem in question and its concreteness or abstractness in operational terms.
- Systemic functionality: the objective possessor of problems as the normative measure of disturbances.
- Contextual relativity: the scope and perspective of the problem which qualifies its extent and relationship with other situations.
- Reflective subjectivity: the awareness of a problem by somebody and the impact it has on sentient beings.
- Dynamic chronology: the change it undergoes through time and the causality of antecedents and consequents.
- Soluble potentiality: the optimal method according to which an intelligent system can deal with its problems.

A properly defined problem must contain information on all of the above six dimensions. On that basis one can distinguish between true and pseudo problems. As an example, for "poverty" to be determined as a problem, it must be: operationally defined, functionally explained, contextually placed, relevantly specified, historically developed, and probably solvable. Only then should it be considered as a rigorous problem to be dealt with in a systematic manner.

Very few empirical problems, of course, can be so completely specified in all their aspects, so as to be scientifically impeccable. For this reason, most problems are moot and fuzzy. In that case, when the parameters of problems are debatable, we speak of "issues." A public issue, then, is joined in order to clarify the above dimensions and thus determine the quality and quantity of given problems.

As in this opening section we have presented the situational aspects of problems, each of the following sections will deal with the remaining five aspects in greater length.

FUNCTION: PROBLEM-MEANING

According to our definition, problems are "disturbing situations." So far, we have explained the "situational" aspect of the definition; now, we do so for the "disturbing" aspect. To begin with, a disturbance is an extraordinary or abnormal stimulus which could upset the steady-state of a system. It is thus an incident creating some dissonance, contradiction, discrepancy or imbalance in a given situation. So qualified, a problematic condition becomes an abnormal state which presents a potential threat to its subject.

This description of a problem requires some explanation and the best way to do that is by systems-analysis. As we used the term "system" above, we meant a set of interrelated-interacting units. This implies the existence of an ordered group of elements undergoing some process in space and time. This systemic process is evident throughout the universe and manifests itself similarly throughout atomic, molecular, biological, human, or social activities. In whatever level one cares to look, "reality" is a conglomeration of such dynamic and open systems.

The essence of a system is some underlying order in its being. It is this order which distinguishes a system from chaos: i.e. a random agglomeration of things in erratic motion. Accordingly, we can postulate that problems cannot exist in chaos; they can only be found in systems. This is because a problem relates to a specific condition in the order of things; without some such order, it would be nonsense to speak of problems.

The next step of this reasoning is that an order implies a norm: i.e., some standard or rule according to which a system usually operates. In this sense, there is a normal condition of the system which a problem could disturb by introducing an abnormal element into it. The threat is that in extreme cases the disturbance may escalate to the point of breaking down the system altogether. For the sake of self-preservation, therefore, a system must be able to contain its problems and maintain its normal steady-state operation.

For example, "starvation" is a problem for a healthy system because, in the first instance, it lowers the organism's normal performance and ultimately may hasten its death. However, the same condition would not be a problem to an obese or abnormal organism; on the contrary, it may prove to be the solution.

From these examples we can see that a problem is whatever interferes with the proper functioning of a system by impeding its optimal performance. Clearly, "proper" and "optimal" are normative criteria of systemic function, against which a problem can be measured: the more this function is disturbed, the greater the problem.

In this sense, a problem may be described as a malfunction of a system from its normal or ideal state. If a system is not working as it should be, there is a problem. Thus, another way of perceiving a problem is to look upon it as a gap between facts and values; a difference between what *is* and what *ought* to be: the wider the gap, the bigger the problem.

This way of measuring the magnitude of a problem implies that we know both the real and ideal conditions of a system, something which is not always so easy. Very often we may be sure that there is something wrong with a particular situation but cannot say exactly why, because we are unable to formulate the norm upon which we judge the discrepancy. The condition of general malaise is an example of such incapacity to specify our desiderata.

By knowing at least the approximate position of normality, one can diagnose the situations beyond it. What lies outside the normal may be described either qualitatively or quantitatively. A quantitative problem is simply a situation of insufficiency (deprivation or underdevelopment) or excess (obesity or overdevelopment); whereas a qualitative problem is a more complex condition of the wrong kind of make-up (malnutrition or maldevelopment). Having too much, too little, or an improper combination causes problems in any system (organic or social). A problem, therefore, may be seen as an imbalance between what a system has and what it needs to function properly. That is why, problems of human needs arise when there is hunger or disease.

If norms are well known, they become ideals, i.e. the goals which the system tries to achieve or maintain. In that case, when the goal of a system is set, the only problems that may arise are those of means or strategy. These are scientific and technical problems, where gaps between knowledge and ignorance are relatively well defined. Cancer or metal fatigue are such problems in which doctors and engineers are working on.

In contrast, poverty or mental fatigue are sociological or psychological problems where norms or ends are either unknown or conflicting. Poverty is a uniquely human social insufficiency syndrome which has no meaning beyond mankind. So when values and goals are nonexistent or contradictory, problems become much more complex and difficult. For that reason, problems of exploitation or disorientation are so insidious. Most of these types of problems may be endemic to the human condition, so they persist through history.

Because they are disturbing situations, problems tend to acquire some negative connotations. Since they are a threat to the well being of a system, problems are to be avoided. It is as if nature abhors problems! And yet, problems can be quite functional in the development of systems. As gaps or imbalances, they present a challenge and so an opportunity for action and correction. Without problems, a system would have little incentive to progress and adapt to changing conditions. Problems can thus serve as stimuli to improve the performance of systems and develop new and better strands.

In that sense, problems are both necessary and desirable in an imperfect and evolving world. By acting as sinks or black holes, they absorb any excess energy which may be generated by chaotic processes. For this reason, it has been suggested that problems be institutionalized or built-into systems as part of their cybernetic mechanism. Be that as it may, the unavoidability of problems forces us to try and understand them so that we may use them for our purposes. We, therefore, continue our search on the different aspects of problems on the next chapter.

STRUCTURE

On the basis of the problem-conceptualization just completed, we now go on to outline the fundamental structure of problems. Structuring a problem means locating its spatial domain and identifying its human content. Problems do not exist in vacuum. They are to be found within a certain place and relate to particular things. Therefore, the analysis of a problem must be able to answer the questions of *where* and *who*. This is what we intend to do in the two sections of this chapter.

CONTEXT: PROBLEM-TOPOLOGY

Real problems take place somewhere in this world. A situation occurs some place far or near, large or small. A problem can, therefore, be located by space and size: two characteristics that would constitute its scope. These two measures may be ranged within a continuum whose extremes are *micro* and *macro* problems. Towards the micro end would be found individual and local problems, whereas towards the macro end would be global and universal ones.

According to this scheme, we classify problems within three main areas: local, regional, and global. Local problems take place in relatively restricted areas or spaces, all the way from an estate to a society. Within this range are found problems involving families, groups, communities, nations, or a combination of these. At the next level of magnitude, are located regional problems involving groups of nations, continents or blocs. The problems of the first, second and third world nations respectively would be placed within these areas. Finally, at the highest level of generality are global problems involving mankind as a whole. These problems could be transnational, inter regional or planetary (including extraterrestrial).

The tabulation on the next page contains the type of problems which could be placed in the various categories we have created, based on the criterion of increasing geographical extent. Reading from top to bottom, the table begins with the micro-problems of local communities and ends with the macro-problems of the world as a whole. Examples of what we consider significant problems in each area have been given at each level.

The representative problem chosen for each level shows the nature of worldly problems as imbalances of some sort. The problem of interference, for example, be it one of the individual versus the state or local autonomy versus world government, involves the question of how entities coexist and cooperate without getting in each other's way. The breakdown of local communities, the rise of the national, state and international conflicts, are all different aspects of the frictions and contradictions among various geographical units.

At the continental level, are the problems concerning an entire culture at a certain point of its development. These problems differ for each cultural area; the major problems of one are not likely to be those of another. Thus the problems of preindustrial, industrial and post industrial societies are not the same. The western world has problems of overdevelopment, whereas the third world suffers problems of underdevelopment; with the second world having those problems peculiar to industrial economies.

Finally, at the global level, problems intersect national and cultural boundaries to extend throughout the world. Problems involving transnational activities, east-west cultural confrontation and north-south income gap, are such examples. At the extreme, the issues of outer space and the high seas, as well as the general problems of world governance, environmental pollution and resource depletion encompass the whole earth as a unit.

The increasing interdependence of the world makes all these problems more and more interrelated, both horizontally and vertically. Local problems may eventually become global and western ones may become eastern. In spite of this overlapping, this geographical delineation of problems is useful for analytic purposes.

CONTENT: PROBLEM-SUBJECTS

As already stated, real problems can only exist in relation to an existing system. A problem must belong to somebody or something. This means that in addition to its location, a problem requires a subject or a theme of activity to which it has a functional relationship. In this sense, we speak of a machine, an organism, a society, or the world having problems because there is a malfunction somewhere in their operation. For this to happen, we assume that these systems have objectives or purposes which the problem hinders from achieving.

Although systems may have intrinsic purposes, in which case they may have objective problems; very often it is human beings who assign them goals, which if they cannot easily attain are considered problematic. In this sense, problems are in the eyes of the beholder as much as in the object itself. This juxtaposition of objective and subjective conditions means that a problem is not only a "state of affairs" but also a "state of mind."

Without taking a solipsistic position, one can admit that there is some truth to the subjectivity of problems, especially in human affairs. Since we are particularly concerned with the problems of this world, one may easily make "man the measure of all things" and look at problems from his point of view. On the assumption that humanity is our system, everything else becomes its environment. Thus problems can either be internal to the system or external between the system and its environment. In the former case, they are personal problems whereas in the latter, they are either social or natural.

The tabulation in the following page elaborates on this distinction. Evidently, that table uses the same conceptual framework as the previous one in its classification of problems. We have retained this uniform trinary taxonomic scheme to facilitate comparison and symmetry. Accordingly, our contextual classification begins by dividing human reality into three broad areas: personal, social and natural. By extension, problems fall into one or another of these categories, depending on whether they involve the internal or external worlds of mankind.

308

Personal problems are inner disturbances or imbalances of human beings. These produce a feeling of discontent or dissatisfaction accompanied by a state of tension and instability. They are incongruities between man and himself, between ego and id, mind and soul. More specifically, personal problems may be grouped under spiritual, intellectual or psychological headings, with some examples given for each one. It should be noted that all cases assume a certain functional norm the denial of which creates a problem (for that reason, "superstition" rather than "truth" is identified as a problem in general terms).

The next large area of problems falls under the "social" label. This type of problems are disturbing situations among people, rather than within them. They are the problems of "man's inhumanity to man," the disorder in interpersonal relations. These problems are manifested in the cultural, political and economic spheres of action, as in the cases of social anomy, power insecurity or wealth inequality. As the examples in the table show, social problems are in the heart of world affairs and relate to both personal and natural dysfunctions.

The latter reflect the imbalances between culture and nature. Humanity, of course, is part of nature and as such cannot escape its laws with impunity; if we do not live according to certain standards, we have problems of health, physiological or psychological. Naturally, no matter what we do, we eventually die. Death is part of the general law of entropy which all things follow in the long run, so it cannot be considered as an objective problem even if life and order try to prolong themselves and postpone their inevitable extinction.

Having given the locational and contextual aspects of human problems, we can conclude this chapter by combining these two dimensions into a single framework. The matrix in the following page has been constructed by using the spatial classification in the vertical and the thematic in the horizontal position. In this manner, the two schemes intersect each other and the nine categories of each one produce eighty-one composite groups of problems.

This two-dimensional classification gives a more precise location of problems than either of the previous one-dimensional lists. Some of the examples given before have now been reproduced in this table to show their position in relation to the combined criteria. Thus, "underdevelopment" is an economic problem found mainly in the third world; whereas the uneven distribution of natural resources creates problems of interregional or interdependent relations.

Apart from the relative arbitrariness of any classification scheme, it is to be noted that the reason for the absence of examples in some of the boxes may be either objective (there are no problems therein) or subjective (none can be found there).

Be that as it may, our problem structuring shows their relativity. What may be problems in one area for some people are quite normal conditions in another place for others. So, an individual problem is not necessarily a systemic one, and *vice versa*. Therefore, the analysis of problems must specify as much as possible whose and where the problem belongs.

Oppression, for example, affects the oppressed differently from the oppressor, although it may be a problem for both. Similarly, undernourishment is found only in certain areas and affects certain people; whereas in other places and for other people, the opposite problem of over nourishment is more common. It is on the basis of this knowledge that one can determine the extent of the problem and thus define its structure both in terms of context and content.

PROCESS

This last chapter of problem-analysis deals with the process by which problems evolve or change. This stage of the study follows logically that of structure, because we now move from the static to the dynamic aspects of problems. Given the way problems were conceptualized and then compartmentalized, we presently try to find some temporal and causal relationships among them. Consequently, we are introducing the element of time and variation into our subject-matter in order to answer the *when* and *how* of problems. The following two sections, thereby, treat the chronological and method-ological aspects of this topic.

PERIOD: PROBLEM-TIMING

Our reality exists in space and time, so real problems are to be found within this framework. As problems take place in a certain location, so they happen at a certain period. The arrow of time may be conceived as a vector of change relative to the constant movement of matter and energy. In existential, open and dynamic systems, problems arise when particular movements tend to deteriorate the structure and functions of the system.

From this dynamic point of view, problems are directly associated with change. More precisely, we might say that a problem occurs whenever a situation calls for change. Problems arise when something must be done; otherwise there are no problems. A *status quo* which suits the system, presents no problems and does not require any alteration.

A situation of optimal homeostasis is not disturbing and presents no problem. Acceptable changes or events are not problems; it is only when the flow of things or the current situation becomes unaccept-able that a problem develops, because it is then when something must be done about it.

Since problems "take time" and involve change, we can classify them on two criteria: timing and duration. The former tells us when a problem happens and the latter how long it lasts. Obviously problems vary in both these dimensions; so we can construct two continual to measure their occurrence. The first one divides problems in three major periods:

- **Past:** Problems of historical interest (ancient or modern);

- **Present:** Problems of current events (contemporary or pending);

- **Future:** Problems of potential outcome (prospective or probable).

Problems change in time. Yesterday's problems are not the same as today's and most likely will not be the same as tomorrow's. Many historical problems which were very crucial once have now become obsolete and forgotten; while new ones have taken their place.

Nevertheless, not all problems come and go; some remain with us for a long time, even forever. The life of problems, therefore, varies from quite short to very long. On this criterion, we divide problems into three main types:

- **Ephemeral:** Temporary problems (momentary or incidental);

- **Seasonal:** Periodic problems (cyclic or repetitive);

- **Eternal:** Perennial problems (endemic or inherent).

Real problems, of course, may straddle these categories in various ways. Some problems which were thought of as obsolete may rise again to haunt us. Others which are considered eternal may disappear with changing circumstances. It is not easy to say which problems are part of the human condition and which are only part of cultural fashion.

In any case, we are not going into further details or more elaborate classification of problems and their examples, (the reader can provide some from one's own experience). What we will do is show how the temporal aspect of problems can be combined with the spatial and contextual dimensions to produce a new relationship among them. The matrix presented in the following page illustrates this space-time relationship.

The fundamental structure of this matrix is the same as that of the previous chapter. The horizontal dimension represents subject and vertical space levels. The visible difference here is that this is a 3x3 matrix, whereas the other was a 9x9 one. This means that we have simplified our categories down to those mentioned and omitted the other ones, in order to focus on those areas of particular interest to world affairs.

On that basic framework, we superimposed two other criteria. The horizontal is that of urgency. This indicates the priority of a problem. Urgency is directly proportional to immediacy: the more urgent, the more prior a problem is. It seems that in our world, the most urgent problems are economic ones and the least urgent political. According to diplomatic activity, the north-south economic problem has replaced the east-west political problem as the most immediate issue of world affairs.

The vertical dimension measures the importance of problems; which is to say the depth to which they affect people. The most important problems are those closer at hand, whereas the least important are those far away. According to survey polls, local or national problems come first; whereas, international or global ones trail last. Combining all these measures, we have the typology shown in the matrix. The nine examples correspond to the different possible permutations among these variables.

On the other hand, it may be said that from the point of view of the global system and the long-run, the significance or importance of problems is the reverse of that shown in the matrix. From the broad and ultimate perspective, it is our treatment of the global-political problems that will determine the existence and shape of our world.

This is particularly so as historical evolution is accelerating. To the extent that change becomes revolutionary (rapid and radical), our reactions become critical (urgent and drastic). Thus, as our lead-time is shortened, we have to look further and wider in time and space in order to survive the rising and spreading of problems.

METHOD: PROBLEM-SOLVING

Closely associated to problem chronology is the process through which they evolve. From this point of view, a problem goes through various stages of development, the most important of which are:

> • **Formative:** The causal ingredients or factors creating a problem;

> • **Critical:** The juncture at which the problem is at its most acute;

> • **Anticlimactic:** The post phase of chronic or solved problems.

The formative stage of a problem, of course, is very significant because it contains the seeds of the disturbance. If we want to prevent problems, it is at this stage that we must prepare to act. This presupposes that one become aware of the developing problem before it reaches the critical stage. Very often the factors which cause a problem are beyond our control; therefore, the only thing one can do is prepare to face the problem when it comes.

It may be, however, that by the proper intervention, the course of events changes and the problem is prevented. In that case, a bit of timely action at an early stage may save much greater effort later on. Knowing the difference between avoidable and unavoidable problems is thus crucial.

If a problem is inevitable, then it reaches a stage when the need for action is at its highest. Since, per definition, problems are disturbing situations, they act as stimuli which draw attention to themselves. This stimulus breaks our complacency and forces us to do something to reestablish an equilibrium. Problems give us the feeling that there is something wrong somewhere, as an unsatisfactory and hence unacceptable condition which one tries to correct. This seems to be the way in which the need to solve a problem will satisfy us and fulfill the demand for harmony within or outside ourselves. Problems are things which bother us; therefore, they prod us to act. If a thing can be left alone, it is not much of a problem.

From what has been said, it would appear that problems call for solutions. Although, not all problems are necessarily solvable, one at least tries to solve them by searching for a way out. It is indeed unusual if one is disturbed by something and does not react to it. Thus, we may say that a solution is what is needed to correct a disturbing condition. Accordingly, problem-solving is a process which attempts to transform an unacceptable situation into a satisfactory one.

As a result, a systematic sequence of such problem-solving process would go as follows:

> • **Study:** The prerequisite information and knowledge about the problem and its parameters (problem-analysis);

> • **Policy:** The sufficient intention to do something about the problem and find a way out of it (solution-strategy);

> • **Therapy:** The necessary action to implement the problem-solving policy and satisfy the need (treatment-execution).

These three areas of activity are indispensable in any rational problem-handling exercise. To begin with, a problem must be perceived by someone, it must be defined and then studied as to its causes and effects. Only by knowing as much as possible about a problem can one hope to solve it correctly. Once this is done, one can evaluate the gravity of the problem and then prescribe a solution.

This may be a plan of action or program of cure to be followed. With such intended plan at hand, all that is left is the actual carrying it out. For complex problems, of course, this means organizing and availing the necessary resources to do the job, as well as undertaking the operation to overcome the obstacles and reach the goals set for the solution.

Problem-solving, therefore, requires a capacity to perform various tasks: semiosis, etiology, analysis, diagnosis, prognosis, therapy, logistics, cybernetics and praxis. Evidently, one does not go through such rigorous algorithm for everyday problems which are often handled instinctively or traditionally. But, as systems become more complicated, so does the problem-solving process. Simplistic solutions to complex problems are not only ineffective but tend to aggravate an already disturbed situation. So, certain technological efforts to buffer human activities from small disturbances may make them more vulnerable to large-scale catastrophes.

In this connection we must say that problems themselves form systems. Complex systems tend to produce a chain of problems which are interrelated in the same way as the system to which they belong. The UIA study already mentioned clustered its 10,000 world problems into 320 overlapping hierarchies, linked by 120,000 relationships of seven types.

Moreover, their preliminary search along nine million pathways identified seven thousand vicious circles of seven problems each. A cycle is a chain of problems, each of which aggravates the next, with self-sustaining positive feedbacks which carry the loop to its ultimate destruction. Simple loops start with three problems, but complex ones go much higher.

This episystem or "problematique", has the following traits:

- **Multiplicity:** Large number or mass of problems;

- **Gravity:** Deep seriousness or weight of problems;

- **Complexity:** Great intricacy or difficulty of problems;

- **Universality:** Widespread or omnipresence of problems;

- **Rapidity:** Fast accelerating evolution of problems;

- **Interactivity:** Manifold interdependence of problems.

Given this problematic situation of complex systems, problem-solving becomes a difficult enterprise which requires increasing time and effort to be done properly. It is for this reason that the science of problems, or problemology, should be developed at this time.

So far, in the relatively simple world of the past, problems could either be left alone to solve themselves or tackled haphazardly and in isolation. Presently, however, such *laissez-faire* attitude is no longer adequate to maintain our artificial systems in working order. Unresolved problems create positive feedbacks which worsen the situation and eventually get out of control.

Hence, a systemic problem-solving methodology must be based in an integrated systems-theory, so as to avoid solving one problem here and now by creating more problems elsewhere later on. The cross-cutting, cause-effect repercussions among problems should make us very careful as to what constitutes a real solution and not simply another problem.

The survey mentioned in the first chapter, identified 6,000 problems which aggravated each other, while only 300 which alleviated each other. With such dangerous relationships, problem-solving becomes a delicate and elusive undertaking. Yet, it is for precisely these reasons that it must be seriously engaged and methodically executed.

CONCLUSION

Global Problematics

Since the presentation of this study has been very succinct, it does not need any further summary at this point. The six parameters of problem-analysis, grouped into three dyads (concept; structure; process) should be clear enough not to require prolonged elaboration. Of course, each and every aspect could be studied in depth and practically applied to actual problem-cases by exhaustive research. Hopefully, this will be done elsewhere; so it does not fall within the purview of this report.

What we will do now is take a synoptic view of the problem-system in the world scale and see how our categories apply to it. As already mentioned, this problem-system has been labeled the "global problematique" and denotes the contemporary situation confronting humanity. This condition is characterized by an intricate and dynamic complex of dysfunctions making up the problem-system.

Following our typology, we can now classify these dysfunctions into six *areas*:

> • **Formal:** The web of disturbances produce a mega-problem of global dimensions, thus increasing system vulnerability.

- **Functional:** The lack or clash of values and goals for individuals and collectives increases the disorientation of the system.

- **Topical:** The complexity of many system variables increases risks of feedback and difficulties of solutions.

- **Spatial:** The great asymmetries of wealth and power among world actors increases dissatisfactions, frictions and conflicts.

- **Temporal:** The rapidity of historical change and technological innovations bring about a storm of crises and revolutions.

- **Procedural:** The magnitude and novelty of the problems out pace and out mode methods and institutions of problem-solving.

In other words, the world-system has become more vulnerable, unstable, asymmetrical and revolutionary, at the same time as its concepts, structures and processes for handling these problems have become anachronistic. The different rates of change have created a widening gap between values, regions, disciplines and institutions, thus increasing the instability of the system. This means that the discrepancies between problems and solutions have been increasing.

The inadequacy of our capabilities or perhaps unwillingness to handle world problems may be illustrated in the following statistics taken from the study already mentioned. The over 1,000 multilateral treaties in force currently, only treat about 250 world problems. The 700 human values accepted today only relate to 350 problems. The 300 Inter-Governmental Organizations and 3,000 Non-Governmental Organizations operating throughout the world are only handling 300 and 700 problems respectively. Finally, about 2,000 disciplines in the world only study about 1,300 problems. When we recall that the grand total of the problems identified was approximately 10,000, these figures show how insufficient are our means for treating the illnesses of our systems.

Nevertheless, there is considerable human potential which could be brought to bear in solving world problems. So far there have been identified 1,400 spiritual and mental potentials and 3,000 awareness modes which could help human development to meet these problems. Together with 230 clusters of dual polarities (good-bad), or 1,000 positive-constructive and 2,000 negative-destructive human values, the world disposes of several thousands of strategies used by international bodies to respond to world problems and promote a better future.

No matter how misleading statistics may be, there is no question that the growth in quantity and quality of world problems is happening at a faster rate than the growth of our mechanisms for their solution. Before this gap becomes unbridgeable, if it has not already reached that stage, there is a pressing need for improving our abilities for problem-analysis and problem-solving. Once we have this increased knowledge, we may hopefully acquire the necessary resolution to apply it in the service of the world. Hopefully, this short study has contributed in this long task.

REFERENCES

Ackoff R.L. *Redesigning the Future*, John Wiley, New York, 1974.

Adams J.L. *Conceptual Blockbusting*, Stanford, 1974.

Arnopoulos P.J.*Conceptual Framework of Human Concerns*, Report to B.E.P, UNESCO, Paris, 1979.

—*Sociophysics*. Nova Science, New York, 1993.

—*Sociopolitics*. Guernica, Toronto, 1995.

B.E.P. "Problem Analysis & Table of Objectives for Medium-Term Plan," UNESCO, Paris, 1974.

Birenbaum A., and E. Sagarin (eds.) *Social Problems*, Scribner, New York, 1972.

Braybrooke D. *Philosophical Problems & Solutions*, Collier-Macmillan, Toronto, 1965.

Brody R. *Problem-Solving*, Human Sciences Press, New York, 1982.

Carnarius S. *Management Problems & Solutions*, Addison-Wesley, Reading, MA, 1976.

Cosmopolitics. Guernica, Toronto, 1997E.

Eden C. *Messing About in Problems*, Pergamon, New York, 1983.

Eyestone R. *From Social Issues to Public Policy*, Wiley, New York, 1978.

Emery F.E. ed. *Systems Thinking*, Penguin, Middlesex, 1969.

Gabus A., and E. Fontela. "Perceptions of the World Problematique," DEMATEL Report. Battelle Institute, Geneva, 1975.

Gordon S. *World Problems*, Batsford, London, 1971.

Henshel R.L *Reacting to Social Problems*, Longman, Toronto, 1976.

Havelock R., and A. Huberman. "Solving Educational Problems," UNESCO, Paris, 1977.

Henderson J.L. *World Questions*, Methuen, London, 1963.

Judge, T. *Encyclopaedia of World Problems and Human Potential*," Union of International Assns., Brussels, 1994.

Lindblom C.E. *Usable Knowledge*, Yale U.P.N.H. 1979.

Mannheim K. *Diagnosis of our Time*, Routledge, London, 1943.

Merton R.K. *Contemporary Social Problems*, Harcourt-Brace, New York, 1971.

Murthy D.N.P. *Mathematical Modelling*, Pergamon, New York, 1990.

E.P.R.C. *Contemporary Societal Problems*, S.R.I. Menlo Park, 1971.

Rachels J. *Moral Problems*, Harper & Row, New York, 1971.

Rastogi P.N. *Policy Analysis & Problem Solving*, Sage, N. P., 1992.

Shumacher E.P. *The Guide for the Purplexed*, Fitzhenry & Whiteside, Toronto, 1977.

Secretariat. "List of Social Concerns," O.E.C.D. Paris, 1973.

Vidal F. *Problem-Solving Methodology*, Dunod, Paris, 1971.

Worsley P. *Problems of Modern Society*, Penguin, London, 1972.

REFORMATION AND ENLIGHTENMENT--THE RECONSTRUCTION OF CIVIL SOCIETY FOR THE 21ST CENTURY

by

John M. Francis

PREAMBLE

We can begin by asking ourselves a question. It is bound to be a difficult question if it is to probe our understanding of the society in which we live and in which we place our hopes and aspirations. As each community becomes more pluralistic, cross-cultural, post-modern, and divided by political allegiances, it follows that we may not even be able to agree on the terms of the question. However, it is an essential part of our struggle with the past that we should find the courage to raise the question and to re-open the debate. The question is this--What is the nature of civil society?

DEFINITIONS

The idea of civil society sprang from the writers and thinkers of the Scottish Enlightenment in the second half of the 18th century and eventually was grounded on the view that the autonomous and moral individual provided the very foundation of social order. All of this is admirably set out in an essay by Adam Seligman contained in the recent book *Civil Society: Theory, History, Comparison* edited by John Hall.[1] As Professor Hall points out in the opening section of this book:

> "Civil society is thus a complex balance of consensus and conflict, the valuation of as much difference as is compatible with the minimum of consensus necessary for settled existence."

Our capacity to live with difference in terms of traditions, cultures, religions and values is therefore the key to the viability of a civil society. It is the means by which in every country the power of the state is balanced by the self-organization of strong and autonomous groups. This is further qualified by the extent to which membership of these autonomous groups is both voluntary and overlapping. In these circumstances the individual is free to express and to sustain intrinsic core values at a personal level, while being equally free to

---

John M. Francis *is an environmental scientist and conservationist at The Scottish Office, St. Andrew's House, Edinburgh, UK.*

criticize and oppose political institutions and structures that owe their allegiance to single ideologies or belief systems to which he or she does not subscribe. For example, with the collapse of Marxist ideology and the command economies of Eastern Europe, it is essential that an implicit faith in the invisible hand of the marketplace (pace Adam Smith) does not simply displace or substitute one set of imperfections in housing, health, nutrition, and social welfare with another. Consequently, we shall need to give much more attention to mechanisms and methods for resolving conflict and building consensus on all social issues which pose problems for the future. In liberal-democratic traditions, a committee or task force appointed by the state is frequently given the investigative role in such matters. A period of fact-finding and analysis then ensues, followed by a formal report and recommendations to ministers or to the elected constitutional body. Increasingly, it has been shown that this benign and often paternalistic approach does not generate the required consensus upon which to develop policies and programs which are valued by the community at large. In key areas of social policy, large numbers of people have to cope with real policy shifts but remain confused about the reasoning behind them. At the same time they are often not well served by the reconstruction or redeployment of the service provision. In countries such as Britain where large scale privatization of public services (gas, water, electricity, and telecommunications) has recently taken place, there are deep misgivings as to whether the efficiency gains have been achieved at the expense of people who can ill afford the increased cost of these services. However, it remains to be seen whether an alternative administration with a stronger sense of communitarian values would be prepared to reverse or intervene in any way in this process.

In other words, the broad consensus about the need for public services has broken down at a community level under the weight of government intervention. The power of the central state is paradoxically increased in the name of deregulation, contracting out of services and the creation of *internal markets*. The official regulators of the privatized industries are given limited powers to control prices in order to prevent overt exploitation, but there has nevertheless been a perceptible shift of economic power from the public to the private sector. Individual shareholders may retain the right of representation at annual general meetings and the like, but they are usually outvoted and outmaneuvered by the block votes of the financial institutions who control the majority shareholding interest. Protest and argument by autonomous groups as custodians of the public interest in these matters are therefore essential if we are to retain the vestiges of a civil society. These examples, drawn from recent experience in Britain, are of course becoming increasingly common elsewhere in Europe. They are almost certainly a mirror to what has already taken place in North America for most of this century. Despite these trends and because of the importance of self-organizing autonomous groups to provide a check on the power of the state, it is appropriate to consider the reconstruction and reformation of civil society as set out in the following paper.

THE LESSONS OF HISTORY

In his essay on *The Possibility of Civil Society*, Victor Perez-Diaz defines the institutional core of civil societies as:

- a government which is limited, accountable and operates under the rule of law;
- a market economy (implying a regime of private property);
- an array of free, voluntary associations (political, economic, social, and cultural);
- a sphere of public debate.

Civil societies can therefore be regarded historically as hybrids or combinations of two different types of association--civil associations and associations as enterprises. Moral sentiments, probably derived from the period of the Scottish enlightenment and attributed to David Hume and Adam Smith, are reflected in both of these arrangements. The morals of the family and of states as enterprises, found on the virtues of intra group solidarity and project outward a fair amount of animosity or hostility to others. This is usually balanced by the strengths of civil associations which are founded on conversational communities with their implicit values of mutual toleration and respect for the procedural rules that regulate specific exchanges."[1]

The tension within this hybrid corresponds to the attempt to live in two essentially incompatible moral environments driven by a precarious dynamic which attempts to find a consensus, supported by the rule of law, to enable society to function in a lively and creative way. The struggle to maintain this consensus or middle path to governance is common to many civil societies of the Western type who are well used to propagating their religion, democratic ideals or scientific knowledge in the name of progress. This confident passage is now showing signs of faltering as the intensity of competition in new markets disturbs and challenges the traditional assumptions about the values of production and consumption in these societies. As Perez-Diaz notes in his essay:

> "Civil societies of the Western type are facing new chal-
> lenges that suggest we are entering an age of uncertainty.
> In fact, uncertainty may prove to be a better name than *the
> end of history*, which proclaims the final triumph of West-
> ern civilization, its expansion and its reforms being just a
> matter of time and patience: such a proclamation sounds
> premature, and unnecessary."

The trends in most nation states facing this dilemma are character-ized by a *sea of troubles*, resulting from the recent economic recession in world trade, increasing competition in global markets for a wide range of goods and services, the threats of urban terrorism, problems of race relations, new elements of environmental degradation and the limitations of the welfare state. The need to define and to manage the construction of an international civil society which provides an external frame of reference for these elements of discontinuity and dissatisfaction was therefore never more apparent. But there is an unfortunate convergence as the international agencies, including the UN itself, appear to be facing their own crisis of identity. What emerges is the opportunity to begin some fresh thinking on the central values and goals of civil society so that we can begin to develop and sustain potential building blocks. These will be considered later in the paper once the wider conceptual framework has been explored.

POWER OF THE STATE: THE ECONOMIC SYSTEM

It is fair to say that both now and in the future the power of the state as reflected in the economic system will be directly linked to the level of scientific and technological development. In those countries, which by most definitions are considered to be highly industrialized, the sustainability of the quality of life and indeed the material standard of living will be related increasingly to the overall efficiency and effectiveness of technological performance in key areas of social policy such as housing, transport, energy and food production, water management and health care. In these circumstances it is reasonable to expect that an increasing proportion of the gross national product of these economies will be allocated to research and development and geared to increasing technological innovation in the years ahead. In most of these countries, typically the Group of 7 which character-ize advanced industrial economies, the market is understood essentially as a decentralized process of decision-making with the linkages dependent on vast numbers of potential consumers and a wide diversity of producers. Apart from rules governing fair competition and quality standards affecting health, safety, and the environment, these market economies are essentially unregulated and depend for their survival on the *invisible hand* as envisaged by Adam Smith in another era.

The state has no authority to intervene in either the production or the distribution of goods and it has no role in overseeing the production and distribution processes. In that sense it is a free market and exposed to fair and open competition. In liberal democracies, therefore, market economies are based on value judg-ments that markets should find their own levels and that the state should not intervene as consumers act to safeguard their own interests; producers in turn act to provide goods and services in the marketplace of a suitable quality and standard and at a price that the markets can bear. Inevitably, these markets are far from perfect and frequently discount significant factors relating to the longer term availability of resources, the external costs of production including environmental factors, and the uneven distribution of certain goods in the marketplace. In the reconstruction of a civil society, it is essential therefore that market economies should not be unfettered but should be compatible with both the needs of ecology and with the demands of social justice. Participation in an increasingly technological society requires that there are new systems of democratic accountability to allow for these choices to be made in a fair and even-handed manner.

Later in this paper attention will therefore be given to the countervailing forces which should be present in any market economy to allow it to function in a way which is compatible with its wider social responsibility. In some countries this may depend upon the development of a *social market economy* whose aims and objectives need to be carefully understood in ideological terms as they represent an interplay between various determining factors. One of these is the overall level of scientific and technological development to which a society is exposed. In turn this requires more detailed technology assessment and foresight exercises to inform the electorate in liberal democracies that they have rights and responsibilities which must be exercised in terms of the long term management of resources and the environment. Following the UN Conference on Environment and Development (Rio de Janeiro, 1992) an international commission on sustainable development has been set up to encourage governments to develop their own strategies and initiatives. The overall aim of this approach has been defined as follows:

- Most societies want to achieve economic development to secure higher standards of living, now and for future generations.
- They also seek to protect and enhance their environment, now and for their children.

The concept of sustainable development attempts to reconcile these two objectives; a widely quoted definition of this concept is "development that meets the needs of the present without compromising the ability of future generations to meet their own needs."[2] The pursuit of sustainable development recognizes that present-day environmental concerns extend beyond the immediate or local environmental impacts to global issues, eg. the protection of the oceans and the tropical forests, the stratospheric ozone layer and the process of climatic change. The principles governing programs of action in response to these concerns are also clearly defined:

- decisions should be based on the best possible scientific information and the analysis of risks.

- where there is uncertainty and potentially serious risks exist, precautionary action may be necessary.
- ecological impacts must be considered, particularly where resources are non-renewable or effects may be irreversible.
- cost implications should be brought home directly to the people responsible--the *polluter pays* principle.

In the broader context of political and economic decision-making, it is recognized that the considerations applied to each of these factors in a particular situation will be a matter of judgment, frequently drawing on scientific analysis and expertise. While environmental cost may have to be accepted in some cases as the consequence of economic development, in others the natural resources, the landscape, wildlife or eco-systems should be regarded as so unique that they should be protected from exploitation. It is in the nature of civil society that groups that identify with particular aspects of the environment should organize themselves in such a way that they can make strong representations to counter the effective power of the state in those areas of legislation and regulatory control where it is in the wider interest of the community to provide the necessary checks and balances on the operation of markets and their freedom to impose external costs on the environment.

POWER OF THE STATE: SCIENCE, TECHNOLOGY, AND INDUSTRY

In considering the potential of any industrialized economy it is important to identify the communities of special interest which allow it to adapt to changing circumstances in the emerging global marketplace. The scientific and engineering community is one of these building blocks for the future. To harness the intellectual capacity of a country so that it can innovate, modernize and grow in economic terms will continue to exercise governments as we approach the third millennium. In Britain a strategy for science, engineering, and technology was produced in the form of a Parliamentary White Paper entitled, *Realizing our Potential* in May, 1993.[3] The opening paragraph of this document clearly underlines the significance of this attempt to integrate science policy and values in the national interest:

> The understanding and application of science are fundamental to the fortunes of modern nations. Science, technology, and engineering are intimately linked with progress across the whole range of human endeavor: educational, intellectual, medical, environmental, social, economic and cultural. They provide--through tools as diverse as mathematical modelling, biotechnology and earth observation from

space--a vital part of humankind's armory for solving the long-standing, worldwide problems, such as poverty and disease, and for addressing new global challenges such as those facing the environment.

It is worth recalling that our industrial revolution which played so large a part in the evolution of the modern world began with the great scientists and engineers of the 18th and 19th centuries. In moving towards the ever fiercer competition of global markets, we should not overlook the lessons of history or the debt that is still owed by those who sought to dominate a market without proper regard for the social and environmental consequences of their actions.

Specific policies were set out in the British White Paper in order to illustrate the immense asset that the scientific and engineering community represents in the life of a nation. However, even in Britain this will not be properly utilized unless further efforts are made to break down barriers which still exist to the public acceptance and recognition of the importance of science and technology to our future. Some of the policy initiatives are worth mentioning here as they are relevant to the perspectives on science, engineering, and technology in other countries:

1. The government's use of funds in its effort in science and technology will be made more explicit and open. Individual Departmental mission statements will be widely disseminated. A Forward Look will be published each year to give the industrial and research communities a clear and up-to-date statement of the government's strategy.

2. Technology foresight, jointly conducted by industry and the science and engineering communities would be used to inform government's decisions and priorities. The process will be carefully designed to tap into the expertise of people closest to emerging scientific, technological and market developments. The aim is to achieve a key cultural change: better communication, interaction, and mutual understanding between the scientific community, industry, and government departments.

3. A new body, the Council for Science and Technology, will draw on the findings of the Technology Foresight Programs. The new council will help ensure that the government benefits from outside independent and expert advice when deciding its own research spending priorities. The information generated by the council will normally be made openly available.

4. Better arrangements will be introduced for drawing together government initiatives in science and technology, coordinating cross-departmental science and technology issues, ensuring value for money from the science and technology which the government applies in its statutory, policy-making and regula-

tory roles,. and monitoring performance against the new Forward Look.

5. Government negotiating positions will be better coordinated across the range of European and international science and technology programs.

6. There will be a new campaign to spread the understanding of science and technology in schools and amongst the public.

Preparation of the White Paper involved extensive consultation with the research communities related to all disciplines in science, engineering and technology and as a result there was a reasonable degree of consensus about what needed to be done in order to achieve a higher profile for science and technology in the life of the nation and at the same time ensure both continuity of effort and adequate resources to sustain the momentum of research and development programs. The introduction of a *technology foresight program* is a central feature of this process and is described in more detail later in the paper.

POWER OF THE STATE: THE ENVIRONMENT

In a paper on the relationship between civic and global environmental change,[4] Timothy O'Riordan has drawn together some important ideas on how to move forward the concept of a socially responsible and accountable science and technology which will in turn be more responsive to the public concern about environmental risks and potentially disastrous ecological changes. The prospect of developing an interdisciplinary approach to a new kind of civic science and technology would represent another possible meeting point between the state and self-determining autonomous groups representing environmental concerns at both a global and a local level. Recent confrontations between Greenpeace and Shell Expro over the proposed deep sea disposal of a North Sea oil loading facility and between Greenpeace and the French government over renewed testing of nuclear weapons in the Pacific atoll of Mururoa, serve to illustrate the depth of feelings and the clear failure of communications between the parties to these disputes. But these are more than simple differences of view about the rights and wrongs of a particular course of action whether by a government or by a multi-national oil company. As Timothy O'Riordan points out in his paper:

> "Civic science is also societal in that society as a whole becomes more of a true partner in political decisions. Adaptive learning also means adaptive listening. This in turn requires structural adjustments in the management of science as well as in the relationship between science

policy and political decision-making to give the civic part
a full voice in the evolutionary process of social learning."

The engagement of a wider public in the development of science
policy will necessarily require those taking part to improve their
understanding of how to handle uncertain and indeterminate
information, how to model futures via open discussion and adaptive
learning, how to build images of future outcomes and apply decision
weights via group mediation techniques, and how to create the
appropriate listening environment for civic sciences to progress. This
is no easy task but the failure to integrate science policy into the
arena of public debate means that decisions are increasingly left to
markets thereby removing access to alternative technological development which might be better suited to meeting society's needs for
housing, transport, energy production and the like. As a result the
state regulatory bodies with concern for the environment are simply
left to remedy the sins of omission by producing measures to control
pollution, clean up waste and generally attempt to minimize environmental impacts which might perhaps have been avoided altogether
if more appropriate technologies had been adopted. It follows that
the scientific community will need to find new ways of representing
the alternative pathways to the general community of interest both
to politicians, potential investors, and the general public. The use of
new procedures for technology assessment and foresight are outlined
below and may represent one of the pathways to ensure that the
available resources are used in a more optimal fashion with proper
regard for the full spectrum of risk and environmental cost.

THE COUNTERVAILING FORCES: SOCIAL MARKET
ECONOMIES

In Western Europe the development of social market economies has
been proceeding for most of the past 40 or 50 years; it has become
the primary objective of the economic order in, for example, the
Federal Republic of Germany and has been adopted as an alternative
to *laissez faire* capitalism on the one hand and centrally controlled or
command economy on the other. This third form of economic order
has attained a high degree of acceptance because it designates the
target of combining the market economy and responsible action by
individual economic agents with the tasks of a social and democratic
constitutional state.[5] Thus, defined it emanates from the lessons of
history and is geared to the flexibility of the market economy and to
the discharge of new social duties. According to these authors a
social market economy is not a closed ideological system; it remains
open to participation by differing school s of thought while respecting much of the tradition of European liberal democracies. In these
circumstances, the process of technological innovation is exposed to
a civil society which is increasingly better informed about the nature

of the risks involved. In the report of the German experience already quoted, this position is carefully set out as follows[5]:

> "Often the dangers connected with new products and processes involving sophisticated technology cannot be readily or fully recognized by those involved in their production, distribution or use. They are also not always able to evade damaging effects caused by the manufacture of certain goods. Hence, the state must ensure protection from dangers, so that method of production is employed, no goods are produced or offered for sale which involve directly or indirectly a disproportionately high level of danger for human beings or the environment. Regulations on consumer policy, health policy and environmental policy are indispensable, alongside the necessary instruction of the population, and must keep up with the current state of knowledge. After careful testing, appropriate limits are to be set to production and use, or conditions imposed. It has proved difficult to limit the dangers posed by the innovation process without slowing it down unduly. A discussion concerning genetic engineering is a clear case in point. But as the objective potential long-run danger involved in the innovation process has increased and our knowledge of the dangers has grown long drawn out processes for planning and giving permission are becoming necessary more and more frequently."

This is a clear indication of the tension that exists in a civil society which is faced with the continuing prospect of rapidly increasing scientific and technological change. Consequently, there is a need for new mechanisms and procedures which are part of a democratic process to allow those autonomous groups which form the core of a civic society to raise significant questions and challenge regulatory systems that are put in place under constitutional arrangements. This aspect of the emerging civil society will be considered further in the following sections of this paper.

THE COUNTERVAILING FORCES: TECHNOLOGY ASSESSMENT AND FORESIGHT

There can surely be no argument that the increasing dependence of the modern world on various forms of new technology needs to be assessed from a variety of standpoints. At the end of the day the selection, implementation and regulation of new technologies is a matter of political decision and regulatory control. Unfortunately, the lessons of history reveal that many of the political decisions governing technological innovation in the past have not been founded on a careful systematic appraisal of the risks involved.

Growing public apprehension and concern about the possible longer-term consequences of developments in various fields, for example, the introduction of genetically modified organisms or the influence of toxic chemicals in the environment, have exposed significant gaps in knowledge and consequently growing demands for wider participation in the process of technology assessment. This is being pursued at a variety of different levels in many countries.

In Britain the White Paper on Science and Technology published in May, 1993[3] established a new procedure which has been taken forward on a year by year basis. This has resulted in a technology foresight program which enables industry and the research community to become closely involved in the appraisal process. A steering group for the program was set up under the chairmanship of the government's chief scientific adviser. Its members were drawn from the industrial, scientific and engineering communities, research charities and government departments, although most of its members were recruited from outside government. The remit of the steering group was to oversee the collection of information on scientific opportunities and potential market applications from a wide cross-section of experts in academia, industry, finance, consumer research and government. The group was also required to devise procedures for the initial and repeat consultation with researchers and industrialists for converting the results into working documents to enable panels of experts to identify those technologies within their sectors which they judge to be of most importance to the country's economy. The latter would be based on an evaluation of the best fit between:

1. trends in scientific research and the current or potential availability of strong research groups (science-push);
2. emerging economic developments and the current or potential availability of firms or organizations with the ability to appropriate research outcomes in order to seize emerging market opportunities (demand-pull).

The next step was to develop procedures for wide and accessible dissemination of the results, including arrangements to extend the partnerships through regional, local and perhaps sectoral networks, wherever possible building on current networking organizations providing both professional management and training opportunities. In a statement of intent associated with this review the government proposed that from 1994 it would publish each year a forward look giving a longer term assessment of:

- the portfolio of publicly-funded work best suited to the broader scientific and technological needs of the country at a time of increasing economic competition, rapid scientific advance and accelerating technological change;
- the extent to which current individual Departmental science and

technology programs are matched to that portfolio, and the prospects of bringing about a close alignment between the two.

This review therefore represents a watershed for British science and technology and the government believes that, over time and reinforced by the results of the Technology Foresight Program, its new annual forward look will form the basis for better-informed decisions between competing priorities which can inform decisions taken during annual public expenditure surveys. The consideration of priorities in the survey will continue to be informed by an assessment, coordinated by the chief scientific adviser, of science and technology proposals across all Departments of State. Inevitably there is a final caveat to be added as a footnote to the new partnership that is now being forged between the science and engineering base, industry and government. This revolves around the fact that basic science is an international enterprise and that progress depends on the rapid sharing of ideas among scientists in different countries. This is an endless frontier limitless possibilities for further work and the pace of change is accelerating. In future, decisions on priorities for publicly-funded scientific research and development will be much more clearly related to meeting the country's needs and to enhancing the well-creating capacity of the country. The contention is that excellence in scientific research is very important; second-rate research is a poor buy. The message to the research councils and other scientific and engineering bodies on the outside of the government is very clear. While these bodies should continue to focus on the value of proposed research in terms of scientific excellence and timeliness, they should take more fully into account the extent to which outcomes could be taken up by potential users. In setting priorities and allocating resources, they will therefore need to take account of the needs of their particular user communities--the relevant industrial or service sectors, private, and public as well as central and local government. This is a turning of the tide away from the public patronage of the pursuit of knowledge for its own sake. It also establishes a vitally important interface for the reformation of a civil society.

That having been said the interface between the confident predictions of the centralized state and the valid concerns of the informed citizen need to be considered carefully. In other European countries, notably The Netherlands and Germany, attempts are being made to engage in a wider process of technological assessment which identifies risks, explores uncertainties and engages the wider interests of environmental groups and other similar bodies. This approach in turn raises questions about the nature of the technology assessment itself and here it is worth quoting from a recent example of a technology assessment under the auspices of the German Ministry for Research and Technology[6] in which the main key words were *participation* and *discourse.*

The more technology assessment is seen as a vehicle to revise in principle the dependence of modern societies on technological dynamism the broader the horizon of problems to be considered. Thus technology assessment has regularly proceeded from the analysis of the consequences to the analysis of the origins of the technology in question. Moving from control to design and from technical options to the social needs. Equally regularly, however, political and pragmatic constraints imposed a return to classical technology assessment orientated towards the control of the consequences of a technology.

It is inevitable in these circumstances that there is a preoccupation with risk in the course of any technology assessment procedure. For those societies where technological innovation is an essential feature of the structure of science and industry, any overt opposition to a particular innovation is likely to rest on the various associated risk factors. It follows that the minimum requirement of a technology assessment should examine the legitimacy of objections which are raised by a concerned public in connection with a new technology. This tension between the concerned citizen or ad hoc group of questioning parties should become a controlling interface within the new order of a civil society. The public has a right to know that considerable efforts are at least being made in procedures of this kind to examine the state of knowledge on controversial subjects with a scientific or technical base. The process of technology assessment must therefore provide answers as to whether the publicly-declared risks do exist in practice, whether advantages claimed for a new process or system exist and whether public criticism is valid. If these conditions are fulfilled then the normal democratic decision-making can take place by elected representatives or an appropriately constituted statutory body. As a result, the emerging consensus on any new technology should provide a guide to politicians, potential investors and official regulators about the viability of a particular technology in the marketplace. The effectiveness of this procedure will in turn reflect the maturity of a civil society in electing not to pursue certain kinds of technology which are considered to pose unacceptable risks and to present an uncertain future.

THE COUNTERVAILING FORCES: THE INTERNATIONAL CONSENSUS ON GLOBAL CIVIL SOCIETY

In the foreword to the report of the Commission on Global Governance,[7] the Co-chairmen Ingvar Carlsson and Shridath Ramphal described some of the important changes that have taken place since the UN Charter was agreed upon and signed more than half a century ago.

1. The need to work together also guided the visionary men and women who drew up the Charter of the United Nations. What is new today is that the interdependence of nations is wider and deeper. What is also new is the role of people and the shift of focus from states to people. An aspect of this change is the growth of international civil society. These changes call for reforms in the modes of international cooperation--the institutions and processes of global governance. ...There is a need to weave a tighter fabric of international norms, expanding the rule of law worldwide and enabling citizens to exert their democratic influence on global processes.

2. We also believe the world's arrangements for the conduct of its affairs must be underpinned by certain common values. Ultimately, no organization will work and no law upheld unless they rest on the foundation made strong by shared values. These values must be informed by a sense of common responsibility for both present and future generations.

The commission argues in its report that the emergence of a vigorous civil society has been assisted by technological advances, particularly in mass media and in communications technology in general. This covers a multitude of institutions, voluntary organizations and networks--women's groups, trade unions, chambers of commerce, farming or housing co-operatives, neighborhood or community-based associations, religious organizations, charitable bodies--the list is endless. These groups provide the means of channelling both the interests and energies of many communities of people outside government, from business and the professions to individuals working towards a multiplicity of desirable social goals. Many of these citizens' movements and NGOs, provide an important source of funding for development and humanitarian work in which their dedication, administrative efficiency and overall flexibility provide a huge pool of complementary support to the official agencies. Their role in resolving conflict and building consensus is becoming increasingly important because if successful it can sideline the need for military intervention or the use of force. There are also broad gains to be achieved through such organizations and networks by enhancing pluralism and strengthening representative democracy.

While these organizations and networks immobilize the energy and commitment of people in communities, there is a tendency to focus on single issues that are giving them strength and expertise on certain subjects and may also inhibit the development of wider perspectives. The process can be assisted by partnerships between UN agencies and their NGO counterparts. Significant advances have been made particularly at recent events such as the UN Conference on Environment and Development in 1992 when more than 1,400 NGOs were accredited to the official conference and many more took part in the parallel Global Forum. This represented the strongest evidence of close collaboration between the official and independent sectors at any UN conference. The commission report indicates that official bodies must reach out to civil society "in a positive spirit and seek its contributions at all stages, including the shaping of policy."

In pursuit of this objective the commission proposes that, pending the evolution of a forum corresponding to a parliamentary or people's assembly within the UN system, a start should be made by convening an annual Forum of Civil Society. This should consist of representatives of organizations credited to the General Assembly as Civil Society Organizations--a new and expanded category of accredited organizations, including existing NGOs but looking to an even wider field such as private sector organizations and citizens' movements. It is further recommended that a forum of 300 to 600 representatives of global civil society would be desirable and practicable and the functioning of the Forum within the UN system will be a matter for negotiation with the UN, particularly the General Assembly.

The purpose of the forum would be to provide direct access to the UN system and by this means to contribute to the deliberations of the UN General Assembly. For example, there is a need for a direct means for civil society to persuade the international community to act in situations where there are grave threats to the security of people as borne out by recent examples in Somalia or Rwanda. The Commission, therefore proposes that there should be a new *right of petition* available to individuals and organizations to enable civil society to activate the UN's potential for preventive diplomacy, and the settlement of disputes where the security of people is or could be endangered by conflicts within states no less than between them. The channel for the petitions would depend upon the formation of a Council for Petitions-high level panel of 5 to 7 persons, independent of governments and selected in a personal capacity to consider petitions and to make recommendations on them to the Secretary General, the Security Council and the General Assembly. These proposals come at a time when clearly there is a need to reinforce and strengthen the nature of UN institutions. Also, the emerging institutions of civil society in many countries would therefore be in a position to contribute to this action and to provide a powerful voice whenever it is most needed to stimulate intergovernmental debate and collective action to redress the situation which imperils *the security of people* as held in trust by the UN Charter.

It remains to be seen whether any of these proposals are exposed to wider debate at a national level but the ideas are sound and warrant wider consideration. It will of course be for others to tease out the ideas in practice and to develop formal guidelines and structures relating to both the proposed Forum on Civil Society and the related *right to petition*. In the remaining sections of this paper we shall therefore concentrate on identifying those emerging institutions which would be needed to sustain it and to build confidence in its effectiveness at an international level.

EMERGING INSTITUTIONS: VOLUNTARY ORGANIZATIONS

In the past there has been a tendency among politicians and other commentators to discount the invaluable contribution of the voluntary sector by the use of dismissive terms--unpaid, part-time, and amateur. However, these attitudes are changing and the reconstruction of civil society is seen to depend more and more upon the willingness of individual citizens to contribute their energy and expertise within a broader organizational framework sustained by salaried professionals who care full-time, non-statutory, and independent. This latter description can be applied to a range of organizations who in any European country can include the staff of voluntary housing associations, community development bodies, environmental pressure groups such as Shelter, WWF and Greenpeace, campaigning groups on behalf of the elderly, disabled or disadvantaged, human rights groups, including Amnesty and fundraising bodies such as Oxfam and Christian Aid.

Each of these groups faces a wider constituency of subscribing *members* or supporters who can in turn provide the platform of popular support for particular issues or concerns identified by the organization. They also represent a potentially large measure of active support which can be mobilized on behalf of communities to achieve practical objectives, eg. community care services or local environment projects.

The hidden strengths of civil society lie in these self-organizing autonomous groups with their powerful networking principles and cadre of committed individuals who have the capacity to catalyze social change at a variety of different levels. The increasing professionalism and operation efficiency of these groups has improved markedly in recent years. Many of them are now able to offer goods and services in the marketplace and while operating as non-profit organizations, they are still capable of generating considerable capital and revenue flows for the mainstream organization in a highly effective manner. Frequently, the subscribing members of voluntary groups, particularly the campaigning bodies and pressure groups, far outstrip the membership of political parties. Consequently, they are in a position to exercise considerable influence on their elected representatives who in turn view them as an expression of popular support or otherwise for a particular cause. This can have advantages and drawbacks for both policy-making and the decision-making process at the center of government.

In certain policy areas, for example, housing and social services, the government is able to achieve added value and to release extra resources if it is seen to march in step with the voluntary sector. However the messages are not always clear and for the most part voluntary organizations would prefer to see their contribution as complementary to the provision and resourcing of public services and not as a substitute for them. The willingness of many voluntary groups to confront areas of social deprivation and to attempt to develop new solutions to long-standing problems in communities and neighborhoods, is frequently attributed to their resilience and power of self-determination.

If a civil society is to thrive, then it must continue to sustain and reinforce the development of these groups. The power of the state to intervene to improve the quality and range of services to any deserving community is usually constrained by the baseline of public expenditure. As individual economies climb slowly out of a recessionary period, it is essential that voluntary sector bodies have the opportunity to prove new ground and to expand their range of activities. Strength in diversity is a sound ecological principle and it could well be applied to the various voluntary groups that go to make up this informal net that is such a key feature of the western type of civil society.

EMERGING INSTITUTIONS: THE AID ORGANIZATIONS

Within the voluntary sector it is remarkable that overseas aid organizations, for example, Red Cross, Oxfam and Christian Aid, Medicin sans Frontieres, have become established at the center of international efforts to provide humanitarian aid whether to the survivors of natural disasters or to refugees in war zones. Intergovernmental arrangements operated by the UN frequently depend on people within these organizations who have a detailed understanding of local situations and the necessary practical skills to ensure that the response time is kept to an absolute minimum. The resilience of these aid organizations is a tribute to their deep structure and fundraising achievements over many years and also to their capacity to recruit loyal and dedicated staff, often on short-term contracts, to undertake specific programs and projects in many of the world's trouble spots.

Most governments continue to struggle towards the official aid targets of 0.7% GDP which is a sufficiently modest goal, but it is still far from being achieved in many cases. It is a true expression of civil society that despite that level of underperformance, voluntary aid organizations have a capacity to circumvent this perceived problem and to mount independent initiatives which spearhead the movement of food, shelter and technical support to where it is most often needed. The unrelenting level of demand for this type of assistance requires a special attitude of mind amongst the project leaders and staff directly concerned. Cheerful optimism and courage at a personal level will not be sufficient to meet the demands of a developing human tragedy which requires a flow of materials, equipment and services managed by professional officers who are able to cope with rapidly changing conditions on the ground. Such key workers are themselves often exposed to considerable risks of disease, injury, and detention but they will not give up easily in the face of these opposing forces. Instead they struggle to maintain a thin lifeline of hope in the face of desperate human need and despair.

It is fair to say that some of these organizations, the International Committee of the Red Cross in particular, now occupy such a position of trust and neutrality which transcends cultural and political boundaries, that they have become a true representative of global civil society. If there is to be a serious commitment towards establishing an annual Forum of Civil Society, then the committee of the Red Cross would be amongst its leading participants, exercising the proposed right to petition the UN system. This would not be simply an exercise in crisis management but a recognition that governments depend on the free expression of ideas and the goodwill of people everywhere to find a solution to some of the world's more intractable problems. The Forum would be assisted by organizations such as the Red Cross to determine the need for resources in particular locations in the interest of peace and justice.

EMERGING INSTITUTIONS: PRESSURE GROUPS AND COMMUNITY-BASED ACTION

The evolution of a global civil society depends upon a wider perception of the need to balance the regulatory power of the state by supporting and sustaining groups of citizens who exercise their franchise outside the constraints of the political process. In many countries in Europe and North America, single issue pressure groups have built their reputation on campaigning zeal and a capacity to highlight deficiencies in the operation of the nation state. This democratic expression of dissent or criticism of the prevailing order does not always convert directly into a political program or ideological response which governments can address. Instead these groups often adopt a position *in the pure light of reason* which allows them to occupy the high ground of moral responsibility while escaping the full rigors of political accountability. These groups therefore represent the *whistle blowers* in an increasingly technological world where choices or alternatives for very large numbers of people in democratic societies are pre-empted by the decisions of governments, international corporations or money markets allegedly taken in the name of progress. Damage to the natural environment and the rapid exploitation of non-renewable resources fall into this category, frequently without appropriate checks and balances being applied at the international level.

It remains to be seen whether a capacity to move international public opinion, for example, by Greenpeace over the French nuclear tests in the Pacific or by Friends of the Earth over the disposal of toxic waste by incineration in the atmosphere, will eventually generate a more reasonable and sustainable response by national governments. But that it all that we are left with, namely, a capacity to raise issues, to query and question scientific judgments based on available facts, observations and figures, and to discover alternative courses of action in the process which will relieve the pressures and difficulties defined by our present state of knowledge.

Another expression of this freedom in civil society is the ability to form community-based groups which encourage leadership and self-determination in order to solve local problems in fields such as housing, social welfare, including the abuse of drugs and care in the community for the young and for elderly people alike. There are examples where these problems can only be addressed on a satisfactory scale if there is a coming together between the community and statutory bodies to form working partnerships or action groups to meet the specific objectives. Programs to address multiple deprivation in urban areas are often geared to this end but there are bound to be many other examples of this type of self-governing community-based action which can achieve objectives that could be met by the state acting alone or in isolation.

AGE OF UNCERTAINTY: VALUE SYSTEMS IN TRANSITION

There is a preoccupation in liberal democracies with reducing the scale and extent of public services that are provided from the taxation base of their economies. The implication that the consumer of health, housing, education, and social welfare should cover the risks of any shortfall in the provision of these services by anticipatory action on the part of the individual or family is fast becoming a part of the conventional wisdom. In these circumstances the spirit of Adam Smith can rest easy as the legendary invisible hand operating in the marketplace allows the costs to fall as they may and prices to reflect the corresponding demand for services.

It is not surprising that the shift in the value system away from the concept of the welfare state as a safety net for all results in some considerable turbulence within the political system of each country that is now required to address these issues. The demographic drive of increasing and ageing populations in most countries in Europe and North America leaves open the question as to whether this is part of the inevitable balancing act required in the interests of sustainability. The vulnerability of capital markets to other kinds of turbulence has been amply demonstrated by events in recent years on the New York, London, and Tokyo exchanges. The confidence in governing parties to withstand currency pressures has been severely tested and the forced devaluation of currencies has been linked to more efficient economic performance and a renewal of confidence amongst the marketmakers. However, the question remains as to whether this represents a historical shift away from collective values and towards individual self-reliance and freedom of choice.

In mixed economies, which will retain a balance between private and public sector investment, the pendulum has begun to swing in favor of the private financing of economic infrastructure, eg. hospitals, roads, bridges, and tunnels, which would in another era have been funded directly from the public purse. Inward investment in conventional manufacturing industry is still the subject of tax breaks or tax holidays, grant incentives and job creation schemes. These paradoxes color the landscape but they also convey a sense of movement in the value system which leaves individuals and communities stranded and with very little means of controlling their destinies. It is against this backcloth that the reconstruction of civil society must take place with increasing emphasis on shared responsibility and mutual respect as the guiding principles.

In the first instance, the burden of defending the public interest in these matters will fall to professional associations and bodies which have the capacity to identify significant technological change and its potential impact on the delivery of services to the general population. Each professional grouping should therefore be capable of identifying a wide range of options for the development and improvement of services which can be put in front of the electorate in order to allow a more informed judgment to be made. Any movement of policy away from the state and towards the community could therefore be identified at a much earlier stage and allow appropriate planning to take place. Elected representatives could then exercise budgetary choices within the framework of a two- or three-year expenditure cycle but would not be able to pre-empt the future by ideological shifts which alter the quality of service provision available to the general population. For example, in recent years the introduction of an internal market and purchaser/provider interface into the British National Health Service has generated differing perceptions as to the overall efficiency and effectiveness of the service across the country. Although waiting lists have fallen considerably in many places, the increasing workload on both medical and ancillary staff has revealed structural weaknesses in the organization of many clinical departments. Consequently, politicians are divided as to whether the NHS is still a service which to all intents and purposes is still free of charge to each patient at the point of service delivery. The fact that increasing numbers of the population resort to private medical insurance is a broad indicator that there has been a significant shift in both access and quality of services provision which does not meet the expectations of growing numbers of people.

Similarly, the provision of primary and secondary education by public authorities in Britain has been subject to similar budgetary pressures. In England, secondary schools that opt out of local authority control are given preferred direct grant aided status by the government which allows them to be virtually self-governing in a manner analogous to schools in the private sector. However, in each case it is important to note that there has been a movement of administrative responsibility from the center of government to a local or community level which may in itself carry certain benefits. As in any business environment it is possible to tract small bundles of resources with far greater effect if this action is carried out near to the point of actual expenditure and service provision. While politicians may argue that this ensures value for money in the purchase of services, it is also fair to point out that this process is also likely to engage more people in systematic planning and resource allocation at a community level. The downside of all of this is that under present arrangements the allocation of responsibility has been largely to non-elective groups who because of their rising power and authority could eventually weaken the base of local democracy. It is essential therefore that these quasi-public bodies and also voluntary organizations operating in the same field are seen to be as broadly representative of the community interests as it is possible to achieve through the full participation of people living in these communities. It follows, therefore, that we should take more time to understand the nature of the communities on which these responsibilities fall.

AGE OF UNCERTAINTY: THE NATURE OF "COMMUNITY"

Civil society requires communities to be composed of organizations which are radically different form those with which we are currently familiar. These organizations will include members of equal personal and productive power and it is this quality which will characterize the relationship between leaders and members of the organizations. In turn the organizations will not seek to "improve" their members as the concept of membership will have a different meaning. The organization will not be a vehicle for "having information" but instead will provide an opportunity of "being" a member (an allusion to Fromm).[8] The focus of the discourse within the organizations will be on the self-disclosure and self-interpretation of its associates. In learning to internalize the purpose of the organization and living within its dialogical community, a process will be modelled which has relevance to the maladaptive social institutions which prevail in the modern world. Progress towards this concept of organization will be achieved by understanding the differences contained in the vocabulary of *group, network,* and *community.* These words tend to be used interchangeably and lack precision. Public policy documents in particular seem unclear about the nature of community. They articulate different levels of need--the needs of individuals, the needs of groups, the needs of community. What do they mean by *community*? Is a community an aggregation of small and large groups, is it a network, or is it a different organism altogether?

The group has been described as a *social aggregation* with an external boundary and at least one internal boundary, for example, between the leadership and membership regions of the group.[9]

Where this boundary is considered to be permeable, individuals will feel empowered to move in and out of leadership roles, forming and reforming task groups as the need arises. A civil association can be interpreted either as a large group with the same boundary issues which challenge small groups or as a set of small groups where members explicitly attend to intergroup relationships. Most groups are challenged by the double task of the management of work and the management of group maintenance. Work can become *busy work* rather than real work and often work is sacrificed altogether because a group is having problems maintaining itself and has lost sight of significant boundary management issues.

A profession network is not a group and should not function as if it is. In this case each member represents a node on the network. Members form and respond to their own reference groups which are engaged in creating other networks. There is no leadership region or membership region in a network, the boundary systems are clearly permeable, the life of different parts of the network ebbs and flows, and the coordinator manages a flexible system which can incorporate both long-life and short-life groups.

The ideal vision of community is therefore of an aggregation of complementary groups and networks. However, the dynamics of the real community fall short of this ideal. This aggregation may characterize the nature of the community rather than aggregation. We may observe the dynamics of envy, the dynamics of splitting and displacement, and the structuring of *systems of defence against anxiety* as they interfere with the real task of building a community.[10] It is assumed that communities are rational and will operate on the basis of reasonable judgments. In reality, we know them to be governed by conscious and unconscious processes which may or may not be made explicit by those elected or nominated to represent the views of these communities.

AGE OF UNCERTAINTY: DIALOGUE AND COMMUNITY

There can be no community without dialogue. Dialogue may be different in every cultural and historical context but human communication is fundamentally the same. It is through ordinary communicative actions that we find solutions to the problems of community. When we travel between linguistic communities we notice that, for example, philosophers are concerned with dialogue as an ideal, while linguists perceive dialogue as describeable. However, the voice of civil society should communicate the values of connectedness and considerateness. The task which should underpin all community ventures is the mutual understanding of the dynamic of groups within systems. We should understand in particular the need which groups have to work towards consensus. This is too often a failed project. The problem is that many citizens are perceived to lack the interest or do not possess the competence to pursue their interest in the process of consensus-building.

Consensus is brought about by sustained discussion. Communities need to learn to discuss. Consensus is achieved through individuals reflecting on, analyzing and articulating their values and commitments with others. Consensus-building is a process, not an end in itself and should not be confused with decision-making. The discourse of decision-making may emerge from reaching a consensus on an issue but decision-making cannot be assumed as a result of consensus. The approach to consensus in the civil society should emphasize the capacity to live with difference. Primarily there must be a recognition that we live in different linguistic communities and different reference groups will tend to talk to each other using their own specialized terminology. On the other hand, we can learn to be effective travellers between linguistic communities if we understand ourselves as speaking a code which may not necessarily be accessible to those with whom we wish to be in dialogue. The primary task for the committed communicator is to identify the codes significant to the process of consensus-building, if possible to acquire a variety of codes and at the very least to become competent in the understanding if not in the performance of different codes.

This learning process is invariably under-estimated by participants in a consensus-building exercise. Public perception of the scientific community, for example, has been damaged because of the lack of analysis of the misunderstandings which have operated in public discussion of issues such as nuclear power and the environment. In the United Kingdom, changes in the management of the health service have meant that there are two different voices, the voice of the internal market and the voice of clinical need. Those who communicate effectively in one community may not travel well in communicating with those whose work is based on a different value system.

Communication breakdown is often portrayed as misunderstanding the content of a message when in reality it is the communication process which is flawed. We speak of disagreement, of understanding the issues which divide a community, while failing to recognize that our understanding is partial, neither fully reflective nor fully rational. The desire to reach consensus may than be an inappropriate goal in that it is associated with the end point of discussion. Mutual understanding can never be finished, it is an ongoing process. Scientists and the wider public need to continue to investigate the differences in their perceptions and whether these perceptions are based in fantasy or reality. Health service staff need to be resolute in voicing their competing claims. Communicative action should be understood as a series of dynamic elements, a developing organism which continues to renew itself. The cycles of agreement and disagreement should be interpreted as entry or exit points within the cycle for further reflection, analysis and definition of strategy.

341

Communities of inquiry which are content-orientated in relation to communication need to be supported by communities of interpreters available to identify process objectives.

These understandings may achieve a better fit between different levels of discourse, for example, the moral, the pragmatic, the ethical, and the political. Each type of discourse has its own purpose, defining a sense of balance between consensus building and decision-making. An understanding of these different levels of discourse as parts of the process would protect the community from the cynicism of citizens who perceive themselves to be disenfranchised from the debates in society through lack of knowledge or articulacy.

There are numerous examples of *town meetings* and *consensus conferences* based on the concepts which have been described. However, their failure is that they have often been community developments unconnected to the political process. They are no more than case studies of a potential methodology. National and local government observers regard them as limited examples of an approach which founders because of the lack of information or communicative competence of community members. Initiators of these events are regarded as unrealistic about the constraints of government administration.

What the detractors fail to see is the connection between one level of discourse and another. Effective management of the boundaries around communities of inquirers, interpreters, and decision-makers would demonstrate how the findings from discourse in one context could be built into discourse in another. It follows that civil associations should primarily be concerned with developing empathy and mutual respect over a particular issue or topic. Dialogue should be approached through the understanding of *self* and *the other* so that "the hope lives on in the gesture of turning to the other with goodwill.[11] The tone of the dialogue to which civil associations should aspire has been defined as:

> "...exploratory and interrogative. It involves a commitment to the process of communicative interchange itself, a willingness to *see things through* to some meaningful understandings or agreements among the participants... It manifests an attitude of reciprocity among the participants: an interest, respect, and concern that they share for one another, even in the face of disagreements."[12]

The writers have explored the different spaces between those who perceive communication as having instrumental value and those for whom communication has intrinsic value. They emphasis reflectiveness and the search for reasonable judgments. What they omit is a focus on the value of the inner dialogue, the act of introspection, which is the necessary precursor to externalized conversation and inquiry. In exploring the values of civil society the tension between the state and civil associations should be reflected in this inner and outer dialogue between the self and the community. This will best be demonstrated by finding a vocabulary with which to communicate personal and professional identity in the communities which we serve.

The notion of a dialogical community requires, above all, attention to the psycho-dynamics of the communication process. The interpersonal perspective, which makes use of moral reasoning, can only be learned if the psycho-dynamic process of lifting feelings into thought and into spoken language is understood. Our understanding of *community* will have meaning if we take the time to explore the boundaries of the personal and professional self, develop understanding of the different levels of person, system and institution which affect the substance and style of communication and begin to understand the interpersonal distortions which occur in our dealings with other people. Reconstruction of public institutions and civil associations alike will therefore depend upon our capacity to interpret and understand behavior, cognition and psycho-dynamics not as discrete elements but as an integrated whole sustaining the moral purpose of a civil society.

REFLECTION

The purpose of the paper has been to invite the reader to consider how the reconstruction of civil society might best be engaged through a renewal of the process of dialogue at international, national, and local levels. The tension between the state as *governor* and the citizen as *governed* is central to this process but the necessary checks and balances to the regulatory system of civil law can only be applied fairly and justly if the appropriate representations are made to the governing parties by civil associations and similar bodies. As national governments become ever more preoccupied with economic management in increasingly competitive world markets, the opportunity to influence and to innovate on domestic and social issues will depend on the emerging consensus amongst civil associations who are concerned about the strength, resilience, and sustainability of their own communities. The preoccupation which is shared by national governments and private corporations over increased efficiency and effectiveness as a business objective will then be countered by the broader appeal of civil associations to human values based on tolerance, mutual trust, democratic participation, and community spirit. These are the values on which the reconstruction of civil society for the 21st century will most depend.

NOTES

1. Hall, John A. (ed.), Civil Society: Theory, History, Comparison," *Policy Press*, 1995.
2. "Sustainable Development: The UK Strategy," *Cm 2426*, HMSO, January, 1994.
3. "Realizing our Potential: A Strategy for Science, Engineering, and Technology," *Cm 2250*, HMSO, May, 1993.
4. "O'Riordan, T. "Civic Science and Global Environmental Change," *Scottish Geographical Magazine*, vol 110 (1), pp. 4-12, 1994.
5. "Common Good and Self Interest," *EKD report*, Evangelische Kirche in Deutschland, March, 1992.
6. van den Daele, W. "Technology Assessment as a Political Experiment," *FS II 94-319*, Science Center Berlin, August, 1994.
7. *Our Global Neighborhood: The Report of the Commission on Global Governance*, Oxford University Press, 1995.
8. Fromm, E. *To Have or To Be*, Jonathan Cape Ltd., 1978.
9. Bramley, W. "Group Tutoring: Concepts and Case Studies," *Kogan Page*, 1979.
10. Menzies, I. "A Case Study in the Functioning of Social Systems as a Defense against Anxiety," *Tavistock Pamphlet No. 3*, Tavistock Institute of Human Relations, London, 1977.
11. Maranhao, T. (ed.), *The Interpretation of Dialogue*, Chicago University Press, 1990.
12. Burbules, Nicholas C. *Dialogue in Teaching: Theory and Practice*, Teachers College Press, New York, 1993.

AFRICA AND THE NEW GLOBALIZATION: CHALLENGES AND OPTIONS FOR THE FUTURE

by

Julius O. Ihonvbere

Indeed, especially in the case of Africa, let us be clear that the task now before us is to ensure that these countries gain more and more from opportunities afforded by the closer integration into the world economy that such a globalized world can offer them. If they fail to take advantage of these opportunities, the risk of their marginalization will only be increased. Michel Camdessus.[1]

The "marginalization of Africa" is not just speculation. Not only are foreign governments closing embassies and cutting back aid flows, but Africa's role in the world economy is also shrinking....Sub-Saharan Africa is seen less and less as a credible or useful economic and diplomatic partner and increasingly as a humanitarian problem for the world. Carol Lancaster.[2]

The plight of the African continent remains the most serious challenge for the emerging world order. World Bank.[3]

The positions above clearly reflect the paradoxical location and role of Africa in the emerging global division of labor and power. The end of the cold war and the increasing integration of the global economy with the triumph of the market and the demise of communism, have posed severe challenges and opportunities for the African continent. On the one hand, there is the opportunity to fully integrate into the emerging global capitalist order to exploit the developments in science and technology, the new information revolution, and the expansion of the global market. Such an integration, it is argued will open up extensive opportunities for trade, investment, foreign aid, and support for other developmental objectives.[4] On the other hand, the changes in the global market hold out the risks of further marginalization, and the redirection of investments and aid to other parts of the world, for a variety of reasons. The complaints about aid and compassion fatigue by the donors is evidence of increasing frustration with the intractable and complex problems and contradictions of the continent. It is contended by those who see the deepening crisis of the region as an inhibition to full and effective participation in the new global order that the legacies of colonial and neo-colonial exploitation and mismanagement, the crisis of the state and society, and conditions of poverty, foreign domination, instability, and institutional and infrastructural decay and dislocation make participation in the global order impossible.[5] Even the World Bank is of the view that Africa's

Julius O. Ihonvbere *is on the faculty of the department of government, University of Texas at Austin.*

future, in the increasingly complex and competitive global order is at best, bleak and uncertain:

> Sub-Saharan Africa will be falling further behind the rest of the world, based on realistic projections of current policies and Africa's current depressed per capita income level, while other developing countries and high-income countries will see their average income levels triple by the year 2030. Sub-Saharan Africa's per capita income will probably be only US$400 by the year 2030, that of the developing countries as a whole will probably reach US$2,500.[6]

This sort of projection raises several questions not just about the future of Africa, but also about its post-cold war relations with other regions of the world. What sort of internal restructurings are needed to empower the region to take advantage of current and future changes in the global order? Is the global system structured in such a way as to make it possible for a debt-ridden, crisis-ridden, and poverty-stricken region to effectively and profitably participate in the emerging global dispensation? How will on-going implementation of orthodox structural adjustment packages as well as difficult political liberalization programs in the context of deepening crisis and global marginalization facilitate or mediate Africa's participation in the new globalization? This paper will attempt to answer some of these questions.

THE CHANGING GLOBAL ORDER: FEATURES, OPPORTUNITIES, AND CONSTRAINTS

Without doubt, the global system is entering a new era. The end of the 20th century has ushered in unprecedented and largely unanticipated changes, at least, not with the rapidity and decisiveness with which the changes occurred:[7] the reunification of Germany with the collapse of the Berlin Wall; the peace talks between Israel and Palestine; the end of apartheid in South Africa and the election of Nelson Mandela as the first black president of that country; the collapse of the Soviet Union as a super power and nation; the widespread adoption of market reform programs as dictated and supervised by the World Bank and the International Monetary Fund (IMF); and the emergence of the United States as the hegemonic military power in the world.[8] As well, we can add a renewed role for the United Nations especially in the areas of humanitarian relief, peacekeeping, and peacemaking; the preponderance of micronationalism; and efforts by the United States to sell the "American way of life" as the only credible alternative left for the entire world in the face of the assumed victory of the bourgeoisie over communism and totalitarianism;[9] and, the deluge of struggles for multipartyism which

346

have altered the political environment. To these we can also add the redundancy of non-alignment as a political/ideological posture in global power relations; the drastic alteration of cold war-based foreign policy platforms; new economic alignments "toward one or others of large economic markets--the US, the European Community (EC) and Japan;" and new immigration restrictions which "display more racist tendencies toward minorities, particularly of African descent."[10] In particular, the end of the cold war and the triumph of the market and the United States have received intellectual support and rationalization from scholars like Francis Fukuyama in his "End of History" thesis, and Samuel P. Huntington in his "Clash of Civilization" postulations.[11]

The changes outlined above have completely altered the content and direction of global social, economic, and political relations. As the World Bank jubilantly declared in its *World Development Report 1995*: "These are revolutionary times in the global economy. The embrace of market-based development by many developing and former centrally-planned economies, the opening of international markets, and great advances in the ease with which goods, capital and ideas flow around the world are bringing new opportunities, as well as risks, to billions of people."[12] Communications are faster, cheaper and more open; the activities of governments are increasingly more open to external scrutiny; and there are more discussions of economic cooperation and integration beyond ideological and political lines. Even Cuba and communist China are doing more business with capitalist economies and carrying out internal reforms along market lines, even if they refuse to admit to such ideological somersaults. A crisis-ridden continent like Africa, with most of the least developed nations of the world, is increasingly caught in the unpredictable and highly sophisticated and competitive vortex of this emerging global order. Unfortunately, Africa was not quite ready for these changes and so, was caught unawares. Africa was not even prepared for the dramatic changes that took place in Africa which culminated in the election of Mandela as president and the vigorous and aggressive expansion of South African businesses into other African economies. Beyond these, however, the new globalization is marked by other critical features which further demonstrate the weakness and vulnerability of the African economy.[13]

One major feature of the new globalization is the increasing powerlessness of the state, at least, as far as regulating the movement of information, ideas, capital, even skills is concerned. As the World Bank admits, "Governments are increasingly seeking to improve the international competitiveness of their economies rather than shield them behind protective walls."[14] The implication is that governments are taking steps to give more autonomy to private initiatives and to cede some political ground to powerful corporations. Rapid changes in information technology have greatly impacted on the autonomy, capabilities, and spheres of action open to the nation state.

Boutros Boutros-Ghali has observed that "(t)he time of absolute and exclusive sovereignty...has passed" and states must "find a balance between the needs of good internal governance and the requirements of an ever more interdependent world."[15] As well, as is evident in Africa, the state is increasingly under pressure and attack, and quite a handful have become stagnant, exhausted or have collapsed out rightly.[16]

The developments in the post-cold war era have opened the way for articulating new patterns of responses to deepening political problems around the world, especially in Africa. This is evidenced in the responses to Somalia, Liberia, The Sudan, Burundi, Rwanda, South Africa, Nigeria, and other spots of crisis.[17] Though these responses have been bedeviled by inconsistencies and other financial and logistical problems, the fact remains that the United Nations is becoming "a central point of constance in the midst of flux."[18] According to Perez de Cuellar, this renewed interest in and role of the UN is clearly evidenced in the exercise of the authority of the Security Council in the manner envisioned in the Charter, the many instances of the General Assembly and the Council reinforcing each other's efforts, the close cooperation between the Council as a whole and the Secretary-General, the growing role of the Secretariat as represented by the Secretary-General in undertaking increasingly diversified missions of peace, and the revitalized role being contemplated for the Economic and Social Council-all these testify to a strengthening of the institutions embodied in the Organization."[19]

The renewed interest (especially by the United States) in the UN is equally the reasoning behind an emerging global moral and political responsibility that has encouraged interventions not only in the states mentioned above, but also in other crisis locations like Haiti and Bosnia at great financial and other costs.[20] When the UN Security Council adopted resolution 688 which states that humanitarian suffering in any member state was a threat to global peace and security, it also laid the grounds for a global response to domestic conditions which might have political and non-political dimensions. This has, of course, strengthened (?) the UN in its responses to and involvement in domestic matters. Yet, there has been a tendency to present the vintage position of the United States and the Western world as reflective of, and representative of the conditions of poor, dominated, vulnerable, and underdeveloped nations.[21] The increasing interest in human rights at the global level has opened up new debates on the issues of sovereignty and autonomy. To be sure, in some instances, as is the case with China, Western nations have been willing to overlook allegations of human rights abuses in order to promote trade relations. However, as the recent execution of Nobel Prize nominee, Ken Saro-Wiwa and eight other environmentalists by the military junta in Nigeria showed, the global community can be swift to action in defense of human rights. In fact, Nigeria was not only suspended from the Commonwealth but many Western nations reviewed diplomatic, trade and aid relations and continue to discuss sanctions as a way of forcing the military out of power.[22] Thus in the area of meting out justice within its borders, the contemporary state can no longer claim an absolute degree of sovereignty. Every action against groups, communities, individuals, dissidents, even coup plotters, come under the very critical scrutiny of international human rights groups and foreign governments:

Today, human rights groups such as Amnesty International challenge the state's claim to be the sole dispenser of justice. In some cases, the International Monetary Fund, the World Bank and other UN agencies have cut aid to the very worst human-rights violators. The US has also been increasingly willing to use aid as a lever, particularly in instances where cold war diplomacy no longer requires it to look the other way, to curb the excesses of its allies.[23]

At no time in the post-Westphalian history of the contemporary state system have non-state actors wielded more relevance, influence, and power than at the moment. The breakdown of ideological orthodoxies and the search for new patterns of socio-economic and power relations have further reduced the relevance of the state in favor of less formal and private structures and institutions. Singular influence and power of election monitors in the current global order attest to the ever growing significance of non-state actors as newly elected or re-elected governments often require their stamps of approval for international acceptability and legitimacy.

On balance, it would appear that scientific, economic, and social factors, rather than political developments, have contributed more significantly to the erosion of state sovereignty and in shaping the character of the new globalization in recent times. As the nations of the world came to depend more on each other, as transportation narrowed distances, as communications made it possible for people to interact and exchange information and ideas, and as nations became readily permeable to the power of new communications systems, the ability of the state to lay claim to some higher level of authority gradually weakened. Of course, since the 1980s with the crisis in the former Soviet Union, and more so since the emergence of the independent republics, the triumph of the market has not only narrowed ideological positions but has also drawn nations together in the struggle to permeate markets, attract foreign aid and investments, and attract new technologies: "Already, capitalism is flourishing in regions as diverse as communist Asia and the former dictatorships of Latin America. Affluence is lifting millions out of poverty, giving many the chance to purchase their first Fiats and Toyotas as well as their first Apple computers and Panasonic VCRs. And inflation is brought to heel in even the most wayward economies."[24] Even if somewhat exaggerated, this view does give a fair idea as to the pervasiveness of market ideas and relations in the contemporary global order. What is instructive, however, is that in most of the on-going discussions about the new globalization Africa is hardly considered or taken seriously. This is in spite of the "encouraging progress...made in transforming sub-Saharan Africa," and the far-reaching socio-economic and political reforms which governments have been forced to adopt to please lenders, donors and international pressure groups.[25] These reform packages, often imposed from abroad and supervised by the multilateral agencies and credit clubs, have served in no small measure to erode the autonomy and sovereignty of African states. The combination of externally designed, imposed, and supervised political and economic condition-alities--structural adjustment and political pluralism--is part of the conditions determining Africa's integration into the emerging global order: as a dependent, vulnerable, weak, dominated, and almost helpless periphery actor in the new division of labor and power.[26]

The complex ways in which the global economy is now connected beyond ideological considerations (China is one of the largest trading partners of the United States, Cuba is working hard to normalize relations, and the US government has normalized relations with Vietnam) seems to have had the greatest impact. For instance, the tendency of Americans "to think about Vietnam as a war rather than a country," has now given way to a vibrant and vigorous competition by Western corporations to capture the Vietnamese market following the July 11, 1995 decision of the Clinton administration to normalize relations.[27] It has become so easy to establish, organize and operate businesses and carry out transactions outside the control of the state. It is not only increasingly true that "(i)nternational trade is the first avenue by which most countries feel the impact of economic integration," but the evidence is in the rising volume of "goods and services traded across borders...accounting for about 45 percent of world GDP in 1990, up from 25 percent in 1970."[28]

There is no doubting the fact that in a world relatively liberated from hard ideological constraints, "new technology is rewriting old concepts of sovereignty and over time will also change national objectives."[29] Recent struggles for democracy in developing coun-tries have benefitted significantly from the cellular phone and fax machines which despotic and repressive governments could not control: "Ideas transmitted by satellite broadcasts, fax machines, and Internet ports are prying open even authoritarian regimes."[30] None of these major technological contraptions is produced or even assembled in Africa. As Walter B. Wriston has noted, the "informa-tion revolution is changing our global economy, transforming national political and business institutions and altering national foreign policy objectives and the methods of achieving them."[31] In Africa, except for a handful of countries like South Africa, business is still performed mostly manually, relying on outdated information, completely oblivious of new possibilities opened up by new technology. From banking to insurance, through import-export activities to information collection, processing, and dissemination, Africa is still decades behind Asia and Latin America, not to mention

Europe and North America.

What has been referred to as the "digital age" with "powerful data networks" is drawing developing nations "into the borderless information economy."[32] Nations of the world really have no choice about joining or opting out of the new information age. To opt out is to be isolated and cut off from the massive flow of ideas and information badly needed to move into the next century. On the other hand, participating in the information age requires a high degree of political openness, administrative flexibility, rapid changes in science and technology, even a revolutionary transformation of the educational system of the country. Internet connections are expanding by 16 percent every month, fiber optics are transmitting 40 billion bits of data per second, and the US army claims that by AD 2000 there will be as many computers as persons in the world. According to Dharan Ghai, "economic restructuring and technological development have reduced the effectiveness of a whole range of institutions that have served to provide social and economic security in the postwar period."[33]. Governments have practically lost the capacity to keep pace with the generation, processing, manipulation, and dissemination of information around the world.[34] The World Bank further supports these claims when it notes that in line with the new global emphasis on the market as the prime mover of growth and development, "technological changes...have made the world easier to navigate--goods, capital, people, and ideas travel faster and cheaper today than ever before. Underlying these changes have been huge reductions in transport and communications costs."[35] So far, African states are not poised to move in the direction of exploiting these new developments. Yet, as African nations wallow in confusion, poverty, superstition, the recycling of outdated information and ideas, and continue to rely on old and already discarded technology, around the world, medical practices, experiments in science and technology, banking services, academic research and so on are being undertaken in cooperation by persons separated by hundreds of thousands of miles.[36] The use of computers, even by faculty members in the sciences, is still a rarity on the eve of the twenty-first century!

All over the world, even in the most developed market economies, governments are rapidly losing control over the flow of money. As the IMF itself has admitted, "this integration of financial markets is not only irreversible, but it can only broaden and intensify in the future. Let us not make the mistake of believing that the answer to financial crises lies in reviewing this globalization through exchange controls and less open markets."[37] The most efficient Central Bank cannot boast of having full knowledge of, or control over, domestic financial transactions. The computer has put within the reach of average citizens the power to execute complex banking transactions within the confines of their homes. Geographical location or currency denominations now mean almost nothing to the new financial market place.[38]

The United Nations Research Institute for Social Development (UNRISD) has revealed that "A single building in New York houses a computer system that moves $1 trillion around the world each business day (more than the entire money supply of the United States). These transactions are linking people internationally as never before."[39] Where does Africa stand in this new globalization of the financial market place? The answer is; "nowhere": the currencies are either worthless (Zaire, Somalia), excessively devalued (Ghana and Zambia) or generally inconvertible. Most of the countries are so poor that their central banks simply exist in name. Others can no longer control inflation, while several countries only do business in the weekly auctioning of foreign exchange in the name of rationalizing the financial market as part of a usually poorly implemented adjustment package. Businesses are not going into Africa because the near worthlessness of the currencies is depressing the market and there are practically no buyers for non-essential commodities and services. Banks are yet to be computerized, and transactions still take forever.

The most powerful actors in the new globalization are transnational corporations. They are rapidly streamlining technology, labor training, utilization, and exploitation; regulations, and production processes. This also includes a strategy to as much as possible, streamline and rationalize consumption around the world to facilitate production and marketing of goods and services without frequent retooling, investments in fixed capital or skill development. The end of the cold war is strengthening the power and influence of the corporations and encouraging them to move into untested waters. The end of apartheid encouraged McDonalds into South Africa, and encouraged South African corporations to move rapidly into neighboring countries.[40] While Western business interests have not been deterred by the uncertainties in the Middle East and Eastern Europe, "the foreign direct investment response has been, at best, hesitant and weak in Africa."[41] As Ellen Johnson Sirleaf has noted, though most African states have developed "new investment codes...; the number of sectors previously reserved for nationals has been sharply reduced; screening procedures have been simplified and one-stop investment centers have been established; the relative equity share that foreigners are allowed to hold in enterprises has been raised; and tax holidays of up to ten years or more are now common," "the annual average flow of foreign direct investment to Africa over the 1985-89 period was $2.6 billion."[42] In the same period, Latin America and the Caribbean received $6.0 billion, the East, South and Southeast Asia received $13.6 billion, North America received $55.8 billion, and Western Europe received $60.8 billion. In fact, of the "23 Sub-Saharan African countries with more than 2 million people, ten had no foreign direct investment inflows and only six had inflows of more than two dollars per capita."[43] It is clear, therefore, that the new globalization is not redirecting resources towards Africa in any credible or substantial sense. Rather, unlike other developing regions, and in spite of the rapidly expanding global financial market, Africa has not expanded its "exports of manufactures," it remains a producer of "primary commodities and ...terms of trade have continued to fall."[44] Increasingly lacking the capacity to generate foreign exchange, and without an appreciable inflow of investments, even to those countries which have clearly decided for open markets and liberal democracy like Zambia, Africa cannot be an effective actor in the new globalization.

CONSTRAINTS OF THE NEW GLOBALIZATION

Africa entered the 20th century as a dependent, foreign-dominated, technologically backward, politically unstable, vulnerable, and marginal actor in the global system. Decades of foreign aid--albeit informed by cold war considerations and calculations, political support for ideological client states, and investments, even if in enclave sectors, produced no appreciable change in the region's unprecedented deterioration, dislocation, and decay. The reasons for this unenviable situation are not lost to observers and scholars of Africa. According to Layashi Yaker, "Africa, potentially the richest continent, with the poorest people, having been exploited for a long time, can and must become a dynamic developing region if there is to be a common future for mankind."[45] Yet, decades of mismanagement, coups and counter-coups, environmental degradation, the exploitation and marginalization of women, misplaced priorities, and the neglect of basic human needs have precipitated distortions and disarticulations in Africa's political economy. As well, unbridled corruption, the privatization of the state and its resources, the suffocation of civil society, the manipulation of primordial loyalties, and criminal abuse of power have also eroded opportunities for creativity, innovation, growth and development. Furthermore, the reproduction and rationalization of neo-colonial economic relations and unequal exchange relations with powerful profit and hegemony--seeking transnational corporations, limited or no investments in science and technology, the neglect and exploitation of the rural areas and rural producers, an urban-based investment pattern and extroverted consumption patterns--have precipitated a huge foreign debt profile and discouraged investment and external support.[46] The net result has been that:
Economic growth proved to be elusive, managing an average rate of only 2.1 per cent per annum (in the 1980s, and much less in the 1990s). This translated into a fall in per capita incomes at the average rate of about 1 per cent per annum. The human and social conditions of the majority of the African people worsened considerably. Poverty increased in both the rural and urban areas; real earnings fell drastically; unemployment and underemployment rose sharply; hunger and famine became endemic; dependence on food

aid and food imports intensified; diseases, including the added scourge of AIDS, decimated populations and became a real threat to the very process of growth and development; and the attendant social evils-crime, delinquency, family disintegration-intensified with a vengeance.[47]

It is precisely these conditions of desperation and weakness that have constrained the ability of Africa to be effectively part of the changing global order in a positive sense. What this means is that Africa will likely remain in the backwaters of the new globalization, reaping most of the negative outcomes and being unable to influence on-going changes. The negative consequences of the new globalization have more implications for Africa's survival, than on-going positive developments: how can Africa protect itself from further manipulation, exploitation, marginalization, and vulnerability?

Clearly, the move towards a globalized political economy is not flawless or without conflict. Only those economies with goods and services to sell, and which can attract investors because of viable political structures, high credit rating, good infrastructure, and an aggressive global agenda will benefit from the emerging global economy. Only those nations with the ability to harness and process information, link up with or develop new technology, and those with the level of skill development relevant for a growing competitive globalized economy will benefit from the emerging order. Africa can hardly make a stake on any of the grounds above. Even Nigeria with its estimated huge population of over a hundred million is in total disarray, bedeviled by tyranny of military rule, corruption, infrastructural decay, violence, and political uncertainty. As well, "approximately 180 million of sub-Saharan Africa's 500 million people can be classified as poor, of whom 66.7 percent, or 120 million, are desperately poor. By every international measure, be it per capita income ($330), life expectancy (51 years), or the United Nation's Index of Human Development (.225 compared to .317 for South Asia, the next poorest region), Africa is the poorest region in the world."[48] The region's sovereignty is under greater pressure and as the state loses the capacity to perform, it also loses credibility abroad and legitimacy internally.[49]

The rapid growth which is accompanying the new globalization is generating severe environmental pressures and problems; the weak and non-hegemonic state remains incapable of constituting law and order; Africa remains so far behind in the development, absorption, and utilization of technology; and it is still unattractive to investors and donors in spite of all the rhetoric about integrating the global economy. European and American corporations are busy exploiting the vulnerability, ignorance, poverty, and desperation of many African states to dump dangerous toxic wastes on their soils and rivers.[50] As transnational corporations compete for market hegemony in Africa (and other parts of the developing world), they are stretching regulations, and utilizing several extra-legal mechanisms to gain one advantage or the other. This has increased corruption, inefficiency, and further eroded the already weak ability of these states to regulate the corporations. Because the developed markets offer better pay and conditions of work, and in the context of deepening systemic crisis in Africa, the brain drain has intensified as hundreds of thousands of the most educated and experienced professionals flee the continent for other parts of the world. In countries like Nigeria, Ghana, Zambia, and Kenya, this has extended to unskilled labor. The new globalization has not stemmed the deepening employment crisis, spiralling inflation, the lack of international confidence in African economies, and the weak structures of state and society which impede creativity and productivity. Automation, the use of robots, reliance on synthetics, stockpiling, and other cost-cutting production and marketing techniques are actually stifling the expansion of the labor force and creating antagonistic stratification within the ranks of the working classes. International negotiations on trade and tariff, intellectual property, labor relations, immigration, use of local resources, pollution, and technology transfer hardly take Africa into consideration.[51]

Given the desperate conditions of African economies, the new globalization, rather than alleviate the region's poverty, is actually consolidating and deepening it. As social and cultural specificities become more pronounced and politicized, African nations increasingly become ineligible for most forms of support from the developed economies. Admittedly, programs sponsored by donors and aid agencies "have achieved negligible or limited results"[52] over the decades, but such poor results have only made it almost impossible for Africa to capitalize on current developments, innovations, and opportunities in the global system. In any case, donors are cutting aid to the poorest nations and expanding investment and support for the more vibrant or promising economies like South Africa, Indonesia, and Malaysia.[53] As a group of NGOs have warned, "(r)educed aid to Africa is likely to mean further environmental degradation, increased disease, conflict and refugee flows. The human costs will be terrible, and the long term financial cost is likely to far outweigh the price of an effective strategy to assist Africa now."[54] The contradictions, negative coalitions, and weaknesses of state and society have been compounded by ethnic, religious, regional, and other primordial contradictions and conflicts which scare away investors and force regimes to divert scarce resources to security, survival, and conflict containment. No serious investor, new globalization or not, would seriously think of investing new capital in Liberia, Togo, Nigeria, Somalia, the Sudan, Zaire, and several other locations of crisis and conflict in the region. As the IMF has warned:

Many others, especially in Africa, are still mired in poverty. What is more, while globalization is a monumental force of economic integration that can benefit the poor countries by speeding their development, it may also lead to the marginalization of those countries that refuse to undertake, or are prevented from undertaking, the necessary structural adjustment effort.[55]

Of course, even if one were to subscribe to the orthodox stabilization and structural adjustment packages of the IMF and the World Bank, African states have failed woefully to put in place successful and sustainable reform programs in the last two decades. In fact, the World Bank has identified only one successful case of adjustment in Africa, Ghana. This claim remains questionable even among Ghanaians:[56]

Despite the efforts to improve the macroeconomic environment, open up markets and strengthen the public and financial sectors, most African countries still lack policies that are sound by international standards. Even Africa's best performers have worse macroeconomic policies than the newly industrializing economies in Asia. Few besides Ghana come close to having adequate monetary, fiscal, and exchange rate policies. And Ghana lags behind other adjusting countries elsewhere-Chile and Mexico for example-in trade and public enterprise reform.[57]

Rather than reduce government expenditure, cut waste, rationalize financial obligations, promote self-reliance, attract investors, control inflation, and encourage productivity among other promised goals of adjustment, African states have been rent by riots, increased state intervention, corruption, economic dislocation, rising unemployment, and general deterioration on all economic and social indicators. While governments in other parts of the world are responding to the new globalization by constructing what has been referred to as the "competitive state,"[58] the beleaguered African state is merely struggling for legitimacy, hegemony, and survival in the face of severe challenges from non-bourgeois communities and constituencies. Based on current socio-economic and political balances, location and role in the global division of labor and power, the level of science and technology development, and the nature of contestations for power, it is doubtful if the new globalization will have much to offer Africa.

BEYOND THE NEW GLOBALIZATION: AFRICA INTO THE 21st CENTURY

Africa has been a victim of too many negative developments in the global system. The continent has been attacked, exploited, colonized, and neo-colonized by powerful external interests for centuries. It was also a victim of the slave trade, and no matter how generous we might wish to be, the continent had not recovered from the ravages, distortion, deformations, and other consequences of the colonial experience.[59] In spite of post-colonial alignment and realignment of political forces, the drastic reconstruction of the political terrain, and changes in the continents relations with the outside world, it is yet to overcome structural impediments to growth, peace, development and democracy implanted in the colonial era.[60] To be sure, local elites and interest groups which benefit from the existing dependent and unequal arrangements continue to rationalize and legitimize the status quo to the detriment of the region.[61] Political independence was not accompanied by socio-economic and cultural liberation, and since the 1960s, Africa has remained the weakest region in the global system, totally incapable of influencing or determining the content and context of global affairs, and dependent on the productive capacities of other nations.[62] As the saying goes, the continent consumes what it does not produce, and produces what it does not consume; it does not set the prices for what it imports and has not control over the prices of what it exports. This is hardly the profile of a region that can enter, find a location, participate or compete in the new globalization.[63] Yet, all is not lost. As J. Brian Atwood has correctly noted, "Africa's future holds both immense potential and enormous difficulties."[64]

For Africa to be an effective actor in the new globalization therefore, some major structural changes must take place. First, a drastic deconstruction and reconstruction of the repressive and exploitative neo-colonial state. Since this state has been identified with all the ills of the region and has been unable to serve as a fountain of protection and inspiration to the people, it becomes rather evident that until this state is restructured to serve the interest of the majority, intervene less in the economy, facilitate an enabling environment for creativity and productivity, Africa will remain mired in the sea of confusion, hopelessness, waste, domination, and instability. As Claude Ake has noted, a state that has no legitimacy cannot be expected to serve as the engine of stability, growth, development and democracy: The state in Africa is plagued by a crisis of legitimacy because of its external dependence, the decision of the political class to inherit the colonial socioeconomic system instead of transforming it, the massive use of state violence to de-radicalize the nationalist movement and impose political monolithism in the face of deep-rooted social pluralism, and the use of force to repress a rising tide of resentment against the failures of the nationalist leadership, especially the mismanagement of development, and the impoverishment of the masses....The post-colonial state is also disconnected from society and exists with it in a relationship of mutual hostility....With minor exceptions, the citizens of the state in contemporary Africa are disconnected from it. They conform to its commands as they must, while committing their political loyalties to kinship groups and political formations within it.[65]

Clearly the state has not been constituted and has not operated as a *state* in Africa; it has operated more like a zig-zag and confused structure with no sense of direction and no sense of mission. It has historically embarked on a project of destruction rather than one of construction; it has squandered rather than generate resources; it has asphyxiated rather than build and reinvigorate civil society; and it has mortgaged rather than liberate the African economy.[66] Unable to legitimately organize an agenda for growth and development, the African state, its institutions and custodians have relied on the manipulation of primordial loyalties, the politics of defensive radicalism and diversion, repression, and asphyxiation of civil society to maintain control. Organizing development in the interest of the people and promoting an agenda which would facilitate participation in the global system has hardly been featured in the overall program of the African state. Reconstructing this state to make it efficient, effective, responsible, stable, legitimate, accountable, transparent, and difficult, if not impossible to privatize, is a major challenge for the future.[67] The reconstruction of the state to reflect and serve the interests of the majority can only come about through the mobilization, education, and full involvement of the people in the on-going struggles to restructure Africa's political landscape.[68]

The second major challenge is the opening up of political spaces. This is directly linked to the recomposition of the repressive neo-colonial state. It would require not just the ending of military and one-party dictatorships, but also the drawing up of viable constitutional arrangements guaranteed by the active role of popular organizations in civil society. There is no alternative to a genuine democratic process in Africa.[69] Conditions of repression, uncertainty, instability, and constant harassment of popular forces only drain already scarce resources, discourage investors and donors, and force desperate and insecure governments to divert resources to survival and so-called security. Only a genuine democratic agenda can bring out the best of the people and their communities, promote popular mobilization, encourage creativity, and redirect resources to critical and productive sectors:

The political and economic revolutions spreading through Africa today will only succeed as the development process become participatory. Africa is experiencing a mushrooming of voluntary organizations of all kinds. These organizations for the substance of "civil society." As democracy increases, and more political decisions are reached through the market place of ideas, these organizations become the building blocks of that political process. Similarly, in the economic realm, the development of effective spokespersons for various economic interests promotes sustainable economic change.[70]

Decades of irresponsible governance, presidents-for-life, one-man rule, one-party states, confused ideological systems, and military dictatorships have set Africa back and consolidated its marginalization in the global system.

The only platform on which this new idea is being articulated or could be effectively articulated is in the on-going struggles for democracy, accountability, social justice, popular participation, gender equality, and the empowerment of the people, their constituencies and communities. Grinding poverty, the failure of adjustment programs, the end of the cold war and reduced external support for dictators, and the emergence of new prodemocracy movements and leaders have played significant roles in promoting the new upsurge of struggles for democracy. Though there are many problems and most of the new victories are still tentative and unconsolidated, it is increasingly being realized that only a truly democratic agenda can move the region away from the decades of neglect, decay, deterioration, and dislocation.

A third agenda relates to regional integration. If the developed economies are taking regionalism very seriously as evidenced in the establishment of the North American Free Trade Area (NAFTA) and the European Union, then Africa should take it even more seriously. To date, the record of regionalism in the region has been very poor: characterized by excessive politicization, lack of political will, disrespect for protocols, weak currencies, petty jealousies, colonial legacies, and pressures from conditions of underdevelopment and dependence. The 1991 adoption of the African Economic Treaty in Abuja, Nigeria equally reflects a high degree of unseriousness. Though it is expected to culminate in the establishment of a common market and the election of an African parliament in AD 2025, the long time span and current emphasis on nationalistic policies, show that the goals will not be attained. In fact, African leaders have not demonstrated an acknowledgement of the deepening crisis of the region, and the fact that regionalism requires the mobilization of all productive sectors and citizens. As well, a collective regional agenda will make no headway until African states open up the political landscape internally, and establish new national orders based on genuine democracy, accountability, and the mobilization of the people for increased productivity.[71]

A fourth issue which African states must contend with in the contemporary era is the revision of traditional notions of "autonomy" or "independence." True, many of the states are young, at least when compared to nations in other parts of the world. But this is no excuse not to learn from past experiences and to repeat past mistakes. Old notions of sovereignty and nationalistic economic policies will only serve, in the context of the changing global order, to consolidate the region's peripheralization in the global division of labor. Regionalism requires that some degree of sovereignty be ceded to larger organizations or institutions of collective action aimed at growth, development, peace and stability. For poor and underdeveloped nations, which have failed to attract sufficient foreign investments and are clearly hundreds of years behind in the new technologies, the essence of regionalism, and the voluntary surrender of substantial degrees of sovereignty cannot be overstated. If African states fail to exploit the current global momentum towards regionalism, the region's marginal location and role in the global order might just become permanent. In Europe, nation-states have demonstrated some desire and resolve to give up a degree of sovereignty in order to enjoy the benefits of regionalism. It is amazing the African governments which willingly (or unwillingly) accepted economic, and later political conditionalities which were openly designed and are supervised by foreign interests still spend much time protecting claims to absolute sovereignty. Even when the nation-states in Africa are clearly incapable of exercising an appreciable amount of regulation, talk less control over political and economic developments within their borders, they still hold on to clearly receding notions of sovereignty. As well, many have no legitimacy to lay claims to, or to exercise sovereignty over their populations given the long-standing records of repression, human rights abuses, and the squandering of national riches. In the new globalization, with the rapid integration of information networks, unprecedented improvements in communications, the borderless information age evidenced in the power of the fax machine, Internet and other networks, as the meaninglessness of border controls to information collection and dissemination, old notions of sovereignty, beyond its legal articulation to capture the sanctity of recognized boundaries, will mean very little. Africa must realize that only through the collective mobilization of resources, planning, design of a viable and interconnected future, can the small, weak, distorted, and marginalized economies survive the on-going competition in the global system.

Finally, the policies outlined above: restructuring of the state, political openness, regionalism, and a revised understanding of the importance of sovereignty, can only enable African states to take national planning, plan discipline, accountability, and the provision of basic needs more seriously. Essentially, this will involve a grand agenda for re-attracting qualified indigenes who now dot every nook and corner of the globe, re-attract donors and investors, strengthen local currencies, promote local accumulation through investment in productive activities, rehabilitate decaying infrastructure, and revitalize the dying educational system. This sort of agenda, anchored on the principles of good governance and an openly democratic system, will encourage the people to become more creative, productive, and supportive of government policies thus reversing the current conditions of anger, alienation, withdrawal, and overt/covert resistance to the state, its institutions, and custodians. As the USAID observed in its recent review of its activities in Africa:

Governments need to be able to supply public services to their people fairly and effectively, while allowing individuals maximum scope and freedom in both the economic and noneconomic arenas. Effective economic management requires macroeconomic stability, an openness to the outside world, and a dependence on market-based solutions. Effective political management requires transparency, responsiveness, and pluralism. Public institutions must be responsive to their constituencies. Most important, governments must expand the political and economic space available in order to empower people to, to allow them to make their own choices and control their own destinies, in both economic and noneconomic spheres.[72]

Though, clearly, the market is not enough, and the state, strengthened and more efficient will continue to play a critical role in Africa's quest for development, the need for very deep-rooted internal restructuring cannot be understated. In other words, a far-reaching and comprehensive new *national* order must precede any effort to find a new location and role in the new global division of labor and power.

NOTES

1. Michel Camdessus, "Closer Integration in Global Economy Vital for Africa." Excerpts from Address at the High-Level Meeting of the United Nations Economic and Social Council (ECOSOC), Geneva, July 6, 1995, reproduced in *IMF Survey* (July 17, 1995), p. 218.
2. Carol Lancaster. *United States and Africa: Into the Twenty-First Century*, Washington, D.C.: Overseas Development Council, Policy Essay No. 7, 1993, p.19.
3. World Bank. *World Development Report 1995: Workers in an Integrating World*, Washington, D.C.: World Bank, 1995, p.122.
4. See "Sub-Saharan Africa: Route to Success Lies in Sound Economic Policies," *IMF Survey*, February 20, 1995.
5. Carol Lancaster. *United States and Africa, op. cit*; Adebayo Adedeji, (ed.), Africa Within the World: Beyond Dispossession and Dependence London: Zed Books, 1993; and Stephen Wright, "Africa in the Post-Cold War World," *TransAfrica Forum* Vol. 9, (2) (Summer 1992), pp.25-37.
6. Mary Chinery-Hesse. "Divergence and Convergence in the New World Order," in Adebayo Adedeji, (ed.), *Africa Within the World*, op. cit., p. 145.
7. Christopher Farrell. "The Triple Revolution," *Business Week* (1994 Special Bonus Issue), November 1994.
8. Robert H. Jackson. "International Community Beyond the Cold War," in Gene M. Lyons and Michael Mastanduno, (eds.), *Beyond Westphalia? State Sovereignty and International Intervention*, Baltimore, MD: Johns Hopkins University Press, 1995, pp. 59-86.
9. Olufemi Taiwo of Loyola University has termed this the "Be Like Mike Syndrome." See his unpublished paper "The Be-Like-Mike Syndrome: An Essay on Contemporary Non-Transitions to Democracy." Department of Philosophy, 1995.
10. Stephen Wright. *Africa in the Post-Cold War World*, op. cit., p. 26.

11. Francis Fukuyama. "The End of History?" *The National Interest* (16) (1989), pp. 3-18; and Samuel P. Huntington, "The Clash of Civilizations?" *Foreign Affairs*, Vol. 72, (5) (Summer 1993), pp. 22-49.

12. World Bank. *World Development Report 1995*, op. cit., p.1.

13. Sadig Rasheed. "Africa at the Doorstep of the Twenty-First Century: Can Crisis Turn to Opportunity?" in Adebayo Adedeji, (ed.), *Africa Within the World*, op. cit., pp. 41-58.

14. World Bank. *World Development Report 1995*, op. cit., p. 51.

15. Cited in Francis Mading Deng. "State Collapse: The Humanitarian Challenge to the United Nations," in I. William Zartman, (ed.), *Collapsed States: The Disintegration and Restoration of Legitimate Authority*, Boulder: Lynne Rienner, 1995, p. 212.

16. See the case studies in ibid. See also Robert Kaplan, "The Coming Anarchy," *Atlantic Monthly*, (February 1994), pp. 44-76; and Steven Holmes, "Africa: From Cold War to Cold Shoulders," *The New York Times*, March 7, 1993.

17. Ruben P. Mendez, "Paying for Peace and Development," *Foreign Policy*, (100), Fall 1995, pp. 19-32.

18. Javier Perez de Cuellar. *Report of the Secretary-General on the Work of the Organization 1990*, New York: United Nations, 1990, p. 4.

19. ibid.

20. According to J. Brian Atwood. Director of USAID, the "international community spent more on peacekeeping operations in 1992 than it did in the previous 48 years combined. In that same year, investments in development declined by eight percent." See his "Sustainable Development and Crisis Prevention. The U.S. Agenda for International Development," *International Politics and Society*, (1) 1995, p. 15.

21. Ingvar Carlsson. "The U.N. at 50: A Time for Reform," *Foreign Affairs* (100), Fall 1995, pp. 3-18.

22. Christopher S. Wren. "U.S. Is Seeking Further Ways to Punish Nigeria for Executions," *The New York Times* (December 17, 1995); Cathy Connors, "Bishop Tutu Asks Stringent Sanctions Against Nigeria," *The New York Amsterdam News* (December 2, 1995); and Hafsat Abiola, "Words are not Enough," *The New York Times*, December 4, 1995.

23. "The End of Sovereignty," in *Great Decisions 1993*, Ithaca, NY: Foreign Policy Association, 1993, p. 7.

24. "Introduction: 21st Century Capitalism," *Business Week*, (1994 Special Bonus Edition), November 1994.

25. Julius O. Ihonvbere. "The Economic Crisis in Sub-Saharan Africa: Depth, Dimensions and Prospects for Recovery," *The Journal of International Studies*, (27), July 1991, pp. 41-69.

26. Carol Lancaster. "Governance in Africa: Should Foreign Aid Be Linked to Political Reform?" in *Africa Governance in the 1990s: Objectives, Resources, and Constraints,* Atlanta: The Carter Center of Emory University, March 1990, pp. 35-41.

27. Allan E. Goodman, "Dateline Hanoi: Recognition at Last," *Foreign Affairs* (100), Fall 1995, p. 144.

28. World Bank. *World Development Report 1995,* op. cit., p. 51.

29. Walter B. Wriston. "Technology and Sovereignty," *Foreign Affairs,* Winter 1988/89, p. 73.

30. ibid. The fax machine was effectively used by prodemocracy forces against the former self-declared life president of Malawi, Hastings Kamuzu Banda. While he was able to censor radio broadcasts and ban newspapers, he could not ban or control the fax machine.

31. ibid. p. 65.

32. ibid.

33. Dharan Ghai, "Preface," to United Nations Research Institute for Social Development (UNRISD), *States of Disarray: The Social Effects of Globalization,* Geneva: UNRISD, 1995, p.v.

34. UNRISD. *States of Disarray,* op. cit., p. 9. This document also notes that "in practice this evolution has been strongly influenced by the economic and political agenda of advanced industrial countries."

35. World Bank. *World Development Report 1995,* op. cit., p. 51.

36. Without doubt, one of the strengths of the U.S. economy is its receptability and adaptability to new ideas and new technologies. This has made production and information dissemination easier and more dynamic. When Gorbachev assumed office as Secretary General of the Communist Party in the former USSR, the country had only 50,000 computers as compared to about 30 million in the U.S. We can understand why the latter was easily ahead of the former in several areas. As well, the CNN's "World Report" is a typical example of cooperation between journalists, reporters, and newscasters located around the world. Of course, Africa participates in this "World Report" thanks to the technological web of Turner Broadcasting.

37. Michel Camdessus. "Close Integration in Global Economy Vital for Africa," op. cit., p.218.

38. Walter B. Wriston. "Technology and Sovereignty," op. cit., p. 72.

39. UNRISD. *States of Disarray,* op. cit., pp. 26-27.

40. Christopher Farrell. "The Triple Revolution," op. cit.

41. Ellen Johnson Sirleaf. "Some Reflections on Africa and the Global Economy," in William Minter, (ed.), *U.A. Foreign Policy: An Africa Agenda,* Washington, D.C.: Africa Policy Information Center, 1994,

p.9.

42. ibid.

43. ibid. p. 9.

44. World Bank. *World Development Report 1995*, op cit., p. 52.

45. Layashi Yaker. "The Case for Solidarity in the South," in Adebayo Adedeji, (ed.), *Africa Within the World*, op. cit., p.132.

46. Julius O. Ihonvbere. "Between Debt and Disaster: The Politics of Africa's Debt Crisis," *In Depth: A Journal of Values and Public Policy* Vol. 4, (1), Winter 1994, pp. 108-132.

47. Sadig Rasheed. "Africa at the Doorstep of the Twenty-First Century," op. cit., p. 41.

48. US Agency for International Development. "Africa: Growth Renewed, Hope Rekindled-A Report on the Performance of the Development Fund for Africa 1988-1992," Washington, D.C.: USAID, n.d., p.20.

49. Julius O. Ihonvbere. "Surviving at the Margins: Africa and the New Global Order," *Current World Leaders* Vol. 35, (6) (December 1992), pp. 1053-1072; and Olufemi Vaughn, "The Politics of Global Marginalization," *Journal of African and Asian Studies* Vol. XXIX, (3-4) (1994), pp. 186-204.

50. Julius O. Ihonvbere. "The State and Environmental Degradation in Nigeria: A Study of the 1988 Toxic Waste Dump in Koko," *Journal of Environmental Systems*, Vol. 23, (3) (1994-95), pp. 207-227.

51. Christopher Farrell. *The Triple Revolution*, op. cit.

52. USAID. *Africa: Growth Renewed, Hope Rekindled*, op. cit., p. 5.

53. *The Reality of Aid '95: An Independent Review of International Aid*, London: Earthscan, 1995.

54. ibid. p. 7.

55. Michel Camdessus. "The IMF in a Globalized World Economy," Third Annual Sylvia Ostry Lecture, Group of Seven (G-7), Ottawa, June 7, 1995. Reproduced in *IMF Survey*, June 19, 1995, p. 194.

56. "Happy 38th Mother Ghana But Where Are We Heading To?" (Editorial), *Ghana Drum* Vol. 4, (3), March 1995.

57. World Bank. *World Development Report, 1991*, Washington, D.C.: World Bank, 1991, p. 8.

58. ibid. p. 33.

59. Walter Rodney. *How Europe Underdeveloped Africa*, London: Bogle L'Ouverture, 1972; and Claude Ake, *A Political Economy of Africa*, London: Longman, 1981.

60. African states have changed their names, constitutions, leaders, ideologies, local government structures, anthems, national pledges, currencies, and built new edifices and institutions in the effort to

consolidate political independence and plan some form of development. Because these are generally superficial and superstructural,
and are often designed to please the tastes and interests of a largely
decadent and unproductive urban-based tiny elite, they have failed
woefully. The structural contradictions which have to do with the
nature of politics, power, production, and exchange relations remain
unaddressed.

61. Walter Rodney. *How Europe Underdeveloped Africa*, op. cit.; Ali
Mazrui, *The Africans*, London: BBC Publications, 1986; and George B.
Ayittey, *Africa Betrayed*, New York: St. Martins Press, 1992.

62. George Ayittey. *Africa Betrayed*, op. cit., p. 8.

63. Edward V. K. Jaycox. *The Challenges of African Development*,
Washington, D.C.: The World Bank, 1992, p. 2. Jaycox also notes that
"The scope and severity of the economic crisis facing Sub-Saharan
Africa is unique in the developing world: declining per capita
income, food shortages, unsustainable debt, and institutional and
environmental neglect. This daunting crisis demands exceptional
response." p. 11.

64. J. Brian Atwood. "Dear Friends," in USAID, *Africa: Growth
Renewed, Hope Rekindled*, op. cit., p.6.

65. Claude Ake. "Academic Freedom and Material Base," in Mahm-
ood Mamdani and Mamadou Diouf, (eds.), *Academic Freedom in
Africa*, Dakar: CODESRIA, 1994, p. 19. See also Claude Ake, "The
State in Contemporary Africa," in C. Ake (ed.), *Political Economy of
Nigeria*, London: Longman, 1985, pp. 1-9.

66. Claude Ake. "Academic Freedom and Material Base," op. cit.

67. Julius O. Ihonvbere. "The "Irrelevant" State, Ethnicity and the
Quest for Nationhood in Africa," *Ethnic and Racial Studies*, Vol. 17, (1)
January 1994, pp. 42-60.

68. Richard Sandbrook and Mohamed Halfani. (eds.), *Empowering
People: Building Community, Civil Associations, and Legality in Africa*,
Toronto: Center for Urban and Community Studies, University of
Toronto, 1993.

69. For a detailed discussion see Julius O. Ihonvbere. "Beyond
Governance: The State and Democratization in Sub-Saharan Africa,"
Journal of Asian and African Studies (50), 1995, pp. 141-158.

70. USAID. *Africa: Growth Renewed, Hope Rekindled*, op. cit., p.14.

71. See the contributions on regionalism, security, and development
in Olusegun Obasanjo and Felix G. N. Mosha, (eds.), *Africa: Rise to
Challenge*, New York: Africa Leadership Forum, 1993. See in
particular the contributions by Bade Onimode, P. Anyang'nyongo,
Wilfred Ndongko and Yoweri Museveni. For a critique of the
current state of regionalism in Africa see Julius O. Ihonvbere, "The

African Crisis, Regionalism and Prospects for Recovery in the 1990s," in Bruce Berman and Piotor Dutkiewicz, (eds.), *Africa and Eastern Europe: Crisis and Transformations*, Kingston, Ontario: Queen's University, 1993, pp. 121-132.

72. USAID. *Africa: Growth Renewed, Hope Rekindled*, op. cit., p. 27.